MICROECONOMICS

MICROECONOMICS

3/e

Paul Heyne
University of Washington

Macmillan College Publishing Company

New York

Maxwell Macmillan Canada

Toronto

Maxwell Macmillan International

New York   Oxford   Singapore   Sydney

Editor(s): Jill Lectka
Production Supervisor: Ron Harris
Production Manager: Paul Smolenski
Text Designer: Eileen Burke
Cover illustration: Juliana Heyne, oil painting "Old World Series: Reds"

This book was set in 10/12 pt. Aster by The Clarinda Company,
and was printed and bound by R.R. Donnelley & Sons Company-Crawfordsville.
The cover was printed by Phoenix Color Corp.

Macmillan College Publishing Company
866 Third Avenue, New York, New York 10022

Macmillan College Publishing Company is part
of the Maxwell Communication Group of Companies.

Maxwell Macmillan Canada, Inc.
1200 Eglinton Avenue East
Suite 200
Don Mills, Ontario M3C 3N1

Library of Congress Cataloging in Publication Data

Heyne, Paul T.
    Microeconomics / Paul Heyne.—3rd ed.
      p.   cm.
    Includes index.
    ISBN 0-02-354441-4
    1. Microeconomics. I. Title.
    HB172.H525 1994
    338.5—dc20   93-15718
                        CIP

Printing: 1 2 3 4 5 6 7 8   Year: 4 5 6 7 8 9 0 1

With gratitude to my joint authors,

Wallie and Ruth

The Theory of Economics does not furnish a body of settled conclusions immediately applicable to policy. It is a method rather than a doctrine, an apparatus of the mind, a technique of thinking which helps its possessor to draw correct conclusions.

John Maynard Keynes

Microeconomics presents, in a slightly revised and expanded form, the "micro" chapters from the seventh edition of *The Economic Way of Thinking*. While I still believe that the best introduction to economics is through a one-term, whole-loaf course, most departments continue to present the principles of economics in two courses. This book is suitable for the microeconomics half of such a sequence. However, it retains throughout the approach and orientation of *The Economic Way of Thinking*.

WHAT ARE WE AFTER?

Introductory economics has long been an easy subject to teach. It's been a hard subject to *take*, but that's another matter. Moreover, the amount of learning that comes out of principles courses bears no reasonable relationship to the amount of teaching that goes in.

Principles of economics has been an easy course to teach because we have used it largely to regurgitate the bits of technique acquired during our own training in economics. There are so many such bits and pieces, and they are so hard for students to grasp, that principles teachers need never worry about what to do today. They can always introduce a new complication or spend the hour clarifying the complication introduced yesterday. And they don't even have to prepare the complications. A single phrase—elasticity, total-average-marginal revenue, long-run competitive equilibrium, marginal-value product, IS-LM, the multiplier—will serve as an adequate text for an entire class session.

What should be the learning goal in the beginning economics course? It is clear from what has already been said that I have little use for what I take to be the usual learning goal: introducing the student to bits and pieces of technique. Why should we want a beginning student to be familiar with the concepts of average variable, average total, and marginal cost, their downward and upward shapes, the necessary intersection of marginal cost at the low point of average cost, and everything else contributing to the demonstration that in the long run, under perfectly competitive conditions, price will be equal to average total and marginal cost for all firms after quasi-rents have been capitalized? To ask the question is to answer it. We have no good reason for wanting a beginning student to know all this. Then why have we continued to teach it?

Part of the explanation lies in our commendable concern to teach *theory.* It is economic theory that gives to economics almost all its predictive or clarifying power. Without theory, we must grope our way blindly through economic problems, conflicting opinions, and opposing policy proposals.

But economic theory has proved itself unusually difficult to communicate. So those responsible for teaching undergraduate economics, struck by the apparent failure of theory-oriented principles courses, have sometimes opted instead for a problems and issues course. In such a course, students typically read and discuss statements by labor leaders, industry representatives, agricultural lobbyists, politicians, and a few domestic radicals or foreign socialists. They look at figures on income distribution, gross national product, employment, prices, and rates of economic growth. They read and discuss the arguments for guaranteed incomes and against planned obsolescence, for free enterprise and against unregulated competition, for nuclear power and against uncontrolled economic growth. And when it is all over, what have they learned? They have learned that opinions abound, with data to support every one of them, that "it's all relative," that every American is entitled to an opinion, and that economics is not a science and is probably a waste of time.

The insistence on teaching theory is correct insofar as it is a denial of the significance of facts without theories. Theory is essential! But what theory? Economic theory, of course. But that begs the real question. What *kind* of economic theory? And in what *context?* Before we can answer, we must know what we're after.

CONCEPTS AND APPLICATIONS

I want beginning students to master a set of concepts that will help them think more coherently and consistently about the wide range of social problems that economic theory illuminates. The principles of economics make sense out of buzzing confusion. They clarify, systematize, and correct the daily assertions of newspapers, political figures, ax grinders, and barroom pontiffs. And the applicability of the economist's thought tools is practically unlimited. Students should come to appreciate all of this in a beginning course.

But they won't unless we, the teachers and textbook writers, persuade them. And we can persuade them only by showing them. *The principles of economics must therefore be taught as tools of analysis.* The teaching of a concept must take place in the context of application. Better, the potential application should be taught first, then the tool. There is so much evidence from pedagogy to support this approach that it's hard at first to understand how any other approach could ever have conquered the field.

"Here is a problem. You recognize it as a problem. What can we say about it?" That's step 1.

"Here is how economists think about the problem. They employ the concept of such and such." Step 2 entails the exposition of some concept of economic theory.

After the applicability of the concept to the original problem has been demonstrated and some of the implications examined, the concept should be applied to additional problems. That's step 3.

It isn't as easy as one-two-three, of course, and I don't mean to imply that it is. The teaching of economic principles requires imagination, insight, a knowledge of current events, and a sense of perspective, as well as familiarity with the formal techniques of economic analysis. Those are all scarce goods. And it presupposes a conviction on the part of the teacher that economic theory really is useful for something more than answering artificial questions and passing equally artificial examinations.

THE VIRTUE OF RESTRAINT

Perhaps no one would disagree in principle with any of the foregoing statements. If so, our practice has been far out of step with our precept. One reason is undoubtedly the obsession with formal technique that characterizes so much teaching of economic theory at all levels. The disciple will very rarely rise above the master. And if the masters in our profession are more concerned with form than content, the effects will be felt at the principles level. We need not debate here the question of how much of the material taught in intermediate and advanced theory texts really belongs there, or what balance should be struck in graduate theory courses between the logic-mathematics and the economics of theory. For the question of what should go into a beginning course can be answered without resolving the other questions. And that answer is: *very little.*

For very little indeed of what might go into a complete and current compendium of economic theory is actually useful in enabling us to make sense of the real world and to evaluate policy proposals. Almost all the genuinely important things that economics has to teach are elementary concepts of relationship that people could almost figure out for themselves if they were willing to think carefully.[1]

The challenge is getting people to *appreciate* these few, simple concepts. To do that, we must practice the virtue of restraint. We must attempt less and thereby accomplish more. An introductory course should distinguish itself as much by what it excludes as by what it incorporates. Unless it is our aim to impress students with the esoteric quality of economists' knowledge, we should teach no theory in the introductory course that cannot be put to work immediately. Otherwise we drown beginning students; they are made to thrash about so desperately that they don't learn to swim a single stroke. Our aim should be to get them swimming and to instill in them the confidence that through practice they can learn to swim better.

Every introductory economics teacher ought to read a short essay by Noel McInnis entitled "Teaching More with Less." Here are three excerpts:

> I dare say that all of us who teach have been guilty of telling our students much more than they cared—or needed—to know. In fact, I would theorize that we have probably been telling them more about our subjects than *we* care to know. That is one reason why we feel compelled to rely on notes to deliver lectures.
>
>   Our present methods of communicating often obscure meaning rather than reveal it. . . . We often see the tragic results of this in our "best" students, who can repeat what we have told them but cannot apply it in a new context so that it

---

[1]A compelling statement of this view was provided by Ely Devons in the first two of his *Essays in Economics* (London: George Allen and Unwin, 1961), pp. 13–46.

means something. Their learning may have been comprehensive, but it has not been comprehending.

Survey courses in almost all disciplines are becoming increasingly impractical because of their compulsive attempt to cover all relevant information. They could be made highly practical once again—or perhaps for the first time—if they were organized to convey the five or six most fundamental organizing and conceptual principles of the discipline, utilizing only the most immediately relevant information to bring the principles to life.[2]

I agree wholeheartedly with McInnis. My implementation of this vision will undoubtedly be found far from perfect. But the teacher who wonders why this or that topic is not treated in the book, or why there is no complete exposition of some familiar portion of theory, should remember that knowledge is imparted by what is left out as well as by what is included. Judgements on relevance and relative importance will, of course, vary. But the argument of McInnis should be faced every time we are tempted to add another jot or tittle to the corpus of what we teach in beginning principles courses.

CHANGES IN THE THIRD EDITION

The third edition of *Microeconomics* has emerged from a thorough reconsideration of exactly what ought to be taught in an introductory course. I have been teaching economic principles to college students for more than 35 years. I continue to enjoy it because I continue to find it challenging. And I find it challenging because I have never gotten it right, as the persistent misunderstandings of my students have repeatedly demonstrated to me. The conviction that I am missing something crucial grew into an obsession over the past few years as a consequence of opportunities given me to teach economics to Russians, Czechs, Slovaks, Hungarians, and Romanians. They can't afford to spend time learning an economics that is merely intellectual aerobics; they need to understand how markets work and what institutions are essential if effective cooperation is to occur in a society characterized by an extensive division of labor.

In the course of careful reflection on all this I discovered how much I remained in thrall to the notion that economics is about *economizing*. In reality, economists have almost nothing that is useful to say about the economizing process.

[2]*Change: The Magazine of Higher Education* (January-February 1971), pp. 49, 50, 51.

What we understand and most people do not is the *exchange* process. Scarcity is a fact, but it's not a mystery. The real mystery, to most people, is the fact that society contains millions of people pursuing incommensurable projects that somehow get coordinated. How does this happen? How do markets work? That is the great puzzle that the economic way of thinking begins to resolve. The important changes in this edition have mostly been undertaken in order to focus more sharply on that puzzle and its innumerable solutions. The most extensive rethinking and rewriting occurred in Chapters 4, 6, 7, 11, and 13.

The Instructor's Guide to the last edition printed answers to all the end-of-chapter questions on perforated pages that could be torn out and made available to students for photocopying. The suspicion that students would learn more from reading a lot of questions with their answers than from perspiring over a few questions has been confirmed for me by experience. But if the answers are to be read by students, they must be less cryptic than they can be when addressed to teachers only. So the Instructor's Guide to this edition will further elaborate many of the answers.

ACKNOWLEDGMENTS

My debts grow larger every year. Before the unpaid interest becomes a crushing burden, I must read the honor roll. Armen A. Alchian and William R. Allen head the list because it was their *University Economics* that first showed me what I ought to be doing in introductory economics courses and because their names both start with "A". Continuing in alphabetical order, I want to express publicly my gratitude for the special insights and generous assistance over the years of Terry Anderson, Yoram Barzel, Robert Bish, Ronald Brandolini, Henry Bruton, Judith B. Cox, John B. Egger, Mary Eysenbach, Robert Higgs, P.J. Hill, Laurie Johnson, Thomas Johnson, Ronald A. Krieger, Charles Lave, Ian Laxer, Frank M. Machovec, Howard Miller, E.C. (Zeke) Pasour, Potluri Rao, Andrew Rutten, Howard Swaine, Peter Toumanoff, Stephen J. Turnovsky, Donald A. Wells, Sidney Wilson, Harvey Zabinsky, and at least half a dozen other economists whose letters have unfortunately disappeared in the clutter of my office. Don't blame any of them for my invincible ignorance; you will never locate the guilty party among so many fine people.

If Jill Lectka of Macmillan had not supported, admonished, and forgiven at all the right times, this revision would have appeared a year later. She understood my desire to re-think everything, but gently yet persistently reminded me that present resources have a higher value than resources in the future. And for the forms and colors whose primacy I so quickly forget in the pale and amorphous world of academia, I am especially grateful to my wife, Juliana.

Paul Heyne

Contents

MICROECONOMICS

THE ECONOMIC WAY OF THINKING

Good mechanics can locate the problem in your car because they know how your car functions when it *isn't having any problems*. A lot of people find economic problems baffling because they do not have a clear notion of how an economic system works when it's working well. They are like mechanics whose training has been limited entirely to the study of malfunctioning engines.

When we have long taken something for granted, it's hard even to see what it is that we've grown accustomed to. That's why we rarely notice the existence of order in society and cannot recognize the mechanisms of social coordination upon which we depend every day. A good way to begin the study of economics, therefore, might be with astonishment at the feats of social cooperation in which we daily engage. Rush-hour traffic is an excellent example.

RECOGNIZING ORDER

You are supposed to gasp at that suggestion. "Rush-hour traffic as an example of social *cooperation?* Shouldn't that be used to illustrate the law of the jungle or the *breakdown* of social cooperation?" Not at all. If the association that pops into your mind when someone says "rush-hour traffic" is "traffic jam," you are neatly supporting the thesis that we notice only failures and take success so much for granted we aren't even aware of it. The dominant characteristic of rush-hour traffic is not jam but movement, which is why people venture into it day after day and almost always reach their destinations. It doesn't work perfectly, of course. (Name one thing that does.) But the remarkable fact at which we should learn to marvel is that it works at all.

Thousands of people leave their homes at about eight in the morning, slide into their automobiles, and head for work. They all choose their own routes without any consultation. They have diverse skills, differing attitudes toward risk, and varying degrees of courtesy. As these passenger automobiles in their wide assortment of sizes and shapes enter, move along, and exit from the intersecting corridors that make up the city's traffic veins and arteries, they are joined by an even more heterogeneous mixture of trucks, buses, motorcycles, and taxicabs. The drivers all pursue their separate objectives, with an almost single-minded devotion to their own interests, not necessarily because they are selfish but simply because none of them knows anything about the objectives of the others. What each one does know about the others is confined to a few observations on the position, direction, and velocity of a changing handful of vehicles in the immediate environment. To this they add the important assumption that other drivers are about as eager to avoid an accident as they themselves are. There are general rules, of course, which everyone is expected to obey, such as stopping for red lights and staying close to the speed limit. That's about it, however. The entire arrangement as just described could be a prescription for chaos. It ought to end in heaps of mangled steel.

What ensues instead is a smoothly coordinated flow, a flow so smooth, in fact, that an aerial view from a distance can almost be a source of aesthetic pleasure. There they are— all those independently operated vehicles down below, inserting themselves into the momentary spaces between other vehicles, staying so close and yet rarely touching, cutting across one another's paths with only a second or two separating a safe passage from a jarring collision, accelerating when space opens before them and slowing down when it contracts. The movement of rush-hour traffic, or indeed of urban traffic at any time of day, really is an astounding feat of social cooperation.

THE IMPORTANCE OF SOCIAL COOPERATION

The traffic example is particularly effective in making us see how much social cooperation we totally fail to notice, because everyone is familiar with traffic but almost no one thinks of it as a cooperative endeavor. But the example is also useful in making the point that we depend on mechanisms of coordination for far more than what we usually think of as "economic" goods. If we had no working procedures to induce cooperation, we could enjoy none of the benefits of civilization. "In such a condition," as Thomas Hobbes (1588–1679) observed in an often-quoted passage of his *Leviathan:*

> . . . there is no place for industry, because the fruit thereof is uncertain; and consequently no culture of the earth; no navigation, nor use of the commodities that may be imported by sea; no commodious building; no instruments of moving and removing such things as require much force; no knowledge of the face of the earth; no account of time; no arts; no letters; no society; and, which is worst of all, continual fear, and danger of violent death; and the life of man, solitary, poor, nasty, brutish, and short.[1]

Because Hobbes believed that people were so committed to self-preservation and personal satisfaction that only force (or the threat of it) could keep them from constantly assaulting one another, his writings emphasize only the most basic form of social cooperation: abstention from violence and robbery. He seems to have supposed that if people could be induced not to attack one another's persons or property, then positive cooperation—the kind that actually produces industry, agriculture, knowledge, and art—would develop of its own accord. But will it? Why should it?

HOW DOES IT HAPPEN?

By what means do the members of a society induce one another to take precisely those complexly interconnected actions that will eventually produce the multitude of goods, tangible and intangible, that we all enjoy? Even a society of saints must use some procedures for inducing positive cooperation *of the right kind* if the life of each saint is to be more than "solitary, poor, nasty, brutish, and short." Saints must, after all, somehow find out exactly what ought to be done and when and where it ought to be done before they can play an effective part in helping others.

Hobbes probably failed to see the importance of this question for understanding life in the "commonwealth," be-

---

[1]Hobbes, *Leviathan, or the Matter, Forme and Power of a Commonwealth Ecclesiastical and Civil,* 1651.

cause the society he knew was far simpler, more bound by custom and tradition, and less subject to rapid and disruptive change than the societies in which we have grown up. Not until late in the eighteenth century, as a matter of fact, did any significant number of thinkers begin to wonder why it was that society "worked"—that individuals pursuing their own interests on the basis of extremely limited information nonetheless managed to produce not chaos but a remarkably ordered society.

One of the most perceptive and surely the most influential of these eighteenth-century thinkers was Adam Smith (1723–1790). Smith lived in an age when most educated people believed that only the diligent attentions of political rulers could prevent a society from degenerating into disorder and poverty. Smith did not agree. But in order to refute the accepted opinion of his day, he had to describe the mechanism of social coordination that he saw operating in society—a mechanism that not only functioned, in his judgment, without the constant attention of government, but worked so powerfully that it often canceled the effects of contrary governmental policies. Adam Smith published his analysis in 1776 as *An Inquiry into the Nature and Causes of the Wealth of Nations* and thereby established his claim to the title Founder of Economics. He did not *invent* "the economic way of thinking." But he developed it more extensively than any of his predecessors had done, and he was the first writer to use it in a comprehensive analysis of social change and social cooperation.

AN APPARATUS OF THE MIND

What exactly do we mean by *the economic way of thinking?* To begin with, it is exactly what the term suggests: an approach, rather than a set of conclusions. John Maynard Keynes phrased it aptly in the statement quoted in the front of this book:

> The Theory of Economics does not furnish a body of settled conclusions immediately applicable to policy. It is a method rather than a doctrine, an apparatus of the mind, a technique of thinking which helps its possessor to draw correct conclusions.

But what is this "technique of thinking"? It is, most fundamentally, an assumption about what guides human behavior. The theories of economics, with surprisingly few exceptions, are simple extensions of the assumption that individuals take those actions they think will yield them the largest net advantage. Everyone, it is assumed, acts in accordance with that rule: miser or spendthrift, saint or sinner, consumer or seller, politician or business executive, cautious calculator or spontaneous improviser.

But don't misunderstand. Economic theory does not assume that people are selfish, or materialistic, or shortsighted, or irresponsible, or interested exclusively in money. None of these is implied by the statement that people try to secure for themselves the largest possible net advantage. Everything depends on what, in fact, people find in their own interest. As we know, some derive enormous satisfaction from helping people. A few, unfortunately, seem to derive satisfaction from actually hurting others. Some find their keenest pleasure in the sight of roses blooming. Others would far rather speculate on urban real estate.

But if people are all that different, how can economic theory explain or predict anything about their behavior merely by assuming that they all act in what they think will be their own best interests? What does the assumption imply except that people do what they want to do, whatever that is?

Matters aren't that hopeless, however, for people don't really seem to be as different in their interests as the preceding contrasts would suggest. All of us regularly and successfully predict the behavior of people whom we have never even met, and we could not function effectively in society without the ability to do so. Rush-hour traffic flow, for example, would be impossible if we could not predict the actions of others who are usually complete strangers. Moreover, in any society that uses money extensively, just about everybody prefers more money to less, because money offers a general command over the resources that can be used to advance one's interests, whatever they may be. This is a most useful fact to know when we are trying to predict the behavior of others.

It is also a useful piece of information when we want to *influence* the behavior of others. And that brings us back to the issue of social cooperation and to a second prominent characteristic of the economic way of thinking. Economic theory asserts that the actions people take in the pursuit of their own interests create the alternatives available to others, and that social coordination is a process of continuing mutual adjustment to the changing net advantages that their interactions generate. That is a very abstract argument. We can make it more concrete by referring once more to traffic flow.

COOPERATION THROUGH MUTUAL ADJUSTMENT

Picture a freeway with four lanes in each direction and with all the entrances and exits on the right. Why don't all the drivers stay in the far-right lane? Why do some of them go to the trouble of driving all the way over to the far left when they know they'll have to come back to the right lane to exit? Anyone who has driven on a freeway knows the answer: The traffic flow is impeded in the far-right lane by slow-moving vehicles entering and exiting, so people in a hurry get out of the right lane as quickly as possible.

Which of the other lanes will they choose? Although we can't predict the action of any single driver, we know that the drivers will disperse themselves quite evenly among the three other lanes. But why does this happen? How does it happen? The answer is also the explanation of what we meant just now by *a process of continuing mutual adjustment to the changing net advantages that their actions generate.* Drivers are alert to the net advantages of each lane and therefore try to move out of any lanes that are moving slowly and into those that are moving faster. This speeds up the slow lanes and slows down the fast lanes until all lanes are moving at the same rate, or, more accurately, until no driver perceives any net advantage to be gained by changing lanes. It all happens quickly, continuously, and far more effectively than if someone at the entrances passed out tickets *assigning* each vehicle to a particular lane.

That, according to the economic way of thinking, is how the social world works. Individuals choose their actions on the basis of the net advantages they expect. Their actions alter, however minutely, the relative benefits and costs of the options that others perceive. When the ratio of expected benefit to expected cost for any action increases, people do more of it. When the ratio falls, they do less. The fact that almost everyone prefers more money to less is an enormous aid in this process, an extremely important lubricant, if you will, in the mechanism of social coordination. Modest changes in the monetary cost and monetary benefit of particular options can induce large numbers of people to alter their behavior in directions more consistent with what other people are concurrently doing. And this is the primary system by which we obtain cooperation among the members of society in using what is available to provide what people want.

HOW MUCH DOES ECONOMIC THEORY EXPLAIN?

Some might object that the preceding paragraph claims too much. "You haven't given a description of `how the social world works' but only of how the economic part of it works. You've described the market system. But that's not the whole of society. In addition to the market or economic sector, we have other institutions (such as the government sector) that operate by different principles and procedures."

That sounds like a reasonable objection, or at least one consistent with the traditional ways in which we've learned to divide up the world. But the economic way of thinking is subversive when it comes to those traditional distinctions. If it makes sense to explain the output of the Bethlehem Steel Company and the Chrysler Corporation as the product of competing interests mutually adjusted, why won't it make sense to explain the output of the United States Congress or the Department of Agriculture in the same way? Why draw a line between "the economy" and "the government"? Isn't every branch and agency of government made up, just like any other social group, of ordinary mortals with a wide variety of interests? The necessity of inducing others to cooperate doesn't stop when the capital city is reached! Or if it does, someone has failed to communicate that fact to the lobbyists, legislative leaders, staff assistants, and executive agents who struggle daily to shape the directions of government action.

To tell the embarrassing truth, economic theorists are highly imperialistic. They tend to think that their way of looking at society explains everything, or at least explains more occurrences more adequately than does any other approach. And so economists have been venturing out in recent years to raid territories traditionally occupied by sociologists, political scientists, historians, and others. Economists don't all agree (and representatives of the raided disciplines *surely* do not all agree) that these excursions have always captured valuable terrain. Some critics of the imperialistic ambitions of economics have even accused it of saying nothing about everything. We won't try to resolve those disputes at this point. But you should be aware in advance that this book will draw no clear lines to mark the boundaries of economics. Instead, we shall fall back on the vague but sensible principle that economic theory should be used wherever it successfully explains or predicts and abandoned for something else whenever it sheds no light.

Economic theory will turn out to be most illuminating when used in the traditional way, to explain the often mysterious workings of what Adam Smith called *commercial society*. "When the division of labour has been once thoroughly established," Smith observed early in *The Wealth of Nations*,

> it is but a very small part of a man's wants which the produce of his own labour can supply. He supplies the far greater part of them by exchanging that surplus part of the produce of his own labour, which is over and above his own consumption, for such parts of the produce of other men's labour as he has occasion for. Every man thus lives by exchanging, or becomes in some measure a merchant, and the society itself grows to be what is properly a commercial society.

The successful coordination of activity in such a society, where everyone lives by specializing and exchanging, is a task of extraordinary complexity. Think for a moment about the activities that had to be precisely coordinated in order for you to enjoy this morning's breakfast. Farmers, truck drivers, construction workers, bankers, and supermarket checkers are just a few of the people whose efforts contributed to the production, processing, transportation, and distribution of your breakfast cereal or toast. How were all these people induced to do exactly the right thing at precisely the right time and place? Economic theory originated and developed largely out of efforts to answer that question. And despite all its imperialistic adventures in recent years, economics still does most of its useful work in explaining the functioning of commercial society, which is what most people probably have in mind when they talk about "the economy."

THE BIASES OF ECONOMIC THEORY

The admission that economics has imperialistic ambitions may not disturb you as much as our admission now that *the economic way of thinking is a biased perspective*. It does not offer an unprejudiced view of society, in which all the facts are presented and all interests are given the same weight. It operates rather with a firm presupposition that *all social phenomena emerge from the choices individuals make in response to expected benefits and costs to themselves*. It rules out anything that cannot be reconciled with this basic presupposition.

Is that a biased perspective or is it not? Consider the emphasis on *choice*. Economic theory is so preoccupied with choice that some critics have accused it of assuming people choose to be poor or choose to be unemployed. That's a fair criticism only if you believe there's no difference between making choices that lead to poverty and choosing to be poor. But there can be no doubt that economic theory attempts to explain the social world by assuming that events are the product of people's choices.

Closely related to this focus on choice is the emphasis economic theory gives to the *individual*. Because only individuals actually choose, economists try to dissect the decisions of such collectives as governments, universities, or corporations until they locate the choices of individual persons who make them up. Does economic theory miss the significance of group action and social bonds by unduly emphasizing the individual? Whatever the merit in this charge, the economic way of thinking definitely does make the individual the ultimate unit of explanation.

Economic thinking is also criticized by some as false or misleading because of its emphasis on calculation and consistency of ends and means. Economists assume that people do not act capriciously, that they compare the expected costs and benefits of available opportunities before they act, and that they learn from and therefore do not repeat their mistakes. But are people really that calculating? Aren't our actions guided more by unconscious urges and unexamined impulses than all this would admit? And is every action really a means to some end? Although economists do not claim that people know everything or never make mistakes, the economic way of thinking does indeed assume that people's actions follow from calculations of costs and benefits. And it does emphasize the instrumental character of human action while neglecting the fact that many important activities—a spirited conversation, perhaps, or a friendly game of tennis—are not engaged in as a means to some end.

Another charge often leveled against the economic way of thinking is that it harbors a *promarket* bias. This criticism, too, calls attention to a genuine and significant characteristic of economic theory, although a characteristic that may not be altogether what it seems to be. Economic theory originated as a study of markets, of complex exchange processes, and economists have learned a great deal over the years about the conditions under which exchange works poorly or well. The economist's alleged promarket bias is probably better seen as a preference for those social institutions and "rules of the game" that make exchange a positive-sum game, a process from which all participants derive benefit.

RULES OF THE GAME

That's a term you're going to meet repeatedly in this book: the *rules of the game*. Whether the "game" is business, government, science, family, school, traffic, basketball, or chess, it can't be played satisfactorily unless the players know what the rules are and generally agree to follow them. Most social interaction is directed and coordinated by the rules that participants know and follow.

When the rules are in dispute or inconsistent or simply not clear, the game tends to break down. The countries of central and eastern Europe that are trying to move from centrally planned and bureaucratically controlled systems of production to decentralized, market-coordinated systems face no greater obstacle than the absence of clear and accepted rules for the new game they are attempting to play. If you have ever traveled in a foreign country with a culture radically different from your own and a language that you didn't understand, you have some sense of what happens when the rules of the game in a society are suddenly and dramatically upset. People don't know exactly what is expected of them or what they can expect from others. Social cooperation declines quickly in such a setting, as mutually beneficial exchanges under the rules give way to hesitant attempts to find out what the rules are and, in the worst of cases, destructive struggles to establish rules that will work in one's own favor.

Property rights form a large and important part of the rules governing most of the social interactions in which people regularly engage. By deciding exactly *what is whose under which circumstances*, they provide the members of society with dependable information and incentives. But a system of satisfactorily clear property rights cannot be created overnight; it will almost inevitably be the product of an evolution over time, in which law, custom, morality, technology, and daily practice interact to establish reliable patterns. A movement away from socialism entails the abolition of old property rights but not necessarily the creation of new ones. The consequence may be chaos rather than market coordination. The road from bureaucratic control of the economy to market control will be a treacherous one for the nations of the former Soviet bloc, with many potholes, washouts, earthslides, and unmapped sections.

BIASES OR CONCLUSIONS?

Let's go back to those four prominent (and interrelated) biases inherent in the economic way of thinking. Are they really biases or prejudices? Why couldn't we call them convictions (or even conclusions) and simply say that economists explain social phenomena by postulating interaction among the calculated choices of individuals, because this enables them to understand those phenomena? Do we say that astronomers are biased because they assume that all the light they observe has traveled toward them at 186,000 miles per second, or that biologists are biased because they assume that DNA molecules control the development of organisms?

The questions we're raising now are important and interesting.[2] But we cannot follow them further without pushing this introductory chapter to an intolerable length. It has long seemed obvious to the author (a prejudice or a conclusion?) that the search for knowledge of any kind necessarily begins with some *commitments* on the part of the inquirer. We cannot approach the world with a completely open mind, because we weren't born yesterday. And completely open minds would in any event be completely empty minds, which can learn nothing at all. All discussion, every inquiry, and even each act of observation are rooted in and grow out of convictions. We cannot begin everywhere or with everything. We must begin somewhere with something. We proceed from where we find ourselves and on the basis of what we believe to be true, important, useful, or enlightening. We may, of course, be wrong in any of these judgments. Indeed, we are always wrong to some extent, since every "true" statement necessarily leaves out a great deal that is also true and thus errs by omission.

We cannot avoid this risk, as some people suppose, by steering clear of theory. People who sneer at "fancy theories" and prefer to rely on common sense and everyday experience are often in fact the victims of extremely vague and sweeping hypotheses. Consider this actual letter to a newspaper from a young person in Pennsylvania who was once "one of a group of teenage pot smokers. Then a girl in the crowd got pregnant. Her baby was premature and deformed and needed two

---

[2]The thoughtful student who would like to pursue these issues further should be sure to read *The Structure of Scientific Revolutions* by Thomas S. Kuhn (Chicago: University of Chicago Press, 1962). This highly readable essay on the history and philosophy of science has had an enormous influence on the thinking of social scientists about the respective roles of assumption and evidence in their investigations.

operations." The newspaper's adviser to the teenage lovelorn printed that letter approvingly, as evidence that the price of smoking marijuana is high.

Perhaps it is. But suppose the writer of that letter had written: "Then the Pittsburgh Steelers won the Super Bowl, and the Philadelphia Flyers took the Stanley Cup." Everyone would object that those events had nothing to do with the group's pot smoking. *But how do we know that?* If the mere fact that the young girl's misfortunes followed her pot smoking is evidence of a causal relationship, why can't we also infer a causal relationship in the case of the Steelers and the Flyers?

NO **THEORY MEANS** *POOR* **THEORY**

The point is a simple but important one. We cannot discover, prove, or even suspect any kind of causal relationship without having a theory in mind. Our observations of the world are in fact drenched with theory, which is why we can usually make sense out of the buzzing confusion that assaults our eyes and ears. Actually we observe only a small fraction of what we "know," a hint here and a suggestion there. The rest we fill in from the theories we hold: small ones and broad ones, vague and precise ones, well tested and poorly tested, widely held and sometimes peculiar, carefully reasoned and dimly recognized.

I.M.D. Little is a distinguished British economist who worked for a time as an adviser to the British treasury. He later wrote an article describing his experiences and discussing the usefulness of economic theory in the world of policymaking. Here is an interesting paragraph:

> Economic theory teaches one how economic magnitudes are related, and how very complex and involved these relationships are. Noneconomists tend to be too academic. They abstract too much from the real world. No one can think about economic issues without some theory, for the facts and relationships are too involved to organize themselves: they do not simply fall into place. But if the theorist is untutored, he is apt to construct a very partial theory which blinds him to some of the possibilities. Or he falls back on some old and over-simple theory, picked up from somewhere or other. He is also, I believe, apt to interpret the past naively. *Post hoc ergo propter hoc*[3] is seldom

---

[3]Literally, "After this, therefore because of this"; the logical fallacy of assuming that A must have caused B if A preceded B in time. The argument of the penitent Pennsylvania pot smoker is an example.

an adequate economic explanation. I was sometimes shocked by the naive sureness with which very questionable bits of economic analysis were advanced in Whitehall. Of course, economists may be too academic in another sense: they may not appreciate administrative difficulties, or may lack a sense of political possibility. But, then, there is no danger of these things being overlooked.[4]

"*Noneconomists* tend to be too academic. They abstract too much from the real world." That isn't the way you usually hear it. But Little is probably correct. "I don't know anything about fancy economic theory," the confident amateur begins, "but I do know this. . . ." And what he says next demonstrates all too often that he was quite right in denying any knowledge of economic theory, but quite wrong in supposing that this preserved him from error. Those who try to reason about complex economic interrelationships without theory usually manage only to reason with very poor theory.

None of this should be interpreted as a wholesale defense of economists, who sometimes like to dazzle the public with complex theorems and exercises in pure logic instead of addressing the questions people are actually asking. Even in the teaching of economics, we have often behaved as if all the students enrolled in an introductory course were aiming at a Ph.D. in the subject, and that it was our duty to begin their preparation for the doctoral exams. That's probably why introductory courses typically offer so many more ideas than students can possibly digest.

This textbook developed out of a growing suspicion that when students found economic theory mystifying and tedious, it was largely because we economists were trying to teach them too much. This book very consciously sets out, therefore, to achieve more by attempting less. It is organized around a set of concepts that collectively make up the economist's basic kit of intellectual tools. The tools are all related to the fundamental assumptions we have discussed and are surprisingly few in number. But they are extraordinarily versatile. They unlock such mysteries as surpluses of scarce goods, business firms that make profits by accepting losses, and different prices charged for "identical" goods—mysteries that are generally conceded to be in the economist's province. But they also shed light on a wide range of issues that are not ordinarily thought of as eco-

[4]I.M.D. Little, "The Economist in Whitehall," *Lloyds Bank Review* (April 1957).

nomic at all—traffic congestion, environmental pollution, the workings of government, and the behavior of college administrators—to mention just a few that you will encounter in the chapters ahead.

It's important to realize, however, that economic theory *by itself* cannot answer any interesting or important social questions. The economic way of thinking has to be supplemented with knowledge drawn from other sources: knowledge about history, culture, politics, psychology, and the social institutions that shape people's values and behavior. Learning the mere techniques of economic analysis is far easier than mastering the art of applying them sensibly and persuasively to actual social problems in their infinite complexity.

But this is not the time to worry about the fact that intelligent applications of economic theory will always be difficult and uncertain. The primary goal of this book is to get you started in the practice of thinking the way economists think, in the belief that once you start you will never stop. Economic thinking is addictive. Once you get inside some principle of economic reasoning and make it your own, opportunities to use it pop up everywhere. You begin to notice that much of what is said or written about economic and social issues is a mixture of sense and nonsense. You get in the habit of sorting the sense from the nonsense by applying the basic concepts of economic analysis. You may even, unfortunately, acquire the reputation of being a cynic, for people who habitually talk nonsense like to cry "cynic" at anyone who points out what they are doing.

QUESTIONS FOR DISCUSSION

1. How much do people have to know about one another in order to cooperate effectively? Contrast the situation of two family members who are planning to take a vacation together with the situation of motorists who are simultaneously using intersecting streets. How are "collisions" avoided in each case? What do you know about the interests, the personality, or the character of the people whose cooperation supplied your breakfast this morning?

2. What do you predict would happen if Los Angeles decided to reserve one lane on each of its freeways for "urgent vehicles," with an urgent vehicle defined as any vehicle whose driver might be late for an important event if the vehicle were to be delayed by congestion in the regular lanes? Do you think drivers would stay out of the urgent vehicle lane? Or would it

become just as congested as all the other lanes? Would such an idea be more likely to succeed in practice if drivers were generally less selfish and more considerate?

3. When Mother Teresa accepted the Nobel Prize for Peace in October 1979 and decided to use the $190,000 award to construct a leprosarium, was she acting in her own interest? Was she behaving selfishly?

4. A newspaper item reported that two-thirds of all mothers who work outside the home "do it for the money, not by choice." Are those really alternatives? Either for the money or by choice?

5. At the present time U.S. commercial airlines will carry an infant under two at no charge if the infant sits on the lap of a fare-paying adult, but will charge for an extra seat if the plane is full and the parents want the child placed in a child-restraint seat. If the government requires that all infants fly in child-restraint seats, the infant will have to have a ticket of its own to make sure that a seat is available. Should the government impose such a requirement? "There is no real choice about the matter," some have argued, "because a child's life is of far more value than the price of an airline ticket." Do you agree with that argument?

6. "In truth, the presence or absence of poverty in this economically advanced society is now a matter open to public choice." Do you agree? Can we choose to abolish poverty in the United States simply because we have enough wealth to do so?

7. What happens when the rules of the game (written or unwritten) decree that important meetings won't start until everyone is present and that late arrivals will incur no penalty? Is it in anyone's interest to be punctual? Are these rules of the game likely to prove satisfactory over time?

8. What are some of the more important rules that coordinate the actions of all those playing the "game" of this economics course? Who decided where and when the class would meet, who would teach it, who would enroll as students, what the textbook would be, when the exams would be given, and so on? Who decides where each student will sit? Do you find it odd that two students rarely try to occupy the same seat?

9. In the early 1980s, when the Polish people had to stand in long lines in order to purchase most consumer goods, the government ordered that every third place in line be reserved for pregnant women or disabled persons. This was presumably done to reduce their discomfort. Do you think it resulted in less standing in line by pregnant women? Do you suppose any women became pregnant in order to be able to cut into the long lines?

10. Here is a paragraph from a *New York Times* News Service article by Celestine Bohlen (published in the *International Herald Tribune* on August 31, 1992) discussing the disintegration of Russian society after the collapse of the Soviet Union and the Communist party:

> Moonshine, tinted and packaged in Chivas Regal whisky bottles, is sold in street kiosks, and drivers of fuel trucks, taking advantage of long lines at

gasoline stations, sell motorists canisters of gasoline laced with engine-fouling kerosene.

Why was this occurring in Russia in 1992? Why do people in the United States almost never have to worry that the whisky or gasoline they buy might have been fraudulently adulterated?

11. What do we mean when we say, "That's just a coincidence; it doesn't prove anything"? How does theory enable us to distinguish relevant evidence from mere coincidence?

12. Would you say that physicians who don't believe acupuncture works are biased if they reject it without trying it? If someone told you that you can get a perfect grade in this course without studying just by regularly chanting the mantra "invisible hand," would you believe him? Would it be a sign of bias or prejudice on your part if you totally ignored this advice even though you are extremely eager for a high grade in the course?

13. Char Cole bought four steaks at the butcher shop on Friday afternoon. Later that evening three friends came over for a barbecue. Do you suppose her purchase of the steaks *caused* the friends to come over? How can you decide which event was more likely the cause and which the effect? If you read that the crime rate increased in a certain city during a time when the purchase of handguns had also increased, would you suspect a causal connection? Which would more likely be the cause and which the effect? How does *theory* shape your answer?

SUBSTITUTES EVERYWHERE: THE CONCEPT OF DEMAND

Y ou must have heard or read statements like these many times in your life:

- Fire safety requires that there be two exits from each apartment unit.
- We need a new car.
- Our state will need large amounts of additional water in the coming decade.
- Traffic surveys have established the need for a new expressway.
- All citizens should be able to obtain the medical care they need regardless of ability to pay.
- There is no substitute for victory.

Fire safety, water, the smooth and rapid movement of traffic, medical care, victory, and even automobiles are all "goods." We say "even" automobiles because some doubts have begun to be expressed about the goodness of automobiles in our congested cities. But you can ask the man who owns one, and a lot of young people who don't. They will assure you that a new car is very much a good. Then what's wrong with those statements?

The element common to all six is the notion of *necessity*. And that is what makes each statement seriously misleading.

Take the first one. Will apartment dwellers who live with only one exit all be injured or killed by fires? Of course not. It's just that the risk is greater with one exit than with two.

But then why not three exits? Or four? Why not go the whole route and make the outside walls nothing but doors? The answer is that, although fire safety is a good, it isn't the only good apartment dwellers are interested in. Low rental costs and low heating and cooling costs are also goods, to say nothing of protection from burglars who notice that multiple exits are also multiple entrances. Moreover, there are other and perhaps better ways to increase fire safety. Extinguishers, alarm sprinklers, and large ashtrays also reduce the risk to apartment dwellers of injury or death from fire. If more than one exit is required, why not also require a fire extinguisher on every wall?

That sensible-sounding statement about apartment exits overlooks three interrelated facts: (1) Most goods are not free but can be obtained only by sacrificing something else that is also a good. (2) There are substitutes for anything. (3) Intelligent choice among substitutes requires a balancing of additional costs against additional benefits.

COSTS AND SUBSTITUTES

Now go back and look at the five other statements. "We need a new car." Who *needs* a new car? Obviously only those who value a new car more than what they must sacrifice to obtain one. That might be a vacation trip this year, new clothes, a lot of movies, and a stereo set. Is it worth it? There are, after all, plenty of substitutes for a new car: an overhaul of the present one, a used car, a bicycle, a car pool, public transportation, moving closer to work, or staying home more often. Intelligent consumers determine their preferences after considering these various costs and benefits.

Consider the third statement: "Our state will need large amounts of additional water in the coming decade." Does any state really need large amounts of additional water? Dams and reservoirs, pipelines, and desalinization plants are ways of obtaining more water. But they have costs. Do the benefits justify the costs? If you think there are no substitutes for water, then you're thinking too academically. You have abstracted in a seriously misleading way from the real world. Probably you're assuming that water is used primarily for drinking, whereas in fact the overwhelming bulk of the water consumed in the United States goes for other uses. Since we shall use the case of water a bit later as an extended working exercise, we can pass this problem by for now. You might want to begin thinking, though, about the substitutes for water in such places of chronic scarcity as Arizona and southern California.

You'll be able to make much more sense out of the water problem and the expressway issue we take up next if you keep in mind that entities like *states* or *cities* never really want anything. Wants and goals are always attached ultimately to individuals. What does the person who says "The people want . . ." really mean? That all the people want it? A majority? Those who count? It is usually a good rule in analyzing statements like those opening this chapter to ask: *Who* wants more water, or more expressways, or more fire safety?

Things are seldom what they seem.
Skim milk masquerades as cream.

The fourth of our misleading propositions—"Traffic surveys have established the need for a new expressway"—leads into one of the vexing issues in city planning. Perhaps it would never have become such a troublesome issue if we had admitted all along that expressways entail costs as well as benefits, that there are excellent substitutes for more expressways, and that intelligent city planning calls for the weighing of additional benefits against additional costs. Those who hope to derive most of the benefits from a new expressway while paying only a small percentage of the costs will not want others to notice the full costs of the expressway or how many substitutes there really are. That's why they pretend that a traffic survey can establish "needs." But a traffic survey only shows how many cars travel given routes *at existing costs to the drivers,* including such nonmonetary costs as delay, danger, and ulcers. Suppose that the cost of downtown parking increased 500%. What do you think would happen to rush-hour traffic? Commuters would form car pools and begin using public transportation. If the cost *to drivers* of commuting were made high enough, through parking charges, toll fees, or some other device, the need for a new expressway could turn overnight into a "need" for an improved public transportation system. It's a strange kind of need that can vanish so quickly in the face of a price change.

The fifth statement sounds humanitarian and liberal. "All citizens should be able to obtain the medical care they need regardless of ability to pay." But how much medical care does any person need? We might all agree that a woman with an inflamed appendix and no money should have an appendectomy completely at the taxpayers' expense if she is unable to meet any of the costs herself. But what of the man with a splinter in his finger? The services of physicians are not free goods, and they would not become free goods even if every physician treated patients without charging a fee. There just would not be enough physicians to go around if everyone consulted a doctor for every minor ill. The lower the price of visiting a physician, the more frequently will people substitute a trip to the doctor for such other remedies as going to bed, taking it easy, or waiting and hoping. One could rather confidently predict that lower monetary fees would result in higher fees of other sorts, like waiting in line for many hours.

What about the sixth statement: "There is no substitute for victory"? It just isn't so. That may be a good battle cry, but it's unrealistic political analysis. Victory is usually obtained by making sacrifices. If the sacrifices reach a certain intensity, people choose compromise or even defeat, although they are then inclined to *say* that they have "no choice." Once again we notice that the intelligent formulation of policy, including foreign policy, flows from a careful balancing of additional expected costs and additional expected benefits.

The word *expected* should be stressed. We live in a world of uncertainty, forced to make choices that will affect our future without knowing for sure just how they will do so. A common mistake in reasoning about economic problems is to assume that there is no uncertainty or that economic decision makers are omniscient. At last report, omniscience was still a virtue denied to mortals. Condemned as we are to living with uncertainty, we can at least keep from making matters worse by pretending otherwise. Be alert for statements, in this book and elsewhere, which assume that completely adequate information is always available. You might even notice that information, too, is a good that has costs of acquisition and for which there are substitutes available.

THE CONCEPT OF DEMAND

The concept of "needs" encourages all-or-nothing thinking. That's why economists prefer the concept of *demand*. Demand is a concept that *relates amounts people want to obtain to the sacrifices they must make to obtain these amounts.*

Ask yourself the following questions: How many compact disks do you want to own? How many times do you want to go out to dinner in a year? What grade do you want from this course?

If you can answer any of those questions, it is because you have assumed some cost in each case. Suppose you said you want an A from this course and plan to get one. What difference would it make if the price of an A went up? The teacher isn't taking bribes; the price of an A *to you* (that's what counts) is the sacrifice you must make to obtain it. Would you still want an A if it required twenty hours of study a week, whereas a B could be had for just one hour a week? You might still want it, but you would probably not be willing to buy it at such a high price when a fairly good substitute, a B, is so much cheaper. And that is what counts. Human wants seem to be insatiable. But when a want can only be satisfied at some cost—that is, by giving up the satisfying of some other wants to obtain it—we all moderate our desires and accept less than we would like to have.

The phenomenon of which we're speaking is so fundamental that some economists have been willing to assign it the status of a law: *the law of demand.* This law asserts that there is a negative relation between the amount of anything that people will want to purchase and the price (sacrifice) they must pay to obtain it. At higher prices, they will want to purchase less; at lower prices they will want to purchase more.

Would you agree that this generalization can be called a *law?* Or can you think of exceptions? Genuine exceptions, if they exist at all, are rare. Why would people be indifferent to the sacrifices they must make? Or prefer more sacrifice to less? That is what a person would be doing who took *more* of something as the cost of obtaining it *increased.*

Alleged exceptions to the law of demand are usually based on a misinterpretation of the evidence. Consider the familiar case where the price of something rises and people increase their purchases in anticipation of further price rises. If you think about it carefully, you will see that this is not an exception to the law of demand. The expectation of higher prices in the future, created by the initial price rise, has increased people's current demand for the item. They want to buy more now so they can buy less later. It isn't the higher price but the changed *expectations* that have caused people to buy more at the present time. We would observe something quite different if the initial price increase did *not* create those changed expectations. Moreover, those whose expectation of further price increases has prompted them to purchase sooner than they otherwise would have done will still consider the sacrifice they must make in deciding how much to buy.

It has sometimes been argued that certain prestige goods are exceptions to the law of demand. For example, people supposedly buy mink coats because the price is high, not low. No doubt there are people who buy some items largely to impress others with how much they can afford to pay. And people sometimes, in the absence of better information, judge quality by price, so that over a limited range at least, their willingness to purchase may be positively rather than negatively related to price. But these seeming exceptions can readily be explained in a way consistent with the law of demand. People are purchasing prestige rather than mere mink, or judging quality by price because they have no better information.

Cases such as these, however, are rare curiosities at most. Whether or not you are willing to call it a law, the fact is undeniable and extremely important: Increases in the price of goods will characteristically be accompanied by decreases in the total amount people want to purchase, and decreases in price will characteristically be accompanied by increases in the amount they want to purchase. It is a serious mistake to overlook this relationship.

MISPERCEPTIONS CAUSED BY INFLATION

One major reason why many people today think that the law of demand doesn't operate is that they have forgotten to take the effects of inflation into account. In an era of rapid inflation, such as the United States and much of the rest of the world have experienced in recent years, most apparent price increases are not real price increases at all. Inflation so distorts our perceptions of relative price and cost changes that we'd better think about it before going any further. An ounce of anticipation may prevent a pound of confusion.

Inflation means an increase in the average *money* price of goods. But because we're accustomed to think of the price of anything as the quantity of money we have to sacrifice to get it, we easily conclude that twice as much money means twice as large a cost or sacrifice. That isn't the case, however, if twice as many dollars have only half as much purchasing power. If the money price of each and every good, including human labor and whatever else people sell or rent to obtain money, were to double, then *no* good would have changed in real price—except money, of course, which would have fallen by one-half. And so a doubling of the price of gasoline won't necessarily induce people to use any less gasoline—*if* at the same time their incomes and the prices of all the other goods they use have also doubled.

All money prices do not, in fact, change in equal proportion as a result of inflation—which is one of the reasons inflation is a problem. But they do tend to move together. Consequently, if we want to examine the effect of a particular price increase, we must first abstract from the effects of a general increase in prices. Suppose, for example, that a college that had been charging its students $2000 per year tuition in 1978 was charging $4000 in 1992. By how much had it raised tuition over this ten-year period? The answer is that it hadn't really raised its tuition at all. Because the purchasing power of money was cut in half between 1978 and 1992, a $4000 tuition in 1992 was equivalent to a $2000 tuition in 1978.

DEMAND AND QUANTITY DEMANDED

There is a general lesson to be drawn from all of this. In using the concept of demand, you must remain alert for the possibility that something else has changed in addition to the price. Your best protection is a clear grasp of the distinction between *demand* and *quantity demanded*. Commentators on economic events often use the word *demand* as a shorthand term for *quantity demanded*. That can and often does lead to error, as we shall see in a moment.

Demand in economic theory is a relationship between two specific variables: price and quantity demanded. You can't state the demand for any good simply as an amount. Demand is always a series of prices and a series of quantities (or amounts) that people would want to purchase at each of those prices. We express that fact by saying that demand is a schedule. A movement from one row of the schedule to an-

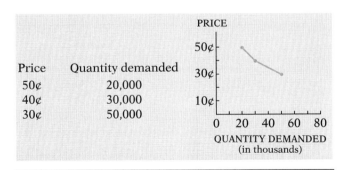

FIGURE 2A   A demand schedule and its complementary curve

Demand is a *schedule* of prices and quantities, not merely a quantity. In Figure 2A, the demand schedule on the left can be turned into a demand curve by connecting the points in the graph on the right.

other should always be called a change in the quantity demanded, not a change in the demand.

MAKING IT GRAPHIC

Many of the concepts economists use can be most easily expressed and understood by means of graphs. The troublesome but important distinction between demand and quantity demanded becomes clear immediately when it's presented on a graph. We can illustrate with the demand for water, as shown in Figure 2B.

(If you happen to be one of that considerable number of otherwise able people whose insides knot up at the sight of a graph, you ought to slow down at this point. Discover for yourself that graphs are not fatal by following carefully to see exactly what Figure 2B is asserting.)

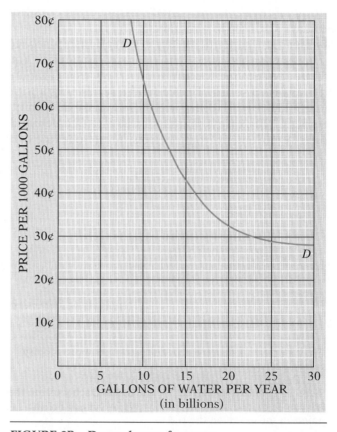

FIGURE 2B   Demand curve for water

The vertical axis shows possible prices that might be charged for water, in cents per 1000 gallons. The horizontal axis shows the quantity of water that would be demanded, or that people would want to purchase, at some of those prices.[1] The quantities are expressed in billions of gallons per year for whatever population the graph is summarizing.

Figure 2B yields the following demand schedule:

Price per 1000 Gallons	Billions of Gallons per Year
74¢	9
50	13
36	18
28	29

If the price happened to be 74 cents per 1000 gallons to begin with and was then lowered to 50 cents, the *quantity demanded* would increase from 9 to 13 billion gallons per year. At a price of 28 cents, the *quantity demanded* would be more than three times as great as at 74 cents. But the *demand* would be unchanged through all this, because the demand is the whole curve or schedule.

For the demand to increase, something would have to occur that made these people want to purchase more water than before *at each price*. A drought, for example, might induce people to water their lawns more frequently. Population growth in the area would also be likely to increase the demand; that is, move the whole curve upward and to the right. A campaign to conserve water, if successful, would decrease the demand, causing the curve or schedule to shift downward and to the left to reflect the fact that, at unchanged prices, people now want to purchase less water than previously.

If you would like to graph an increase in the demand for water, plot the quantities in the second column below on Fig-

[1]It's unfortunate that economists ever chose the word *demand* to describe the desire to purchase; but they've been using it in this way for several centuries and it's too late to change now. The economist's concept of demand carries absolutely none of the word's ordinary connotations of authority or threat, as in *non-negotiable demand*. Demand as the economist thinks of it is preeminently negotiable.

ure 2B. If you prefer to graph a decrease in demand, practice with the third column.

Price per 1000 Gallons	Billions of Gallons Demanded per Year	Billions of Gallons Demanded per Year
70¢	15	5
60	16	7
50	18	10
40	22	13

THE DIFFERENCE IT MAKES

A short editorial in *The Wall Street Journal* a number of years ago revealed the perils awaiting those who think such verbal distinctions are too trifling to bother with. The editorial writer wanted to chide an Agriculture Department economist for his ignorance of economics, an ignorance supposedly revealed by his stating that "the power of the U.S. consumer movement" had brought the price of coffee down again after it had hit a high of $4.42 a pound. Not so, said the *Journal's* editorial writer: "The coffee market is behaving the way the basic textbooks say a market behaves: Prices go up, demand falls, and prices come down."

The basic textbooks say nothing of the sort. On the contrary, they say that the editorial writer has confused the quantity demanded and the demand. When the price of coffee went up, the quantity demanded fell. Period. If the consumer movement managed to change people's attitudes toward serving and drinking coffee (some people got so angry about the price rises that they wouldn't drink coffee for a while at *any* price), then the consumer movement did succeed in changing the demand. And if the demand falls, *then* the price comes down. The *Journal's* mistaken logic implies, if you think about it carefully, that the price will bob up and down indefinitely, since when the price comes down again, demand ought to increase once more, causing the price to go up, whereupon the demand will fall, causing the price to go down. . . .

But it's all just a confusion of thought introduced by a careless use of terms. Think of price and quantity demanded as objects on the opposite ends of a seesaw, and demand as a large, lighter-than-air balloon to which the seesaw is attached. When price goes one way, quantity demanded goes

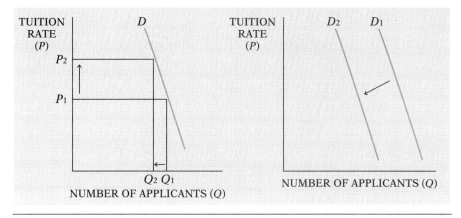

FIGURE 2C   Demand curves for a university education
   If a university raises its tuition rate, the number of applicants will decrease.
That is shown in Figure 2C on the left. The price (P) goes up and the quantity demanded (Q) goes down, but the demand curve itself does not change, so there is no
further effect we can predict.
   If, however, students decide that a university education is less valuable than
they previously supposed, then the demand will fail. That is shown on the right. The
demand curve (D1) shifts to the southwest (D2).

the opposite way. Changes in the demand (movements of the
balloon up or down) will exert simultaneous pressure in the
same direction on both the price and the quantity demanded.
The demand for any good is the product of biological realities, social relationships, psychological factors, and a broad
assortment of economic variables, such as income and the
price, quality, and general availability of substitutes. All these
forces combine to create the demand for a particular good,
the relationship that will exist between changes in its money
price and changes in the quantity people will try to obtain.
Unless the demand is changing (the balloon is ascending or
descending), price and quantity demanded will always move
in opposite directions.
   To put it most simply: The one change that will *not* cause
a change in the demand for bicycles is a change in the price
of bicycles. If a combination of rising incomes, environmental
concern, and new interest in outdoor exercise induces more
people to want bicycles, the demand for them will increase.
And both the price and quantity demanded may well increase
as a consequence. Something like this happens frequently.
You have grasped the distinction between demand and quantity demanded if you see clearly why this in no way contra-
dicts the law of demand. An increase in demand may pull up
both price and quantity demanded. But it will still be as true

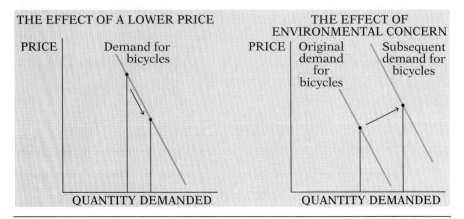

THE EFFECT OF A LOWER PRICE

THE EFFECT OF ENVIRONMENTAL CONCERN

FIGURE 2D   Demand curves for bicycles

with the high demand as with the low demand that a smaller quantity will be demanded at higher than at lower prices. And this is what the law of demand asserts. Economic theory isolates the money price of goods for special attention because of the exceptionally important role that money prices play in adjusting and coordinating people's behavior.

MONEY COSTS AND OTHER COSTS

None of this implies, however, that the price in money that must be paid for something is a complete measure of its cost to the purchaser. Indeed, sometimes it is a very inadequate measure (as in the case of the student who wanted an A). Economists know this at least as well as anyone else. The concept of demand definitely does not suggest that money is the only thing that matters to people. Confusion about this point has done so much to create misunderstanding that we might profitably take a moment to clarify the matter.

Ponder the cases of April Shauers and her coworker May Flours. April is a dedicated environmentalist who lives out her commitment by walking or taking the bus almost everywhere she goes. May despises public buses and uses her car for any trip longer than fifty yards. However, April does drive her car on family outings, because the cost of bus fare for all six Shauers would be too hard on the budget. And May suppresses her aversion to public buses whenever she has a meeting downtown, because the outrageous prices at the downtown parking garages are more than she's willing to pay. April

and May face the same money prices for driving and for taking the bus but make sharply contrasting decisions because of
different values, preferences, and circumstances.

To assert that people purchase less of anything as the
cost to them increases does not imply that people pay attention only to money, or that people are selfish, or that concern
for social welfare does not influence behavior. It does imply
that people respond to changes in cost and—a crucial implication—that a sufficiently large change in price can be
counted on to tip almost any balance. Money is a common
denominator, something to which everyone pays attention because they can all use it to further whatever projects they happen to be interested in. Changes in money prices are therefore
a useful device for coordinating people's behavior. That's why
economists give such changes so much of their attention.

WHO NEEDS WATER?

People are creatures of habit, in what they think as well as
what they do. Perhaps this also explains why so many have
trouble recognizing the significance of substitutes and hence
such difficulty appreciating the law of demand. Water provides an excellent example.

Back in the mid-1960s the first of a string of serious water shortages hit New York City. Several years of less than
normal rainfall had depleted the city's reservoirs, and there
was great fear that New York would run short of water during
the summer unless consumption could be sharply reduced. A
few brave souls suggested that the city should install more
water meters and raise the price of water. The suggestion was
not taken very seriously because, as everyone supposedly
knows, water is a necessity. "People won't go thirsty just because the price of water goes up a little, or even a lot," said
the critics. And so New York launched a massive campaign of
education plus legal threat to try to get its citizens to be more
sparing in their use of water.

Lawn sprinkling and car washing were condemned.
Restaurants were told not to give customers a glass of water
with their meals unless they specifically asked for it. The ornamental fountains of the city were turned off—largely as a
symbolic gesture, since the water in the fountains is recircu-
lated. Citizens were asked to refrain from keeping their beer
cool by letting the shower drip on it. One of the more amus-
ing aspects of the campaign was a set of ads for a particular
Scotch whiskey that urged people to drink their Scotch with

water. The word *water* was crossed out in the advertisement and *soda* was written above it, with an appended admonition to save water by drinking soda.

The water shortage was relieved not by any of these trivial measures but by a providential end to the drought. New Yorkers thereupon went back to their old familiar habits to await the next drought. It came in 1980, and in January of 1981 the mayor of New York City, warning that "there will be a calamity" unless residents conserve water, signed a law imposing fines of up to $1000 on "water wasters." Fortunately, the rains came soon thereafter, enabling New Yorkers to return to their dangerous conviction that the forces of nature, not human beings, cause water crises. Unfortunately, that conviction has by now made water crises a chronic condition in New York City.

The best way to turn a drought into a calamity is to pretend that water is a necessity. The truth is that there are many substitutes for water, a fact that becomes glaringly obvious as soon as we break loose from the habit of assuming that people do nothing with water except drink it.

Here are just a few of the substitutes for water in New York City: dirty automobiles, brown lawns, bricks in the toilet tank, low-flow shower heads, plumbers, migration, larger refrigerators (to hold the beer that would otherwise be cooled in the shower), plus a host of small inconveniences. The trick is to persuade people to *use* these substitutes: to call the plumber, for example, and have that leaky toilet repaired rather than allow it to continue wasting fifty gallons of water a day. To flush less frequently. To tolerate a dirty automobile. To put an ice cube in their glass of drinking water rather than let the tap run for several minutes to cool it. In the case of industries using huge quantities of water, to sacrifice the advantages of a New York location in favor of locating near more plentiful water supplies. Or to install recycling equipment.

But what is the best way to induce the use of substitutes? Educational campaigns and moral exhortation can help. But how much? Most people are expert rationalizers when their own interest is involved, and it is all too easy to put off calling the plumber until the end of the month, or next month, or the month after that, always fully intending, of course, to do one's civic duty and get that leak repaired.

What about criminal penalties for wasting water? Enforcement becomes a problem here. Are the police to stage surprise raids to catch people cooling their beer in the shower? Shall we fine a person for rinsing a glass too many times before taking a drink? What constitutes *criminal* waste?

A quite different approach is available. Is there any way to enlist almost everyone in a conscientious effort to seek out and use substitutes for water? A sizable increase in the price of water just might do the job. Wouldn't the careless house-holder call the plumber more quickly if that leaky toilet cost more per month than the plumber would charge to fix it? Wouldn't people accept dirty automobiles more readily, or at least not let the hose run the whole time they were washing the car, if water became very expensive? There is some price for water at which it becomes cheaper to buy a new refrigera-tor than to use the shower as a cooler. Industries that use large quantities of water will tend to locate elsewhere if the price of water is high in their area of first choice.

And so it goes. There are substitutes for anything. A higher money price will induce some people to find and use some of those substitutes. And the higher the price, the more will substitutes be used.

TIME IS ON OUR SIDE

If you are at all the suspicious sort of person, you will have wondered whether all these changes might not take too much time to be helpful. That is a healthy suspicion. Changes in the amount purchased will be greater for any given price change the longer the time period allowed for adjustment.

Check this out for yourself with a mental experiment. Suppose the price of water has been 30 cents per 1000 gallons for twenty years and it is raised overnight to 60 cents. What substitutions for water will be made *right away?* What substi-tutions would you expect to observe after a month or two had passed? What substitutions would you expect to observe over the next ten years—assuming that everyone expects the price to remain at the higher level?

An even better example is gasoline. How high will the price of gasoline have to go before Americans reduce their consumption? Don't answer without first noting that the price hasn't gone up by nearly as much as the newspaper headlines suggest. It's the *relative* price that matters, and much of the increase in the price of gasoline since 1972 is merely an inflation-induced rise in its *money* price. The 1972 price of 38 cents per gallon for regular would have been about $1.15 by 1992 *if gasoline prices had merely gone up at the rate of infla-tion.* The question is nonetheless a good one: How large a rel-ative price increase will it take to cut gasoline consumption by 10 percent or 25 percent or even 50 percent? The answer clearly depends on the time allowed for adjustments. People will buy cars that use less fuel, will move closer to work, and will arrange car pools if the price of gasoline rises far enough, but they won't do so at once. It will also take time for automotive engineers to increase the fuel efficiency of cars and for buses and airlines to expand their schedules.

By taking our examples almost entirely from the area of household decisions, we may have obscured the important fact that customers include producers as well as consumers. Business firms use water and gasoline, too, and they sometimes use so much that they are exceptionally sensitive to price changes. You'll be neglecting some of the major factors that cause demand curves to slope downward if you overlook the contribution producers make to the demand for many goods. In the case of water, location decisions are often made on the basis of the expected price of water, and those decisions then affect the quantities demanded in different geographic areas.

But it takes time for customers to find and begin to use substitutes. It also takes time for producers to devise, produce, and publicize substitutes. As a result, the amount by which people increase or decrease their purchases when prices change depends very much on the time period over which we are observing the adjustment. Occasionally, even a rather large price increase (or decrease) will lead to no significant decrease (or increase) in consumption—*at first*. And this sometimes causes people to conclude that price has no effect on consumption. A very mistaken conclusion! Nothing in this world happens instantly. People, creatures of habit that they are, must be allowed time to prove that there are substitutes for anything.

PRICE ELASTICITY OF DEMAND

It is extremely cumbersome to talk about "the amount by which people increase or decrease their purchases when the price changes." But this is an important relationship with many useful applications. So economists have invented a special concept that summarizes the relationship. The formal title of the concept is *price elasticity of demand*.

That's an appropriate name. Elasticity means responsiveness. If the amount of any good that people purchase changes substantially in response to a small change in price, demand is said to be elastic. If even a very large price change results in little change in the amount purchased, demand is said to be inelastic.

Price elasticity of demand is defined precisely as *the percentage change in quantity demanded divided by the percentage change in price.* Thus, if a 10 percent increase in the price of eggs leads to a 5 percent reduction in the number of eggs sold, the elasticity of demand is 5 percent divided by 10 percent, or 0.5. To be completely accurate, it is *minus* 0.5, since price and amount purchased vary inversely. But for simplicity we shall ignore the minus sign and treat all coefficients of elasticity as if they were positive.

Whenever the coefficient of elasticity is greater than 1.0 (ignoring the sign)—that is, whenever the percentage change in quantity purchased is *greater* than the percentage change in price—demand is said to be elastic. Whenever the coefficient of elasticity is less than 1.0, which means whenever the percentage change in quantity purchased is *less* than the percentage change in price, demand is said to be inelastic. Compulsive learners will want to know what is said when the percentage change in quantity is exactly equal to the percentage change in price, so that the coefficient of demand elasticity is exactly 1.0. You may file away the information that demand is then *unit elastic.*

You can begin to familiarize yourself with the uses of this concept by asking whether demand is elastic or inelastic in each case below. Each case is discussed in the subsequent paragraphs.

"People aren't going to buy much more no matter how far we cut the price."

"This is a competitive business. We would lose half our customers if we raised our prices by as little as 2 percent."

The demand for salt.

The demand for Morton's salt.

The demand for Morton's salt at the Kroger store at Fifth and Main.

"The university's total receipts from tuition would actually increase if tuition rates were cut by 20 percent."

"It's odd but true. Wheat farmers would gross more money if they all got together and burned one-quarter of this year's crop."

THINKING ABOUT ELASTICITY

"People aren't going to buy much more no matter how far we cut the price." If a businessman doubts that even a very large price decrease will do much to increase his sales, he believes

that his demand is highly inelastic. He will obviously not want to lower his price under such circumstances, for he will lose more through the lower price than he will gain through the larger volume. But if people don't respond very much to a price cut, will they also be relatively insensitive to a price hike? If they are, a businessman out to increase his income will want to raise his price. Businessmen typically complain that prices are too low. Then why don't they raise their prices? The answer, of course, is that they would usually lose too many customers if they did so. It is the elasticity of demand that determines whether or not a businessman can add to his money receipts by raising his prices.

"This is a competitive business. We would lose half our customers if we raised our prices by as little as 2 percent." The businesswoman making this statement is saying in effect that she faces a highly elastic demand: A 50 percent decline in quantity demanded would follow a mere 2 percent increase in price. The coefficient of elasticity is 25. The demand is very elastic indeed. Another way of putting it would be to say that her customers are extremely sensitive to any price change. And that makes it difficult for her to raise her prices, however eager she might be to do so.

The demand for salt. What makes demand curves elastic or inelastic? The availability of good substitutes is the most important factor. Another is the significance of the item in the budget of purchasers. If the expenditure on some good is large relative to the income or wealth of purchasers, they will be more sensitive to any change in its price.

Apply this to table salt. One pound of salt lasts a long time and costs a few pennies an ounce. So who cares? Shoppers will be relatively insensitive to any change in the price of salt. Moreover, salt has few good substitutes. You would not be inclined to put sugar on your eggs if the price of salt rose dramatically, just as you would not cut the pepper and double the salt if the price of salt fell substantially.

Adam Smith observed in *The Wealth of Nations* that "salt is a very ancient and very universal subject of taxation. . . . The quantity annually consumed by any individual is so small, and may be purchased so gradually, that nobody, it seems to have been thought, could feel very sensibly even a pretty heavy tax upon it." Moreover, salt was one of "the necessaries of life" in Smith's terminology. We can object to the term *necessary* and express Smith's meaning more accurately: Salt has few good substitutes. The result is a highly inelastic demand and an apparently irresistible temptation to some governments to levy taxes on salt.

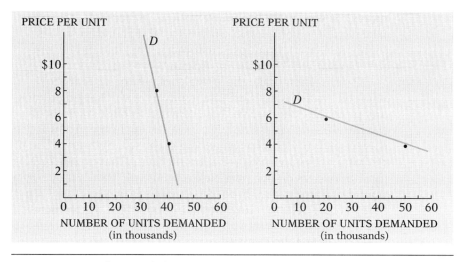

FIGURE 2E   Inelastic and elastic demand curves
    Given the relatively inelastic demand curve in Figure 2E on the left, reducing the price from $8 to $4 will cause only 5,000 additional units to be demanded. Total receipts from sales would fall from $280,000 to $160,000.
    With the relatively elastic demand curve on the right, 30,000 additional units will be demanded if the price is lowered from $6 to $4. Total receipts from sales will rise from $120,000 to $200,000.

But it's possible to exaggerate the inelasticity of even the demand for salt. Householders in wintry regions sometimes sprinkle table salt on their sidewalks or porch steps to melt the ice. If salt were ten times as expensive, many would substitute chopping and scraping for salt.

The demand for Morton's salt. Why would the demand for Morton's salt be less inelastic than the demand for salt? Because there are good substitutes—namely, other brands of salt. The Morton Salt Company is not in the privileged position of ancient governments, which could raise the price of *all* salt. If someone in the marketing department at Morton chanced to read Adam Smith and was inspired by him to double the price, the grocery stores that are Morton's customers would purchase from other salt manufacturers.

The demand for Morton's salt at the Kroger store at Fifth and Main. If there are more good substitutes for Morton's salt than for salt, there are even more good substitutes for Morton's salt sold at the local Kroger store. We have moved from a very inelastic to what is probably a highly elastic demand for the same quantity. And that is why you aren't victimized when you purchase salt. You might be willing to pay $5 a pound if salt were not available at a lower price. But fortunately for you, there are many options. Sellers who tried to take advantage of the fact that the total demand for salt is highly inelastic would lose customers. The demand for *the salt they sell* will be quite elastic.

People often make the mistake of assuming that those who sell "vital necessities" can get away with charging almost any price they choose. We have learned to be suspicious of the phrase *vital necessities.* Now we see again the grounds for this suspicion. Food has as good a claim as anything to the title "vital necessity." But the relevant fact is that *no one buys food.* Shoppers do not purchase a pound of "food"; they buy a pound of hamburger, or bacon, or calf's liver. And there are many sellers selling many kinds of food. All of which means that there are excellent substitutes for specific food commodities, and hence the demand curves are highly elastic. So sellers are for the most part closely constrained in the prices they can charge.

ELASTICITY AND TOTAL RECEIPTS

"The university's total receipts from tuition would actually increase if tuition rates were cut by 20 percent." The university's total receipts from tuition are the product of the tuition rate and the number of students who enroll. If a 20 percent decrease in the tuition rate results in an increase in tuition receipts, then there must have been a more than 20 percent increase in enrollment. The percentage change in quantity demanded is greater than the percentage change in price, so demand is elastic.

This suggests a simple way of thinking about elasticity. Keep in mind that the quantity demanded will always move in the opposite direction from the price. *If the price change causes total receipts to move in the* opposite *direction from the price change, demand must be elastic.* The change in the quantity purchased has to be larger in percentage terms than the price change because total receipts are nothing but the product of price and quantity. And that is the definition of an elastic demand. *If a price change causes total receipts to move in the* same *direction as the price change, demand must be inelastic.* The change in amount purchased was not large enough to outweigh the change in price. And that is the meaning of an inelastic demand.

Don't jump to the conclusion that the university will always be in a better financial position, given an elastic demand, if it lowers its tuition. True, lower tuition charges will mean larger receipts whenever demand is elastic; but a larger

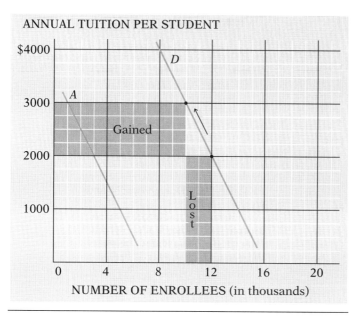

FIGURE 2F   Demand curves for a university education

Assume that the line labeled D in Figure 2F shows the demand for your university's services as an institution of undergraduate education. If the university raises its tuition rate from $2,000 to $3,000, it will lose 2,000 enrollees and the $2,000 in tuition each would have paid, or $4 million. But it will obtain an additional $1,000 from each of the 10,000 students who continue to enroll, or an additional $10 million. So total tuition receipts will rise by $6 million when the tuition rate rises, which is evidence of an inelastic demand.

Test your understanding by figuring out whether the parallel demand curve labeled A is also inelastic between $2,000 and $3,000. You should conclude that it's not. Total tuition receipts decline from $6 million to $3 million when tuition is raised from $2,000 to $3,000. So demand is elastic. Do you see why the demand curves, despite having the same slope, nonetheless have different elasticities between any two prices? It's because the percentage change in the quantity demanded is so much greater in the case of A. A change from 3,000 to 1,000 is a far larger percentage change than is the change from 12,000 to 10,000.

enrollment probably also means larger costs. The university must decide in such a case whether the addition to total receipts will be larger than the addition to total costs. (But problems of pricing strategy must be deferred until we reach Chapter 9.)

"It's odd but true. Wheat farmers would gross more money if they all got together and burned one-quarter of this year's crop." The logic of the preceding case also applies here. Farm-

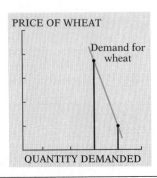

FIGURE 2G   Demand curve for wheat
Farmers would receive more income if one-fourth of the wheat crop simply disappeared, because the demand, as shown, is inelastic.

ers can gross more money while selling less wheat only if the percentage change in price is greater than the percentage change in the amount sold. Demand would have to be inelastic. The only difference is that we have reversed the causal relationship assumed till now. We have been tacitly assuming that sellers set the price and buyers respond. This is not always the best way to look at the price–quantity relationship. In some industries, such as agriculture for the most part, it is more useful to assume that the quantity available for sale will determine the price. We'll be talking a lot about this later. For now it is only important to notice that the relationship between changes in total sales and changes in price depends on the elasticity of demand.

Farmers may never have heard about elastic or inelastic demands. But when they lobby for government controls on production, they are usually very much aware of the relation between price and the amount that is sold. Like Molière's famous Monsieur Jourdain, who spoke prose for forty years without knowing it, you can make good use of demand elasticities without ever having heard the term.

THE MYTH OF VERTICAL DEMAND

Let's go back to the beginning. In the six statements with which we began this chapter, what was implicitly assumed about the elasticity of demand? Our objection to each statement, you recall, was that it ignored the fact that all goods have substitutes and that substitution does occur when prices change. In other words, demand curves are *not* completely inelastic. A completely inelastic demand curve would graph as a vertical line. You would be wise not to look for such demand curves in the real world.

The law of demand can now be expressed in the language of elasticity: *There is no such thing as a completely inelastic demand* over the entire range of possible prices. Most purchasers will respond at least a little to changes in the cost to them, and all purchasers will respond to a sufficiently large change. If this seems too obvious to bother mentioning, consult your daily newspaper for evidence that it is by no means obvious to everyone. Well-intentioned people and some not so well intentioned talk constantly of basic needs, minimum requirements, and absolute necessities.

Demand curves are rarely as inelastic as orators suppose. This does not imply, of course, that they are always elastic. That is a more difficult question, to be answered by looking at each case. But as we shall subsequently discover, it is a very important question for anyone who wants to decide how well our economic system functions.

ONCE OVER LIGHTLY

Every good has substitutes: other goods that will be used in its stead when the cost of using the original good rises, goods for which the original good will become a substitute when their cost rises. Pork replaces beef when the price of beef goes up, and a restaurant beefsteak takes the place of a movie when theater tickets become more expensive.

By talking about "needs" we can sometimes win arguments we might otherwise lose. Needs are actually wants of many different urgencies.

People want more or less of a good as the cost those people must pay decreases or increases.

The concept of *demand* is preferable to the concept of *need,* because demand relates the amounts that people want to purchase to the sacrifices that must be made to obtain these amounts.

The "law of demand" asserts that people will want to purchase more at lower prices, less at higher prices—assuming that something in addition to the price has not changed to offset this consequence.

The money cost of a good is only one part of the cost that affects people's decisions.

A sufficiently large change in money cost (price) can usually overcome the effects that nonmoney costs exert on people's decisions.

A change in price will usually induce a larger change in amounts purchased when more time is allowed for consumers and producers to learn about and invent new substitutes.

Price elasticity of demand is a measure of the percentage change in the quantity of a good demanded relative to the percentage change in its price.

Demand is (price) elastic when the percentage change in quantity demanded is greater than the percentage change in price. Demand is inelastic when the percentage change in quantity demanded is smaller than the percentage change in price.

Price elasticity of demand depends on the importance of the price relative to one's income, but even more on the quality and price of available substitutes.

More separate sources of supply for a good imply better substitutes for any particular good and hence a more elastic demand.

Total receipts or expenditures move in the opposite direction from price when demand is elastic and in the same direction as price when it is inelastic.

The concept of "needs" implies a perfectly inelastic demand curve—an extremely rare phenomenon.

The demand for a good refers to the *schedule of relationships* between price and quantity demanded and must be distinguished from the quantity or amount that is demanded. The quantity of a good demanded changes with its price. But a true change in demand will alter both price and quantity demanded.

QUESTIONS FOR DISCUSSION

1. A Gallup Report quoted by *The Wall Street Journal* in January 1985 found that the average U.S. family says it needs at least $252 per week after taxes "to get by." College graduates reportedly needed $301 a week on the average, but high-school graduates needed only $250 a week. While Democrats said they could get by on $251 a week, Republicans needed $298. Do you think college graduates and Republicans really have more needs, or more expensive needs, than high school graduates and Democrats? What explains these differences?

2. According to a National Automobile Safety Study conducted by Northeastern University and reported on by *The Wall Street Journal* in February

1986, 16 percent of all surveyed consumers said they would "definitely buy" an air-bag safety system for their automobiles if one were available for $500. Only 5 percent of them would "definitely buy," however, at a price of $1000. What does this imply about the "need" for air-bags on the part of those people who are convinced that air-bags will work? What does the study suggest in general about the "need" for life-saving goods?

3. U.S. courts decided in 1977 that prohibitions on advertising by lawyers were illegal. Since that time many legal "clinics" have sprung up, advertising standard legal services at lower than ordinary fees. Would you agree with the results of a survey showing that about 60 percent of all middle-income Americans have "unmet legal needs"? What are some "legal needs" that many people will only have if they can hire a lawyer cheaply?

4. Most systems of hospitalization insurance substantially reduce the cost to the patient of hospitalization, sometimes to zero. How does this affect hospital use? Why? Evaluate the argument that it does not affect hospital use since "no one gets sick just because hospitals are cheap or avoids getting sick because they're expensive."

5. In 1967 the president of the American Medical Association was quoted as saying that medical care was a privilege and not a right. Today the AMA officially proclaims that "health care is the right of everyone." What quantity and quality of health care do you suppose they're talking about? Is a liver transplant, for example, the right of everyone with a diseased liver?

6. Here is a paragraph from a front-page story that was published in August 1988 in *Workers World* during a record-breaking heat wave in the midwestern United States:

> Shouldn't air conditioning be a right? Why should it only be accessible to those who can afford it? Only a system which defines human worth based on how much money you have would reject the simple solution that in these crisis weeks everyone who needs air conditioning must have it.

Who "needs" air conditioning? Do people in wealthy nations like the United States "need" air conditioning more than people in much hotter but also much poorer nations, such as Bangladesh or Niger? Did anyone "need" air conditioning before it had been invented?

7. The contention that certain goods are "basic human needs" carries a strong suggestion that access to those goods should be a matter of right, not of privilege. But the assertion of rights logically entails the assertion of obligations. Your right to vote, for example, entails the obligation of election officials to accept and count your ballot; your right to use your own umbrella implies an obligation on the part of others not to borrow it without your permission. If "health care is the right of everyone," who has the obligation to provide health care to everyone? Who currently accepts the obligation to provide people with health care? How are they persuaded to accept these obligations?

8. Here is a classroom exercise that might be fun and also sharpen your ability to recognize substitution possibilities. Let one person come up with two goods that seem to have no connection and challenge others to construct a plausible set of circumstances in which one would be a substitute for the other. (Avoid the easy, though correct, answer that all goods are in the last analysis substitutes inasmuch as the acquisition of each uses up scarce time or income.)

9. The advertising slogan of Maker's Mark whiskey is: "It tastes expensive . . . and is."

   (a) Isn't the seller foolish to advertise the high price? Or will people buy more at higher prices? Does this contradict the law of demand?

   (b) A waiter at Jean-Louis, a restaurant in Washington, DC, often patronized by eminent politicians, says, "It is good to be known as expensive. People know they can impress their guests here." What does he think people are purchasing when they go to Jean-Louis for dinner?

10. "Electricity, by its nature, . . . will not yield much to conservation, whether inspired by government mandates, price, or ideology. It is the energy form of choice." Do you agree with that assertion from a letter to the editor of *The Wall Street Journal* (October 17, 1986)? Is electricity the energy form of choice *without regard to price?* Why do some urban transit systems use diesel buses while others operate electric buses? Why do some people heat their homes with oil or natural gas while others use electric heat?

11. A front-page article in *The Wall Street Journal* of May 13, 1980, was headlined: "Europe's Drivers Don't Reduce Gasoline Use Despite Soaring Prices." In the continuation of the story on a back page, the reporter revealed that pump prices had increased 120 percent in Great Britain from 1973 to 1979 while the general price level had risen by about 140 percent. How would you criticize that headline?

12. If the government forbids motorists to drive more than 55 miles per hour, does everyone stay within the 55-mile limit? What are the costs of going faster? What are some of the costs of going faster that do not fall on the speeding motorist? Do these latter costs affect motorists' decisions? Why might the fact that faster driving uses up more of the nation's scarce petroleum reduce the speed of some drivers but not others?

13. Why do people live in New York City if the costs of doing so—high rents, noise, dirt, congestion, the risks of being robbed or assaulted—are so high? Is it true that most of them "have no choice"? What do you think would happen if the costs mentioned were significantly reduced?

14. Here is a question from a letter to the editor of a Seattle newspaper protesting a proposal to reduce gasoline consumption by imposing a tax of 50 cents per gallon. "How could you or anyone think that such a tax

would reduce gas consumption when a doubling of the price, consisting of considerably more than 50 cents a gallon over the past two years, has not reduced consumption one iota?"

(a) What does this letter writer think the demand curve for gasoline looks like?

(b) Do we have any evidence on whether or not he is correct?

(c) The writer recommends the elimination by law of nonessential uses and mentions as an example rural mail deliveries six days a week. Would we be eliminating a nonessential use of gasoline if all rural carriers took Saturdays off? Why don't we eliminate Tuesday and Thursday deliveries as well and save even more gasoline?

15. "Coffee Prices Sink as Demand Wanes." Does that newspaper headline use the word *demand* correctly? Would you expect those falling prices to be associated with more or with less coffee consumption?

16. Higher prices for beef, automobiles, or television sets will lead to a reduction in the *amount of each demanded.* Think of some specific changes (such as in tastes, prices of substitutes, quality of complementary goods) that would cause the *demand* for each to increase so that more might actually be demanded at higher prices. Why is this completely consistent with the law of demand?

17. Does the graph in Figure 2H, employed by some medical organizations to predict a "doctor glut," use the concept of demand in the same way that economists use it?

18. Do the following statements use the word *demand* correctly? Or should the term *quantity demanded* be substituted?

(a) When OPEC raised the price of oil in the 1970s, the demand for oil fell.

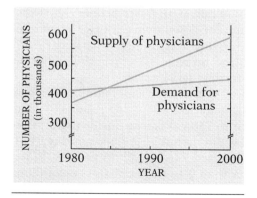

FIGURE 2H   **Demand and supply curves for physicians**

(b) Inflation has increased the demand for oil.

(c) When the Iran–Iraq war broke out, oil refiners panicked, and their panic increased the demand for oil and sharply raised its price.

(d) The 55-mile-per-hour speed limit has reduced the demand for oil.

(e) Price controls imposed by the United States in the 1970s on domestic oil producers, by keeping down the price of U.S.-produced oil, increased our demand for OPEC oil.

19. A change in expectations can cause a change in demand. Explain how this could lead to a situation in which a price decline was followed by a decrease in the amount purchased.

20. Is it strictly true that a change in the price of a good causes a change in the quantity of that good demanded but *not* a shift in the demand curve for the good?

  (a) What effect did the large increases in the price of gasoline in the 1970s have on the demand (curve) for fuel-efficient cars?

  (b) What effect did this have after several years on the original demand (curve) for gasoline?

  (c) How did the increase in the price of heating oil in the 1970s affect the demand for housing insulation? How did this eventually shift the demand for heating oil?

  (d) Can you think of similar processes through which changes in the price of other goods would lead over time to shifts in the demand for those goods?

  (e) If the price of a good returned to its previous level after a time but the quantity demanded did not, would this be evidence that the demand had changed in the interim?

21. The graphs in Figure 2I show the demand for bus service (left) and the demand for downtown parking space (right) in an imaginary city. If the city raises bus fares from p_1 to p_2, the demand curve will not change, but the quantity demanded will fall. With fewer people riding the bus, what will happen to the demand for downtown parking? What effect will this have on downtown parking rates? With higher parking rates, more people will want to ride the bus. So what effect will the higher bus fare have after all on the demand for bus service?

22. According to a 1983 report by the American Planning Association, the average four-member household uses about 345 gallons of water daily. The report broke that down into 235 gallons for inside use and 110 for outside use. Of the "inside" water, about 95 gallons per day went to flush toilets. Drinking and cooking used 9 to 10 gallons per day. Water rates vary; but they are rarely higher than 0.1¢ (that's $0.001) per gallon. Would a doubling or even a quadrupling of water rates work a serious hardship on poor people?

23. On June 18, 1985, *The Wall Street Journal* ran an article entitled "Denver Turns on to Xeriscape," describing efforts to persuade Denver residents

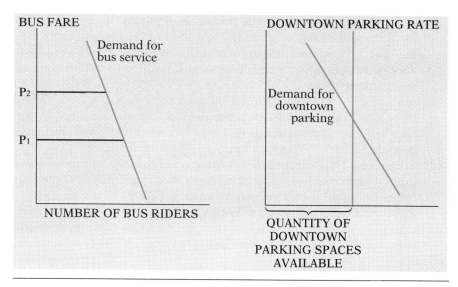

FIGURE 2I   Demand curves for bus service and downtown parking

to avoid "a consumer water crunch" by growing lawns that require little irrigation. (*Xeriscape* is the technique of gardening in dry climates.) The predominant grass in Denver lawns is currently Kentucky bluegrass, which requires about 18 gallons of added water per square foot each summer to thrive in the arid climate. Buffalo grass, by contrast, will do well on half as much water.

(a) How much extra would a homeowner with a typical 5000-square-foot lawn pay in water costs to enjoy Kentucky blue rather than buffalo grass at a price of 60¢ per 1000 gallons? Is this likely to affect the decisions of many homeowners?

(b) The schedule of water prices for Denver users with a ¾-inch main in June 1985 was actually 74¢ per 1000 gallons for the first 15,000 gallons per month, 60¢ per 1000 for the next 35,000, 46¢ per 1000 for the next 650,000, and 42¢ per 1000 gallons for all consumption beyond 700,000 gallons per month, with a minimum charge of $2.65 per month. How much do the first 4000 gallons cost under this pricing scheme?

24. A 1980 drought in the northeastern United States produced, early in 1981, numerous water-rationing schemes in the states, cities, and towns of the region. The following bits of information were gleaned from a *Wall Street Journal* feature of February 25, 1981:

(a) Greenwich, Connecticut, limited users to 45 gallons of water per day. One resident predicted they would soon be drinking Perrier. Is that likely?

(b) In Randolph, Massachusetts, people were paying 10 cents per gallon for deep-well water, because the low level of the town's reservoirs had given the water from them an offensive taste. What would have been a cheaper way for the citizens of Randolph to obtain good-tasting drinking water?

(c) Many cities and towns banned "nonessential uses of water." Which of these uses, in your opinion, is nonessential: macaroni manufacture, beer brewing, lawn sprinkling, filling of swimming pools, ordinary household use (cooking, cleaning, showering, flushing)?

(d) When New Jersey imposed rationing on about 200 communities, it limited each resident to 50 gallons per day. How many people have "essential uses" for 50 gallons of water per day?

(e) Per-capita water use in New York City at the onset of the drought was 190 gallons. How much of that do you think went for "essential uses"?

25. How do you think the development of other copying machines affected the elasticity of demand for Xerox machines?

26. Is the demand for prescription drugs elastic or inelastic? Why? Do you agree with the statement sometimes made that the prices charged for prescription drugs can be freely set by the manufacturers, since people must buy whatever the doctor prescribes?

27. How does ignorance affect elasticities of demand?

28. How might the development of science and technology affect demand elasticities?

29. Does a society's transportation system in any way affect elasticities of demand? How?

30. The demand for aspirin at currently prevailing prices seems to be highly inelastic. What do you think would happen to the elasticity of demand if the price of aspirin relative to everything else were five times as high? Fifty times as high? Why?

31. In 1977 Brazil was supplying about one-third of the world's coffee exports. When a frost wiped out about 75 percent of Brazil's 1976–77 crop, the price of green (unroasted) coffee rose 400 percent. What was the approximate price elasticity of demand for coffee? Why was it so low?

32. Harvest-time rains in California in the spring of 1978 destroyed a portion of the lettuce crop. As a result, the price for a 24-head carton loaded in California hit a record of $18 on May 1, 1978. On June 29, after new crops had come in, the price was $2.75. What does all this suggest about the demand for lettuce? What attitudes and practices on the part of households and restaurants contribute toward making the demand for lettuce very inelastic with respect to price?

33. In a January 1984 *Wall Street Journal* article on Chicago's attempt to attract more transit riders with lower fares, Joseph L. Schofer, research di-

rector at Northwestern University's Transportation Center, was quoted as saying that "lower fares never make up for loss of revenues. Even when losing riders by increasing fares, revenue usually goes up. It's a law of economics." What exactly is the "law of economics" Mr. Schofer seems to be defending? Would you agree in calling it a "law of economics"?

34. When William Bennett was director of the Office of National Drug Control Policy, he sent a letter to Ann Landers attacking one of her correspondents who had advocated the legalization of drugs. Here is one paragraph from the letter: "Drugs would become much cheaper—at least one-fifth the cost. Then five times as many people could and would buy them. We would then have five times as many addicts. This means instead of only 100,000 addicted babies being born to addicted mothers each year, we would have half a million." What assumptions is he making about the demand for drugs?

35. The Congressional Budget Office concluded in 1984 that adding access charges of $2 to $6 per month to the bills of phone subscribers would not induce many users to give up their phones—as some critics of the charges had maintained. "Demand for local telephone service is quite inelastic," according to the CBO report.

(a) If the cost of local phone service rose from $12 to $18 per month, what percentage of telephone subscribers would have to give up their phones for the demand to be described as elastic?

(b) What percentage do you estimate would actually do so? What is the coefficient of elasticity that you are estimating?

36. Price elasticity of demand can be calculated by dividing the percentage change in the quantity demanded by the percentage change in the price.

(a) What is the coefficient of elasticity between the two points of the demand schedule in each of the cases shown below?

Price per Ticket	Tickets Demanded	Price per Cup of Coffee	Cups of Coffee Demanded
$2	200	35¢	600
$1	400	70¢	300

(b) If you divided 100% by 50% in the ticket case, and 50% by 100% in the coffee case, you got very different coefficients (2 and 0.5, respectively) for what are actually identical relative changes. The different results come from using the larger price and the smaller quantity as the base from which to calculate the percentage change in the first case, and using the smaller price and the larger quantity as the base in the second case. But the coefficient of elasticity should be the same between two points regardless of the direction in which the change is measured. How can this problem be handled?

(c) What is the coefficient of elasticity in each of these cases if you use the *average* of the prices and quantities between which the change is occurring as the base for calculating the percentage changes?

(d) In both cases, total expenditure (price times quantity) does not change when the price changes. What does this imply about the elasticity of demand between the prices given? Does this implication agree with your answer in (c)? (It should.)

37. Figure 2J shows a hypothetical demand curve for strawberries.

(a) What price per case would maximize the gross receipts of strawberry growers? [Peek at part (d) of this question rather than waste too much time trying all sorts of different prices. The price that maximizes gross receipts will be found at the midpoint of a straight-line demand

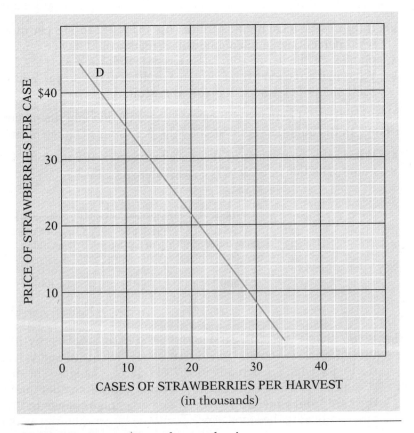

FIGURE 2J   Demand curve for strawberries

curve when the curve is extended to the axes. If you see why, good. If not, it's a bit of knowledge with only academic usefulness anyway.]

(b) If the price of strawberries is determined by the total quantity harvested in conjunction with the demand, what size crop will result in the price quoted in part (d)?

(c) What would the gross receipts of strawberry growers be if the crop turned out to be 30,000 cases?

(d) Can you prove that the demand for strawberries is elastic above a price of $24 per case and inelastic below that price?

(e) If strawberry growers can make more money by selling fewer than 30,000 cases, why would they ever market that much? Why wouldn't they destroy some of the crop rather than "spoil the market"?

38. Here is a puzzling headline from a front-page story in *The Wall Street Journal* of October 12, 1992: "Natural-Gas Prices Surge, and Producers Aren't Happy at All." Why would natural-gas producers be *unhappy* about a large increase in the price of their product?

(a) The article explains how a series of unrelated events reduced the quantity of natural gas available to consumers and prompted a 140% increase in the price of natural gas between February and October of 1992. What does this suggest about the elasticity of demand for natural gas, at least in the short run?

(b) Would you expect to observe a considerably different elasticity of demand for natural gas in the long run? Why?

(c) How does a comparison of the short-run and long-run demands for natural gas explain the producers' unhappiness about their current prosperity?

39. See if you can clarify this analysis: "If half of our forests were destroyed in a fire, the value of the remaining lumber would be greater than the value of all the lumber in the country before the fire. This absurdity—that the whole is worth less than a half—shows that values are distorted in a market economy."

40. Here's a question for those who wondered why price was graphed along the vertical axis in Figure 2A, which is the standard procedure in economics, rather than along the horizontal axis, where the independent variable usually goes. Is price in fact the independent and quantity the dependent variable? If quantity depends on price, on what does price depend? Who or what determines prices?

OPPORTUNITY COST AND THE SUPPLY OF GOODS

Y ou have already been introduced to the central concept of this chapter. If you failed to notice, that's because we didn't call it by its proper name. But several times in the preceding chapter, in talking about the relationship between price and quantity demanded, we pointed out that the amount of any good that a person will want to purchase is determined by the good's cost to that person, or the value of the sacrifice required to obtain it. That is the definition of *opportunity cost,* a concept that ties together the law of demand and the principles governing supply. We shall try to convince you in this chapter that it makes sense to think of cost as *the value of sacrificed opportunities.*

COSTS ARE VALUATIONS

Everyone will concede that demand reflects people's values. But supply, many believe, is the material side of economics, governed by costs of production that are objective realities, in contrast with such subjective factors as people's values and preferences. That belief is in error. Supply and cost are also based on valuations. To help you see this, we shall detour through a college dormitory on a Monday night in the fall, where the following exchange takes place.

"Hey, Jack, do you want to go see the new Wim Wenders movie? It closes after tonight."

"I'd like to, but I can't. We've got a Russian test tomorrow, and I'll flunk if I don't cram some vocabulary."

"Forget it. You can borrow my vocabulary cards in your free period tomorrow. An hour with the cards right before class is a B for sure."

"Well—trouble is, the Redskins and Miami are on TV tonight and I'd rather watch the game if I don't have to study."

"We'll go at six and be back for the kickoff."

"All right. Just let me see how much money I've got—five, six, seven, eight dollars—to last until I get paid on Thursday. And I'm out of meal tickets!"

"Eat peanut butter sandwiches! I thought you wanted to see the movie."

"I do. O.K., I'll let my stomach shrink until Thursday. Should we leave at quarter to six?"

The real cost of any action (going to a movie, buying a pair of jeans, manufacturing a lawnmower, moving to Halifax, raising beef cattle, building a hardware store, taking out an insurance policy) is the value of the alternative opportunity that must be sacrificed in order to take the action. The cost for Jack of going to the movie was at first calculated as a passing grade (given up!) in Russian. When his friend showed him how to reduce that cost, Jack looked at the next most valuable opportunity he would have to sacrifice if he went to the movie: watching the Monday night football game, a game he particularly wanted to see. His friend eliminated that cost for him, and Jack turned to the money cost. But money wasn't the real cost. The real costs that dollars and cents represent are the opportunities given up when the money is spent in one way rather than another. The five or six dollars Jack will spend for the movie represent some meals he would have liked to eat but is willing to sacrifice in order to see the film.

PRODUCERS' COSTS AS OPPORTUNITY COSTS

The theory of supply in economics is not essentially different from the theory of demand. Both assume that decision-makers face alternatives and choose among them, and that their choices reflect a comparison of benefits and costs. The logic of the economizing process is the same for producers as it is for consumers.

When we think about producers' costs—asking ourselves, for example, why it costs more to manufacture a ten-speed bicycle than a redwood picnic table—we tend to think first of what goes into the production of each. We think of the raw materials, of the labor time required, perhaps also of the machinery or tools that must be used. We express the value of the inputs in monetary terms and assume that the cost of the bicycle or the table is the sum of these values. That isn't wrong, but it leaves unanswered the question of why the inputs had those particular monetary values. The concept of opportunity cost asserts that those values reflect the value of the inputs in their next-best uses, or the value of the opportunities forgone by using the inputs in the production of bicycles and picnic tables.

Manufacturers' costs of producing a bicycle will be determined by what they must pay to obtain the appropriate resources. And, because these resources have other opportunities for employment, they must pay a price that matches the "best opportunity" value. The value of forgone opportunities thus becomes the cost of manufacturing a bicycle. This makes excellent sense, for the meaningful cost of obtaining one more bicycle is the value of what must be given up or sacrificed or forgone in order to obtain that bicycle.

Consider the example of the picnic table. Part of its cost of production is the price of redwood. Assume that the demand for new housing has increased recently and that building contractors have consequently been purchasing a lot more redwood lumber. If this causes the price of lumber to rise, the cost of manufacturing a picnic table will go up. Nothing has happened to affect the physical inputs that go into the table, but its cost of production has risen. Because houses containing redwood lumber are now more valuable than formerly, table manufacturers must pay a higher opportunity cost for the lumber they want to put into their picnic tables. When Hurricane Andrew devastated southern Florida in 1992, the price of plywood quickly rose across the entire United States. Plywood took on a greatly increased value for people whom Andrew had made homeless, and everyone who wanted to use plywood for other purposes now had to pay this new opportunity cost.

The concept of opportunity cost also explains how labor enters into production costs. Workers must receive from their employers a wage that persuades them to turn down all other opportunities. A skilled worker will be paid more than an unskilled worker because and only insofar as those skills make the skilled worker more valuable somewhere else. Workers who can install wheel spokes while standing on their heads and whistling "Dixie" are marvelously skilled. But our bicycle manufacturer will not have to pay them additional compensation for that skill unless their unusual talent makes them more valuable somewhere else. That could happen. A circus might bid for their talents. If the circus offers them more than they can obtain as bicycle producers, their opportunity cost to the manufacturer rises. In that case the manufacturer will probably wish them goodbye and good luck and replace them with other workers whose opportunity cost is lower.

When the National Basketball Association and the American Basketball Association merged into one league, what happened to the opportunity cost of hiring physically coordinated seven-footers? With two leagues, each player had two teams bidding for his services. What either team was compelled to pay to get him was determined by what the other team was willing to pay, and both were willing to pay a lot if they thought he would make a big difference in ticket sales. When the leagues merged, however, the right to hire a particular player was assigned to a single team, and the opportunity cost of hiring a well-coordinated seven-footer fell. When the players' union subsequently secured the right of players (under certain circumstances) to switch to another team if they chose, the opportunity cost of hiring basketball stars rose again. It's not surprising that owners of professional athletic teams prefer one league to two and vehemently argue that giving players the right to switch teams will destroy balance and hence the quality of the game.

Let's take a more ordinary case. If a large firm employing many people moves into a small town, the cost of hiring grocery clerks, bank tellers, secretaries, and gasoline station attendants in the town will tend to go up. Why? Because grocery stores, banks, offices, and gasoline stations must all pay the opportunity cost of the people they employ, and these people may now find better opportunities for employment in the new firm. Suppose the new firm is interested in hiring women exclusively; then only the opportunity cost of hiring women will increase at first. But that will pull women out of some jobs, thereby creating additional opportunities for men and causing the opportunity cost of male workers to rise.

The resource that most clearly illustrates the opportunity-cost concept is probably land. Suppose you want to purchase an acre of land to build a house. What will you have to pay for the land? It will depend on the value of that land in alternative uses. Do other people view the acre as a choice residential site? Does it have commercial or industrial potentialities? Would it be used for pasture if you did not purchase it? The cost you pay for the land will be determined by the alternative opportunities that people perceive for its use.

CASE STUDIES IN OPPORTUNITY COST

Let's examine some other cases of varying costs to see how the concept of opportunity cost explains familiar but often misunderstood phenomena.

Why, in the last fifty years, has the cost of getting a hair-cut gone up so much more than the cost of goods generally? It's because people who want barbers to cut their hair must be willing to pay them enough to keep them in the trade. If productivity in haircutting had kept pace over the last fifty years with productivity in manufacturing, barbers would have been able to maintain their incomes by trimming more heads per hour. But with productivity virtually unchanged, only a higher price per head could keep them working in the barber shop. We who want our hair cut by professionals have bid up the price of haircuts to meet the rising opportunity cost to barbers of working at a job in which productivity never increases.

Why is it often so much harder to find a teenage babysitter in a wealthy residential area than in a low-income area? The frustrated couple unable to find a babysitter may complain that all the kids in the neighborhood are lazy. But that is a needlessly harsh explanation. Teenage babysitters can be found by any couple willing to pay the opportunity cost. That means bidding the babysitters away from their otherwise most valued opportunity. If the demand for babysitters in the area is large because wealthy people go out more often, and if the local teenagers receive such generous allowances that they value a date or leisure more than the ordinary income from babysitting, why be surprised to find that the opportunity cost of hiring a babysitter is high?

Why did the cost of obtaining a college education rise so steeply during the 1960s? A very large part of the explanation lies in sharply increased instructional costs, made up partly of higher faculty salaries and partly of reduced teaching loads. But how did these developments come about? Ask your friendly neighborhood professor and she will probably tell you about the long years that must be spent getting a Ph.D. and the impossibility of doing research while teaching twelve hours. Any good member of the professorial guild will assent to the virtues of those arguments. But no good economics professor will be much impressed with their cogency as an explanation of why professors earned more and taught less at the end of the decade than at the beginning.

The rapidly rising demand for professors provides the explanation. State legislatures poured money into building new

colleges and expanding old ones; the federal government responded to the fear of Soviet scientific superiority by appro-
priating vast sums for higher education and for research,
which gave teachers new opportunities; the World War II
baby boom became a college-student boom in the 1960s; and
a larger percentage of the population became persuaded that
a college degree was a passport to the good life. The government and private industry meanwhile increased their demand
for the services of highly trained persons, widening the range
of opportunities for people with extensive education. The net
result was a vastly increased demand for the services of college professors. College professors, too, are scarce resources
with opportunity costs. A larger number of them were obtained by bidding them away from alternative employments
with the offer of higher salaries and reduced teaching loads.
(All college professors know that it is easier to raise their incomes by finding a better opportunity elsewhere than by
reciting their virtues to their current deans. Deans are more
attentive to the recitals of professors with alternative opportunities.)

If you have grasped the argument, you should see why
the salaries of many college professors declined in the 1980s.
Inflation partially concealed that decline; but once we have
adjusted for changes in the value of the dollar, we can see
the same factors that pulled faculty salaries up in the 1960s
pulling them down in the 1980s.

Why does the high-school dropout rate decrease during a
recession? The opportunity cost of remaining in high school
varies with the job market for teenagers. A decline in job opportunities reduces the opportunity cost of remaining in
school for some young people; therefore, fewer drop out.

Why are poor people more likely to travel between cities
by bus and wealthy people more likely to travel by air? A simple answer would be that taking the bus is cheaper. But it
isn't. It's a very expensive mode of transportation for people
for whom the opportunity cost of time is high; and the opportunity cost of time is typically much lower for poor people
than for those with a high income from working.

Do you have the idea? Figure out for yourself the cost of
going to college. If you include in your calculations the value
to yourself of whatever you would be doing if you were not in
college, you have grasped the principle of opportunity cost.

A final example. Consider the case of a woman who runs
a small grocery store all by herself. She says that she does
pretty well because she has no labor cost. Is she right? The
cost of her own labor is not a monetary outlay, but it certainly

is a cost. And that cost can be measured by the value of the opportunities she forgoes by working for herself.

COSTS AND ACTIONS

The economic way of thinking recognizes *no* objective costs. That offends common sense, which teaches that things do have "real" costs, costs that depend on the laws of physics rather than the vagaries of the human psyche. It's hard to win a battle against common sense, but we must try.

Perhaps we can disarm common sense most quickly by pointing out that "things" have no costs at all. We are talking about costs relevant to supply, of course—costs that have an effect on people's decisions to make goods available. "Things" cannot have costs in that sense. Only actions can. If you think that things do indeed have costs and are ready with an example to prove it, you are almost certainly smuggling in an unnoticed action to give your item a cost.

For example: What is the cost of a baseball? "Five dollars," you say. But you mean that the cost of *purchasing* a baseball at the local sporting goods store is five dollars. Since purchasing is an action, it can entail sacrificed opportunities and thereby have a cost. But note the smuggled-in action. With other actions, the cost of a baseball changes. The cost of *manufacturing* a baseball is quite different. *Selling* one has yet another cost. And what about the cost of *catching* one at the ball park by spearing a line-drive foul with your bare hand, where the sacrifice may be the opportunity to wear an unbroken nose the rest of your life?

Let's return to the case of a college education. What does it cost? The answer is that "it" cannot have a cost. We must first distinguish the cost of *obtaining* a college education from the cost of *providing* one. As soon as we make that distinction, we should also notice something that has been implicit in everything we've said so far about costs, either in this or the preceding chapter: Costs are always cost *to someone.* The cost of obtaining an education usually means the cost to the student. But it could mean the cost to the student's parents, which is not the same. Or, if that student's admission entailed the rejection of some other applicant, it could even mean the cost to John (who was refused admission) of Marsha's obtaining entrance to the first-year class. Those will all be different.

A great deal of fruitless argument about the "true cost" of things stems from a failure to recognize that only actions have costs, and that actions can entail different costs for different people. The ongoing debate about reinstituting the military draft is an excellent example. Let's take a look.

THE COST OF A VOLUNTEER MILITARY FORCE

Selective service, as it is euphemistically called, has been around for a long time. Although almost everyone regards it as undesirable in itself, many Americans still seem to think of it as the only way to secure an adequate supply of military personnel at an acceptable cost.

There may be good arguments for the draft, but the familiar argument that an adequate volunteer army[1] would cost too much is not one of them. The Department of Defense and others who worry about the relative costs of a conscripted and a volunteer military are conveniently bypassing the question of cost to whom. Are we talking about the cost to taxpayers, enlisted personnel, Congress, or the Pentagon? They are very different.

What is the cost to a young person of becoming a soldier? The best way to find out would be to offer a bribe and to keep raising it until it was accepted. If Marshall would enlist for $5000 per year, Carol for $8000, and Philip for no less than $60,000, these represent the opportunity costs of Marshall, Carol, and Philip. The cost of drafting all three, *to them*, would then be $73,000, even though the government can conceal this fact by offering far less in wages and then compelling each to serve.

The opportunity cost is a function of forgone alternative employment opportunities and all sorts of other values: preferences with respect to life-style, attitude toward war, degrees of cowardice or bravery, and so on. When the government bids for military personnel, raising its offer until it can attract just the desired number of enlistments, the government in an important sense actually minimizes the cost of its program. For it pulls in those with the lowest opportunity costs of service—everyone like Marshall but no one like Philip. Under a draft, this could occur only through the most unlikely of coincidences. Figure 3A provides a simple way to grasp the argument.

There is a supply curve of military volunteers. The argument that people won't voluntarily risk their lives is refuted

---

[1] In some contexts, a volunteer means someone who works without pay (volunteer firefighters, hospital volunteers). That is *not* the case with the volunteer military force, where payment of an attractive wage is the key to success.

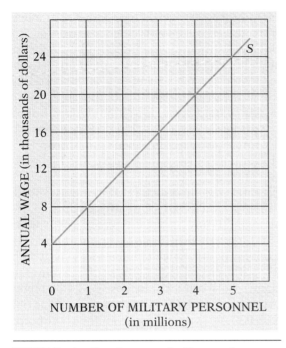

FIGURE 3A   Supply curve of military volunteers

by the fact that people do—not only military volunteers but also police, steeplejacks, and even skiers. Whatever its precise position and slope, the supply curve will certainly incline upward to the right. Some people (those who assign low value to their available alternatives) will volunteer at a very low wage. But three million volunteers can be secured, on our assumptions, only if the wage offer is at least $16,000 per year. That would mean a wage bill of $48 billion annually. But because taxpayers don't like to have their taxes raised, Congress is reluctant to approve such a huge appropriation. And the people in the Department of Defense care very much about the likes and dislikes of the people in Congress. They can cut that upsetting bill in half by offering only $8000 and compelling enlistments. The published cost will now be only $24 billion. Hurrah for cost savings!

But what of the costs to those who make up the armed forces? The cost of the *volunteer* army (to the volunteers) under our assumptions would be $30 billion. That is the value of the area under the supply curve up to three million men and women, or the sum of the values of the opportunities forgone by those who enlisted. The other $18 billion paid out by the government is a transfer of wealth from taxpayers to members of the military who would have enlisted at a lower wage but who nonetheless receive the higher wage that is required to induce the enlistment of the three-millionth volunteer.

What will be the cost of a *conscripted* army to those who are drafted? We can't say, except that it will certainly be larger. Only if the draft happened to hit exactly those and only those who would have enlisted under a volunteer system would the cost be as low as $30 billion. That is most unlikely. The more draftees who are grabbed from the upper, rather than the lower, end of the supply curve, the higher will be the cost to the conscripts. For example, a man who would have volunteered at a wage of $9000 is offered only $8000. He rejects the offer, and he is subsequently not drafted. Instead, a person who would only have volunteered at $24,000 is drafted—and paid $8000. The net result is that taxpayers save $8000 by obtaining for only $8000 services for which they would have had to pay $16,000 under an all-volunteer system. But someone whose opportunity cost is $24,000 has been substituted for someone whose opportunity cost was only $9000. That's a $15,000 increase in cost from the standpoint of those who serve.

The military draft does *not* reduce the cost of maintaining a military establishment. It rather transfers that cost from the shoulders of taxpayers to the shoulders of the draftees. That may in your judgment be one of the least of its faults, or it may be outweighed in your mind by presumed advantages. But at least it's a consequence that economists can point out.

COSTS AND OWNERSHIP

Everyone who has been in the armed forces knows horror stories about the inefficient ways the military makes use of its personnel. A highly skilled accountant is put to work painting barracks, and the commissary books are kept by someone who counts on his fingers. The stories are probably exaggerated. Nonetheless, we have grounds for predicting that personnel will tend to be used in such wasteful ways in the military more often than in civilian life.

Why? Because, in civilian life, those who employ people are usually compelled to pay them their opportunity cost. When you have to pay accountants the wages of accountants, you don't have them paint barracks—at least not if you're an employer with regard for the profitabililty of your enterprise. On the other hand, what is the cost to a sergeant of assigning a highly skilled recruit to a task that requires no skill at all? If the sergeant happens to resent the recruit for his air of superiority, real or imagined, then transferring him to a job more suited to his abilities might actually entail the sacrifice of a valuable opportunity for the sergeant—the opportunity to humiliate someone he dislikes.

Two conclusions emerge from the foregoing analysis. First, resources tend to be utilized thoughtlessly and carelessly when users don't have to pay the opportunity cost, or the value of the resources in their next-best use. Second, users are most often compelled to pay the opportunity cost of resources when those resources are clearly and definitely owned by someone. A man who is drafted does not "own his own labor," because the law has deprived him of the power to decide where and for whom and on what terms he will work. And so he can't insist on receiving his opportunity cost when Uncle Sam beckons—as he can when United Soapchips wants his services.

The point also applies, of course, to nonhuman resources. If no one owns a resource, there is no one to insist that potential users of the resource pay the value of the opportunities sacrificed by their use. The resource will consequently tend to be underpriced. And underpriced resources, as we shall see time and again in a variety of situations, tend to be used with little care or thought for the consequences. The incentive to economize is weak when the cost of using is low.

A NOTE ON ALTERNATIVE SYSTEMS

Don't fail to notice that the concept of opportunity cost is fully applicable to a socialist society in which resources are allocated by government planners. To economic planners in the former Soviet Union, the cost of building a railway from Lubny to Mirgorod was the value of whatever could otherwise have been done with the resources. But if government officials have the power to obtain valuable resources without having to bid for them, how will they discover the value of the resources in alternative uses? Recall the remarkable workers who could install spokes in bicycle wheels while standing on their heads and whistling "Dixie." In the absence of circus owners willing to bid for their services, how would central planners ever find out that they were too valuable to be assigned to bicycle production?

A distinguishing characteristic of different economic systems is the way in which they assign costs to alternative actions. Where resources are privately owned, competing bids and offers generate prices that approximate opportunity costs to resource owners. Where resources are not clearly owned by anyone, this process cannot operate. What takes its place? Who determines the relative value of this railway line and that one, or of using steel for railroad tracks versus using it to build trucks, or of improving transportation versus improving the quality of what is transported, or of more and better consumer goods versus additional leisure? In the absence of the information that competing bids and offers create, the economic planners are fairly free to impose their own, private evaluations on the alternatives before them. Remember that intelligent choices presuppose good information. An effective economic system will be one that transmits reliable information to decisionmakers and gives them strong incentives to use the information so provided.

PRICE ELASTICITY OF SUPPLY

The concept of elasticity is every bit as important in the case of supply at it is in the case of demand. The formal definitions are the same: the percentage change in the quantity divided by the percentage change in the price. In the case of supply, price and quantity will vary in the same direction, reflecting the fact that it takes a higher price to induce suppliers to offer for sale a larger quantity. The supply is relatively elastic if the percentage change in the quantity supplied is greater than the percentage change in the price, and it is relatively inelastic if the percentage change in the quantity supplied is less than the percentage change in the price.

This book puts completely inelastic *demand* curves in the same family as unicorns: the family of nonexistent phenomena. Completely inelastic *supply* curves are another matter. While it takes no time to start demanding less when the price of a good rises, it does take time and often quite a bit of time to start supplying more when the price of a good rises. Even a significant increase in the price of a good may consequently produce no increase at first in the quantity of the good supplied. With time, however, potential suppliers will reorganize the resources available to them and will almost always be able to supply a larger quantity in response to a higher price.

If additional quantities of the resources required to produce a particular good can be readily obtained at no higher cost, the supply curve for the good will be close to completely elastic. In such a case a very modest rise in the price will induce suppliers to increase by a very large amount the quantity offered for sale.

The supply curve of military volunteers portrayed in Figure 3A is an in-between case. The price elasticity varies along the curve, decreasing steadily from 2.0 between $7 and $9 to 1.2 between $23 and $25.

Pause for a moment to be sure you have understood the concept of price elasticity of supply. As we shall see in the next chapter, it is the relative elasticities of supply curves and demand curves that determine what effects changing circumstances will have on the quantities of goods exchanged and the prices at which they exchange.

DO COSTS DETERMINE PRICES?

When sellers announce a price increase to the public, they like to point out that the increase was compelled by rising costs. The business press publishes frequent announcements of this kind, and it's rare indeed when the announcement fails to include an expression of regret that higher costs made this unfortunate step necessary. In Chapter 9 we'll explore more fully the principles that guide sellers when they're setting prices. All we want to do now is use the concept of opportunity cost to examine critically the basic notion that prices are determined by costs. We want to show you that it makes as much sense to assert that costs are determined by prices. More accurately, we shall argue here that *costs always depend on demand.*

DEMAND AND COST

We can begin with an example discussed earlier in this chapter. Does it make sense to claim that the price of getting a haircut has gone up because barbers' wages have risen? If people weren't willing to pay high prices for haircuts, how could barbers' wages rise? The price people are willing to pay to have their hair cut professionally is one important factor that causes costs—that is, wages—to be what they are.

Plastic surgeons receive high wages for their services. Is this why it costs so much to have a face lift? Not exactly. The causal relationship also runs in the opposite direction. It's the fact that people are willing to pay a high price for cosmetic surgery that makes the cost of hiring a plastic surgeon so high. Few people have the requisite skills, of course, and their acquisition is difficult and time consuming. That's why the demand for cosmetic surgery raises the income of the surgeons rather than merely increasing the number of people willing and able to provide the service. But the cost to any one person of the services of a plastic surgeon is obviously not independent of the demand of others for plastic surgery.

When the owners of professional football teams announce in the summer that ticket prices will be raised in the fall, they like to blame the increase on rising costs, especially the high wages that must be paid to the players. But why do the players receive such high wages? It can't be that their work is so dangerous and grueling, because it was just as dangerous and grueling in the days when players received only a few hundred dollars for the season. It's the demand, the willingness of many people to pay high prices to watch, that has made football players such valuable resources. Soccer players in the United States receive far less, not because they work less hard, but because soccer isn't that popular in this country.

One of the most interesting cases of the relationship we're stressing is found in agriculture. The average price per acre of farm real estate in the United States rose 267 percent from 1971 to 1981, more than twice as fast as the general price level increased over the same period. Consequently, anyone who decided to go into farming in 1981 found that he had to pay a high price to obtain productive land. It would clearly be misleading to assert that the high cost of land was the cause of high food prices. It was the demand for land, determined in large part by the demand for agricultural products, that pulled up the cost of farming land. When farmers argue for higher government support prices for their crops because land costs so much, they are ignoring the fact that higher support prices will tend to pull up the price of the land on which those crops can be grown. It will do so by enhancing the value of the opportunities available to one who owns the land.

Similarly, the sharp declines in agricultural land prices in the 1980s were the result, not the cause, of lower farm commodity prices.

Consider the case of a farmer whose land lies near a large city. As the suburbs expand, residential developers offer to buy the land for a price that is three or four times higher than the price it can command as agricultural property. If the farmer refuses to sell because he wants to stay in farming, it is very unlikely that he will complain about the rising cost of land. But farmers who *rent* land near large cities often do just that. The landowner will understandably want to sell the land to developers unless the tenant farmer is willing to pay three or four times more rent. We can certainly sympathize with the tenant farmer dispossessed by the growth of the suburbs. But it's important that we see why he's being asked to pay a rent so much higher than before: It is the demand for the land that is raising the cost of farming on it.

Note that if *tax assessments* are based on what is called "highest and best use," then the owner who wants to remain in farming can legitimately complain that he can't afford *not* to sell. In those circumstances he is required to pay taxes based not on his own use of the land, but on the use to which the land would be put by the highest bidder.

But let's push the analysis a bit further. Suppose the farmer himself owns the land he's cultivating, and that the county does not raise the assessed value of the land when suburban developers bid up its price because public officials want to keep the land in farming. Will the policy succeed?

The cost to the farmer of maintaining the land in agriculture is the net value of the opportunities he thereby forgoes. By rejecting an opportunity to sell, he gives up the income he could obtain from investing the sales proceeds. If his annual net income from the farming operation is $5000 per year, he will be losing a large sum each year if he refuses to sell the land for $300,000, since $300,000 can earn far more than $5000 per year in such low-risk investments as U.S. government bonds.

What about the value to the farmer of remaining a farmer? Might he not, in selling his land, be giving up a valuable opportunity to lead a good, simple, honest, and satisfying life? Probably not. If he really does value farm living so highly, he can buy a replacement farm in some location where suburbanites aren't competing for the land. If he chooses not to do this, we have evidence that he doesn't place all that high a value on the agricultural life. In either event, the cost to him of continuing to farm on the land that the developers want goes up as soon as the developers bid up the price. That means he is less likely to continue farming that land, which means in turn that he is more likely to increase the supply of land available for suburban development.

CONSUMER PRICES AS OPPORTUNITY COST

In all these examples we've tried to show that the costs of productive resources like labor and land are prices determined by demand. That, in fact, is what's meant by calling them opportunity costs. We can just as easily argue that the prices of consumer goods are, in reality, costs—opportunity costs that measure the value of the goods in alternative uses.

Take, for example, the case of lobster. Sad to relate, so few lobsters come to market that it just isn't possible for all of us to have as many as we could enjoy. More are brought to market as higher prices offer larger incentives to lobster fishermen; but the demand in recent years has increased considerably faster than the supply, and the price has consequently risen sharply.

The higher price can be viewed as the opportunity cost of the resources engaged in bringing lobsters to market. But when the lobsters have all been brought to market on a given day, so that the quantity is, for that day at least, completely fixed, then the price should be viewed as the opportunity cost of the last potential purchaser who was persuaded by the high price to do without lobster. Think of it as follows: Lobsters have many alternative uses, at least as many as there are potential lobster eaters. Lobsters have only one function, it is true, from the aggregate point of view. (We're notorious for ignoring the values and preferences of the lobster.) But the consumption of a lobster by one gourmet prevents its consumption by another. Lobster lovers in effect bid against one another for the limited supply. As the price rises, more and more potential consumers are reluctantly persuaded to do without. The price that clears the market, that makes the quantity demanded equal to the quantity supplied, will be the price that just barely persuades the most reluctant of the disappointed lobster lovers to go home from the seafood market with ocean perch or flounder fillets. It is *that person's* opportunity cost that is expressed by the market clearing price.

The point of all this is that people don't pay what lobster is worth to them, but rather what lobster is worth in its most valued alternative use: as food for the consumer who was just barely deterred by the price from making a purchase. It's the opportunity cost of this disappointed lobster lover that the price reflects, as well as the opportunity costs of the resources that might have been used to bring additional lobsters to market.

How many coffee drinkers realize that when the price of coffee soars because of a freeze in Brazil, they are continuing to pay a price based on cost? It's not the cost of *growing* the coffee that determines the new, much higher price; it's the opportunity cost of those coffee lovers who must be persuaded (by a rising price) to sacrifice the caffeine they covet to others who are less willing to give it up and therefore willing to pay more.

But now we have moved into the question of scarcity and its social management. That is the topic for Chapter 4.

CASE STUDY: SUPPLY CURVES ARE DEMAND CURVES

The case study shows how both demand curves and supply curves reflect the estimated value of alternative opportunities.

Ira Tennforte owns and operates a tax-accounting business out of two adjoining offices in a six-unit office building. He would like to have more space, but he has to pay $1000 per month. However, if the rent fell to $900, he would take a third unit. At $700 he would expand into four units; at $580 he would rent five units; and at $500 per month he would be willing to rent the entire complex. On the other hand, if his rent rose above $1300, he would contract his operation into a single office. And he would leave the building entirely and possibly give up the business if the monthly rent for an office rose above $2500.

The information in the preceding paragraph describes Ira Tennforte's demand schedule for office space.

| | Number of |
Monthly Rent	Offices Demanded
$2500	1
1300	2
900	3
700	4
580	5
500	6

That demand schedule would also describe Ira Tennforte's supply schedule in the event that he purchased the building in which he had been renting space. Would he occupy all of the offices himself if he owned the building? It depends on the going rental rate. If he can get more than $2500 for his offices, he will rent all six to others, since, as we know, $2500 is the most an office is worth to him in his business. If the going rent is between $2500 and $1300, he will occupy one office and supply five for the use of others. If the market rental rate is below $1300, he will use two and hence supply four. Below $900 he will demand three and supply three. He will supply two offices if the rental rate falls below $700, only oine if it is less than $580, and none at all if he can't get even $500 in rent.

Here is Ira Tennforte's supply schedule:

| | Number of |
Monthly Rent	Offices Supplied
$501	1
581	2
701	3
901	4
1301	5
2501	6

Ira Tennforte's supply curve is the mirror image of his demand curve. Whether Ira chooses to occupy an additional office or instead make the office available for others to rent depends on the going price of office space, not on who owns the building.

ONCE OVER LIGHTLY

Supply curves, as well as demand curves, reflect people's estimates of the value of alternative opportunities. Both the quantities of any good that are supplied and the quantities that are demanded depend on the choices people make after assessing the opportunities available to them.

Supply depends on cost. But the cost of supplying is the value of the opportunities forgone by the act of supplying. This concept of cost is expressed in economic theory by the assertion that all costs relevant to decisions are opportunity costs—the value of the opportunities forsaken in choosing one course of action rather than another.

Insofar as the resources utilized in producing goods can be obtained only through competitive bidding, costs of production will reflect the value to the resource owners of the alternative uses of those resources. This implies that producers will want to suppress competitive bidding for the resources they use, if they can find an effective way to do so.

The value of a human being may be infinite, but the wages of human beings in any task will be much closer to the value of their services in alternative employments than to infinity.

Many disagreements about what something or the other "really costs" could be resolved by the recognition that "things" cannot have costs. Only actions entail sacrificed opportunities, and therefore only actions can have costs.

Costs are always the value of the opportunities that particular people sacrifice. Conflicting assertions about the costs of alternative decisions can often be reconciled by agreement on whose costs are under consideration.

Prices rise to the level of opportunity costs insofar as the owners of resources insist on being paid their value in the next-best use. This discourages a careless use of resources and assigns resources to those uses on which people place the highest monetary value.

Supply curves slope upward to the right because higher prices must be offered to resource owners to persuade them to transform a current activity into an opportunity they are willing to sacrifice. The price elasticity of supply is the percentage change in the quantity supplied divided by the percentage change in the price.

Demand curves slope upward to the left because higher prices persuade resource users to sacrifice a current activity for their next-best opportunity.

Demand helps determine costs. Costs contribute to the determination of prices. The prices of goods affect the demand for other goods that they complement or for which they can substitute. From the perspective of opportunity cost, everything depends on everything else.

QUESTIONS FOR DISCUSSION

1. A prominent hospital in New England decided in 1980 to turn down a request by staff surgeons to perform heart transplants. The general director of the hospital objected to the statement that this decision was "based largely on cost considerations." On the contrary, he insisted, "the decision was based largely on the limited physical resources and highly trained personnel of the hospital. For each heart transplantation operation," he pointed out, the hospital "would have to turn away a number of other patients who receive less resource-draining open-heart surgery that is much more predictably beneficial to them than heart transplants currently are." Do you agree that the decision was not based on cost considerations?

   (a) What is the valuable opportunity forgone when the hospital performs a transplant operation?
   (b) Why didn't the hospital simply hire more surgeons and buy more physical resources if "cost considerations" were not the reason for the hospital's decision?
   (c) What do you suppose prompted the hospital's general director to insist that the decision was *not* based on cost considerations?

2. Here is a statement from the economics textbook most widely used in American colleges before 1860: "The qualities and relations of natural agents are the *gift* of God, and, being His gift, they *cost us nothing.* Thus, in order to avail ourselves of the momentum produced by a water-fall, we have only to construct the water-wheel and its necessary appendages, and place them in a proper position. We then have the use of the falling water, without further expense. As, therefore, our only outlay is *the cost of the instrument* by which the natural agent is rendered available, *this* is the only expenditure which demands the attention of the political economist."

   (a) What was the cost to a nineteenth-century mill owner of using a waterfall to power his mill if he owned the site of the waterfall?
   (b) What was the cost to the mill owner if someone else owned the site?
   (c) Under what circumstances would use of a waterfall to power a mill actually have cost nothing?
   (d) Why do modern "political economists" disagree with Francis Wayland and pay attention to the cost of using "natural agents"?

3. The acres of grass surrounding the Taj Mahal in Agra, India, are often cut by young women who slice off handfuls with short kitchen blades. Is this a low- or high-cost way to keep a lawn mowed?

4. By taking an airplane one can go from D to H in one hour. The same trip takes five hours by bus. If the air fare is $90 and the bus fare is $30, which would be the cheaper mode of transportation for someone who

could earn $6 an hour during this time? For someone who could earn $30 an hour? $15 dollars an hour?

5. At a sufficiently high price for gasoline, almost everyone would choose to leave the car at home and use public transportation to commute to and from work. But that price will differ vastly from one person to another. Why might it be higher for self-employed than for salaried people? For executives than for clerks?

6. What would be the effect on the cost to students of completing high school if legislation denied drivers' licenses to anyone under the age of 18?

7. Why did the cost of hiring domestic servants increase dramatically during World War II? What would you have replied to people who said that servants "just weren't available"?

8. Explain the following statement by a military recruiter: "There's nothing like a good recession to cure our recruiting problems."

9. A severe hurricane passing through a populated area will blow out a lot of windows and thereby cause a huge increase in demand for the services of glaziers. If glaziers respond by raising their hourly rates, the cost to homeowners of having their windows repaired will rise. But does a hurricane raise the cost *to glaziers* of repairing windows? Or are glaziers who raise their rates merely taking unfair advantage of the situation?

10. Smith, Ricardo, Marx, and Keynes are potential tutors for students in introductory economics. Each wants to work 8 hours a day at his best available monetary opportunity. Students regard their services as perfect substitutes: As far as students are concerned, an hour of tutoring is equally valuable whichever of the four provides it.

    Marx is willing to tutor 8 hours a day for $4 an hour, because his next-best opportunity, fomenting revolution, currently pays only $3.99 an hour. Ricardo can work 4 hours a day at Merrill Lynch for $13.99 an hour; after that he's reduced to selling shoes for $4.99 an hour. Smith's best alternative is teaching moral philosophy at the local college for $7.99 an hour, 8 hours a day. Keynes has an 8-hour-per-day job, paying $11.99 an hour, raising money for the local symphony.

    (a) Construct the supply curve of tutoring services from these data on the graph in Figure 3B.
    (b) Show how the supply curve would change if Merrill Lynch hired Ricardo full time.
    (c) Show the change that would occur if someone offered Marx a job as a newspaper reporter at $9.99 an hour.
    (d) How would the supply curve change if the public suddenly became much more interested in learning something about moral philosophy?

11. The supply curve on the graph in Figure 3C shows the wage rates that would have to be offered by business firms to obtain various quantities of hours of envelope stuffing on any given day.

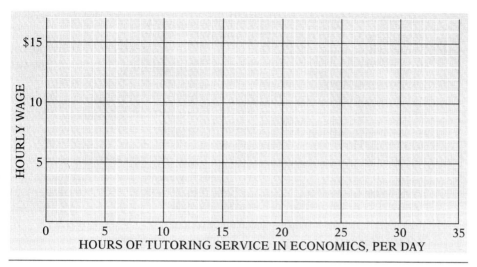

FIGURE 3B   Supply of tutoring services

(a) What wage rate will firms have to offer if they want to hire 400 hours of envelope stuffing?

(b) What will be the firms' total expenditure on the wages of envelope stuffers?

(c) What will be the total opportunity cost to the envelope stuffers of stuffing envelopes? (Hint: Each square represents $20: 20 hours times $1.)

(d) What is the price elasticity of supply between $4 and $6? Between $6 and $8?

12. (a) It has been argued that a volunteer army would discriminate against poor people, because they tend to have the lowest-value alternatives to

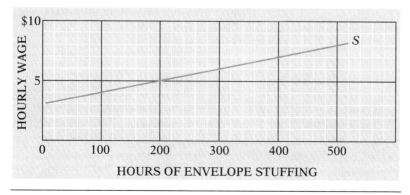

FIGURE 3C   Supply curve for envelope stuffing

military service and hence would dominate the ranks of volunteers. Do you agree with the analysis and the objection?

(b) Some critics have argued that if the military relied exclusively on volunteers, the armed forces would be filled with people of such low intelligence and skills that they could not operate sophisticated weapons. International Business Machines relies exclusively on "volunteers," and *its* employees are not predominantly people of low intelligence and skills. What's the difference between the armed forces and IBM? How would you reply to the argument of these critics?

(c) Another frequent criticism of a volunteer military is that we don't want "an army of mercenaries." How high does the military wage have to be before the recipient becomes a mercenary? Are officers compelled to remain in the armed services? Why do they stay in? Are they mercenaries? Is your teacher a mercenary? Your physician? Your minister?

13. Why might a multinational corporation with identical plants in different countries pay different wage rates to workers in the two countries even though their skill levels are the same? Does this strike you as unjust? Why might the *higher-paid* workers object?

14. If people are offering to pay $100 for $10 (face-value) tickets to the Big Game, and someone gives you a ticket, what does it cost you to attend the game? Would you be more likely to attend if someone gave you a ticket than if you had to purchase one for $100? Would you be more likely to attend if someone gave you a ticket than if you had to purchase one that you could buy (through an inside source) for $10?

15. Rising commercial rents in San Francisco in recent years have induced many corporations to move their offices out of the city. Can a San Francisco firm that owns its own office building simply ignore rising rents?

16. Henrietta George bought her large, old house 48 years ago for $2000. She could get $200,000 for it today if she chose to sell it. About how much do you suppose it's costing her per month to continue living in her large, old house?

17. What is the cost per ticket to a professional baseball club that offers 50 free tickets to an orphanage? Does it matter for what game the tickets are offered? Why would it probably cost the ball club more to give the tickets to college students than to poor orphans?

18. Think about the cost of television commercials. What enters into the cost of a 30-second commercial plugging Friendly Fred's Ford Dealership? How do you explain the fact that the same commercial will cost $90 on Wednesday morning but $1600 right before a big football game? Local television stations are often asked to donate time for public-service spots. Does this cost the station anything? Do you think that station owners' religious beliefs make them more willing to donate time on Sunday mornings than on weekday mornings?

19. The network advertising fee per 30-second spot during Super Bowl XVIII was $484,000. Did that reflect the network's estimate of the cost of providing a 30-second advertising spot? What made the cost so high?

20. Why do parking lot fees vary so widely from city to city in the United States? The all-day rate in Manhattan, for example, is often $20. In Atlanta, it is likely to be less than $5. Does this difference reflect the greater greed of New York City parking-garage owners?

21. In 1977 a Seventh Day Adventist congregation in Manhattan purchased a former synagogue for $400,000. Several years later the congregation decided to sell it because the maintenance costs were running $100,000 per year, too much for the 80-family congregation to pay. In 1982 a developer paid the congregation $2.4 million cash for the property. (The information is taken from a *Wall Street Journal* article of September 27, 1982.)

   (a) What would it have cost the congregation to continue using the building?
   (b) Would you say that it is greed that prompts congregations to sell large, old churches in downtown areas to commercial developers?

22. Most mobile-home owners own their homes but pay rent for the land on which the home sits. Some municipalities have recently begun to impose legal limits on the amount by which the owners of mobile-home parks can increase the rent they charge for their sites. One argument given in defense of such rent controls was that zoning regulations against mobile-home parks made it difficult for mobile-home owners to move to a new site when faced with a huge rent increase.

   (a) What determines the rent a mobile-park owner can charge for a site?
   (b) To what cost, if any, is this charge related?
   (c) How do zoning regulations against mobile-home parks affect the rents park owners can charge?
   (d) Do you agree with the mobile-home owner who, when faced with a large increase, protested indignantly, "my home gives value to that pad of dirt"?

23. A number of American cities have passed rent-control ordinances in recent years. These ordinances often try to restrict rent increases to the amount of the owners' cost increases. Use the analysis of this chapter in thinking about these questions:

   (a) What is the cost to a landlord of renting an apartment to you for $150 if someone else is willing to pay $250?
   (b) What determines the cost to a potential landlord of purchasing an apartment building?
   (c) What effect will a rent-control ordinance have on the cost of purchasing an apartment building?

(d) What effect will a rent-control ordinance have on the cost to land-lords of letting an apartment unit stand idle, or of using it themselves, or of allowing relatives to live in it rent-free?

(e) What concept of cost do you think supporters of rent controls have in mind when they speak of basing maximum rents on landlords' costs?

24. Are hand-carved redwood flamingos that sell for $150 valuable because they take so many hours to carve? Or do people spend many hours carving redwood flamingos because they are valuable? Does the value of an object ever depend on what people know about how it was produced? Would a flamingo be more valuable if people thought it had been carved by Pope John XXIII than if they thought you had carved it?

25. Many Americans today seem to be much more "pressed for time" than were their grandparents. This is rather odd in view of the fact that today's homes and workplaces are full of so many time-saving devices to which our grandparents had no access. How would you account for this? If you can't think of an explanation, ask yourself what causes anyone to feel "pressed for time." What happens to the cost of engaging in an activity, whether it's for business or for pleasure, when attractive alternative opportunities suddenly present themselves?

26. "In the Middle Ages people believed in a just price for goods, not determined by supply and demand, but by the cost of raw material and labor." Assume that the author of that statement is accurate in his historical facts, and correct his economic analysis.

SUPPLY AND DEMAND: A PROCESS OF COORDINATION

In the late summer and autumn of both 1989 and 1990, as the system of central economic planning in the USSR disintegrated, news reports regularly told about unharvested food rotting in rural areas while grocery store shelves stood empty in the cities.

How could a thing like this occur? Why didn't someone transport that food to the cities where it was so much in demand? Collapse of the system of bureaucratic control just does not provide an adequate explanation. People should be able to move food out of the fields and into the hands of hungry people without explicit orders from above.

FAILURES OF COOPERATION

Or so one would suppose. But think more carefully and concretely. Who owned the food that was going to waste? Who had authority to harvest it? Who owned harvesting equipment? Who could authorize the use of the equipment? Who owned trucks to transport the food to the cities? Who had fuel for the trucks? How was the food to be distributed once it arrived in the cities? The mere fact that food is going to waste in the fields while people are hungry in the cities is not enough to get food actually moving from farms to urban pantries. The right people must first acquire the appropriate information and incentives.

When people want something done (they want food made available, for example), and are willing to pay what others

79

want for doing it (as in the former USSR in 1989 and 1990), but it nonetheless does not happen, we have what looks very much like a failure of cooperation. Such cases are worth thinking about.

Here is a simple one of a type that all of us have probably encountered. Each day several hundred cyclists use the bicycle lane to cross the bridge. Every now and then an accident will scatter broken glass all over the bicycle lane. Each one of those several hundred cyclists, encountering the broken glass for the first time, would willingly pay one dollar to have it swept up. That means the cyclists would be collectively willing to pay several hundred dollars to obtain an action that any number of people would be happy to perform for less than $10. Nonetheless, hundreds of bicycles will ride through that broken glass day after day until weather and traffic finally disperse it. This is a failure of cooperation. Why does it occur?

TRANSACTION COSTS

It occurs because the costs of arranging the transaction are too high. It isn't enough that demanders are *willing* to pay what suppliers *would* require. Someone must arrange the actual transaction: collect money from the cyclists and see to it that the glass gets swept up. And that's not easy to do, as it turns out. If it were easy, we wouldn't see so much glass in bicycle lanes. An enterprising person who resolved to profit from repairing this failure of cooperation would have to flag down cyclists, explain the situation, persuade them of his own honesty, induce them to admit how much they want to see the glass removed, and finally talk them into handing over a sum of money that reflects the strength of their desire, while all the time most of them are wondering to themselves why *they* should pay when the benefits are going to go to so many others.

Failures of this sort are the consequences of *transaction costs: the costs of arranging contracts or transaction agreements between demanders and suppliers.*

Transaction costs explain the "wasteful" situation that prevailed in the former USSR in 1989 and 1990. The word *wasteful* is set between quotation marks because it's not at all clear that what happened really was wasteful. It's not wasteful to let food rot rather than consume it if the costs of getting the food to consumers exceed the value of the food. And that was apparently the case. Transaction costs are just as real and no less important than the costs of harvesting and transporting.

Such a situation would be much less likely to develop in the United States, where fields, food, farm machinery, trucks, warehouses, and retail stores are privately owned. Under a system of clearly defined property rights, people with information about the situation would have strong incentives to acquire control of whatever resources were needed to move the food from where it had no use to where it did. And within a system that allows for free exchange among property owners, the necessary resources will quickly and at low cost come together under the control of those who can put them to valuable uses.

Contrast the frustrating situation in the former USSR with the way that ice, plywood, building tools, and everything else needed for emergency relief and reconstruction move into areas of the United States that are hit by hurricanes, such as Charleston after Hugo in 1989 or Miami when Andrew struck in 1992. The crucial difference is the well-established system of clearly defined property rights in the United States along with the extensive freedom that people have to trade those rights as they choose. This has produced over the years a vast network of institutions in the United States that keep transaction costs low for almost all the exchanges in which people engage with any frequency or regularity. (The thoughtful reader will shrewdly note that people frequently and regularly engage in particular transactions only *because* the transaction costs are low.)

The concept of transaction costs enables us to explain many of the more puzzling dilemmas of modern societies, where people seem to behave in ways that are contrary to their own best interests. We will use the concept in Chapter 13, for example, to explain why people so often spoil their own environment, and in Chapter 14 to explain why the majority of the voters in a democracy often fail to get their way. The concept is especially important for those societies that are now attempting to make a transition from central economic planning and bureaucratic control of economic decisions to market-coordinated systems.

MARKET SYSTEMS

Market systems are often referred to as "automatic" or "self-adjusting" or spoken of in other ways that give the impression that they function without the intervention of human beings. This is a serious mistake. Market systems are entirely composed of demanders and suppliers, live human beings pursuing the projects that interest them, negotiating arrangements to obtain what they want from others by offering others what they in turn want to obtain. When economists use the terms *supply* and *demand,* they are really talking about these kinds of continual, on-going negotiations.

The negotiations rarely take place in committee meetings. They are rather the daily bids and offers that we extend in the many societies in which we participate. These bids and offers presuppose well-defined rules of the game, including well-defined property rights. We take for granted most of the relevant rights and obligations when we enter into a negotiation. "Will you do this for me if I do that for you?" Usually we don't even have to ask. We just walk uninvited into the pizzeria, seat ourselves at an unoccupied table, and instruct an attendant to prepare a medium pizza with green peppers, black olives, and extra cheese. The attendant doesn't ask what we're willing to do in return, but simply assumes we will pay the posted money price.

The many transactions that made this moment possible—that constructed the pizzeria, grew the peppers, shipped the olives, milked the cows, and arranged the requisite lines of credit for all these activities—also had to be negotiated. All these negotiations succeeded because the transaction costs were sufficiently low. And the transaction costs were low because the transactions occurred within an extensive set of institutions that has evolved over time as market participants worked to lower the costs of the transactions in which they wanted to engage. Think of specialized manufacturers, specialized retailers, specialized providers of every kind of service; the principles of financial accounting, the rules of the road, the customs of the trade in varied lines of business; banks, credit-reporting agencies, highly organized stock exchanges; the classified sections of daily newspapers, the telephone companies' Yellow Pages, lists of brokers and suppliers that can be obtained on a moment's notice; the rules of the common law, police to enforce these rules and courts to resolve disputed issues, plus private systems of arbitration to supplement the system of public law. The nations that are currently attempting to move from central planning to market systems face the obstacle of high transaction costs at almost every turn, because they lack many of the institutions that are crucial to the effective working of market systems. Can these nations now create by design what evolved without design in the long-established market economies? Can they create quickly the complex institutions that have elsewhere come into existence through a slow, evolutionary process? Can they overcome the problem of high transaction costs rapidly enough to satisfy the aspirations of their citizens, who are impatient to enjoy the promised rewards of a market system? The success of the reform programs in the nations of the former Soviet bloc is going to depend largely on the answers to those questions.

THE COORDINATING ROLE OF MONEY PRICES

Why do almost all the exchanges in a commercial society (Adam Smith's term for a society characterized by extensive specialization and exchange) take place *for money?* Why don't more people engage in barter, exchanging what they produce directly for what they want? Why do they go through the medium of money?

The answer is that money lowers transaction costs. The advantages of using money rather than employing a barter system are enormous. The cost of arranging exchanges would be far greater, and our wealth as a consequence far less, if there were no money in our society to facilitate the process. In an economic system limited to barter, people would have to spend an inordinate amount of time searching for others with whom they could advantageously exchange. A violin maker would have to find a grocer, a haberdasher, an electricity generator, and a glue supplier, among many others, each willing to accept violins in return for the goods that they produce. All that time spent on searching would be time not available for violin making, and the production of violins would decline steeply. Aware of the high transaction costs attached to almost every exchange, people would increasingly try to produce for themselves most of whatever they wanted. Specialization would decline dramatically in a society confined to barter, and everyone would be much poorer. The evolution of some kind of money system in almost every known society, even when conditions were extremely unfavorable to it, is eloquent testimony to the advantages of using money.

Money has another advantage in addition to the fact that everybody is willing to accept it in exchange. The amount of it offered in exchange can be adjusted up or down by very small as well as very large amounts. Half of a violin that I have made is worth nothing to someone who wants to play, and two of my violins will usually be worth far less to a buyer than twice what one is worth. So if I have specialized in making violins in a society without money, I will pretty much have to buy one violin's worth of anything I want to purchase, even if that much will spoil before I can use it or I would really like a lot more. But if I have sold my violins for money, I can buy a little bit more or a little bit less of what I want with no trouble at all. And I can raise the exchange value of my violins by a small amount if I sense that my customers are willing to pay more for them than before, or lower their exchange value by just a little if I think this would secure some sales that I wouldn't otherwise get.

The ability to make small adjustments is essential to the coordination of a commercial society. Consider a gallon of gasoline. If we are to be able to fill our tanks at the self-service island on Tuesday evening at 5:30, just the right number of people with just the right abilities and command over just the right physical resources must cooperate at just the right times and in just the right ways to explore, drill, pump, pipe, refine, truck, and store. That intricate system is coordinated basically by means of adjustments in money prices. The people who regularly accomplish this spectacular feat of coordination don't do it because they love us and know how much we want gasoline, but to further the innumerable and diverse projects in which they happen to be interested. Their efforts mesh because those efforts are coordinated by the continually changing signals that money prices emit.

We must insist again that the crucial importance of money prices to the working of our society implies nothing about the character or morality of our citizens. People pay attention to money prices insofar as they want to economize, that is, to get as much as possible of what they value from the resources they command. They don't pay attention *exclusively* to money prices, of course; that wouldn't make sense. They do, however, change their behavior when prices change, in order to "take advantage" of the new situation signaled by the new prices. This is what causes markets to clear and self-interested behavior to become cooperative action.

THE BASIC PROCESS

Supply and demand analysis is the most basic tool in the economist's kit. To master the economic way of thinking, you must first learn to think in terms of supply and demand. The beginning step is to convince yourself that all the important factors affecting exchange can be usefully divided into two categories: factors affecting demand and factors affecting supply.

Let's practice with a few simple examples. What will happen to the price of wheat and the amount harvested in the United States if the wheat crop fails disastrously in Russia and Ukraine? The first question to ask is whether that crop failure will affect the demand or the supply *in the United States.* Since U.S.-grown wheat is an excellent substitute for wheat grown elsewhere, a large crop failure elsewhere will increase the demand for U.S. wheat. The demand curve will move toward the northeast. That will cause both the price and the quantity offered for sale to increase.

Which will increase more: the price or the quantity offered for sale? That is going to depend on the elasticity of supply. If a small price increase leads to a large increase in the quantity supplied, the supply is elastic; in that case, a large increase in demand will raise the price of wheat just a little while substantially increasing the quantity of wheat available. On the other hand, if even a very large increase in the price produces just a small increase in the amount offered for sale, the supply is inelastic, and a large increase in demand will result in a much higher price but little increase in the amount of wheat available for consumption.

Which is it in fact? Is the supply of wheat in the U.S. elastic or inelastic? That is going to depend primarily upon the time period we are thinking about. A sudden and unanticipated increase in the price of wheat will not lead at first to a very large increase in the amount offered for sale because it takes at least several months to grow additional wheat. There will be *some* immediate increase in the amount offered for sale, because there is always a substantial amount of wheat in storage being held for sale in the future. When the increase in demand bids up the current price, those who are holding wheat for future sale will choose to sell at least some portion of it now. In the short run, however, the supply of wheat is highly inelastic.

In the longer run, the supply of wheat has shown itself to be highly elastic. Farmers respond to the expectation of higher prices by substantially increasing the amount planted and eventually harvested. The conclusion to which we come, therefore, is that the crop disaster in Russia and Ukraine will probably cause a sharp jump in the price of wheat at first, but that this will be followed after a time by an increase in the quantity supplied and a return of the price to somewhere near its original level.

How will all this affect the price of soybeans? When the price of wheat rises, will consumers substitute soybeans for wheat? If they do, that will increase the demand for soybeans and cause the price of soybeans to rise. Substitution in consumption is unlikely to be significant in this case, however, and it probably would not have a discernible impact on the demand for or the price of soybeans. But there is another type of substitution to consider: substitution in production. When farmers decide to devote additional acreage to wheat production, they withdraw that land from other uses. If land suitable for growing soybeans is also suitable for growing wheat, then the increase in the expected price of wheat will raise the opportunity cost of growing soybeans, and the supply curve of soybeans will consequently shift toward the northwest. The price of soybeans will rise as a result while the quantity of soybeans exchanged declines.

A LITTLE PRACTICE

Try your hand at the following questions. What will happen to the price of lakefront lots if rising incomes induce many additional families to look for vacation cottages? Would you predict a large or a small increase in the price of such lots?

What effect do you think a surge in multiple-choice testing would have on the price of no. 2 pencils? By how much do you think the price would rise?

What effect would you predict on the price of gasoline in your state if the state government substantially raised the retail tax on gasoline?

The first case describes an increase in the demand for lakefront lots. I would predict a substantial jump in the price of such lots, because the supply is probably very inelastic. It is usually quite costly to create additional lakefront lots, and so the quantity available for purchase will not increase much even in response to the prospect of a much higher price.

A surge in multiple-choice testing would cause the demand for no. 2 pencils to increase. I would predict a large increase in the production of no. 2 pencils with no significant increase in their price. Additional no. 2 pencils can probably be supplied easily and quickly and at no increase in the cost of producing them if the demand increases. The supply curve is highly elastic.

The third case is a bit harder. The increase in the retail tax will definitely raise the cost of selling gasoline. But will it raise the price by the same amount? Or will the suppliers absorb some portion of the tax? A good way to see what's going on here is to ask under what circumstances suppliers would be willing to pay some portion of the tax themselves rather than pass it all along to consumers. What about a retailer whose station is situated near the border of another state with much lower gasoline taxes? A good substitute for the gasoline sold in Kansas City, Missouri, is the gasoline sold in Kansas City, Kansas. Everyone won't always want to drive to another state to

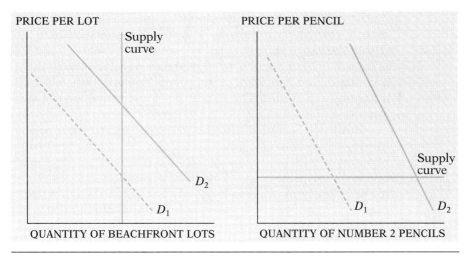

PRICE PER LOT

Supply curve

D_2

D_1

QUANTITY OF BEACHFRONT LOTS

PRICE PER PENCIL

Supply curve

D_1 D_2

QUANTITY OF NUMBER 2 PENCILS

FIGURE 4A   Demand curves for beachfront lots and number 2 pencils
     When all the beachfront lots in an area have been developed, an increase in the demand for such lots will only raise the cost of purchasing one because the supply has a very specific limit.
     A huge increase in the demand for number 2 pencils, however, occasioned perhaps by a surge in multiple-choice testing, will probably not raise the cost of purchasing one. That's because more can be supplied, in any quantity desired, at a constant opportunity cost.

save a few pennies on gasoline, of course, but some will do so regularly and others will do so occasionally. And that might be all it takes to make the demand curve quite elastic. In that case, those in the business of selling gasoline in the state that hiked its tax might choose to raise their prices by considerably less than the amount of the tax increase rather than lose too many of their customers.

THE URGE TO FIX PRICES

To a demander, the price of a good is its cost. Demanders consequently tend to look on rising prices as an imposition. To a supplier, prices represent income. So suppliers see falling prices as a threat. That's probably why so many people don't appreciate the coordinating role that price changes play and why they often try to get government to prevent the changes from occurring. The consequences will usually be quite different from what was intended, however, because price fixing amounts to suspending the working procedure for securing social coordination.
     Figure 4B presents a hypothetical demand curve for gasoline in the United States, labeled *DD*, with the price per gallon

on the vertical axis and the number of gallons demanded per month on the horizontal axis. The demand is very inelastic within the range shown: a large percentage increase in the price will lead to a much smaller percentage decrease in the quantity demanded. That's a reasonable assumption, well supported by experience. The substitutes for gasoline are not very attractive to most of the people who use it.

But there *are* substitutes for gasoline: joining a car pool, moving closer to work, buying a smaller car, taking the bus, planning ahead, getting more frequent tune-ups, or staying at home. As the price of gasoline rises, so do the sacrifices people must make in order to buy it. As a result, although a few may choose not to reduce their consumption at all, most people will find ways to economize at least a little, and some will decide to curtail their purchases substantially as the price goes up. The demand for gasoline is not totally inelastic.

Figure 4B also shows a relatively inelastic supply curve of gasoline, labeled *SS*. The element of time, which plays such a large role in determining the responses of users to price changes, performs an even larger part in determining the responses of suppliers. Gasoline in storage can be quickly re-

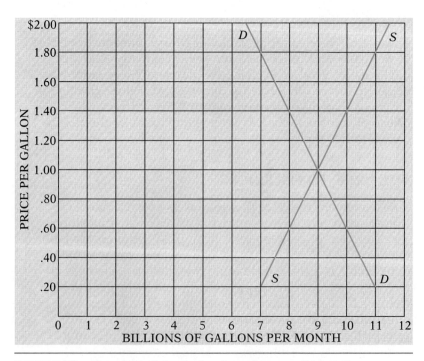

FIGURE 4B   Hypothetical demand and supply curves for gasoline

leased for sale if a higher price makes selling more attractive than storing. But time is required to import gasoline from abroad in response to a higher price. Still more time is required to increase the flow of gasoline from the refineries by switching over from the production of other refined products, such as heating oil. And far more time will necessarily elapse before additional refinery capacity can be created in response to the higher price of gasoline.

What about the availability of crude oil? Weren't the gasoline shortages of 1973–74 and 1979 the result of inadequate supplies of the basic raw material? We must answer carefully if we are to avoid begging the question. Iran's political turmoil in 1978 and 1979 certainly disrupted the flow of oil imports into the United States. But other OPEC countries had the capacity to step up their rate of production and thereby compensate for the Iranian cutbacks. They did not do so, because they wanted the price of crude oil to rise. But that is precisely our point. More than enough oil could have been supplied in 1979 to keep the refineries running at 100 percent of capacity if the refineries—and ultimately the consumers of refined products—had been willing and able to pay the price. We must add the word *able*, because the ability of consumers and refiners to offer more money for gasoline and for crude petroleum was deliberately restricted by law in the United States.

The market-clearing price of gasoline in Figure 4B, the price that makes the quantity demanded equal to the quantity supplied, is $1 per gallon. Why didn't the government allow the price of gasoline to move to the market-clearing level (sometimes called the *equilibrium level*) in the 1970s? Why did the U.S. government instead impose ceiling prices on the sale of petroleum and petroleum products in the 1970s? Judging by the statements made at the time, the price controls were designed to prevent "oil companies" from obtaining large, unearned profits at the expense of low-income consumers. Proponents of the controls failed to point out, however, perhaps because they didn't realize, that by freezing prices the government was disconnecting a crucial link in society's system of mutual adjustment and cooperation.

THE "POPULAR PERSPECTIVE"

That raises yet another question. Why don't advocates of price controls recognize the consequences of what they are calling for? Some of them probably know very well but expect to benefit personally from price controls. The majority of

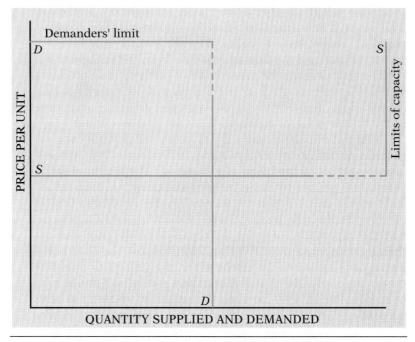

FIGURE 4C   The popular perspective on supply and demand

those who support price controls in such situations, however, are quite likely sincere in their belief that freezing prices by law protects vulnerable people while doing little harm. They probably hold what we shall call the Popular Perspective on supply and demand.

According to the Popular Perspective, those who supply particular goods won't supply any at all below their cost of producing the goods, which is characteristically thought of as a constant fixed by the facts of nature. Once the price rises above that minimum level, they will be willing to supply as much (or as little) as consumers are willing to purchase, up to the limits of their capacity. Consumers will be willing to purchase however much they "need," regardless of the price—at least until some upper limit is reached, at which point they will be compelled to do without the good altogether. According to the Popular Perspective, then, supply curves are completely elastic (horizontal) at a price equal to the cost of production, and demand curves are completely inelastic (vertical) at the quantity "needed"—which, like the cost of production, is pretty much determined by natural facts.

In this way of thinking, prices do not coordinate decisions; they merely redistribute wealth. Price controls on gasoline, therefore, will only keep oil companies from exploiting a crisis to get rich at the expense of helpless motorists. Who but an oil company executive or stockholder could reasonably object to emergency price controls if supply and demand conform to the Popular Perspective?

How many people actually hold the Popular Perspective? Probably no one holds it clearly and consciously. It's one of those views that make little sense when thought through carefully but that may nonetheless be widely held because so few people take the pains to think carefully, especially when they know in advance what they want to believe. We'll come back a number of times to the Popular Perspective in the pages ahead. It's one way of accounting for some of the most perverse but persistent public policies.

The economist's perspective is quite different. Demand curves slope downward to the right because purchasers can choose among substitutes and will do so as the relative prices of those substitutes change. And supply curves slope upward to the right because suppliers can also choose among alternative activities and will do so as their prospective benefits and costs change. In the economic way of thinking, supply and demand is a process of mutual accommodation. Changing circumstances affect demand or supply. When demand increases relative to supply, the price rises. The higher price persuades demanders to take less, thus leaving more for others, and persuades suppliers to produce more. When supply increases relative to demand, price falls. The lower price persuades demanders to substitute this good for other goods and persuades suppliers to shift their efforts toward the production of other, more highly valued goods.

SCARCITY AND COMPETITION

No one blames the thermometer for low temperatures or seriously proposes to warm up the house on a cold day by holding a candle under the furnace thermostat. People do, however, often blame high prices for the scarcity of certain goods and act as if scarcity could be eliminated by enforcing price controls. That just isn't so.

Scarcity is a relationship between desirability and availability, or between demand and supply. In a society where everyone is terrified of snakes, snakes may be rare but they cannot be scarce. In another society, where snakes are valued as

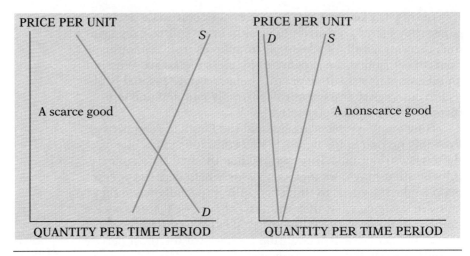

FIGURE 4D   Supply and demand curves for a scarce and a nonscarce good
     When everyone can obtain as much of a good as they want at no cost, that good is not scarce. Of course, the money price that must be paid will rarely be the entire cost of obtaining a good.

food, they could be quite common but nonetheless scarce. *A good is scarce whenever people cannot obtain as much of it as they would like without being required to sacrifice something else of value.*

Now it follows immediately that if a good is scarce, it must be rationed. In other words, a criterion of some kind must be established for discriminating among claimants to determine who will get how much. The criterion could be age, eloquence, swiftness, public esteem, willingness to pay money, or almost anything else. We characteristically ration scarce goods in our society on the basis of willingness to pay money. But sometimes we use other criteria in order to discriminate.

Harvard University each year has many more applicants than it can place in the freshman class, so Harvard must ration the scarce places. It discriminates on the basis of high-school grades, test scores, recommendations, and other criteria.

Only one person at a time can be president of the United States. Since many more people than one want the position, we have evolved an elaborate system of discrimination in the form of conventions and elections. Although there is considerable doubt about just what the criteria for discrimination are, the system does discriminate. We end up every fourth year with only one satisfied candidate.

Joe College is the most popular man on campus and has young women clamoring for his favor. He must therefore ration his attentions. Whether he employs the criterion of beauty, intelligence, geniality, or something else, he must and will discriminate in some fashion.

The other side of discrimination is competition. Once Harvard announces its criteria for discrimination, freshman applicants will compete to meet them. The criteria for selecting a president are studied carefully by the hopefuls who begin competing to satisfy those criteria long before the election year. If the women eager to date Joe College believe that beauty is his main criterion, they will compete with one another to seem more beautiful.

Competition is obviously not confined to capitalist societies or to societies that use money. The point is of fundamental importance: *Competition results from scarcity* and can be eliminated only with the elimination of scarcity. Whenever there is scarcity, there must be rationing. Rationing is allocation in accord with some criteria for discrimination. Competition is merely what occurs when people strive to meet the criteria that are being used.

Of course, the criteria used do make a difference. If a society rations on the basis of willingness to pay money, members of that society will strive to make money. If it uses physical strength as a primary criterion, members of the society will do body-building exercises. And if the better colleges and universities use high-school grades as an important criterion for selection, high-school students will compete for grades. They might be competing for grades to acquire other goods as well (status among classmates, compliments from teachers, use of the family car), but it is odd for colleges to complain of grade grubbers when their own rationing criteria promote grade grubbing.

COMPETITION WHEN PRICES ARE FIXED

What is going to happen, then, when a good like gasoline becomes more scarce but its money price is not allowed to rise? We will certainly see increases in the nonmonetary costs of purchasing it, for gasoline is scarce and therefore *must* be rationed. If by law we suppress the rationing device of monetary price, other rationing criteria will have to be used, whether by drift or by design. Potential purchasers of gasoline will attempt to discover the new criteria being used to discriminate among buyers, and they will compete against one another in trying to satisfy those criteria. Their competition will raise the total cost—price plus nonmonetary costs— and will continue raising it until the quantity demanded no longer exceeds the quantity supplied.

The gas line is probably the best example. When people think they may be unable to purchase as much gasoline as they would like to buy at 60 cents a gallon, they try to get to the station early before the stocks have all been sold. But others have the same idea, so that the lines form earlier and grow longer. Waiting in line is unquestionably a cost. As this cost rises, the law of demand comes into play: Consumers drive less when they expect to have to pay $12 plus half an hour's wait for a fill-up than when they can fill their tanks for a straight $12.

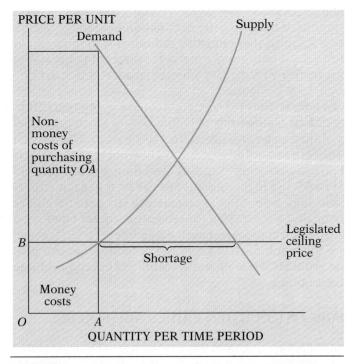

FIGURE 4E   Supply and demand curves with a legislated ceiling price

Look at Figure 4E. If the money price of a good is held down by law to *OB*, a quantity of only *OA* will be supplied. While demanders would like to purchase far more than *OA* at the low price off *OB*, they obviously cannot succeed in purchasing more than suppliers make available. That will be the quantity *OA*. The quantity demanded will be constrained to match the quantity supplied by an increase in nonmoney costs of purchasing.

Some drivers may decide to hunt around rather than wait in line. They will pay their additional cost in time and gasoline spent on searching. Others will strike deals: a fill-up out of reserved supplies in return for a tip to the station operator, or the payment of a special fee for parking at the station, or an agreement to have service work performed there, or maybe tickets to the theater for the station owner. All these ways of competing for gasoline raise the cost of obtaining it. And the cost will continue rising until it finally reduces the quantity demanded to match the quantity supplied.

Competition among people—whose combined desires to purchase a good cannot all be fully satisfied at the prevailing money price—will bid up the cost of purchasing it. Usually it is the money price that rises in such a situation. Whenever other components of the cost of purchasing a good start to climb, we can be fairly certain that some kind of social pressure (such as legislated price controls) is holding down the money price. And when that occurs—that is, when lengthening lines, longer searching, or special arrangements come into play to ration a good because the quantity demanded is greater than the quantity supplied *at the prevailing money price*—we have a shortage of that good.

The economist's concept of shortage zeroes in on the money price. Shortages exist only when money prices are not able to perform the function of rationing scarce goods to competing demanders. *We spot a shortage in real life whenever we find the nonmoney costs of acquisition rising to ration scarce goods.*

THE SUPPLIER'S ROLE IN RATIONING

We expect to see the money price of a good rise when the good becomes scarcer. Why? Because it is almost always in the interest of suppliers to raise the money price rather than see some other component of the acquisition cost increase. What does the owner of a gas station gain, after all, when customers wait in line for 30 minutes? Nothing (and maybe less than nothing if they are all less pleasant people by the time they get to the pump). But an increase of 20 cents in the money price of a gallon of gasoline is simultaneously an addition of 20 cents per gallon to the station owner's wealth. An increase in nonmoney costs usually entails an increase in what the economist calls *deadweight costs*. These are *costs to the purchaser that are not simultaneously benefits to the seller.* The cost of waiting in line is a perfect example.

Deadweight costs are closely linked to transaction costs. If there were no transaction costs, demanders would never wait in line. They would instead agree upon a system to allocate priority in purchasing that did not require anyone to wait for service. In reality the costs of negotiating and enforcing such an agreement are much higher than the costs of queuing, and so gasoline purchasers do sometimes wait in line. But they do so only where price controls have ruled out the quick and easy way to get rid of deadweight costs: an increase in the money price.

If sellers have it in their power to transform a deadweight cost into a benefit for themselves, they will want to do so. And whenever sellers are free to raise the money price of the good they are supplying, they have ready at hand a simple tool for making that transformation. Notice what a handy and versatile tool it is. Everyone values money because its possession confers command over a whole universe of other goods. Everyone is accustomed to paying money for goods. The seller is usually the owner or agent of the owner with an acknowledged right to change the money price. The money price can be minutely adjusted, up or down, in a search for the price that most completely converts the buyer's cost of acquisition into the seller's benefit from supplying.

All of this explains why changes in money prices are the usual response to changes in relative scarcities, and why economists view changing money prices as such a crucial means for securing social coordination. No doubt there are goods that *cannot* and other goods—most people would agree—that *should not* be rationed by means of changing money prices.[2] But it is a fact well worth noting that where this procedure for achieving social coordination is not available, cooperation on any extensive scale becomes much more difficult to achieve.

APPROPRIATE AND INAPPROPRIATE SIGNALS

What will suppliers do if the law prevents them from raising their prices in a situation of obvious shortage? They will probably look for alternative ways to turn the situation to

---

[2]It would be difficult to assign all residents on a city block the precise amount of street illumination for which each is willing to pay. And we apply a variety of derogatory terms to people who ration their affections by the criterion of money price.

their advantage. Gasoline retailers may decide to lower the cost *to themselves* of selling by reducing their daily hours of operation and closing altogether on weekends. If they can sell their entire weekly allocations in 20 hours, why should they bother to stay open for 120 hours a week? This response to the shortage will tend further to increase the cost to *buyers* of purchasing gasoline: they will face even longer lines, will be forced to cancel or curtail weekend traveling, will more frequently find themselves stranded because of the inability to obtain fuel, and will pay additional costs through searching, worrying, and even endangering their lives by improperly siphoning and storing gasoline.

Those who supply or demand gasoline are not peculiarly selfish or inconsiderate. The costly chaos that we actually witnessed in recent years at the gasoline pumps simply demonstrated how dependent we are on changing money prices to secure effective cooperation in our complex, interdependent society and economy. When prices are not permitted to signal a change in relative scarcities, suppliers and demanders receive inappropriate signals. They do not find, because they have no incentive to look for, ways to accommodate one another more effectively. It is important that people receive some such incentive, because there are so many little ways and big ways in which people *can* accommodate—ways that no central planner can possibly anticipate, but which in their combined effect make the difference between chaos and coordination. Changing money prices, continuously responding to changing conditions of demand or supply, provide just such an incentive, because, contrary to the Popular Perspective, supply curves slope upward to the right and demand curves slope downward.

IS THERE A *BETTER* SYSTEM?

To say that money prices perform this function is not to say that they perform it perfectly. They certainly don't. In subsequent chapters we'll be looking at the limitations of social coordination through a price system as well as at its accomplishments. We'll ask under what circumstances money prices are less likely to reflect people's preferences in an adequate way, and we'll discover that ignorance, market power, collusive arrangements, disagreements about property rights, and inequalities in society all interfere with the "ideal" operation of the price system. But we do not discard the first law of motion (which says that bodies in motion tend to remain in motion) just because there is friction in the actual world. It would be a similar mistake to overlook the achievements of the price system just because it fails to coordinate flawlessly.

A system that rations scarce goods by means of money prices will, of course, allocate the goods to those who are willing to pay. Consequently, when rationing occurs by means of price, poor people tend to get less than rich people. That, in fact, is the very meaning of *rich* and *poor* when used in an economic context. But it is not the whole picture. Price rationing accommodates all sorts of other differences among people as well, differences that will prove extremely difficult to handle fairly under any other form of rationing.

Suppose we decide to ration gasoline by means of specially issued coupons. How will the government allocate those coupons? It would not be fair to allocate the same number to a single person as to a family of seven, but neither would it be fair to give seven times as many coupons to the family. It wouldn't be fair to allocate an equal number of coupons to each licensed driver, and it wouldn't be fair to assign coupons to each owner of an automobile. (This would encourage people to stock their driveways with clunkers.) People who live in dense metropolitan areas probably travel shorter distances on average and also are more likely to have access to public transportation. Fairness therefore suggests that they should receive fewer coupons than those who live in thinly populated regions of the country. But some people in New York City regularly drive farther than some people in Silverton, Colorado. Would a system that ignored the special circumstances of individuals be fair? How could coupons be awarded fairly to a traveling sales representative in west Texas and an elderly woman in Cedar Rapids who drives only to church? Should the person who hates to drive receive as many coupons as someone who enjoys driving?

And what about business users? (An adequate rationing system must take account of the fact that diesel fuel and gasoline compete for scarce petroleum and scarce refinery capacity.) If farms, taxicab companies, commercial fisheries, and trucking firms—to mention just a handful of businesses that use large amounts of motor fuel—are allotted "all that they need," they will turn out to "need" more than anyone had anticipated. If we therefore create a government agency charged with determining the specific quantities to which each individual firm is entitled, what criteria will it use to make its decisions? Past consumption? Probably. But in an economy where new firms are continually born and old ones die, where some businesses expand and others decline, where technology is constantly changing and so is demand, how can past consumption be an adequate guide to current allocation?

The unfairness of its decisions might be the least of the agency's worries. Because business firms supply inputs to other business firms, as well as final goods to consumers, mistakes that were not quickly caught and corrected could have a domino effect. An error in allocation could close down an entire industry by inadvertently preventing the manufacture or transportation of some seemingly minor but actually crucial input. The intricate interdependence of a modern, industrialized economy could not long be maintained in the face of arbitrary allocations of motor fuel among business firms.

INFLATION AND RENT CONTROLS

Popular hostility to rationing by means of money prices grows in periods of inflation, because people mistakenly assume that an increase in money prices means a decline in their level of living. It's hard for most of us to see that our money incomes tend to rise right along with the prices of the goods we buy. When expenditures on a particular good take up a large percentage of our monthly budget, we become especially sensitive to increases in that good's price. If in addition the price of the good changes infrequently, and therefore by large jumps when it does change, we grow even more indignant about increases in its price. And popular indignation is fertile ground for the growth of legislative interference with the movement of money prices.

Rent controls are far and away the best example. Although grocery and clothing prices creep slowly upward in a period of inflation and are therefore commonly ignored, rents tend to remain fixed for longer periods of time—and then to do their advancing with a bound. A rent increase from $350 to $425 also makes a big dent in the budget and seems unreasonably steep, even when the average prices of the other goods we buy have increased by more than 50 percent since the last rent increase. People look for scapegoats in such circumstances, and landlords (the word itself stirs resentment) are prime candidates.

There is an unusual irony in the case of residential rents, an irony that greatly aggravates the problem. Because residential rents are exceptionally "sticky" prices, tending to lag behind the rate of change in other prices, the average level of rents tends actually to fall during rapid inflations. Thus, whereas the average level of prices paid by consumers more than doubled from 1967 to the end of 1978, rents increased slightly less than 70 percent. So rents actually declined by about 15 percent.[3]

But this fall in rental prices was caused by a malfunction of the price system, not by any change in underlying conditions of demand or supply. The result in one American city after another was *declining vacancy rates.* These low vacancy rates, themselves a result of underpriced housing, then became a further argument for rent controls. "We cannot permit rent gouging when the vacancy rate is less than 1 percent." Or even better: "We must impose rent controls until the vacancy rate rises to an acceptable 3 percent." Since the low vacancy rate is the product of low rents, that is an argument, whether recognized or not, for permanent rent controls. Note that the suppliers who are thus singled out and specifically forbidden to raise their prices are suppliers whose prices are already failing to keep pace with inflation.

When law or custom keeps money rents below the level at which the quantity demanded equals the quantity supplied, other ways of rationing will evolve. Landlords might discriminate on the basis of age, sexual preference, personal habits, family size, letters of reference, pet ownership, length of residence in the community, or willingness to abide by petty regulations. Tenants who were lucky enough to be in a rent-controlled apartment when the controls were imposed will hang on to as much space as possible for as long as they can and will try to pass the unit on to a friend or to sublease when they do vacate. Landlords will lower the quality of the services they provide, since they know that there is a long line of tenants waiting to move in if any current tenant becomes dissatisfied.

All these responses will lead to demands for costly administrative review boards and for additional legislation prohibiting particular landlord responses. The long-term result may be the eventual disappearance of landlords, as existing buildings are allowed to deteriorate or are turned into condominiums, and new rental units are not constructed. But even the most unrelenting foe of landlords must concede that it will be hard to find an apartment to rent when none is being offered.

---

[3]The ratio of rents to all consumer prices, which by definition was 100/100 in 1967, had become 170/200 in 1978; so rents in 1978 were at only 85 percent of their 1967 levels when measured in relative prices. That constitutes a 15 percent decline.

SURPLUSES AND SCARCITY

Many people use the word *surplus* to suggest that a particular good is not scarce. But this doesn't make a lot of sense. Let's consider the much discussed problem of farm surpluses.

Agricultural surpluses have been a continuing concern in the United States for many years. Farmers and their supporters maintain that the prices of agricultural products should go up at about the same rate as the prices of other goods. They have persuaded Congress to establish parity prices: prices that preserve the ratio that farmers had enjoyed from 1910 to 1914 (prosperous years for farmers generally) between the prices they received for their crops and the prices they paid for the goods they bought. A common policy goal was 90 percent of parity.

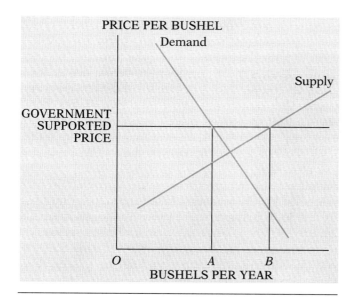

FIGURE 4F   Supply and demand curves with a government-supported price
According to Figure 4F, the quantity demanded at the government-supported price is *OA*. Since the quantity supplied is *OB*, the surplus created by the price-support policy is *AB*. In a broader sense, however, no surplus actually exists, because the government purchases the quantity *AB*. The quantity supplied, *OB*, equals the quantity demanded: *OA* by the private sector plus *AB* by the Commodity Credit Corporation. The CCC "wants" this quantity insofar as it "wants" to keep the price from falling below the supported level.

Through the Commodity Credit Corporation, an agency of the Department of Agriculture, the federal government offers to store for farmers, free of charge, any crops for which they cannot find a market at the established parity price, meanwhile lending the farmers the value of the crops they choose to store. These are nonrecourse loans, which means that farmers can simply pocket the loan and let the Commodity Credit Corporation keep the stored produce. In effect farmers use the government as a buyer of last resort in order to be sure of receiving the target price for any "supported" crop. The resulting surpluses do not mean that wheat, corn, cotton, and other supported crops are not scarce. They simply mean that Congress is unwilling to let key farm prices fall to the level at which the quantity demanded for current consumption will match the quantity farmers want to produce.

The American Medical Association has long been warning about an imminent surplus of physicians. If we don't stop training so many physicians, says the AMA, we will soon be burdened with more than we need. But there is no precise number of physicians "needed" by any population. When members of a profession talk about the number "needed," they almost always mean the quantity demanded *at the current price.* Of course, a lower price for their services is precisely what they don't want to see. And that makes them reluctant to admit that lower prices would also produce lower incomes for physicians and an eventual reduction in the number of physicians practicing. Do you detect the Popular Perspective at work?

Surpluses of teachers also became a problem in recent years, at least for the teachers. From the standpoint of school boards and local taxpayers, the problem looked more like an opportunity. At lower wage rates, school districts would be willing to hire more teachers. And at lower wage rates, some of those now offering to teach would decide to seek careers elsewhere. If salary scales cannot be reduced, either because of union contracts or just because it "wouldn't be right" to lower the pay of those to whom we entrust the hearts and minds of our youth, other ways are usually found to balance the quantity supplied and the quantity demanded. Salary scale increases that are less than the rate of inflation reduce the real wage. School boards can also add to the duties of teachers, lowering the wage per unit of product by getting more product for a given salary.

If these measures are insufficient to balance quantity supplied with quantity demanded, other criteria will of necessity be used to ration out the scarce supply of teaching positions. (A surplus of teachers is a shortage of teaching positions.) Seniority is an obvious and common rationing criterion. It's one that appeals to long-established teachers, but not one that younger or prospective teachers find very attractive. And certainly it does little to promote a situation in which those most eager to teach are also most likely to end up in the classroom.

SUPPLIERS WHO DON'T CARE ABOUT THE PRICE

When a good becomes more scarce, competition from demanders tends to bid up its price. Suppliers are usually happy to cooperate in letting this occur, because they benefit from higher prices. What will happen, however, when a good becomes more scarce but those who supply the good have nothing to gain from letting its price rise?

A good example is landing space at some of the nation's busiest airports. The Federal Aviation Administration predicts that as many as 50 U.S. airports will face serious congestion problems by the end of the century. Why is this occurring?

An increase in demand, even a huge, rapid increase in demand, won't necessarily create a shortage. There is no current shortage of personal computers, to take a dramatic example. And when more people want to fly, the airlines simply offer more flights. They hire more people and buy more airplanes, if they must. That costs them money, of course, but those are expenses the airlines are happy to incur, because they expect their additional revenue to exceed their additional costs.

The bottleneck appears at the airports because the airports and the airspace surrounding them are not privately owned and hence are not priced to earn a profit. The additional travelers who bring joy to the heart of the airline managers are a pain in the neck to those who manage the airports, because those who "own" the airports and the airspace around them have no interest in charging higher prices when the goods they supply become more scarce.

YOUR VERY OWN AIRPORT

The easiest way to grasp the essential point might be to suppose that you owned National Airport in Washington, DC, one of the most crowded in the country, and that you were free to operate as you saw fit. The "congestion problem" would disappear immediately, transformed into "full-capacity operation." (Do theater owners worry about congestion when they've sold all the tickets?)

The various airlines would still be eager to schedule more flights into National, because it's just a few minutes from the Capitol and hence the airport preferred by most travelers to Washington. But you would make them bid for the scarce landing slots, because you (money-grubbing rascal that you are) want to squeeze as much revenue as you can out of the landing fees. In the resulting competition, the price would rise to reflect the opportunity cost of the first *excluded* bidder. You would make a mint. But you would also have allocated the available landing slots to those who valued them most highly, as measured by their willingness to pay a landing fee that clears the market.

Won't travelers suffer, however, from your mercenary maneuver? It's quite likely that the airlines would tack a little extra onto the ticket price under this system for flights into National Airport. But that would in effect ration the scarce landing space at National to those passengers who placed a high value on the convenience of landing close to downtown rather than an hour away at Dulles Airport far out in Virginia.

In fact, many passengers would be better off if passengers flying into National had to pay a premium. That would induce the airlines to divert more flights to the uncrowded, almost deserted runways of Dulles. As a result, many passengers who didn't want to go to downtown Washington in the first place, or who were merely making a connection in Washington, would be able to enjoy the convenience and greater safety of Dulles Airport.

Moreover, if there is any way for you to expand the capacity of your airport, you will investigate it carefully. And if the cost of the expansion is less than the value of the expansion, as measured by the willingness of the airlines and ultimately of travelers to pay for landing, you will quickly and expeditiously carry through the expansion. You won't behave like the FAA, which cries "crisis" but announces a program to upgrade air-traffic-control equipment only *over a ten-year period.*

Flight delays, near collisions, and other evidence of a shortage of airspace can be traced directly to our system of airspace ownership. The rules of the game make it next to impossible for those who value scarce airspace most highly to bid it away from those who value it far less. The transaction costs are much too high when the landing slots are not privately owned. A slow, small, propeller-driven plane carrying half a dozen passengers will be allowed to land at Washington's National Airport or Chicago's O'Hare at a peak hour, thereby delaying two jumbo jets with 600 passengers, because the rules of the game make it almost impossible for the 600 passengers to bid the landing slot away from the six. Supply and demand are still at work, but they don't produce a great deal of mutual accommodation in cases like this.

PRICES, COMMITTEES, AND DICTATORS

The central economic task for a society is to secure cooperation among people in using what is available to obtain what is wanted. Effective cooperation among large numbers of people who barely know each other requires that the terms of exchange be clear, simple, and standardized so that transaction costs can be kept down.

Money prices are a device of extraordinary effectiveness for simplifying, clarifying, and standardizing. Have you ever wondered why committees achieve so little while consuming so much of their members' time and energy? It's because committees are such poor devices for simplifying, clarifying, and standardizing the available options. If a committee does manage to evolve procedures for performing these tasks, it ceases to behave like a committee—instead, it becomes a cooperative venture.

There's another method for getting work done through committees, of course: by letting one person make all the decisions. Dictators do get things done quickly. And dictatorial decision making can also perform, in the larger society, some of the simplifying, clarifying, and standardizing functions of the price system. The other side of the coin is that the price system makes social cooperation possible in the absence of dictators. That's a definite plus for all those who don't care much for dictators.

An even stronger objection to dictators is that they don't know nearly as much as all the people whom they are trying to direct. The price system pays attention to and coordinates not only the preferences but also the special knowledge of all demanders and suppliers. If the Popular Perspective were correct, it wouldn't take a whole lot of knowledge to run a modern economy. Producers could simply be ordered to produce the specific quantity of everything that people "need" at each item's predetermined cost of production. But the truth is that supply curves are not completely elastic at some cost of production decreed by technology, and demand curves are not perfectly inelastic at the quantities "needed." We live in a delightfully kaleido-scopic world characterized by continual change and constant discovery. The collapse of central planning in the former USSR and its client states has once again illustrated the woeful inability of dictators to manage effectively the day-to-day business of a commercial society.

ONCE OVER LIGHTLY

The coordination of decisions in a society characterized by extensive division of labor is a task of enormous complexity, requiring the continuous daily negotiation, renegotiation, and monitoring of millions of agreements to exchange.

An effective market economy features numerous institutions that have evolved to reduce transaction costs, which are the costs of arranging contracts or transaction agreements between suppliers and demanders.

A system of money prices that change readily in response to changing conditions of supply and demand is an essential mechanism for coordinating behavior in highly specialized economic systems.

Supply and demand is the process of interaction through which relative prices are determined. It is a process of mutual adjustment and accommodation.

Changes in relative prices create incentives to change behavior: to use less and provide more when prices have risen, to use more and provide less when prices have fallen.

Scarcity is a relationship between availability and desirability, or between supply and demand. A good ceases to be scarce only when people can obtain all they want at a zero opportunity cost.

Scarce goods must be rationed in some fashion. Rationing entails the use of discriminatory criteria to determine who gets how much. Competition is the attempt to satisfy whatever discriminatory criteria are being used to ration scarce goods.

When a good becomes more scarce, but prices are prevented from rising, a shortage develops: the quantity demanded at the prevailing price is greater than the quantity supplied.

A surplus is a situation in which the quantity of a good supplied exceeds the quantity demanded at the prevailing money price. Any good, whatever its scarcity, will exist in surplus supply if its price is fixed at a high enough level.

When competition is prevented from raising prices, it will raise other components of the cost of acquisition. These are often deadweight costs: costs to demanders that, unlike money payments, are not benefits to suppliers.

Suppliers usually have an incentive to convert deadweight costs into benefits for themselves by raising money prices when a shortage appears.

When suppliers do not benefit from higher prices, perhaps because the scarce resources are not privately owned, money prices will be less responsive to changing conditions of scarcity, and cooperation in the use of scarce resources will be more difficult to secure.

Allocating rights and obligations by means of monetary prices discriminates in favor of those with high monetary incomes. But it also allows individuals to obtain special consideration for their particular wants and abilities in social assignments of benefits and tasks.

QUESTIONS FOR DISCUSSION

1. Here is a good question to get you thinking about supply and demand as a process of coordination. Millions of Americans change their residences each year, many moving long distances to new and strange areas. How do they all find places to live?

   (a) Who sees to it that every individual or family moving to a new state finds someone in that state willing to sell or rent them a house or apartment that suits their tastes and circumstances?
   (b) Who oversees construction planning so that those states that are growing most rapidly manage to expand their stock of housing at a rate that matches their population growth?

2. A *Wall Street Journal* article of January 3, 1983, was headed, "Moving House Isn't Easy to Do in China, Where Government Is the Only Landlord." The government not only owns all housing in China; it also keeps rents down to a level equal to about 3% of an average worker's income.

   (a) In the United States, 3% of an average worker's income would be about $50 a month. Would you expect to have trouble locating housing in an American city where rents were limited by law to $50 a month? What effect do the low rents in China have on vacancy rates?
   (b) Under these conditions, how could a Chinese family that wanted to move to another city do so? How could they find a place to live in the new city? How could they persuade someone in the new city to vacate housing space for them?
   (c) The Chinese government maintains housing-exchange stations in all the major cities. Why would transaction costs be much higher with a

housing exchange than with a system of private ownership and changing prices when it comes to facilitating trades among millions of people who want to move?

3. List some of the institutions that lower transaction costs for Americans who must sell a house and buy another house in order to move from one city to another.

4. If you want to help people who live in an area that has just been devastated by a hurricane, what are the best items to send them?

5. If the desire for more money is an indication of a selfish and materialistic attitude, as many people seem to think, why do churches and charitable organizations work so hard to acquire more of it?

6. A major step toward mastering the economic way of thinking is learning to reason in terms of supply and demand. Here are some questions on which to practice. It would be a good idea to take a piece of scratch paper and sketch the demand or supply curves described or inferred in each case below.

   (a) If a huge increase in the demand for soybeans results in almost no increase in the price of soybeans, what can you conclude about the supply of soybeans?

   (b) If a large fall in the cost of growing corn results in almost no decrease in the price of corn, what can you conclude about the demand for corn?

   (c) What effect would you predict on the price of rental housing in an area where several major employers have recently closed down or moved away? Would you expect the effect to be large or small, and why? (Your answer in this question and the ones that follow is less important than the reasoning with which you arrive at those answers.)

   (d) If unanticipated changes in weather conditions cause large annual variations in the quantity of wheat harvested in the United States, would you expect large or small annual fluctuations in the price of wheat? Why?

   (e) What effect do you think the development of synthetic fabrics had on the price of cotton?

   (f) It has been estimated that meat eaters indirectly consume five times as much grain per capita as those who consume grain directly. Does this imply that meat eaters take food from the mouths of others? Be sure to refer in your answer to the price elasticity of supply of grain.

   (g) What effect would you expect an increase in the property tax rate to have on residential rents? Would you expect the effect to be different in the long run from what it is in the short run?

   (h) What effect would you expect on the price of gasoline if automobile makers succeeded in doubling the number of miles that drivers can obtain per gallon?

7. The summer of 1988 saw a record-breaking drought in the U.S. agricultural heartland. In the autumn of 1988, experts were predicting the largest jump in U.S. crop acreage since World War II. What prompted farmers to undertake such a public-spirited response to the situation created by the drought?

8. A letter to the editor recommends: "Gasoline should be rationed, if it becomes necessary, according to need—real need." How will the rationing authorities determine *real need?*

9. Evaluate for their fairness toward single-car and multiple-car families the following proposed systems for rationing gasoline:

   (a) People whose license plates end in odd numerals can buy only on odd-numbered days; people whose plates end in even numbers buy on even-numbered days.
   (b) People are required to choose one day of the week on which each car will *not* be driven. They are assigned numbers (1 through 7), which they must display. Any car being driven on the prohibited day is ticketed by police.
   (c) No one may buy gas on Sundays.
   (d) No one may buy less than $10 worth of gasoline.

10. Is smallpox virus rare today? Is it scarce? What's the difference?

11. Many ceiling prices were fixed by law in World War II. How were scarce goods rationed?

12. State colleges and universities set very low tuition. How do they ration scarce facilities? Who do you think gains from this system? Why might professors and administrators of state schools prefer *not* to have scarce facilities rationed by means of higher prices (tuition)?

13. There are no toll charges for driving on many urban expressways during the rush hour. How is the scarce space rationed?

14. Parking space is often sold on college campuses at a zero price. How is the scarce space rationed? If all students who bring cars onto the campus are charged $100 a year by the college as an automobile registration fee, is that fee a rationing device?

15. The government did not impose controls on sugar prices in 1974, and the price per pound rose about 600 percent. Did the high price cause any more sugar to be available in 1974 than would have been available at a lower, controlled price? Do you think there would have been any refined sugar available on grocers' shelves if the government had frozen the price near its original level? Where would it have gone?

16. What do you think would have happened had the government imposed price ceilings in 1977 when the price of coffee increased about 400 percent? What do you think would have happened had the government imposed price controls in 1978 when lettuce prices increased by about the same percentage?

17. If a ceiling of $1 per pound were placed on lobster sold at retail, where could you go to eat a lobster?

18. A May 1979 wire-service story reported that a San Diego Chargers' football player got so upset waiting in line to buy gasoline for his Rolls-Royce that he purchased a gas station. "I bought it for my friends' convenience, too," Johnny Rodgers said. Do price controls keep the wealthy from obtaining more than the poor?

19. One reason that local governments sometimes impose rent controls is precisely to prevent money prices from rationing scarce residential space. Do the controls succeed in doing this? How has it happened, do you suppose, that most of New York City's rent-controlled apartments are occupied by relatively wealthy people?

20. When federal environmental rulings forced stricter limits on street parking in midtown New York, parking-garage rates rose. Why? New York's consumer affairs commissioner called for a crackdown on parking-garage "gougers." What would happen if parking-garage rates were held down by law?

21. If the distribution of income were completely equalized, would everyone purchase the same quality automobile? Against whom do automobile prices discriminate? Under an equal income distribution, would all families of the same size want to own or rent the same quantity and quality of housing space? Against whom do rental prices discriminate?

22. Suppose the Department of Defense decides to close a military base along the seashore and to turn the land over to private citizens. The land is close to heavily populated areas and offers choice view lots.

    (a) If the lots are allocated by means of a lottery, who will end up building on them?
    (b) Some lots are clearly more desirable than others. Will more expensive houses tend to be constructed on the more desirable lots if the lots are allocated by lottery?
    (c) Were you assuming in the answers above that the government places no restrictions on reselling? What difference will it make if the rules of the lottery declare that lottery winners cannot sell their lots for five years after acquisition, on penalty of forfeiture?
    (d) Is it fairer to allocate the lots by a lottery than on the basis of willingness to pay?

23. Help the Federal Communications Commission decide how to award scarce broadcast licenses for low-power television stations among the 5000 competing applicants by indicating the principal advantages and disadvantages of the following systems. Award the licenses:

    (a) To the highest bidders.
    (b) To the most qualified applicants.
    (c) By lottery.
    (d) By a lottery that favors groups currently underrepresented in the ranks of broadcast license holders as long as the lottery winners are qualified.

Can you understand why the FCC, when instructed by Congress to use method (d) above, replied that it lacked the ability to devise a system that would withstand lawsuits from disappointed applicants?

24. Utah annually sells 27 licenses to hunt buffalo in a 1500-square-mile area of the state. The fee is $200 for residents and $1000 for nonresidents. Because the state receives more than a thousand applications each year, it holds a lottery to decide who will get the 27 licenses.

   (a) Why do you suppose Utah doesn't sell the licenses to the highest bidder?
   (b) Do you think people who receive a license should be allowed to sell it to someone else?
   (c) What effects do you think a lottery system *with freely transferable licenses* would have?

25. A parking space in the 1500-car garage under the Boston Common cost $110 a month in 1988, according to a November 7 article in *The New York Times.* Those who want to rent a space could expect a seven-year wait, according to the state agency that runs the garage. Is the rate too high, too low, or about right, in your judgment? What do you think would happen to the monthly parking rate if the garage were privately owned? Why doesn't the state raise the rate?

26. If the supply of turkeys in a particular November turned out to be unusually small, do you think a turkey shortage would result? Why or why not?

27. If you travel through the western states in the summer, you are much more likely to encounter a shortage of camping spaces than of motel rooms. Why?

28. Think about a registration scheme under which students would have to pay higher tuition for 10 o'clock classes and would receive discounts for taking 8 o'clock classes. Would you favor such a plan? Why do colleges *not* charge higher prices for the hours in greater demand? A student willing to pay a friend $5 to stand in line for him and grab a 10 o'clock section might protest vigorously if he were charged an extra $3 to take a 10 o'clock class—even though the $3 fee gets rid of the line that he was willing to pay $5 to avoid. If you think these apparently inconsistent responses are plausible, how would you explain the contradiction?

29. In an article in *Energy* (Vol. 8, No. 8–9, 1983) economist Charles Lave has written:

> Perhaps a virtue of price-oriented solutions (in the energy sector) is that people already know how to solve problems that way; there is continuity with the past. And perhaps the drawback of bureaucratic solutions is that they lack this continuity and instead require people to learn and understand a new set of behaviors.
>
> We vastly underestimate the complexity of the familiar. The distribution and sale of gasoline seemed a trivial thing until the government tried to manage it in 1973 and 1979.

(a) Does this explain in any way the "contradiction" pointed out in the preceding question—that we are *familiar* with bureaucratic solutions in school systems?

(b) Does Lave's suggestion explain why something like the system discussed in the the text for allocating scarce airspace is unlikely to be implemented? Would such a system require a sharp break with familiar patterns of behavior?

(c) How do complex systems ever become familiar? Who introduces them? Why does anyone ever try to introduce a new and complex system to replace an old and familiar but less "efficient" one?

(d) No one would want to open a gasoline station unless a large number of people owned and drove automobiles. But few people would be willing to invest in an automobile if gasoline stations were not readily available. It's easy to think of similar conundrums, but surprisingly hard to find a real-world example of one. How are such chicken-and-egg dilemmas resolved in practice? Why did people buy television sets before there were television stations or create stations before people owned sets?

30. Why do restaurants have such different pricing policies for different items? With napkins, for example, the policy usually is to charge no price and let customers have as many as they want. With beverages, a price may be charged with additional servings available at no fee or a reduced fee. With other items, customers pay a set price for each unit consumed. If your answer is that napkins don't cost very much, how do you account for the fact that grocery stores don't let their customers take as many napkins as they want free of charge? And why do cafeterias typically charge per pat of butter while sit-down restaurants will usually provide additional butter at no extra charge if the customer requests it? What accounts for these differences?

31. The text maintains that the price system is an institution that secures social cooperation in large part by simplifying options. Another institution that does this effectively is the traffic light. Are traffic lights fair? How much attention do they pay to the special circumstances of the drivers who approach them? Would you prefer a system of traffic control that always gave the right of way to the motorist on the more urgent errand?

32. The graph in Figure 4G reproduces the original data of question 10 in Chapter 3 in the form of an opportunity cost curve, or supply curve. It adds to those data a demand curve, showing how many hours of tutoring students would want to buy at various prices.

(a) What will students have to pay for an hour of tutoring in economics? How many hours will they buy?

(b) The opportunity cost to Marx of tutoring was given as $3.99—the wage he could get for fomenting revolution. If you know this fact and consequently ask Marx to tutor you for $5 an hour, he will tell you

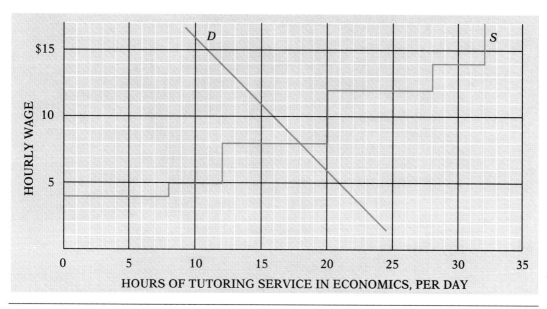

FIGURE 4G   Hypothetical demand and supply curves for economics tutoring

that the opportunity cost to himself of tutoring you is $8. Is he right?
Or is he just trying to exploit you?

(c) If Merrill Lynch offers Ricardo full-time work at $13.99 an hour,
he will no longer be willing to supply 4 hours of tutoring per day
for $5 an hour. What will happen to the price of tutoring service as
a result?

(d) If the demand for tutoring service doubled (i.e., twice as many hours
were demanded at each price as previously), what would happen to
the price of tutoring services and to the number of hours supplied?

(e) If the demand tripled, what would be the price and the number of
hours supplied?

33. The graph in Figure 4H presents a hypothetical demand curve for wheat
labeled D, and the aggregated opportunity-cost curves of all wheat farmers, labeled S for supply.

(a) Why will the price of wheat move toward $2.50? What would occur if
the price were $2.75? If it were $2.25?

(b) Suppose wheat farmers persuade the government to "support" the
price of wheat at a "fair" price of $3.75 per bushel, by itself purchas-
ing for $3.75 a bushel any wheat farmers can't sell at that price or
higher. What will this do to the total demand for wheat?

(c) How many bushels of wheat will the government have to buy and
store? (Why can't the government simply buy the wheat and then re-

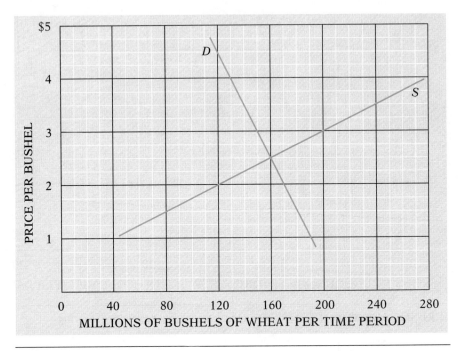

FIGURE 4H   Hypothetical demand and supply curves for wheat

sell it?) Is this properly called a *surplus?*

(d) What would happen, under the supply and demand conditions depicted, if the government told wheat farmers they should sell their wheat for whatever they can get on the market, and then collect from the government a subsidy of $1.25 for every bushel sold? What will be the price of wheat? How many bushels will be exchanged?

(e) What will be the cost to the taxpayer of the support program? Of the subsidy system? Are there any other advantages that one method of aiding wheat farmers has over the other?

34. How do taxes imposed on the purchase or sale of a good affect its price? Does it matter whether the government requires the purchaser or the seller to remit the tax?

Figure 4I presents a supply curve and a demand curve for soybean oil. The market-clearing price is 20 cents per pound.

(a) Suppose the government levies a tax on all soybean oil sold, requiring sellers to remit 5 cents for every pound they sell. How will this affect the cost of supplying soybean oil and hence the supply curve?

(b) When the supply curve rises by 5 cents a pound, what does the mar-

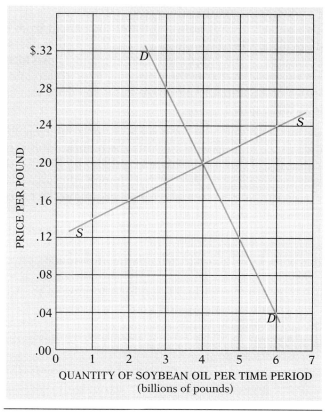

FIGURE 4I   Supply and demand for soybean oil

ket-clearing price become?

(c) How much *more* do demanders pay per pound as a result of the tax? How much *less* do suppliers receive (after payment of the tax)?

(d) The government ordinarily requires sellers rather than buyers to remit sales taxes in order to simplify the task of enforcing and collecting the tax. (Think about what would happen if consumers in states with sales taxes had to keep track of their purchases and send monthly checks to the government.) You can get some practice in reasoning with the aid of supply and demand concepts by figuring out what the market-clearing price would be and who would ultimately bear the burden of the tax in the soybean oil case if the government required purchasers to remit the tax. (Assume away all problems of enforcement.)

(e) What would be the effects if the government offered a 5-cent-per-pound subsidy to suppliers in order to boost their incomes?

(f) What would be the outcome if the 5-cent-per-pound subsidy were offered to demanders rather than to suppliers?

(g) Will demanders always obtain most of the benefit from a subsidy and suppliers always bear a smaller part of the burden of a sales tax? What features of the supply and demand curves produce those results in this case? What is the price elasticity of demand between the quantities of 3.5 and 4.5 billion? What is the price elasticity of supply between these quantities?

35. Should parents with one television set and three children allocate program choice to the sibling who submits the highest money bid? Suppose they allocated the choice to the highest bidder *and* divided the winning bid between the two losers. Would that change your answer? If you think it is preferable for parents to make this decision on the basis of fairness and what is best for the children, would it also be preferable for the Department of Energy to allocate scarce energy resources among competing citizens according to the department's sense of what would be most fair and in everyone's best interest? What is the difference between the two cases?

36. Far fewer babies are currently offered for adoption in the United States than couples want to adopt. Would you be willing to let the available children go to the highest bidder? What consequences would you predict from such a system? By what criteria are scarce babies currently assigned to prospective adopters?

37. Federal law currently prohibits the sale of human organs for transplant purposes. At the present time people are dying while waiting for suitable organs to become available. It seems almost certain that more organs would become available if financial incentives were offered to prospective donors. Would you be in favor of allowing this? What consequences would you predict?

38. Renters in Honolulu currently must pay three times as much and renters in Chicago twice as much for an apartment as renters in Colorado Springs. Is that fair? Why does it occur? Should the government offer subsidies to Honolulu and Chicago renters? What would happen if it did?

MARGINAL VALUES AND ECONOMIC DECISIONS

Economic analysis is basically marginal analysis. Many economists even use the word *marginalism* to refer to what we have called "the economic way of thinking." *Marginal* means *additional.* Economic theory is marginal analysis because it assumes that decisions are always reached by weighing additional costs against additional benefits. Nothing matters in decisionmaking except marginal costs and marginal benefits.

DECISIONS AT THE MARGIN

Suppose that the love of your life phones you at 9 P.M., while you're studying desperately for your physics exam the next day. He wants to come over for a couple of hours. You tell him you have to study. He pleads. You say no. He asks plaintively, "Is physics more important than me?" And if you've grasped the economic way of thinking, you respond without hesitation: "Only at the margin."

    If that doesn't stop his whining, tell him to enroll next term in an economics class, and go back to your studies. The issue of *his value* versus the *value of physics* just doesn't arise in this situation. The question, rather, is whether an additional two hours with him at this time is worth more than an additional two hours with your physics text.

    Since you don't want to alienate him, you might explain a little further. Ask him which is more important to him, water or toothpaste. If he answers, "Water," you've got him. For he undoubtedly *uses* water as if it had no value at all. And he would probably refuse indignantly to pay as little as 5 cents for a drink of water if someone tried to charge him that price in a restaurant. Why? Because it is the value and importance of *additional* water in his actual situation that affects his behavior, not the value of water in the abstract. What he and you are each willing to give up to obtain a drink of water is *not* what you would be willing to pay if you were dying of thirst in a desert; it is what you are willing to pay when you're surrounded by faucets and fountains that offer virtually unlimited quantities of water at the turn of your wrist.

He is thinking in terms of "all or nothing." But that just isn't the choice when he phones on the evening before your exam. In fact, that is rarely the choice we face when we're called upon to make decisions. It's usually more of this and less of that versus more of that and less of this. The economic way of thinking rejects the all-or-nothing approach in favor of attention to marginal costs and marginal benefits.

THE IRRELEVANCE OF "SUNK COSTS"

When you pass through the cafeteria line, pick up the tuna lasagna, and pay the cashier $1.90, you incur a cost: the value of whatever opportunity you will have to forgo because you've spent $1.90. Then you take your first bite and suddenly wish you hadn't selected this item. What will be the cost to you of leaving the lasagna on your plate?

It will *not* be $1.90—or $1.80, if we assume your first bite consumed about ten cents' worth of tuna lasagna. That cost is history. The cost of leaving the lasagna on your plate will be the value of whatever opportunity you forgo by doing so. Do you have a dog that would enjoy pasta with tuna, cheese, and spicy tomato sauce? If so, the cost of leaving the lasagna is the opportunity you forgo (by not asking for a doggie bag) to see your dog's eyes light up and its tail wag.

The price you paid is what economists dismiss as a *sunk cost*. Sunk costs are irrelevant to economic decisions. Bygones are bygones.

> *The Moving Finger writes; and, having writ,*
> *Moves on; nor all your Piety nor Wit*
> *Shall lure it back to cancel half a Line,*
> *Nor all your Tears wash out a Word of it.*

Of course, we must be certain that a cost is really sunk, or fully sunk, before we decide to regard it as irrelevant to decisionmaking. If you were to purchase a new motorcycle and immediately afterward regret your decision, what would be the cost to you of continuing to own the motorcycle? Clearly, you would not be forced to say, "I did it and now I'm stuck." You could resell the motorcycle. By not doing so you would incur a cost (a benefit forgone) equal to its resale value. The genuine sunk cost would therefore be only the difference between what you paid for it and what you can get by selling it. That is the irrelevant part of your cost. *In the economist's way of thinking it is no cost at all, for it represents no opportunity for choice.* It may be cause for bitter regret and the occasion of some education in the dangers of impulse buying, but it is no longer a cost in any sense relevant to the economics of present decisions.

Yet we all know that people do not consistently reason things out in this way. Many people who made such a purchase and then regretted it would be tempted to retain possession of the motorcycle rather than sell it for substantially less than the original price. They might justify this action by saying "I can't afford to take the loss." But they already took the loss! They made a mistake, and their full loss occurred when they made it. If they nonetheless choose to keep the motorcycle, they are probably practicing self-deception. They persuade themselves that a motorcycle gathering cobwebs in the garage has the same value as the money they paid to put it there, and more value than the opportunities forgone by keeping it there. But the only relevant cost now is the opportunity forgone *by not selling.*

THE CASE OF THE LAS VEGAS CAPER

Let's practice this approach. Suppose you own a television retail store, and one of your suppliers is sponsoring a gigantic Dealers Contest. For every television set you buy (no returns allowed), you receive one day in Las Vegas with all expenses paid. You gleefully order 28 sets, and your wife starts planning your two-week holiday together.

Upon your return from Las Vegas, you begin wondering how you will sell all those television sets. One month later you're still wondering. It seems that none of your customers is interested in that brand or model. You are about ready to give up and store the whole lot in the back workroom.

Then you get an offer from an orphanage in some distant city to take all those sets off your hands for $4000. You know that a businessman can't make money by selling below cost, so you sit down to figure out the cost of the sets. You paid $140 apiece to the supplier. Moreover, you have had them in your store for a month tying up valuable floor space. You borrowed the money to buy them at 12 percent annual interest. You also had various handling costs, which you estimate at $400. And you spent $160 on advertising in a vain effort to move the sets. By estimating $280 as the cost of display space tied up for a month, you arrive at a figure of $4800. You write back to the orphanage that you would be willing to sell the lot at cost for $4800, forgoing any profit on the transaction in the interest of charity. The orphanage replies that $4000 is their top price, since they can get the sets they want somewhere else for that price. But you are a good businessman, you know that losses don't make profits, and you refuse.

You were actually a rather poor businessman. Every one of the "costs" you enumerated in arriving at your total of $4800 was a *past expenditure* and hence no cost at all. *The proper stance for making cost calculations is not looking back to the past, but forward to the future.* Your costs, if you sell, will be the opportunities thereby forgone, or what you can get for the sets if you do not sell to the orphanage. You know the market fairly well and you estimate you could get $1120 by selling them for junk. The marginal cost of selling to the orphanage is therefore $1120. Your gain from selling to the orphanage is consequently $2880. Any loss that you're worrying about should be assigned to experience and the glorious memories of Las Vegas. It is irrelevant for decisionmaking purposes.

MARGINAL EFFECTS GUIDE DECISIONS

The word *marginal* means in economics exactly what it means in everyday speech: situated on the border or edge. The concept is of fundamental importance in economic thinking, because economic decisions, like all effective decisions, always involve *marginal* comparisons. That is, they always have to do with movements at the border, with positive or negative *additions.* What will be the *additional,* or *marginal,* cost that results from this decision? And how does it compare with the marginal cost of alternative decisions? If you think about it for a moment, you will discover that opportunity costs are always expected marginal costs. The term *marginal cost* does no more than bring into strong relief an aspect of opportunity-cost thinking.

It's important not to get the marginal concept mixed up with the notion of *average*. You may have no intention of confusing marginal with average; if so, what follows may only plant in your head the seeds of a bad idea. Let's hope it doesn't. A simple production schedule of a hypothetical zerc manufacturer will illustrate the distinction.

Number of Zercs Produced	Total Cost of Producing Zercs
42	$4200
43	4257
44	4312
45	4365

A little long division reveals that 42 zercs can be produced at an average cost (total cost per unit) of $100; the average cost is $99 for 43 zercs, $98 for 44, and $97 for 45. A little subtraction reveals, however, that the cost of producing the 43rd zerc is not $99 but $57. The incremental expenditure, or the extra cost, incurred by producing the 43rd zerc, is its marginal cost. The marginal costs of the 44th and 45th zercs are $55 and $53, respectively. It is clear that marginal cost can be more or less than average cost and can even differ substantially from average cost. It should also be clear that for a zerc manufacturer trying to make production decisions, it is the marginal costs that should guide him. Shall we produce more? Or less? Marginal cost is the consequence of action; it should therefore be the guide to action.

Are business people then not interested in average costs? Unless they receive sufficient revenue to cover all their costs they will sustain a loss. They won't willingly commit themselves to any course of action unless they anticipate being able to cover their total costs. They might therefore set up the problem in terms of anticipated production cost per unit against anticipated selling price per unit. But notice that the *anticipated* costs of any decision are really *marginal* costs. Marginal cost need not refer to the additional cost of a single unit of output. It could also refer to the additional cost of a batch of output, or the addition to cost expected from a decision regarding an entire process. Decisions are often made in this "lumpy" way.

For example, no one plans to build a soda-bottling factory expecting to bottle only one case of soda. There are important economies of size in most business operations, so that unless business people see their way clear to producing a large number of units, they won't produce any. They won't enter the business. They won't build the bottling factory at all. The entire decision—build or don't build, build this size plant or that, build in this way or some other way—is a *marginal* decision at the time it is made. Remember that additions can be very large as well as very small.

Whether or not business people cast their thinking in terms of averages, it is expected marginal costs that guide their decisions. Averages can be looked at after the fact to see how well or poorly things went, and maybe even to learn something about the future if the future can be expected to resemble the past. But this is history again—admittedly an instructive study—whereas economic decisions are always made in the present with an eye to the future.

THE COST OF DRIVING

The Hertz Corporation conducts an annual study of automobile operating costs to determine how much it costs motorists per mile to drive the cars they own. Hertz takes into account depreciation over the life of the car, license fees, insurance premiums, interest on the automobile loan, maintenance, and of course gas and oil. They then announce that it costs so many cents per mile to drive an intermediate-size car if the car is owned four years and driven 10,000 miles per year.

But what does this really tell us? Does it offer any guidance to someone who is trying to decide whether to drive or to take the bus to work each day? Or to someone weighing a commercial airplane against the family car for a vacation trip? Let's suppose you have been asked by your college to drive your car to a conference. You plan to attend the conference whether you drive your own car or not. The college offers you 25 cents a mile. Will it pay you to drive, or should you say no and hitch a ride with someone else? If you go about deciding by trying to calculate whether the cost to you of owning and operating a car is less than 25 cents a mile, you're being foolish. It makes no more sense to speak of the cost per mile of owning a car than to speak of the cost per mile of owning a house. Neither houses nor cars are *owned per mile*. They're owned per month or per year, but not per mile. If you nonetheless decide to divide the cost of owning by the miles driven, you will come up with numbers that tell you the more you drive, the less it costs. That just isn't so. Each time you drive, you *add* something to your costs. In order to decide whether or not to drive, you must know the marginal cost of driving.

Costs of purchase, license, insurance, borrowing, plus maintenance and depreciation not due to operation are all unrelated to your decision whether or not to drive. That is why they are irrelevant. The relevant cost is the marginal cost: How much extra will you be out of pocket if you drive? Be sure to include not only the cost of gas but also the costs of oil, tire wear, and mileage-induced repairs. Insofar as cost can be expected to vary proportionately with mileage driven, it can properly be expressed as so many cents per mile. If it is less than 25 cents, as it probably would be, you make money by driving your car. As long as the marginal cost remains less than the price paid by the college, you gain from every additional mile "produced" and "sold."

Are the costs of purchase, license, insurance, borrowing, and time-related depreciation *completely* irrelevant? Shouldn't you be allowed to cover these costs, too? After all, you have to pay them even if they are not related to the trip you've been asked to undertake.

You are certainly free to ask the college for as high a mileage rate as you choose. And if you have no scruples, you are even free to trot out all your sunk costs and wave them righteously. There is ample precedent for such action. But the one person you don't want to confuse is yourself. Only marginal costs are relevant to your decision, whatever price the college finally agrees to pay you.

Perhaps you've begun to suspect that it's our example that is irrelevant. We're interested, after all, in ordinary business decisions, and whatever may be true of the student driver as entrepreneur, businesses surely have to cover *all* their costs, not just marginal costs. It would seem so. But it isn't so. There is no more necessity to cover sunk costs in the business world than there is in our case study.

The plain fact is that each year many businesses fail to cover sunk costs. But most of them don't stop operating. We can illustrate by supposing that you bought your car with the intention of driving it for the college. When you made up your mind to become a sort of taxi operator, you hoped to make enough money to pay your way through college. So you purchased a car, the license, and insurance. You probably would not have done so had you expected the college to offer only 25 cents a mile. Maybe you had reason to believe they would pay you 50 cents. Your calculations in these circumstances might have run as follows:

Purchase price: $8000.00
License: $200.00
Insurance: $500.00
Gas and oil: $0.08 per mile
Maintenance: $0.04 per mile
Chauffeur service: $6.00 per hour

Your problem now is the familiar one of adding apples and oranges. Or even worse, adding apples and velocity. How can you add $8000 to 8 cents per mile and $6 per hour? Obviously you can't.

You could, however, turn all these figures into costs per year, much as Hertz does. The license and insurance are annual costs. The purchase price could be converted into an annual figure by estimating annual depreciation and adding the annual interest charge on your initial outlay of $8000. But you can't state the other costs on an annual basis without knowing how far and how long you'll be driving. You must anticipate. Remember what we said earlier: the significant costs and benefits in economics are *expected* costs and benefits. That means they're uncertain. But uncertainty is a fact of life, and if you want to be a student entrepreneur, you'll have to live with it. So you estimate that you'll obtain so many miles and so many hours of business per year. You can then plug in your estimate and obtain numbers for gas and oil, maintenance, and chauffeur services per year.

Now you can do your addition and come up with a figure for the annual cost of doing business. You can then take the mileage estimate you used to calculate gas, oil, and charges for wear and tear, multiply by the rate you expect to be paid, and thereby calculate prospective revenue per year. If the anticipated annual revenue exceeds the anticipated annual cost, you take the plunge and buy a car. If it doesn't, you don't.

So sunk costs are relevant? Of course not. Until you take the plunge, they aren't sunk. They are marginal. They are additions to cost that you are thinking about incurring. That's the essence of being marginal. And as long as they're marginal, they are relevant. But only that long! Until you commit yourself in some way to a business operation, *all* your costs are marginal. Once you have committed yourself, the situation has obviously changed. If you want to maximize your profits (or minimize your losses, which comes to the same thing), you must produce and sell all those units of output whose anticipated marginal cost is less than the anticipated price to be set by the college, which is the marginal benefit.

WHO PAYS SUNK COSTS

But if a business firm doesn't cover its sunk costs, who does? Who pays the bill for mistaken decisions in the past? We're going to look more closely at that issue in Chapter 11, when we introduce the concept of the entrepreneur. For now, though, we can say that the costs are paid by *the investors who provided the means by which the mistakes were made.* They had hoped to profit; but matters failed to turn out as expected, and so they take a loss.

Consider a simple case. Amber Crombie and her husband Fitch pay $250,000 to buy a lot and build a home overlooking beautiful Lake Lilypad. They expect to receive more than $250,000 worth of benefits from living in their comfortable new home with its breathtaking view. Soon after moving in, however, they notice that Lake Lilypad supplies an odor as well as a view. The smell gets progressively worse. Finally, Amber and Fitch decide they can't stand it any longer and will have to move. When they put their house on the market, however, the best offer they get is $60,000, from a couple with chronic nasal congestion. What will happen next?

Amber and Fitch must compare marginal benefits and marginal costs. They will weigh the odor-reduced benefits from continuing to live in their house against the cost of doing so, which is $60,000 forgone. In other words, would they choose to buy this house, knowing what they now know, if the total price were $60,000? If not, they should sell.

What about the other $190,000 they've invested? That's the loss they incurred by paying $250,000 for something that has turned out to be worth only $60,000. They can't avoid that loss by staying in the house, at least not if they themselves place a lower value on the house than what the congested couple is willing to pay. They have sustained a $190,000 reduction in their wealth. And their loss will be even greater, under our assumptions, if they try to avoid the loss by not selling.

Suppose, however, that the Crombies had put up only $75,000 of the original cost, and had taken out a bank mortgage for the remaining $175,000. Who bears the loss in this case? The bank will want the mortgage paid off when the sale goes through; but the sale proceeds of $60,000 won't come close to meeting the Crombies' indebtedness. If they have no other assets with which to satisfy the bank, the bank might decide to prevent the sale. But what is there then to stop the Crombies from defaulting on the mortgage and turning the house over to the bank? Whereupon the bank will sell the house to recover its investment, and get . . . $60,000 from the nonsmelling couple. In that case the Crombies will have lost $75,000, their original investment, and the bank will have lost $115,000, the difference between what it loaned and what it recovered by foreclosing on the mortgage and selling the property.

There are other possibilities, of course. The Crombies may decide that the (expected future!) loss of honor and credit worthiness is a cost too high to accept, in which case they won't default, but will faithfully continue to pay the bank long after they have abandoned the house on Lake Lilypad. There is a good chance that the Crombies or the bank will try to shift the loss to whoever can be found responsible for the odor, or, if no villain can be located, whoever should have warned the Crombies about the fumes from Lake Lilypad.

Whatever ultimately occurs, the cost of buying the lot and building the house were incurred when these steps were taken. All but $60,000 of that is a sunk cost and a loss. Mortgage payments in this case are the marginal cost of retaining possession, or, if the Crombies sell but continue paying, the marginal cost of retaining their credit rating and their honor.

THE RISING COST OF MEDICAL CARE

Let's use this way of looking at costs and decisions to see if it can clarify the controversy over rising medical costs and how to contain them. We will look first at physicians' fees.

People often assert that physicians charge high prices in order to recover the cost of their education. Could this be true? The argument implies that dullards who take an extra year to finish medical school will set higher-than-average fees, and geniuses who breeze through in less than the normal time will set lower-than-average fees. We don't see that occurring. The argument also implies that physicians who went through college and medical school on full scholarships will establish lower fee schedules than those who had to pay their own way. That implication is not confirmed by observation either. Suppose a recent medical school graduate learns that she has only two years to live. Could she raise her fees enough to recover the full cost of her education in her two remaining years of practice? The argument makes no sense. To a practicing physician, the cost of a medical education is entirely in the past and consequently irrelevant to current decisions.

Does the cost of acquiring a medical education have no effect, then, on physicians' fees? The answer is that it affects fees indirectly by influencing the supply of physicians' services. The prospect of many arduous years in preparation deters people from premedical programs. The necessity of forgoing income for all those years and of borrowing money to live and to pay tuition decrease the anticipated attractiveness of a physician's life. The expected future cost of going through medical school thus restricts the number that will eventually supply physicians' services. (This restriction is in addition to others, of course: not everyone who wants to graduate from medical school is able to do so.) All of this ultimately affects the prices physicians charge. But to see exactly how it does so, we must push our analysis further.

The fees that physicians charge for seeing patients are indeed related to costs, but the relevant costs are *the costs of seeing patients*. What is the cost to physician X of seeing patient A? What opportunity does physician X thereby sacrifice? In the common case today it will probably be an opportunity to care for patient B. What determines the value to the physi-

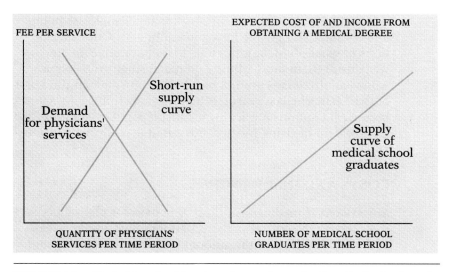

FIGURE 5A   Market for physicians' services and supply of medical school graduates

cian of that opportunity? It will be the fee that patient B is prepared to pay.

In other words, people bid for the scarce time of physicians on the basis of their demand for physician care. This demand interacts with the supply of physicians' services to determine the cost of a visit to the doctor, or the price that physicians will be able to charge. The more that physician X can get from seeing other patients, the higher is the cost of tending patient A. Note that this is not determined by the value of the time the physician spent in school, but by the value of the physicians' time *to patients*. The point is a most important one. If the demand for physicians' services increases but there is no increase in the amount of such services supplied, demanders will simply raise the cost of medical care, essentially by trying to bid it away from other people. In short, we who call for appointments determine the cost of physicians' services.

Physicians are not required to raise their fees when demand increases faster than supply, and many do not. They can instead allow other elements of the cost to rise. "I can't get you in before Thursday." "You can come into the office and wait, if you want to, but the doctor may not be able to see you." The less that fees rise in response to increased demand, the more queuing costs tend to rise. As a result, those who would have been willing to pay more money will tend to surrender some portion of available medical services to those willing to sit for hours reading old magazines.

The reasons for the large increases in recent years in the demand for physicians' services are many. People are living longer, and older people have more ailments. Our expectations of what physicians are able to do have gone up, and so we consult them more often. And increasingly, the people who visit physicians are not required to pay the marginal cost of that visit. The last reason is an especially important one, because it contains a warning against a popular "solution" to the problem of rising medical costs that is really no solution at all.

COSTS AND INSURANCE

Any system of medical insurance that pays for physicians' services lowers the cost to patients of obtaining those services—and thereby increases the amount people will want to purchase. It doesn't much matter for the present argument whether the insurance system is a public one financed wholly out of taxes or a private system under which the beneficiary pays all the premiums. So long as patient A's decision to visit the doctor has no discernible effect on the amount patient A must pay, the relevant price is zero. It's true enough that if beneficiaries go to the doctor more often, premiums (or taxes) will have to be increased. But those additional payments will be made by the policyholders (or taxpayers) whether they decide to see their physicians or, alternatively, to stay at home, get plenty of rest, and drink lots of liquids. The additional payments are sunk costs, and so they cannot affect decisions.

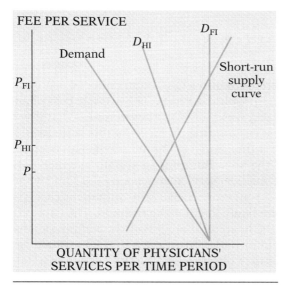

FIGURE 5B   Supply and demand curves for physicians' services under various insurance plans

Figure 5B portrays the demand for and short-run supply of physicians' services. In the absence of any insurance system for paying physicians' fees, the market-clearing fee will be at P. However, if patients expect to have their fees fully paid by insurance, they will demand the quantity they would want with a zero fee and will be indifferent to the fee charged. The demand under "full insurance" will consequently shift to become the line labeled D_{FI}, and the market-clearing fee will rise to P_{FI}. (D_{FI} is not a true demand curve, because it graphs the quantity demanded against the fee charged, not the fee paid.)

If the insurance pays only one-half the fee for service, the "demand curve" will shift to D_{HI}, showing that the quantities demanded without insurance will now be demanded at fees precisely twice as high. The market-clearing fee will be P_{HI}.

The marginal monetary cost to the patient of a visit to the doctor is zero when insurance pays the entire fee.

Here is the catch in the insurance approach to the problem of medical costs. If we respond to higher costs by offering larger insurance benefits, we subsidize the use of these scarce services. But that increases the demand, bids up the cost, and necessitates yet another increase in benefits. It also makes people ask why we don't do something to keep medical costs down! We will certainly not keep them down as long as our response to the problem is one that pulls them up by increasing the demand for medical services faster than the supply is increasing.

HOSPITAL COSTS

The question of *who pays* is also important in the case of another, even more important, contributor to rising medical care costs—hospital services. The average cost of a hospital room in 1985 was more than seven times what it was in 1965. It is almost certain that an increase this large would not have happened if the people using the rooms had been the ones who paid the bills. But under a system in which patients' payments for medical service are exactly the same whether they enter the hospital or receive only outpatient care, patients are much more likely to enter the hospital. The care is usually better in the hospital than outside it, and physicians can more easily monitor patients' progress in the hospital. On top of that, insurance often covers the full cost of hospital care, while paying only a part of outpatient care. That's a direct invitation to people to increase the demand for scarce hospital services, and it quite predictably produces a steadily mounting level of room charges.

Hospital administration also demonstrates that sunk costs do have their uses. Suppose a particular hospital adds a 200-bed wing and purchases a lot of sophisticated new laboratory equipment. Once these decisions have been taken, the costs associated with them are sunk costs. But that doesn't mean they can't be useful to the hospital's administrators. If the government and private insurance companies have agreed to make payments to the hospital based on the hospital's cost of providing service to patients, and if the hospital gets to decide what counts as cost, every dollar of those sunk costs will be used. The sunk costs will be "spread over" each patient, according to whatever formula enables the hospital to recover them as quickly as possible without unduly antagonizing those who must pay.

Cost *to whom?* Benefit *to whom?* That's always the best way to pose the question of costs and benefits if you want to find out why some policy is being followed. If the benefits from a hospital's ownership of all the most modern equipment accrue largely to its medical staff, if the cost of not pleasing the medical staff falls primarily on the hospital's administrators, if the cost of acquiring that equipment is borne entirely and uncomplainingly by government, insurance companies, or philanthropists, then hospital administrators will purchase expensive equipment even if it is rarely used—and the cost of hospital-care services will soar. In recent years insurers and government have started to pay hospitals a fixed fee for particular services rather than just reimburse the hospitals for whatever costs they claim to have incurred. Hospital administrators as a consequence now have more reason to control costs and less reason to pretend that sunk costs are costs of providing particular services.

COST AS JUSTIFICATION

The economic analysis of costs is an especially treacherous enterprise for the unwary, because costs often have an ethical and political as well as an economic dimension. Many people seem to believe that sellers have a right to cover their costs, have no right to any price that is significantly above their costs, and are almost surely pursuing some unfair advantage if they price below cost. This way of thinking, in which cost functions as *justification,* has even infiltrated our laws. Legislated price controls, for example, usually allow for price increases when costs go up but refuse to permit any price hikes that are not justified by higher costs. And foreign firms selling in the United States can be penalized for "dumping," if a government agency determines that they sold in this country at prices "below cost." In circumstances such as these, when costs become a rationalization rather than a genuine reason for decisions, all statements about costs must be inspected for evidence of special pleading.

Prices *ought* to be closely related to costs, in popular thought, because costs supposedly represent something real and unavoidable. The most enthusiastic advocates of rent control will agree, at least in principle, that landlords should be allowed to increase their rents when the cost of heating fuel goes up. They will never agree—if they did, they wouldn't advocate rent controls—that landlords should be allowed to raise rents merely because the demand for apartments has increased faster than the supply. That would be "gouging," "profiteering," or "a rip-off," because it is unrelated to cost. But such a rental increase is just as surely related to cost as is an increase in response to higher heating bills. When the demand for rental apartments increases, tenants bid against one another for available space, thereby raising the cost to the landlord of renting to any particular tenant. What another tenant would be willing to pay for the third-floor corner apartment in the Hillcrest Arms creates the landlord's marginal cost of continuing to rent to the present occupant. The case seems to be different with higher heating-fuel prices but really is not. The cost of fuel oil is also determined ultimately by the bids of competing users in relationship to the offers of suppliers. Cost is always the product of demand and supply.

When you grumble to your butcher about the high price of hamburger, the butcher will deny all responsibility. "They keep raising the cost to me," he will say. If you were to investigate further to find out who "they" are and why "they" keep raising the butcher's cost, you would eventually discover that "they" are "we"—we who like hamburger and bid against one another for it. To see exactly how this works, imagine a sudden and unexpected increase in the demand for hamburger, occasioned perhaps by splendid summer weather and a surge of backyard cookouts. The first effect will be a depletion of butchers' hamburger inventories. When butchers find their hamburger inventories low and the demand continuing strong, they will increase their orders for beef suitable for grinding. With this happening all over the country, meat packers will in turn find their inventories of beef reduced and will try to buy more cattle. But the increased demand for cattle will encounter a relatively inelastic supply curve, and the price of cattle will rise. The packers who must consequently pay more for cattle will increase the price to the butcher, who can then honestly say "they raised the cost," without for a moment suspecting that "they" are in front of the checkout stand, not back at the wholesale meat market. The cost of hamburger in the supermarket is determined by the interactions of demanders and suppliers.

PRICE, COST, AND SUPPLIERS' RESPONSES

We can easily imagine circumstances under which such a surge in the demand for hamburger would *not* increase its cost to the butcher. Suppose that the increased demand for hamburger is accompanied by a *decreased* demand for round steak, chuck roast, and other beef cuts that can be used to make hamburger. The meat packers and the butchers may be able, under those circumstances, to produce the additional hamburger being demanded without increasing their demand for cattle. In that case, there would be no additional bidding for cattle to raise their price, create higher costs for the butcher, and hence produce a higher price for hamburger at the meat counter.

The passage of time can have a similar effect. Suppose the increased demand for hamburger is part of a general, widespread increase in the demand for beef. The demand for cattle will increase at the livestock market, the price per pound will rise, and consumers will end up paying more for beef.[1] The competitive bidding of consumers will have increased the price.

But that will trigger a new kind of competitive bidding, some of which will go on within the mind of single livestock growers. The higher price for cattle will make resources more valuable in cattle production than they were previously and will consequently "bid" some resources away from other uses—growing hogs, raising soybeans, feeding chickens, or working less at the business of feeding cattle. The more effective the higher price is in pulling additional resources into cattle growing, the less will the price of cattle (and hence the price of beef) increase as a result of the original increase in its demand. But the supply adjustments that we're now describing take time. That's why supply curves are typically more elastic in the long run than in the short run.

Let's summarize what we've been trying to say in this section. An increase in the demand for any good (hamburger, medical care, rental apartments) will bid up the cost of acquiring the good (its price) to the extent that it does *not* cause a larger quantity to be supplied. Or looked at from the other side, an increased demand for any good will *not* raise its price to the extent that suppliers respond by making larger quantities available. The responses of suppliers will depend on the marginal cost of transferring resources out of their current uses into the production of the good for which the demand has increased.

If resources can be shifted at marginal costs only slightly above those already prevailing, the increased demand will lead to a larger output rather than a higher price. But as the supply of such resources is used up, progressively higher

---

[1] Don't forget that this higher price will also have the effect of decreasing the quantity demanded. Consumers will end up increasing their monthly beef consumption by less than they had originally intended—before their increased demand raised the price.

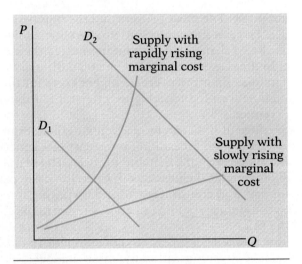

FIGURE 5C   Effect of marginal cost on supply curves
        Figure 5C shows that the effect of a change in demand on the price of a good depends on the marginal cost to suppliers of responding. Marginal cost will rise slowly if an increased demand readily attracts additional resources into production of the good. However, if the resources required to expand production must be enticed from highly valuable alternative opportunities, marginal cost will rise steeply.

prices will have to be offered to cover the rising marginal cost of shifting less suitable resources. Since resources are more mobile, or less rigidly specialized to one use, in the long run than in the short run, the marginal cost of additional output will usually rise less when adequate time has been allowed for adjustments than when suppliers are restricted entirely to those responses that are immediately available to them.

        Summaries tend to be both abstract and obscure. You can make the preceding paragraph more concrete and thus more comprehensible by testing each step of the argument against some real-life situation with which you're familiar. (The case of rental housing in the vicinity of your college might be an excellent example on which to practice.)

ANOTHER NOTE ON ALTERNATIVE SYSTEMS

Is all this just the economics of capitalist societies? Or does it also apply to communist and socialist societies? The principles we have described are the general principles of economizing, applicable wherever resources are scarce. The central planners in a socialist state also operate within the constraints imposed by scarcity: the resources available to them have alternative uses; substitution possibilities are pervasive; one good can usually be achieved only by giving up some other good. Rational planners will calculate the opportunity cost of contemplated actions, treating sunk costs as irrelevant and paying attention only to marginal costs.

There will nonetheless be important differences. Suppose that the minister of coal production in a socialist state is trying to decide how much coal should be mined this month. He can increase coal production by using more workers or employing them for longer hours, or by using more machinery or better machinery. The relevant cost to the society of doing so is the value of whatever is given up through his decision, or the marginal (opportunity) cost. If he obtains new machinery in order to increase coal output, society loses what could otherwise have been produced with the aid of that machinery, or what could have been produced with the resources employed in the construction of the new machinery. The real cost to the larger society of increased coal production is therefore decreased production of locomotives, or cement, or farm tractors.

If the minister can expand coal production by using machinery already in place that would otherwise stand idle, the opportunity cost is much lower and may even be zero. The sunk cost of the equipment is irrelevant. Notice, though, that the marginal cost will be greater than zero if the machinery has any alternative use, including use as scrap metal.

The differences emerge when we ask how all these costs are calculated. In a society where workers own their own labor and must therefore be induced through monetary bribes (wages) to work in particular ways, the wage measures the opportunity cost to workers. The wage must be sufficient to attract them from their (subjectively) next-best alternative. But if workers can be compelled to do what the state dictates, the wage need not bear any relation to the opportunity cost as determined by the workers. (We saw in Chapter 3 how that occurs under a military draft.) In moving from an eight- to a ten-hour day, the miners might be sacrificing two hours of leisure. Whether this is worthwhile would depend on the *planners'* valuation of the extra coal produced in relation to the *planners'* valuation of the leisure forgone.

It would be clearly wrong under any circumstances to suppose that the cost of producing the extra coal can be determined from the *average* cost of coal production. Some have argued that marginal cost considerations are relevant only in an economy guided by the pursuit of private profit. It is true that in a capitalist society entrepreneurs will not choose to produce anything whose marginal cost of production to them exceeds its value to the consumer as measured by its price. But it is just as true that in a socialist society the central planners and enterprise directors will want to produce nothing whose marginal cost exceeds its marginal value.

The major difference lies in the different rules of the game under which opportunity costs and prices are calculated. In a system characterized by substantial private ownership and control of resources, competitive offers to buy and sell resources interact to establish scarcity prices and opportunity costs expressed in monetary units. An enormous quantity of information summarizing a vast range of alternatives is thus distilled into the prices that in turn guide the choices of decisionmakers.

In no economic system past or present have prices ever summarized perfectly the available range of opportunities. And under certain circumstances, as we shall see later, they may do so in a fashion so inadequate as to be politically unacceptable. The relevance of all this for making a choice between alternative economic systems is a complex issue that cannot be resolved exclusively by economic arguments.

In any economic system, however, the following general principles will be applicable:

- Real costs are opportunity costs, the value of opportunities forgone.
- Sunk costs are irrelevant, because they are costs that the decision cannot affect.
- Opportunity costs are always additional or marginal costs, the costs expected to result from the decision under consideration.
- Some method of assigning indexes of value to alternative opportunities must be used in any economic system, or decisionmakers will be operating blindly.
- Supply and demand, or the market process of competing bids and offers, creates indexes of value for decisionmakers by placing price tags on available resources.

The supply and demand process also operates in socialist societies. But where the rules of the game do not clearly assign to particular persons rights to control and exchange specific resources, this process will not generate indexes of scarcity to guide allocation and coordinate activity.

ONCE OVER LIGHTLY

The economic way of thinking is a marginal way of thinking. It assumes that demanders and suppliers pay attention to the marginal (additional) benefits and costs of the actions they are considering: How much extra benefit or extra cost will this decision entail?

Supply curves reflect costs. All costs capable of influencing supply will have three interrelated characteristics that should be watched for: They will belong to actions, not to things; they will be opportunities forgone by particular decisionmakers; and they will be the expected, not-yet-incurred consequences of decisions at the margin.

Past expenditures cannot be affected by present decisions: They are sunk costs and hence irrelevant to decision-making.

Opportunity costs are necessarily marginal costs: They are the additional costs that a decision entails.

If costs per unit are to be used in making supply decisions, the units must be related to the decisions. The cost per mile of owning a car or the cost per bushel of owning a farm are both meaningless, because "owning" is not a decision that produces either miles or bushels (although it may be a precondition for such decisions).

Because economic decisions are based on future or expected consequences, they always entail some degree of uncertainty. The expectation that future revenue will cover future costs is often frustrated in experience.

The common notion that prices ought to be related to costs generates a substantial amount of confusing rhetoric among suppliers who want to justify (or others who want to condemn) a particular price.

Costs are not something independent of demand. The demand for goods helps to determine the cost of supplying them.

Increases in demand for a good will result in higher prices, rather than additional output, to the extent that resources cannot be shifted into production of that good. To the extent that resources can be shifted with no significant rise in marginal cost, the increased demand will result in additional output rather than higher prices.

Under a system characterized by private ownership and control of resources, the forces of supply and demand will establish relative prices that function as indexes of scarcity. It will ordinarily be in the interest of private decisionmakers to be guided by these indexes in their decisions to demand or to supply.

QUESTIONS FOR DISCUSSION

1. In what sense do relative prices reflect relative value? Here is a question to help you think about it. Suppose that the average wage of a hairdresser is twice the average wage of a child-care worker, and that prompts the following comment: "By paying hairdressers twice as much as child-care workers, this society is saying that people who cater to human vanity are twice as valuable as people who care for our children." Is that true in the situation summarized in Figure 5D? D_{hd} portrays the demand for hairdressers and D_{ccw} the demand for child-care workers. S_{hd} portrays the supply of qualified hairdressers and S_{ccw} the supply of qualified child-care workers. The market-clearing wage is $10 for hairdressers and $5 for child-care workers.

   (a) In what sense precisely is a hairdresser worth twice as much as a child-care worker in this society?
   (b) Since the demand for child-care workers seems to be considerably greater than the demand for hairdressers, why do hairdressers command twice as high a wage?

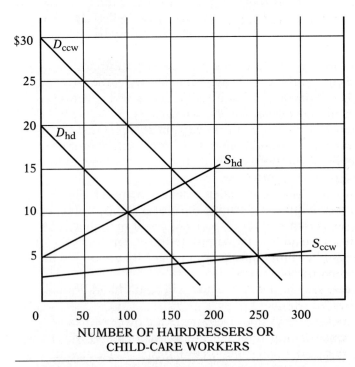

FIGURE 5D   Demand and supply for services of hairdressers and child-care workers

(c) Do the *supply* curves tell us anything about the relative value people place on styling hair versus caring for children? If the social esteem attached to a particular job increases, what effect will this have on the supply of qualified people willing to work at that job? What effect will that have in turn on the market-clearing wage rate for the job?

(d) Use the information provided on the graph to make an argument that this society in fact places more than twice as much value on the services of child-care workers as it places on the services of hairdressers.

2. Test your understanding of the marginal principle by helping Paul Behrer decide how much fertilizer to apply to his parsnip patch. We'll keep the problem simple by assuming that, as Paul applies additional fertilizer, the only cost that changes is the cost of purchasing fertilizer. Here is how yields increase as fertilizer is added:

Bags of Fertilizer Applied	Parsnip Yield in Tons
1	12
2	22
3	28
4	32
5	35
6	37

Paul can sell all the parsnips he raises for $2 a ton. Fertilizer costs $10 per bag, but Paul receives quantity discounts: 2 bags for $18, 3 for $24, 4 for $30, 5 for $35, and 6 for $42.

(a) What is the marginal benefit to Paul, in dollars, of applying fertilizer? In other words, how many dollars does Paul add to his receipts from parsnip sales each time he applies an additional bag of fertilizer?

(b) What is the marginal cost of applying additional bags of fertilizer? In other words, by how much do Paul's costs change each time he adds a bag of fertilizer?

(c) How many bags should Paul apply if he wants to make as much money as possible from parsnip production?

3. The photocopy machine in the library costs $295 per month to rent. The rental fee covers repair service, toner, developer, and 20,000 copies per month. The library also pays 1 cent for every copy beyond 20,000, plus one-half cent for every sheet of paper used.

Harriet Martineau has to read a 20-page journal article for tomorrow's class. She is willing to pay 50 cents for a photocopy of the article; but she will read it in the library if she has to pay more than that.

(a) What is the highest price per page Harriet will be willing to pay to use the copier?

(b) What is the lowest price per page the library should be willing to accept? What additional information must you have in order to answer?

(c) Harriet just found out she is supposed to read a second article for tomorrow's class, an article full of complex graphs. Harriet badly wants her own copy of this article and will pay whatever she has to pay to get one. What is now the highest price Harriet will be willing to pay to use the library copier? (You must supply some information from your own experience to answer.)

(d) How does the $295 monthly rental fee affect the price the library will want to charge users of its copier?

4. In 1981, when AT&T was the exclusive provider of long-distance telephone service in the United States, a cost specialist for the company estimated the cost of a daytime telephone call from New York to Los Angeles at 68.9 cents for the initial period and 33 cents for each additional minute. The 68.9 cents included 11.3 cents for maintenance, 3.3 cents for operator services, 4.4 cents for business services such as sales and advertising, 2.7 cents for pricing and billing, 8.2 cents for depreciation and amortization, 10.6 cents for general purposes, 12.9 cents for taxes, and 15.5 cents for earnings.

(a) When these calculations were made, AT&T was charging less than 25 cents for a one-minute call from New York to Los Angeles. Was the phone company losing money at that rate? Or don't some of those costs have to be met at night and on weekends?

(b) AT&T presented these data to the Federal Communications Commission, which oversees long-distance rates, and asked for permission to set a fee of 74 cents. Does that fact help explain which items the cost specialist included?

(c) Does it actually cost the phone company less when people place long-distance calls at night or on weekends? What is the marginal cost to the phone company of a call from New York to Los Angeles? Why might it differ with time of day and day of the week?

(d) An AT&T advertisement in 1989 said: "AT&T's daytime prices are so low, you can call anywhere in the U.S. for 28¢ per minute or less." A footnote explained that this was the average price per minute for a 10-minute call, dialed direct. Do you think the cost of providing long-distance telephone service fell by that much in the 1980s?

5. How long will you search for a $20 bill that you lost if you value your time at $5 an hour? Suppose you know that you lost it somewhere in

your bedroom. Would it ever be rational for you to search more than four hours? Use the concepts of sunk cost and expected marginal cost to explain how a rational person who values time at $5 an hour could *search indefinitely* for a lost $20 bill.

6. An airline is thinking about adding a daily flight from Denver to Billings. It has estimates of the number of passengers who would use the flight. What costs should and should not be considered in deciding whether the anticipated revenue is sufficient to make the flight profitable?

7. The city of Seattle owns a marina and rents space to boat owners. City officials decided in 1981 to set rental rates that would yield a 5 percent profit on the estimated cost of replacing the facility. They said this would call for an approximate doubling of moorage fees over the next three years.

   (a) What does the estimated cost of replacing the facility have to do with the cost of renting out moorage space?
   (b) The most important part of the facility is the ocean water that fills Puget Sound, on which the marina was constructed. Should the estimated cost of replacing the ocean be included in the price? (If you argue that it should *not* be included because the ocean is a free gift of nature, go back and check your answer to question 2 at the end of Chapter 3.)
   (c) At the time they announced their intention to raise the fees, city officials estimated the waiting time for a space at 17 to 20 years. What does this have to do with the cost of renting out moorage space?

8. According to an article by economist Terry Anderson in *The Wall Street Journal* of September 30, 1983, farmers in the Imperial Irrigation District of California are required to pay only $6.50 an acre-foot for water that may cost taxpayers as much as $300 an acre-foot to deliver.

   (a) At which number—$6.50 or $300—will Imperial Valley farmers look when deciding whether to irrigate a little more or a little less?
   (b) Do these figures demonstrate that irrigation is not really worthwhile in the Imperial Valley?
   (c) Why would anyone pay $300 to supply an acre-foot of water that is worth only $6.50 to the demander?
   (d) What do you think the demand curve for water in the IID looks like? What about the opportunity-cost curve of supplying water to the IID?

9. In order to decide whether or not to drop intercollegiate football, your school undertakes a study of the program's cost. To what extent do you think the following budget items represent genuine costs?

   (a) Tuition scholarships to players.
   (b) Payments on the stadium mortgage.
   (c) Free tickets to all full-time students.
   (d) Salaries of the athletic director, ticket manager, and trainer.

10. What determines the cost to a university of providing parking spaces on campus for faculty, staff, and students? Why would a parking facility probably cost an urban university more than it would cost a university located in a small town? If monthly parking fees are higher for students than for faculty, does this mean it costs the university more to provide parking for students?

11. The American Society of Internal Medicine is not happy with the schedule of relative fees that insurers use to compensate for different kinds of medical service. The ASIM maintains that internists are grossly underpaid relative to surgeons. It wants fees set by taking into account the time and effort required to learn the particular skill (e.g., cardiac surgery or diagnosis of an infection) and the time it takes to perform the service. (See "Doctors Debate How to Split the Fees" by Harry Schwartz, *The Wall Street Journal*, January 15, 1985.)

   (a) Does the ASIM proposal violate the maxim that sunk costs are irrelevant?

   (b) What consequences would you predict from implementation of this proposal? If surgeons' fees fell and internists' fees rose, would a shortage of surgeons and a surplus of internists develop?

   (c) If an internist and a surgeon are both necessary to the successful completion of a particular medical procedure, how can the relative importance of each one's contribution be assessed?

12. (a) What differences would you expect to observe in the fees set by three young physicians just setting up practice if one financed her education by borrowing and must now make payments of $4000 per year for 15 years, another had his entire education paid for by his parents, and the third went all the way through on government-provided scholarships and grants?

   (b) Evaluate the argument, put forward in a *Newsweek* column of March 19, 1979, that the government could lower our doctor bills by paying for the entire education of physicians, thus making it unnecessary for physicians to recover the costs of their education (plus interest) by raising their fees.

   (c) The author of the *Newsweek* article asserts that "you and I" will have to cover the cost of the doctors' loan repayments in our fees because these payments "are a legitimate cost of doing business." What difference does it make whether particular payments are or are not "a legitimate cost of doing business"? Suppose all physicians practicing in an area were required to pay $5000 a year to the local crime syndicate as protection money. Would these payments be "a legitimate cost of doing business"? Would they affect doctors' fees?

13. In June of 1988, the Canadian Horticultural Council filed a petition with the Canadian Revenue Department claiming that U.S. apple growers

were selling American red and golden delicious apples in Canada at prices below cost.

(a) U.S. growers admitted that they had sometimes sold below cost, but they blamed this on the huge harvest. Do you agree that a huge harvest could push prices down *below cost?* Cost to whom of doing what?

(b) In response to the petition, the Canadian government sent long questionnaires to U.S. packing houses, seeking information on the cost of planting new orchards and building new packing plants and cold-storage warehouses. The head of a U.S. apple growers association objected on the grounds that the cost of orchards and plants many years old is lower than the cost of new ones. Can you resolve this dispute?

14. The Department of Defense awards you a cost-plus-10% contract to build missiles in your garage. Which of the following may you legitimately include in your costs?

(a) Original cost of constructing the garage, adjusted for inflation and depreciation.

(b) Weather damage to your car from parking it outside because your garage is full of missile-making machinery.

(c) Cost of lengthening the garage by four feet so the missiles don't extend into your driveway where neighborhood children might accidentally set one off.

(d) Cost of the course you took at the community college to qualify as a missile maker so you could win the government contract.

(e) Cost of the math courses you took years ago which turned out to be prerequisites for the course on missile making.

(f) Cost of your elementary school education, since you wouldn't be able to manufacture missiles if you didn't know how to read.

(g) Cost of the tetanus shot you received when you were three years old, which saved your life and thereby enabled you to become a successful defense contractor.

(h) Cost of psychological counseling whereby you seek to overcome depression when your children scorn you as a member of the military-industrial complex.

15. Backers of the B-2 bomber have argued that it would be wasteful for Congress to stop their manufacture because so much has already been spent to develop the B-2. Advise Congress on how to deal with this argument.

16. Your boss tells you in an angry voice, "I don't care what you learned in economics. If you don't include all our sunk costs in your report and recommendation, I'll fire you." Are the sunk costs now irrelevant to your decisionmaking?

17. Should the casualities already incurred in a war be taken into account by a government in deciding whether it is in the national interest to con-

tinue the war? This is obviously not a trivial question. And it is a much more difficult question than you might at first suppose, especially for a government depending on popular support.

18. What does it cost you to sleep through one of 30 lectures in a course for which you paid $300 in tuition?

19. Do students put more effort into courses when they have to pay higher tuition to take the courses?

20. Do hot dogs taste better at the ball park, where they cost twice as much as they ordinarily cost? Do they taste better *because* they cost more?

21. Would you expect to find any people who don't particularly like Ingmar Bergman's movies attending a Bergman film festival if the price of the festival ticket is $5 for 10 movies? Would you expect to find many people who aren't enthusiastic about Bergman attending a Bergman festival where the price is $50 for 10 movies? Does your answer to this question change your answer to the preceding question about hot dogs at the ball park?

22. The economist's rule, "sunk costs are irrelevant," is like a string around your finger. It reminds you to consider only marginal costs, but it cannot identify the marginal costs. That requires informed judgment. You could sharpen your judgment by trying to enumerate and assess the marginal costs of retaining or not retaining your college apartment over the summer vacation. Try to calculate the minimum rental from subleasing that would persuade you to retain it for fall reoccupancy.

23. Here is what it would cost you to fulfill your long-time ambition to own and operate a small ski resort:

To acquire the land	$200,000
To acquire the ski lift	100,000
To acquire a shelter	20,000
To operate the lift and sell tickets	50 per hour

You plan to be open 50 hours a week for 20 weeks in the year. You therefore anticipate operating costs of $50,000 per year. You will be able to borrow the $320,000 you need to get started under a 20-year loan. Your annual payments on the loan (principal and interest) will come to $43,000 per year.

(a) What is the minimum amount of annual revenue from the sale of lift tickets that you will have to anticipate in order to take the plunge and invest $320,000?

(b) Suppose your actual revenue in the first year of operation turns out to be $60,000. Should you go out of business?

(c) You can occasionally earn $600 by opening your resort for 8 hours on weekdays (when you would ordinarily be closed) for the benefit of special charter groups. This revenue will cover your operating costs of $400 for the day; but since your operating costs are only 54 percent of your total costs, you would need about $750 in revenue to make it worth your while to open. Or would you?

(d) If you spend $10,000 a year on advertising in your second year, and as a result increase your total revenue to $75,000, was the decision to advertise a good one?

(e) What are your options if it turns out after several years that you cannot do any better financially than you did in your second year of operation? Should you go out of business? If you decide you can't afford to lose $28,000 a year on a ski resort, what are your options? Suppose the best offer you get when you put the facility up for sale is $100,000 for land, lift, and shelter. Should you sell?

(f) If the lender forecloses because you default on your payments, what will he do with the property? Should the lender foreclose or allow you to spread out the length of your loan so that your payments are reduced to an amount you can meet out of your revenue?

24. The graph in Figure 5E shows the demand for and the supply of residential rental space in an imaginary city. The market-clearing rent is $300 per month.

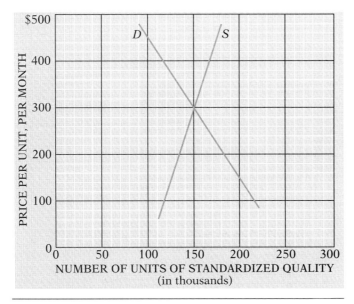

FIGURE 5E   Hypothetical demand and supply curves for residential rental space

Then two events occur: (1) Inflation causes the value of money to fall by one-third; (2) the city and state dramatically lower the property-tax rate, so that landlords' net income from residential rental property rises by one-third.

(a) How would you expect these two events to affect the demand for and supply of residential rentals? What would happen to rents? Distinguish between short-run and long-run effects.
(b) What difference would it make if the property-tax reduction were confined exclusively to residential property?
(c) If rents rise in the short run as a consequence of these occurrences and the city responds by imposing rent controls, what will be the longer-run effect?

25. Figure 5F portrays a supply curve of physicians' services and a demand curve for those services. The market-clearing fee is $30.00.

(a) To what position will the demand curve shift if the government agrees to pay the entire fee charged by physicians? What will consequently happen to the market-clearing price? (Hint: What quantity will people demand at a zero price?)
(b) What will happen to the demand curve and to the market-clearing price if the government commits itself to pay one-half of physicians'

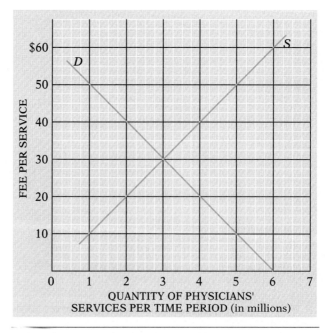

FIGURE 5F   Demand and supply for physicians' services

fees? (Hint: When the fee *charged* is $30, what is the fee *paid* by consumers? What quantity will they want to purchase at this price?)

(c) What will be the market-clearing price if the government pays 80 percent of the fee charged by physicians?

26. What is the relationship between costs and prices? The three parts of this question ask you to analyze some specific cases.

   (a) It costs a lot of money to build and equip a halibut fishing boat. Is that why halibut is so expensive to purchase? What is the relationship between the price of halibut and the cost of a fully equipped halibut fishing boat?

   (b) Do people in poorer neighborhoods pay more for groceries because grocers must charge more to cover the higher costs associated with higher crime rates? What is the relationship between the price of groceries and the cost of insurance in high-crime areas?

   (c) Does the United States government offer price supports to farmers who grow certain crops because the cost of growing those crops is high? Or is the cost of growing certain crops high because the government offers price supports to farmers?

27. You usually pay $1 a bottle to purchase seven bottles of your favorite soda each week. Last Saturday the store held a special promotion on the occasion of the opening of its new parking lot, and you were able to buy your weekly supply for just 50 cents a bottle. Your neighbor has just come over to say he ran out of soda during a party and would like to purchase a couple of bottles if you have any on hand. What would be a fair price to charge him?

28. The *American Economic Review* published in its September 1986 issue a fascinating article by Daniel Kahneman, Jack L. Knetsch, and Richard Thaler that bears on the relevance of costs. It is titled "Fairness as a Constraint on Profit Seeking: Entitlements in the Market." The authors report on and interpret the results of a public opinion survey designed to determine the rules of fairness people use in evaluating actions by business firms.

   Here is one hypothetical situation that was described in the survey and the respondents' evaluations:

   > A grocery store has several months' supply of peanut butter in stock which it has on the shelves and in the storeroom. The owner hears that the wholesale price of peanut butter has increased and immediately raises the price on the current stock of peanut butter.

   Of the 147 respondents surveyed, only 21% thought this was acceptable behavior while 79% deemed it unfair.

   (a) The wholesale price of peanut butter in stock is a sunk cost. Is it relevant to pricing decisions for a seller who shares the majority view on fairness in pricing?

(b) How could it be relevant to a seller who personally holds the minority view but also knows that his customers will find out what he has done if he raises the price on "old" stock?

(c) The economist does not distinguish a sum of money *paid out* from a sum of money *not received:* both are equally costs. The majority of the public apparently does distinguish, because it holds that sellers may raise their prices to cover higher wholesale cost payments but may not do so merely because consumers are willing to pay the higher prices. Can you defend the popular distinction, or do you think it is simply the product of failure to understand what's going on?

EFFICIENCY, EXCHANGE, AND COMPARATIVE ADVANTAGE

Efficiency is the virtue most consistently praised by economists. That should occasion no surprise, since efficiency and economy are practically synonyms. Both terms refer to the effectiveness with which means are used to achieve ends. Getting as much as possible out of the scarce resources available—that's what we mean by efficiency and by economy.

Voices have begun to appear in our society in recent years suggesting that we place too high a value on efficiency; that we sometimes sacrifice more valuable goals to achieve an efficiency that isn't worth what it costs us. Could this be true? Anyone who thinks about it carefully will discover that there is something logically odd about this critique of efficiency. While the critics may have valid and important points to make, it cannot be true that we are paying too high a price for efficiency.

TECHNOLOGICAL EFFICIENCY?

If efficiency is to have any useful meaning, it must be understood as a ratio of one thing to another. Engineers use a definition of efficiency that seems to satisfy this test. They define efficiency as the ratio of the work done by a machine to the energy supplied to it, and that ratio is usually expressed as a percentage. From the engineering standpoint, a diesel locomotive is more efficient than a steam locomotive because, per unit of potential energy contained in its fuel, the diesel does more work.

153

This definition is unsatisfactory, however, when we think about it more critically. Efficiency cannot be measured by the ratio of energy output to energy input because, by the laws of thermodynamics, that ratio is always unity for any process. The engineer's efficiency is rather a measure of *work done* in relation to energy input. But what constitutes "work done"? Doesn't that depend on what is wanted? What qualifies as "work"? Engineers actually call a steam engine less efficient than a diesel because with a steam engine a higher percentage of the energy input is *wasted*. Strictly speaking, however, even wasted energy does work. It just doesn't do any *useful* work. That means it doesn't do work that anybody wants done. All of which implies that efficiency is not a purely objective or technological matter but depends inevitably on valuations.

EFFICIENCY AND VALUES

Efficiency is inescapably an evaluative term. That's the first point to be grasped. It always has to do with the ratio of the *value* of output to the *value* of input. Efficiency will always have an objective component, of course; our likes and dislikes don't determine the potential heat in a pound of fuel. But physical facts by themselves can never determine efficiency. It follows that the efficiency of any process can change with changes in valuations, and because everything depends on everything else, any change at all in any subjective preference is in principle capable of altering the efficiency of any process.

Let's go back to the question of the relative efficiency of diesel and steam locomotives. Each can be put into operation only with the use of a large number of inputs; not only coal or oil and locomotive operators but also all the inputs used in manufacturing the locomotives, the inputs that went into the fabrication of these inputs, the inputs that went into the fabrication of the products that were inputs in the process of producing the products that were inputs in the manufacture of the locomotives, and so on, without any discernible limit. Anything that changes the value of anything that contributes to a locomotive's operation can in principle alter its efficiency.

We don't need any farfetched illustrations to make the essential point. An increase in the value of oil relative to coal, if it is large enough, can by itself transform their relative efficiencies so that a coal-fired steam locomotive becomes more efficient than a diesel. It follows that these relative efficiencies depend on the demand for and supply of oil and coal, and hence on such factors as the motoring habits of the general public, the political situation in oil-producing countries, and the value placed on the environmental effects of strip-mining coal. Perhaps it never occurred to you that the relative efficiency of the old steam locomotive was affected by the efforts of the United Mine Workers!

"Wait a minute," says a voice from the rear of the room. "Aren't you talking now about something other than efficiency? I'll grant you that it costs a railroad less per ton-mile of freight to use diesels than to use coal-fired steam locomotives. But that's not the same as being more efficient. If coal became cheap enough, some railroads might go back to using their old steam locomotives. But that would be because the old locomotives were cheaper, not because they had become more efficient."

From the standpoint of the railroad, however, cheaper *is* more efficient, because the relevant values are monetary values. The illusion of a purely technological efficiency dies hard, but it deserves to be stomped until it's dead. No machine, no process, no arrangement is so efficient that it cannot be rendered inefficient (or so inefficient that it cannot be made efficient) by an appropriate change in values.

THE MYTH OF MATERIAL WEALTH

In emphasizing the essential role of valuations in any measure of efficiency, we are also rejecting the common belief that economics has to do peculiarly with the "material": with material wealth, material well-being, or material pursuits. It just isn't so, and the word *material* actually makes no sense when attached to such words as *wealth* or *well-being*.

Of what does wealth consist? What constitutes your own wealth? Many people have drifted into the habit of supposing that an economic system produces "material wealth," like cars, houses, basketballs, breakfast cereals, and ball-point pens. But none of these things is wealth unless it is available to someone who values it. Additional water is additional wealth to a farmer who wants to irrigate; it is not wealth to a farmer caught in a Mississippi River flood. A food freezer may be wealth to an Alabaman but not to an Eskimo. The crate in which the freezer was delivered is trash to an adult but a treasure to a small child, who sees it as a playhouse.

Economic growth consists not in increasing the production of *things* but in the production of *wealth*. And wealth is whatever people value. Material things can contribute to wealth, obviously, and are in some sense essential to the production of wealth. (Even such "nonmaterial" goods as love

and peace of mind do, after all, have some material embodi-
ment.) But there is no necessary relation between the growth
of wealth and an increase in the volume or weight or quantity
of material objects. The indefensible identification of wealth
with material objects must be rejected at root. It makes no
sense. And it blocks understanding of many aspects of economic life. Trade (or exchange) is the best example.

TRADE CREATES WEALTH

Trading has long had an unsavory reputation in the Western
world. This is probably the result of a deep-seated human
conviction that nothing can *really* be gained through mere exchange. Agriculture and manufacturing are believed to be
genuinely productive: They seem to create something genuinely new, something additional. But trade only exchanges
one thing for another. It follows that the merchant, who profits from trading, must be imposing some kind of tax on the
community. The wages or other profit of the farmer and arti-
san can be obtained from the alleged real product of their efforts, so that they are entitled in some sense to their income;
they reap what they have sown. But merchants seem to reap
without sowing; their activity does not appear to create anything and yet they are rewarded for their efforts. Trading,
some have thought, is therefore social waste, the epitome of
inefficiency.

This line of argument strikes a deeply responsive chord in
many people who still retain the old hostility toward the merchant in the form of a distrust of the "middleman." Everybody wants to bypass the middleman, who is pictured as a
kind of legal bandit on the highways of trade, authorized to
exact a percentage from everyone foolish or unlucky enough
to come his way.

However ancient or deep-seated this conviction of the un-
productiveness of trade, it is completely erroneous. There is
no defensible sense of the word *productive* that can be applied
to agriculture or manufacturing but not to trading. Exchange
is productive! It is productive because it promotes greater efficiency in resource use.

Many have taken a fatal wrong turn at the very beginning
in considering this question by assuming that exchange, unless it is fraudulent or coerced, is always the exchange of
equal values. The exact reverse is true: exchange is never an
exchange of equal values. *If it were, it would not occur.* In an
informed and uncoerced exchange (and this is what we mean
by genuine exchange), both parties gain by giving up some-

thing of lesser for something of greater value. If Jack swaps his basketball for Jim's baseball glove, Jack values the glove more than the ball, and Jim values the ball more than the glove. Viewed from either side, the exchange was unequal. And that is precisely the source of its productivity. Jack now has greater wealth than he had before, and so does Jim. The exchange was productive because it increased the wealth of both parties.

"Not really," says that contentious voice from the rear. "There was no real increase in wealth. Jack and Jim feel better off, it's true; they may be happier and all that. But the exchange didn't really produce anything. There is still just one baseball glove and one basketball."

But the manufacturers of the baseball glove and the basketball didn't "really" produce anything either; they just rearranged materials into more valuable patterns. And isn't that essentially what occurs when people trade? Our suspicion of exchange is evidence of our material bias, a bias obviously shared by that voice from the rear. Both Jack and Jim do have greater wealth after their exchange.

Recall what we concluded earlier about efficiency: It is measured by the ratio of one *value* to another, not by physical ratios of any sort. You can think of Jack's and Jim's exchange as an act of production. Jack used the basketball as an input to obtain the output of a baseball glove. For Jim the glove was the input and the ball the output. The result of the productive process (the exchange) was an output value greater than input value for both parties. Nothing further is required to make an activity productive. The exchange expanded real output.

PROPERTY RIGHTS AND EFFICIENCY

The case of Jack and Jim is simple and straightforward. Their exchange of the basketball and the baseball glove was an efficient reallocation of resources. It's an easy case because Jack and Jim were the only people in the story and they reached an agreement. Other cases are less simple.

Suppose Jean owns an apartment building that Jill wants to buy and convert into an office complex. Would this be an efficient move? Jean doesn't think so, which is why she continues to rent space to residential tenants. But Jill thinks the building would be worth more as an office complex. Who will win their argument?

There probably won't be any argument. Jill will decide what she expects the building to be worth to an owner who has converted it to offices and Jean will decide what the building is worth to someone who keeps it as apartments. Both will calculate their valuations in the common denominator of money. If Jill's valuation is higher, Jean will sell to Jill and the building will become an office complex. If Jean's valuation is higher, Jill won't be able to meet Jean's asking price and the apartment building will remain.

Where property rights are clearly defined, people don't argue about what is more efficient: Owners decide. And those who disagree can become the new owners by backing their opinions with sufficient money.

But now let's complicate the story. What about the tenants in Jean's apartment building? What if they want to continue living where they do now? Then they must offer to pay enough additional rent to Jean to make the building more valuable as apartments than as offices. And if they can't afford that? Then they cannot demonstrate, in the way that counts, that the building is indeed more valuable when kept in its present use. What counts are monetary bids offered to the owner.

If that strikes you as heartless and mercenary, you might want to think about it a little longer before coming to a final conclusion. This is the way in which we settle the allocation of most resources in our society. We let owners decide and we require those who disagree to purchase the property rights if they want to override the owners' decisions. This system for settling the allocation of resources has become the dominant system, the system most people prefer to use, because it holds down transaction costs. It substitutes clear and quick exchanges for murky and prolonged committee meetings.

Keep in mind, however, that every exchange takes place within a framework provided by the laws of the land and other relevant rules of the game. Most cities have zoning laws, for example, that rule out certain uses of property no matter what the owner decides. Moreover, the members of a society can and often do use the political process to change the rules of the game in order to promote some outcome that they think they prefer. This is especially common in the case of real estate transactions. Governments at all levels, in the name of many worthy-sounding goals, have passed a great variety of laws to set restraints on how owners may use their land or buildings. They have, for example, prohibited the conversion of buildings from one use to another, either absolutely or by imposing expensive conditions on the conversion. Such legislative acts create new property rights even while they are restricting or abolishing others. And they alter the allocation of resources.

Here is an interesting example reported on in 1987 by *The Wall Street Journal*. A New York City developer had to construct a 31-story office tower in Manhattan *around* a brownstone on the building site because a single tenant refused to move. The tenant took advantage of New York City landlord-tenant laws that prohibit owners from evicting tenants even when they have sold the building for another use. The developer, who evidently underestimated the tenant's attachment to that site, offered her the choice of other apartments and eventually a cash offer of $650,000 to relocate, but she would not budge. And because she would not budge, the apartment building could not be torn down. The tenant had a property right, created by the landlord-tenant laws, and she exercised it. She demonstrated by her actions that she placed a lower value on living three blocks away with an additional $650,000 in the bank than she placed on continuing to live in her old four-story brownstone without that $650,000.

Whatever you want to call the result, you can't properly call it inefficient. You could, if you wished, criticize the landlord-tenant laws that created this particular tenant's property rights. But that would require a more complicated argument than a simple charge of inefficiency. It would require us at minimum to take into account questions of fairness and to ask about the long-run consequences of laws that arbitrarily alter the property rights of owners.

THE EFFICIENCY OF INTERNATIONAL TRADE

Popular thinking hangs on tenaciously to the notion that some countries may be able to produce almost everything at a lower cost. If wages in Mexico or Italy are lower than in the United States, won't Mexican and Italian manufacturers be able to produce just about anything more cheaply than U.S. manufacturers can do it? How can the United States compete with countries that tolerate wage rates, even for skilled workers, below our legal minimum? In Mexico and Italy, however, you could find workers arguing that they can't compete with America's low-cost techniques of mass production. And the suspicion would properly arise that something is wrong with the argument.

The basic flaw in such arguments is their neglect of opportunity cost. It is *logically* impossible for one country to be more efficient than another in the production of everything. And that becomes apparent as soon as you remember to calculate efficiency as a ratio between what is produced and what is consequently *not* produced. The real cost of producing anything is the value of what is given up in order to produce it. Calculations in dollars, yen, pesos, and francs (or working hours) all too easily obscure these real costs of production.

Suppose that Japan and the United States each produced only three goods: grain, textiles, and radios. Suppose further that competition had moved prices in both countries to levels that reflected the opportunity costs of each good, with these results:

Prices per Unit of Good (Identical Quantity and Quality)		
	United States	Japan
Grain	30 dollars	9,000 yen
Textiles	20 dollars	4,500 yen
Radios	50 dollars	13,500 yen

Which country is the more efficient or lower-cost producer of these goods? Before we can answer, we must find some way of comparing costs. What measure is available?

Dollars and yen clearly won't do. It's obviously absurd to suggest that the United States is more efficient in producing all three goods simply because the dollar prices are lower than the yen prices. That would be true only if a yen had the same value as a dollar. We shall see in the later chapter on international exchange how the relative values of national currencies are established. It's enough for now to note that this is a blind alley because currency exchange rates only reflect the value of currencies; they indicate nothing about costs of production.

Some people might want to use the labor time invested in the production of these goods as the ultimate measure of their relative costs. To do that we would first have to find some common denominator for labor of different skill and effectiveness plus some way of translating such other inputs as machinery and land into units of labor time. And even if we could find a satisfactory way to do this, we would still be forced to adopt the arbitrary assumption that an hour of labor in Japan is as valuable as an hour of labor in the United States. But is it? Attitudes toward work and leisure are culturally determined, and there is no good reason to assume that an hour of working time is exactly as "costly" in one country as in another.

Then how can we decide which country is the lower-cost producer of these goods? The answer is: *There is no way at all to do so.* All we can do is determine that one country or the other is the more efficient producer of a particular good *relative to some other good or goods.* This is the meaning of *comparative advantage.*

Take radios, for example. The price ratios show that in the United States, a unit of radios costs either 1 ⅔ units of grain or 2 ½ units of textiles. It costs that much because that's what is given up in obtaining one unit of radios. In Japan, a unit of radios costs 1 ½ units of grain or 3 units of textiles. Those are the quantities of grain and textiles that are given up in Japan when additional radios are produced. It follows, then, that Japan is more efficient than the United States in producing radios *relative to grain,* but less efficient *relative to textiles.*

Which country is the more efficient textile producer? If you've gotten the idea by now, you will immediately ask: relative to what? A unit of textiles costs ⅔ unit of grain and ⅖ unit of radios in the United States, and ½ unit of grain and ⅓ unit of radios in Japan. So Japan is the more efficient (lower-cost) producer of textiles relative to both grain and radios.

The United States in turn is the lower-cost producer of grain relative to textiles: 1 ½ units of textiles are given up to produce a unit of grain, versus 2 units of textiles given up in Japan. The United States is also the lower-cost producer of grain relative to radios: ⅗ unit of radios is the cost of a U.S. unit of grain; ⅔ unit of radios is the Japanese cost.

Don't lose the point in all the fractions. *A nation can become an inefficient producer of good X simply by becoming a fabulously prolific producer of good Y.* When you become extraordinarily good at one thing, it is costly for you to do anything else. If Japan starts to produce radios and television sets at a lower cost than they can be produced in the United States, that does not imply that U.S. radio and TV manufacturers have failed in some fashion. It could just as well mean that U.S. productivity has been increasing rapidly in other industries.

TRANSACTION COSTS AND EFFICIENCY

"Hold it just another minute," interjects the voice from the rear that seems to have infiltrated Chapter 6. "United States farmers can surely produce rice at a lower opportunity cost than Japanese farmers can do it. But the Japanese nonetheless choose to grow domestically most of the rice they consume rather than import it from the U.S. Your concept of efficiency obviously doesn't apply to international trade."

There are some Japanese, many but by no means all of them rice farmers, who insist that foreign rice just doesn't taste as good as Japanese rice, and that is why Japanese consumers prefer the domestic product. The weakness in this explanation is that it doesn't explain why the Japanese government severely restricts rice imports. If the Japanese people really didn't want to eat foreign-grown rice, the government would not have to keep it out; the market would do the job. Japanese farmers faced with this counterargument often respond that rice produced in Japan is a symbol of Japanese culture, like sumo wrestling, and therefore deserves a market protected from foreign competition. They may be right. How does one place a monetary value on national symbols?

The undeniable fact is that Japanese consumers pay a great deal more than they would otherwise have to pay for the food they eat, because Japanese farmers and their allies have persuaded the government not to let a whole lot of foreign-grown food into the country. It is quite likely that the free import of food into Japan would save Japanese consumers so much money each year that they could afford to retire every Japanese farmer at his current income level and still be better off than they are under the present system of trade restrictions.

Similarly, American motorists pay much more for the cars they drive because U.S. automobile manufacturers and their allies have persuaded the U.S. government to restrict the importation of Japanese automobiles. Some calculations have suggested that U.S. government restrictions on automobile imports protect the jobs of U.S. automobile workers at a total cost to automobile buyers of more than $230,000 per job (in 1993 dollars). That is a lot to pay to preserve just one job. It seems altogether likely that a payment of half that amount would be far more than enough to persuade each and every automobile worker who would lose his job to drop his objection to Japanese imports and look for a job in another industry.

Does all this mean that it would be efficient to abolish these restrictions on free international trade? Not if we remember to take transaction costs into account. What we actually have here is another example of cooperative failure. It is often the case that those who benefit from a particular government policy gain less in monetary terms than the monetary cost that the policy imposes on those whom it harms. It is tempting to call such policies "inefficient" and to say that efficiency would be enhanced if those who pay the costs of the policy offered monetary payments to the beneficiaries to persuade them to give up the policy. But unless we can find some way to actually collect and transfer the payments, the policy will not change. And that will be conclusive proof that the expected marginal costs of making the change *when we include the transaction costs* are actually greater than the expected marginal benefits of the change. If this were not the case, the change would occur. The persistence of such "inefficient" trade restrictions demonstrates that no one knows how to get rid of them at a sufficiently low cost.

Transaction costs are just as real, just as important impediments to the production of additional wealth, as any other kind of cost. When we want to evaluate the efficiency of a policy proposal by comparing the expected value of its benefits with the expected value of its costs, realism requires that we take full account of the transaction costs.

THE PURSUIT OF COMPARATIVE ADVANTAGE

Suppose that the dean appoints Professor Klunk head of the economics department, even though Professor Svelte wants the position and is far superior to Klunk as a teacher, as a scholar, and even as an administrator. Can the dean defend his decision when Svelte complains? "How could you make that Klunk the head of our department?" he asks indignantly. The dean must point out that Svelte is such a fine teacher and scholar that the college cannot afford to have him spend his time in administrative activities. The opportunity cost is too high. Klunk may take all morning just to order new pencils, but if the students hate his classes and he never publishes anything of value, the cost to the college of a whole day spent by Klunk on pencil purchases might be zero. While Klunk is a poorer teacher, scholar, and administrator than Svelte, he is so much worse than Svelte at teaching and research that he has a *comparative advantage* in administrative work. Anybody can acquire a comparative advantage over others in doing absolutely anything just by being sufficiently lousy at doing everything else.

No one except economists ever goes through the mind-numbing calculations presented in the case of Japanese versus U.S. grain, textiles, and radios, and even economists do it only in order to explain to students the logic of comparative advantage. In the real world, people pursue their comparative advantages simply by choosing the option that they find most attractive, all things considered. The dean appoints Klunk, John Elway plays football rather than baseball while Bo Jackson chooses baseball over football, American apparel makers buy Japanese textiles, and Japanese millers purchase grain from the United States because, in each case, they believe that is the best way to obtain whatever they want. In most of these decisions, relative prices provide fundamental information. We consider our various abilities and the wages we can command at the different tasks we are capable of performing and choose the job that we think will best further the projects in which we are interested. Americans looking for textiles find Japanese products less expensive than domestically produced textiles of similar quality. Japanese farmers choose not to raise wheat because they know that they could not raise enough to earn a satisfactory living, given the fact that they could not sell it above the price at which U.S.-grown wheat was available to Japanese millers. In short, they behave as if the least costly way to achieve a given objective was the most efficient way. And in doing so they continuously coordinate these processes of cooperative interaction and mutual accommodation that comprise the economy.

None of this implies that anyone pays attention exclusively to prices, which would be an absurd and impossible way to behave. It means rather that relative prices guide people's decisions when other things are equal. The other things that must be equal—or to be quite accurate, must be *thought* to be equal—include an enormous array of factors from the technological to the psychological. Consider a homeowner, for example, who wants to eliminate broad-leaved weeds from a lawn. Would it be more efficient to dig them out with a hand tool or to spray them with a herbicide? The homeowner's decision will reflect a judgment on the effectiveness of each procedure in killing the root, on likely damage to ornamental shrubs, on the desirability of exercise, and on the joys of yard work, and not just the relative prices of herbicide and hand tools. But those relative prices nonetheless play a crucial coordinating role.

DISAGREEMENTS ON VALUES

If efficiency is finally an evaluative concept, expressing the ratio of output value to input value, anything at all can be inefficient to a person who holds the appropriate values. If Professor Svelte places a sufficiently high value on the authority and prestige that he associates with the job of department head, then from his point of view he would be a more efficient choice than Klunk as head of the economics department. And if Svelte threatens to resign unless he gets the appointment, the dean will have to weigh a new cost in deciding whether it would be more efficient to appoint Klunk or Svelte: the cost of losing Svelte's services altogether.

There are people to whom both teaching and research are utterly without value. There are also people to whom a grassy knoll by the side of the road is a waste of space unless it displays a billboard. A person who neither visits wilderness areas nor derives satisfaction from knowing that they exist will correctly condemn as inefficient every legislative decision to create new wilderness preserves. Flying between cities rather than driving is a much more efficient travel arrangement for someone who gets car sickness than for someone who enjoys the scenery. And someone somewhere may even believe that Rembrandt wasted time by not painting with a six-inch-wide brush.

We could multiply such examples indefinitely, but the point is surely clear. *What we value determines what we will consider efficient or inefficient.* It follows that disagreements in society about the relative efficiency of particular projects will usually be disagreements about the relative value to be assigned to particular goods—or the relative disvalue of particular nongoods. Knowing this won't settle any controversial issue. But failing even to recognize what we're arguing about surely makes the resolution of controversy more difficult.

The question is not, "What is *really* more efficient?" but rather, "Who has the *right* to make particular decisions?" Crawling out of a sleeping bag to climb a mountain is atrociously inefficient to someone who plans to crawl back into that sleeping bag in the evening and is merely looking for the shortest distance between those two points. Fans of mountain climbing strenuously disagree, of course. But that creates no social conflict, because we all agree that individuals should have the right to decide for themselves whether it's more valuable to put their bodies on mountain peaks or to keep them in bed during vacations. When we do *not* agree on who has which rights, that's when we get into vehement arguments about whether it is "really" efficient, for example, to clear-cut forests or to strip-mine coal.

EFFICIENCY, VALUES, AND PROPERTY RIGHTS

You should be able to see now why we insisted at the beginning of this chapter that the common critique of efficiency is logically confused. A society that placed "too high a value on efficiency" would be one that placed too high a value on using its resources in the most valuable way. That's an odd notion at best. The real target of the critics has to be either the values people hold or the rights they exercise.

Suppose a mineral exploration company came to the conclusion that there were large quantities of chrome, vanadium, and manganese under the ground in Yellowstone National Park and requested permission from Congress to search for them. Can you imagine the cries of outrage that would greet such a request? "Profiteers with no respect for nature!" "Greedy materialists willing to destroy an irreplaceable national heritage!" And someone would surely say: "Efficiency and economic growth are not worth pursuing if they deprive us of everything that makes life worth living."

The issue in such a case, however, would not be efficiency and economic growth versus nature, wilderness, or anything else that makes life worth living. The issue would rather be *what is efficient,* or what constitutes genuine economic growth. There is nothing intrinsically more efficient about mining than about meditating. It is not necessarily the case that economic growth proceeds faster when manganese is extracted from the mountain than when trout are extracted from a stream. To decide whether it would be efficient to mine in Yellowstone Park, we must set the expected value of what would be obtained from mining against the expected value of what would thereby be lost. Chrome, vanadium, and manganese have no value that we can talk about apart from the purposes to which people intend to put them. And the same is true of the vistas, the tranquility, or the unblemished land and water that mining would destroy.

The issue comes down to this: *By what process should the prospective benefits and costs of mining in Yellowstone Park be evaluated?*

When the rules of the game establish clear and secure property rights, they implicitly decide by what process prospective benefits and costs are to be evaluated for decision-making purposes. If I decide to open my windows and turn up the thermostat on a cold winter day, I am using resources efficiently as long as I have an uncontested right to allocate all the resources I'm using. If, on the other hand, I am cooling off someone else's living space, or if someone else is paying the heating bills, my property rights are likely to be challenged. Then the issue becomes *not* the efficiency of my preferred arrangements but rather my exclusive right to value the inputs and the outputs in what I am doing.

When property rights are clear, stable, and exchangeable, scarce resources tend to acquire money prices that reflect their relative scarcity. Decisionmakers then pursue efficiency by using these prices as information. To say that the prices are "wrong" because they don't reflect the *real* value of certain costs or benefits amounts to rejecting the process by which those prices were determined. It is a critique not of efficiency but of the existing system of property rights, and of the rules of the game of which they form a part.

COMPARATIVE ADVANTAGE: THE ECONOMIST'S UMBRELLA

The term with which economists summarize almost everything we have been discussing in this chapter is *comparative advantage.* It might even be thought of as a term to summarize the entire collection of concepts presented thus far. To pursue comparative advantage means simply to sacrifice that which is less valuable for the sake of something more valuable.

Why do demand curves slope downward to the right? Because people pursue their comparative advantage. A rise in the price of any good means that its users will now be able to obtain the satisfaction it provides at a *relatively lower cost* by using some substitute.

How is the opportunity cost of any resource established? Through the pursuit of comparative advantage. People bid for a resource after estimating the potentiality of that resource *relative to other resources* for providing whatever they're after.

Why are only expected marginal costs and not sunk costs relevant to decisionmaking? Because expected marginal costs reflect the *comparative advantages of alternative decisions,* whereas sunk costs can never do more than reflect the comparative advantages of past decisions. But no one makes decisions with the hope of affecting what happened yesterday.

It is comparative advantage—the advantage resources have over other resources in particular uses *relative to other uses* —that determines the most efficient way to employ one's resources.

An Appendix: THE ARITHMETIC OF COMPARATIVE ADVANTAGE

Imagine a society with only two goods and three producers. We shall call the goods M and S, which you may think of, if you wish, as material goods and spiritual goods, respectively.

The producers we'll call Ann, Ben, and Cal. In a given period of time (e.g., a day), each is capable of producing the following quantities of M or S:

- Ann can produce 8 Ms or 4 Ss or any linear combination between, such as 6 Ms plus 1 S, or 5 Ms plus 1 ½ Ss, or 2 Ms plus 3 Ss, and so on.
- Ben can produce 3 Ms or 3 Ss or any linear combination in between.
- Cal can produce 1 M or 2 Ss or any intermediate linear combination.

Ready for the question? Who would you say is the most efficient producer of spiritual goods in this drastically simplified economy? Check the data before answering.

Do you agree that it's Cal? Or did you mistakenly suppose it was Ann, who is in fact the *least* efficient producer of Ss in this society? If you failed to identify Cal correctly as the most efficient producer of Ss, you weren't using the concept of opportunity cost in your calculations.

What does it cost when Cal produces an S? The cost of an action is the sacrifice that action entails. Since Ms and Ss are the only goods in this society, the only way we can state the cost of producing an S is in terms of forgone Ms. Now look at the data. Cal forgoes the production of ½ M to make an S. Ben sacrifices 1 M when he makes an S. And Ann, who is such a prolific maker of Ms, gives up 2 Ms for each S she produces. The conclusion is obvious. Cal is the lowest-cost producer of Ss, and Ann is the highest-cost producer of Ss.

Suppose you are the commissar of production in this little society, and you want to produce the maximum quantity of Ss that can be obtained consistent with producing the minimum quantity of Ms required to keep the society going. Let's further assume that 1 M per day is enough to keep everyone alive and functioning; your production plan therefore calls for 1 M plus as many Ss as can be turned out with the resources that remain.

If you order Cal to produce that required 1 M, in the mistaken belief that he's an inefficient S producer, while instructing Ann and Ben to concentrate exclusively on Ss, you'll find yourself at the end of the day with the 1 M you ordered plus 7 Ss: 4 from Ann and 3 from Ben.

If, however, you recognize that Cal is your most efficient S producer, who must therefore be kept exclusively on S production, and that Ann should produce the single M you want because she's your most *inefficient* S producer—then you'll end up with 2 Ss from Cal, 3 from Ben, and 3 ½ from Ann, for a total of 8 ½ Ss, along with the required single unit of M. If more is better than less, you're better off by 1 ½ Ss per day when you assign Ann rather than Cal to M production.

What would the output have been if you had told Ben to produce the 1 M? Then you would have gotten 4 Ss from Ann, 2 from Ben, and 2 from Cal, for a total of only 8 (plus the 1 M).

What's going on here? Nothing at all strange if you remember to wear the spectacles of opportunity cost. What it costs you, as commissar, to have any person produce an M or an S is the value of what you thereby forgo. When Ann produces an S, you give up 2 Ms. When Ben produces an S, you lose 1 M. But when Cal produces an S, only ½ M is sacrificed. From your point of view, therefore, Cal is clearly the lowest-cost producer of Ss and Ann is the highest-cost producer.

When we look at the costs of M production, we see that it costs you ½ S when Ann produces an M, 1 S when Ben produces an M, and 2 Ss when Cal produces an M. Ann is therefore the lowest-cost producer of Ms, which is why you got the most of what you wanted by assigning Ann to M production. Does this counterintuitive result—namely, that fumble-fingered Cal, who can't turn out much of anything, is nonetheless the most efficient producer of spiritual goods— does this affront to common sense perhaps arise from the fact that we put a dictator in charge? Not at all. It is entirely a result of the logic of opportunity cost.

Let's stage a coup, get rid of the commissar of production, and allow Ann, Ben, and Cal to decide individually what they want to produce.

They would presumably begin by deciding what each preferred to consume. Let's suppose that Cal, a well-balanced person, wants 1 M and 1 S. He's got a problem. There's no way he can produce that much. If he produces the M he wants, he'll have to go without S altogether. If he produces the 1 S he wants, he'll have to get along with only ½ M.

Now let's further suppose that Ben is an equally well-balanced person and wants to consume 1 ½ Ms and 1 ½ Ss, which is exactly what he's capable of producing. If Ben and Cal know and trust one another well enough, they can arrange an exchange that will be advantageous to Cal without making Ben any worse off. Cal could agree to specialize exclusively in S production. He would then keep one of his Ss for his own use and give the other to Ben. That would enable

Ben to produce 2 ½ Ms, since he would now have to produce only ½ S for his own use. Keeping 1 ½ Ms for himself and giving the other to Cal would leave Ben no worse off than before. But Cal would now have obtained, through specialization and trade, the greater wealth that he wanted but hadn't been able to achieve on his own.

Does it look like a trick? Perhaps it is, but not in the sense of an illusion or something deceptive. It's the trick that all of us perform every day in order to supply ourselves with the goods that we want but can't even begin to produce for ourselves. We all specialize in the production of those goods in which we think we have the greatest *comparative advantage* and then exchange our products for the goods we really want. Just as Jack found that he could use a basketball as an input to produce a baseball glove that he wanted more than the basketball, so Cal found he could use an extra S as an input to obtain the M he wanted. That in essence is what we all do.

In a world where people can arrange and carry out exchanges with one another at low cost, people will find it in their interest to specialize and trade. They'll discover that specialization can bring them more of what they want, whether they want material goods, spiritual goods, leisure, or even a chance to make more of everything available to others. If Michael Jordan, a basketball player of extraordinary ability, had decided it was his primary aim in life to make more food available to the destitute in Chicago, he would still have worked as a professional basketball player. That's where his comparative advantage lay. He could "grow" far more food by playing basketball for pay and using the proceeds to "hire"

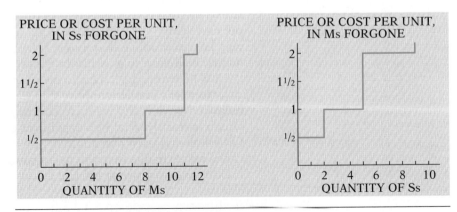

FIGURE 6A   Supply curves for Ann, Ben, and Cal

farmers than he could ever have grown by sitting on a tractor. And the farmers of northern Illinois "grow" entertainment for themselves by specializing in grain production and using the proceeds to buy a color television set on which to watch Michael Jordan play.

You don't have to be "better than others" to pull this trick off. Cal can benefit from trading with Ben even though he's less productive than Ben in both spiritual and material goods. He can even gain from trade with Ann, who has the ability to turn out in a day twice as many Ss and eight times as many Ms as Cal. The important fact is that Ann has a *greater* advantage over Cal in Ms than in Ss. That means Cal has a *lesser disadvantage* with respect to Ann in Ss than in Ms. And that in turn implies that both Ann and Cal may be able to benefit from trading with each other after specializing in that good in which each has the *comparative advantage*.

ONCE OVER LIGHTLY

Efficiency depends on valuations. Although physical or technological facts are certainly relevant to the determination of efficiency, they can never by themselves determine the relative efficiency of alternative processes. Efficiency depends on the ratio of output *value* to input *value*.

Exchange creates wealth, because voluntary exchange always involves the sacrifice of what is less valued (input) for what is more valued (output). Exchange is as much a wealth-creating transformation as is manufacturing or agriculture.

People specialize in order to exchange and thereby increase their wealth. They specialize in activities in which they believe themselves to have a comparative advantage.

Comparative advantage is determined by opportunity costs. No person, no group, no nation can be more efficient than another in every activity, for even the most highly productive agents must have some activities in which they are less highly productive. If you're four times as intelligent, three times as strong, and twice as beautiful as another person, then that person has a comparative advantage in beauty—and you, handsome as you are, have a comparative disadvantage in beauty.

A social system with clear property rights and few restrictions on exchange generates money prices that help people who are pursing their comparative advantage to discover in exactly which direction their advantage lies.

Disagreements about whether some process or arrangement is or is not efficient are at root disagreements about the relative weights that should be given to different people's evaluations. They are therefore disagreements about the rules of the game, or about who should have what rights over which resources.

QUESTIONS FOR DISCUSSION

1. Here is a criticism of shopkeepers and other middlemen written several centuries ago that still finds echoes today. "Their meer handing of Goods one to another, no more increases any Wealth in the Province, than Persons at a Fire increase the Water in a Pail, by passing it thro' Twenty or Forty hands."

   (a) Why would persons at a fire bother to pass a pail of water through forty hands if doing so increased no one's wealth?
   (b) It's true that the physical quantity of water is not increased when the water changes hands (some will even be spilled), just as the physical quantity of goods is not increased by the transactions of middlemen. But what about the *value* of the water and of the middleman's goods?
   (c) Does wealth depend on physical quantities or on valuations?

2. Many people enjoy the sight and sounds of a steam locomotive.

   (a) Should these aesthetic pleasures be included in the valuable output of a steam locomotive, right along with the value of the freight that is hauled?
   (b) If the owners of railroads could somehow collect a fee from all those who enjoyed seeing and hearing steam locomotives, would they include aesthetic pleasures in the value of a steam locomotive's output?
   (c) Would the efficiency of steam locomotives increase if a low-cost way were found to extract from steam-locomotive buffs a fee proportioned to the pleasure they derive from seeing and hearing them?

3. Is it efficient to feed a family using large quantities of frozen "convenience" foods? Under what circumstances could these expensive grocery items provide the lowest-cost inputs for producing the output of family dinner? What questionable premise is being used by someone who says that shoppers are wasting money by paying twice as much for convenience foods as they would have to pay for dinner items they prepare themselves?

4. Many Americans regularly drive their own cars to work rather than use public transportation or form a car pool.

   (a) How do you know that each person in a single-passenger vehicle during the rush hour is behaving efficiently?

(b) The people riding the bus are also behaving efficiently. How can (a) and (b) both be true simultaneously?

(c) What is actually being asserted by someone who says that it's inefficient for so many commuters to take their own cars to work?

5. The United States used wood as a fuel in metallurgy long after the British had changed to coal. Was this evidence of technological backwardness in the United States? If the United States was technologically backward, how would you explain the fact that all sorts of machines for woodworking were perfected in the United States in the first half of the nineteenth century? Fireplaces are often said to be inefficient ways to heat a room. Why then were they so widely used in the United States in the nineteenth century in preference to stoves? (Hint: Larger logs can be used in fireplaces.) Why did stoves become more popular as wood prices increased?

6. Is it more efficient to build dams with lots of direct labor and little machinery or with lots of machinery and little labor? Why will the answer vary from one country to another?

7. Which is more efficient: Japanese agriculture with its carefully terraced hillsides or American agriculture with its far more "wasteful" use of land? How have relative prices in the two countries brought about these different methods of farming? How have opportunity costs entered into the formation of these relative prices?

8. Attorney Fudd is the most highly sought-after lawyer in the state. He is also a phenomenal typist who can do 120 words per minute. Should Fudd do his own typing if the fastest secretary he can obtain does only 60 words per minute? Prove that Fudd is *not* twice as efficient as his secretary at typing, that he is in fact *less* efficient at typing, and that he should therefore retain a secretary.

9. In seeking to show that population growth threatens to exhaust the world's agricultural resources, the Worldwatch Institute has pointed out that in 1988, for the first time in its history, the United States ate more food than it grew.

(a) By what measure do you suppose the U.S. ate more food than it grew in 1988? Volume? Weight? Calories? Or monetary value?

(b) If official trade accounts show that U.S. food imports exceeded food exports in any given year, this will mean that the dollar value of the imports was greater than the dollar value of the exports. Why would such figures *not* be persuasive evidence that the U.S. had lost the ability to feed itself?

10. The Boeing 767 uses less than 110 pounds of jet fuel per seat per 1000 miles. The older 727 uses about 155 pounds of jet fuel per seat per 1000 miles. But the 767 costs far more per seat to purchase. Which of the planes should an airline purchase if it is interested in efficiency? Does the price of jet fuel affect the answer? How might the decision to purchase a

used 727 rather than a new 767 turn out to be not only more economical but also more conserving of natural resources?

11. It has often been claimed that under a capitalist system business firms will sometimes continue to use obsolete equipment rather than the new, "most efficient" equipment because they have a lot of money tied up in the old equipment. Does this make sense? What is the relevance to such decisions of "money tied up"? When would an airline that has "money tied up" in 727s elect to replace them with 767s?

12. You own and occupy a large brick house in an old residential neighborhood. The area is being rezoned to allow multiple family occupancy and apartment buildings. How would you go about deciding whether to (a) continue to occupy the house as a single-family dwelling, (b) divide the house into several apartments, or (c) tear down the house and erect a new apartment complex? If you were to choose (b), could you be accused of retarding the economy by failing to adopt the most up-to-date equipment because of your vested interest in obsolete equipment? Does this differ from question 11?

13. A May 1979 letter to the editor of *The Wall Street Journal* wondered why, in view of the gasoline shortage, such "utterly wasteful uses of gasoline" as auto racing were still permitted. The writer also urged that such "obvious waste" be curtailed in the public interest. Is auto racing an utter and obvious waste of gasoline? Try to construct a clear and defensible definition of *waste* that would indict auto racing but exonerate other uses of automotive gasoline at a time when there might be a gasoline shortage.

14. Grain farmers have many options when it comes to preparing the soil. They can plow and then thoroughly harrow a field before planting, they can practice minimum tillage, or they can go so far as to plant without preparing the ground at all. Heavy tilling buries and thus kills weeds and insects. No-till farming requires careful and extensive use of herbicides and pesticides and also produces slightly lower yields. Explain how each of the following will affect the relative efficiency of maximum tillage and no-till farming:

   (a) Higher prices for diesel fuel.
   (b) Improved herbicides and pesticides.
   (c) Tougher government controls on stream and lake pollution caused by chemicals used in agriculture. (Note: Untilled ground is more likely to retain the chemicals put into it.)
   (d) Farmers adopt the same attitude toward their fields that some suburban homeowners have toward their lawns: they find satisfaction in looking at a broad, well-tended expanse of land.
   (e) Higher prices for land.

15. Some critics of U.S. agriculture argue that highly mechanized production techniques in farming are inefficient because the energy consumed by the machinery used to grow food exceeds the amount of potential energy

available in the food that is grown. Does this argument make any sense? Is energy the ultimate measure of value?

16. A pumped-storage reservoir is a reservoir that an electrical utility drains during hours of peak demand in order to generate electricity, then refills during hours of slack demand by pumping water back up into it.

    (a) The electricity generated by the falling water is inevitably far less than the electricity used to refill the reservoir. Does this mean the practice of using pumped-storage reservoirs is inefficient?
    (b) If you think it's inefficient or wasteful to use two watts of electricity to create one watt, why do you suppose the utilities do it? Can it be profitable to behave inefficiently?
    (c) If you believe that inefficient behavior can sometimes be profitable, would you ever want to condemn such behavior as not in the general or long-term interest of society? Why or why not? Under what circumstances?

17. The Sevier River in Utah has been used for about a century to irrigate farm land in central Utah. Recently, a 3000-megawatt, coal-fired electrical generating plant was proposed for this area. The generating plant would require about 40,000 acre-feet of water per year from the Sevier River. Operation of the generating plant would mean less water for agriculture.

    (a) Is the water of the Sevier River used more efficiently when it grows food or when it generates electricity?
    (b) Can you answer this question by comparing the value of food with the value of electricity? (Hint: Value is determined at the margin.)
    (c) If farmers who own rights to Sevier River water sell their rights to the power company, is the water allocated to its most valuable use?
    (d) Who are some of the parties who might be adversely affected by the farmers' decision to sell their water rights?

18. Have you ever noticed how few gasoline stations are found in the center of large cities? With such heavy traffic one ought to be able to do an excellent business. Why then are there so few?

19. The key to question 18 is the high price of land in the center of large cities. Would it make sense for the city government, which has the right of eminent domain, to take over some of this land in order to provide "vitally needed service stations"?

20. Land has become so expensive in Beverly Hills and Westwood, California, that developers estimate it would require more than $25 million to construct a supermarket with adequate parking space in these communities, according to *Parade Magazine*, January 20, 1985.

    (a) Why has the land become so expensive?
    (b) There is only one supermarket in all of Beverly Hills and central Westwood. Why?

    (c) At these land prices, supermarket construction is not a profitable investment project. Might it nonetheless be efficient to have another supermarket or two in the area?

21. In a June 6, 1985, article titled "On the Waterfront: Tugs, Barges Battling Quiche and Fern Bars," *The Wall Street Journal* discussed the gentrification of waterfront property.

    (a) A Seattle land-use specialist who wants to halt this development said, "A condominium can be built anywhere, but the shipyard it replaces can't move two miles inland." Why is that not a conclusive argument?

    (b) Maritime interests in Boston have objected to a plan to turn unused piers into housing and parkland on the grounds that the now vacant piers may be needed someday. Why is this an inconclusive argument?

    (c) Marine businesses complain that they cannot outbid developers for waterfront land and so need zoning help and other protection from local government in order to keep down the price of goods that move by water. Why should the cost of water carriage be kept down by government action?

22. The New York City woman who refused to move from her apartment despite being offered a payment of $650,000 seems to have placed a very high value on continuing to live in that particular apartment.

    (a) *High* is a relative term. Is it possible that she did not in fact place a particularly high value on continuing to live in that apartment but did place a very low marginal value on money?

    (b) What would induce a person to place a low marginal value on money?

    (c) Do you think that wealthy people sometimes waste money on stupid purchases?

23. Is it efficient for cars to have bumpers so strong and heavy that the car will sustain no damage in collisions at speeds up to 5 miles per hour? How would you answer such a question if you were a car buyer? If you were an automobile manufacturer? If you were a federal official charged with setting minimum standards for automobile bumpers?

24. In view of the high cost of transporting milk from the mainland United States, is it efficient for Hawaii to produce within its own borders all the milk its citizens consume? What difference does it make to your answer to know that Hawaiian dairy farmers import all their cattle feed? If it is inefficient to import milk into Hawaii, why does the state's Milk Control Board receive requests to import milk from other states? Is it efficient for the Milk Control Board to deny these requests, as it has regularly done?

25. A 1984 study issued by the Congressional Office of Technology Assessment concluded that a high-speed rail system capable of moving passengers between U.S. cities would probably not be able to attract enough

riders to stay in the black. Does this imply that it would be inefficient to construct such a system?

26. Bonneville Dam is the oldest dam on the Columbia River, and its navigation lock is much smaller than the locks on the seven dams farther up the river. As a result, Bonneville is a bottleneck for Columbia River barge traffic, with barges sometimes compelled to wait 10 hours for passage.

   (a) By what process could the federal government, which owns and operates the dam, decide whether it would be efficient to construct a new lock at Bonneville?

   (b) The Burlington Northern and Union Pacific railroads operate tracks along the northern and southern banks of the Columbia River. They argue that a new lock should be constructed only if barge owners and towboat operators are willing to pay for it. Barge and towboat people respond that the benefits of the lock would extend far beyond themselves, and that this justifies a government subsidy for the proposed new lock. Would other beneficiaries be able to avoid paying for the benefits they receive if the federal government financed the new lock through a fee paid by the towboats and barges that use it?

27. Chapter 4 discussed the problem of increasing airport congestion, using Washington, DC's crowded National Airport and the near-deserted Dulles Airport as a case study. Airlines prefer to fly into National because it's only 10 minutes away from downtown Washington; Dulles is almost an hour away.

   (a) Is it efficient for airlines to choose National over Dulles when scheduling their flights? Would that efficiency change if the government charged a higher landing fee at National?

   (b) Is it efficient for passengers to choose a flight into National over one into Dulles? Would their relative efficiencies change if ticket prices for flights landing at National rose by twice the price of a cab from Dulles to the Capitol?

   (c) In 1966 the FAA decreed that flights coming into Washington from any city more than 650 miles away had to land at Dulles. Was this an efficient order? What effects do you think it had?

   (d) The Transportation Department has been floating proposals recently to buy and sell landing rights at National and other busy airports. Some critics of this proposal object that the larger airlines would buy all the slots. Do you think this would occur? What sort of factors would determine how much any airline was willing to pay for a particular landing slot?

   (e) This situation appears to indicate a set of cooperative failures. Passengers who value their time most highly are unable to exchange with passengers who value it less highly, and airlines that could make extremely profitable use of landing slots cannot obtain them from other airlines for whom the slot is less valuable. What is the source of the high transaction costs standing in the way of more effective cooperation?

28. Airlines are willing to overbook flights because they know that people who make reservations do not always show up. Sometimes, however, this results in more people holding reservations at the gate than there are seats on the flight.

   (a) Is overbooking efficient from the airlines' standpoint?
   (b) Is overbooking efficient from the standpoint of passengers?
   (c) As a consequence of a 1976 court case that Ralph Nader won against an airline that had "bumped" him, the federal government adopted a rule requiring airlines to compensate people who were denied boarding despite holding a confirmed reservation. As a result, the airlines started to ask for volunteers who were willing to take a later flight whenever a flight turned out to be overbooked. Who benefited from this new regulation?
   (d) If passengers can in effect sell their confirmed reservations when a seat shortage arises, why can't passengers sell their right to land at a crowded airport when a shortage of landing slots arises?
   (e) Prior to 1976, the airlines often denied boarding to passengers who were flying on urgent business in favor of passengers who were not in any particular hurry to reach their destinations. This would seem to be a cooperative failure. What was the crucial step that lowered transaction costs sufficiently to transform the frustrating situation prior to 1976, when the last persons to show up at the gate were denied boarding, into the current system, where only volunteers are denied boarding?

29. Bent Grasz spent $100,000 to plant grass, flowers, shrubs, and trees and make his home a landscaping showplace. The city is suffering from a drought this summer and has prohibited all watering of lawns and gardens. Bent would be willing to pay several thousand dollars if necessary to obtain the water he needs to irrigate adequately. Many of Bent's fellow citizens would be willing to conserve the amount of water Bent wants in return for a payment far less than Bent is willing to offer.

   (a) Is there room here for everyone to become better off through exchange?
   (b) Why can't people ordinarily sell the water they conserve in a drought to someone else who wants it more than they do?
   (c) Suppose the city responded to the drought not by prohibiting watering but by tripling the price of water. Would this make Bent happy?
   (d) If the city distributed the extra revenue from higher water prices to water users, an equal amount going to each customer, would this cancel out the effect of the price increase? Who would be better off and who would be worse off under such a system (better or

worse than under the system of restrictions on use but no price increase)?

(e) How do high transaction costs prevent Bent and his neighbors from cooperating to everyone's advantage? Who is in a good position to lower these transaction costs?

30. During the 1970s, the federal government maintained extensive and complex controls on the prices of petroleum and petroleum products.

(a) Why would you expect these controls to lead eventually to greater scarcity of petroleum products in some areas than in others, or to what were called "supply imbalances"?

(b) When the U.S. Department of Energy authorized oil companies to move as much as 5 percent of their supply among and within the states to "relieve imbalances," the companies generally declined to do so. How could the oil companies know where to move oil and how much to reallocate with prices fixed by law?

(c) The Department of Energy authorized the governors of states to move this 5 percent of supply when the oil companies declined the invitation. How were the governors able to allocate petroleum products efficiently when the oil companies could not do so?

(d) In a March 16, 1981, letter to the editor of *The Wall Street Journal*, the Commissioner of the New Jersey Department of Energy argued that the oil companies' refusal to accept the authority granted to them and their decision to hide "timidly behind government controls" demonstrates the inadequacy of "the free-market philosophy." Is this a sound argument?

31. Is it possible to assess the efficiency of the federal government's 55-mile-per-hour speed limit?

(a) What is the output or desired result whose value would go in the numerator of the efficiency ratio? What is the input or cost or forgone opportunity whose value would go in the denominator? How would you choose appropriate values once you had decided on the appropriate output and input?

(b) Suppose we use fuel saved as the output of the 55-mph limit and time lost as the input. What might we use as appropriate value weights so that we can decide whether the value of the output is greater than the value of the input?

(c) If we include in the output not only fuel saved but also the lives saved, won't our assessment inevitably conclude that the 55-mph speed limit is efficient? How can we set a finite value on a human life?

(d) Economist Charles Lave has calculated that the 55-mph speed limit causes Americans to spend 102 extra years driving in order to "save one life" and suggests that 102 years traveling in an automobile rather closely fits his personal notion of hell (*Newsweek*, October 23,

1978). List a few ways in which 102 years could be used to "save" far more lives than one.

(e) Far more lives would be saved if we required that all motorists be preceded by a person on foot carrying an orange flag. Would such an arrangement consequently be even more efficient than a 55-mph speed limit?

(f) Who gains from the 55-mph speed limit? Who loses the most?

32. If you saw a bumper sticker that said "Eliminate Government Waste—At Any Cost," would you laugh, cry, or cheer?

33. Efficiency is a relationship between ends and means. When we decide that a process is inefficient, we seem to be concluding that inappropriate means are being used to achieve some end.

(a) Can ends or goals be inefficient?

(b) Can you think of any ends or goals that are not also means to further ends?

(c) The chairman of a government committee studying manned space flight in the late 1950s said that they chose to send men to the moon because this "represented a true end objective which was self-justifying and did not have to be supported on the basis that it led to a subsequently more useful end." Do you agree that putting astronauts on the moon was a pure end and not a means to some further ends?

INFORMATION, MIDDLEMEN, AND SPECULATORS

The costs and benefits that affect decisions to demand or to supply are always *expected* costs and benefits. Producers decide to supply so many units of X because they expect to pay no more than a certain amount for the required resources and to receive at least some larger amount than that from selling X. Consumers decide to purchase a product because they expect to receive some benefit from its possession greater than what they expect to pay for it. But the future is uncertain, so expectations are often frustrated by events. Decisions turn out to be mistaken. And mistakes are costly.

Because of all the interdependencies that characterize our highly specialized economic system, mistaken decisions will often have costly consequences for many more people than the ones who made the decision. If refiners don't build up adequate inventories of crude oil, motorists may have to wait in line for gasoline. If physicians don't anticipate the adverse side effects of a drug, a patient may die. And if manufacturers overestimate the demand for their product, employees who sacrificed other opportunities to work for those manufacturers may find themselves unemployed.

Since mistakes are costly, people try to avoid making them. Unfortunately, avoiding mistakes is costly, too. The way to eliminate mistakes is to acquire more information before acting. But information is a scarce good with its own costs of acquisition. It may be less costly, as a result, to accept some mistakes than to acquire the information that could have prevented them. One mistake we can all avoid is the mistake of assuming that information is a free good. We shall see as we proceed through this chapter just how often that mistaken assumption seems to influence our attitudes and actions.

REAL ESTATE AGENTS ARE
INFORMATION PRODUCERS

"How to save about $900 and lose $3000 . . . right on your own home."

That was the headline under which the National Association of Real Estate Boards ran an advertisement urging people to use the services of a realtor in selling their homes. The ad continued:

> Don't laugh. It could happen. For instance, suppose you decide to sell your house. Yourself. You decide it's worth $15,000, and you sell it for $15,000. Great. But how did you arrive at that price? By guesswork. It takes a lot more than that to determine a property's value. It takes a Realtor who knows houses and what they're worth. Suppose he said your house was worth $3000 more. A fair price to buyer and seller. It could happen. Of course, you'd save the Realtor's fee. But at quite a cost.
>
> So when you decide to sell a house, use your Realtor. He's not just anyone in real estate. He's the professional who is pledged to a strict code of ethics. That's good. Especially if you want to make the best sale you can. Or for that matter, the best buy.

That ad is eloquent testimony to something mentioned in Chapter 6: the public's deep-rooted suspicion of middlemen.[1] The fact that the realtors' association thought the ad worth running is strong evidence that such a suspicion exists, and the argument used in the ad is further evidence. For the ad seems designed to obscure the realtor's function while defending it, almost as if the truth is more than the public would tolerate.

Suppose, we might ask, that the realtor said your house was worth $3000 *less:* "A fair price to buyer and seller." Isn't it just as likely that homeowners selling their own houses will guess too high as too low? Or even more likely in view of the hopeful optimism typical of so many homeowners? Then the use of a realtor will cost the owner twice over. And just what constitutes a "fair price"? Moreover, if the realtors obtain

---

[1]It is also testimony to the inflation and the relative increase in housing prices that have occurred since the early 1970s. While $15,000 today may buy a garage, it won't buy much of a house.

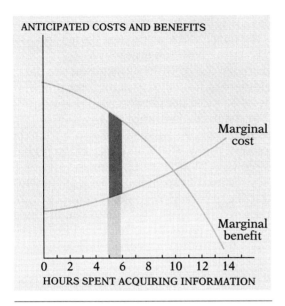

ANTICIPATED COSTS AND BENEFITS

Marginal
cost

Marginal
benefit

0 2 4 6 8 10 12 14
HOURS SPENT ACQUIRING INFORMATION

FIGURE 7A   Marginal cost and marginal benefit curves for information

You avoid costly mistakes by acquiring information before you decide. But acquiring information is itself costly. So you must compare the
cost of acquiring more information with the anticipated benefit (in costly mistakes avoided).
Someone in the situation portrayed in Figure 7A
who had spent 5 hours acquiring information
would want to spend an additional hour searching, because the anticipated benefit from that 6th
hour would be the entire vertical column, while
the cost would be only the gold portion of the
column. The proper amount of time to spend is
10 hours; after that, further inquiry is worth less
than its cost.

The trouble with this approach is that we
can rarely anticipate with any accuracy the benefit from further inquiry. The benefit will depend
on what we discover, and we don't know what
we will discover. If we did know, we wouldn't
have to search. The problem here is related to
the one you encountered earlier if you thought
about Discussion Question 5 at the end of Chapter 5. We can't know when to stop searching or
inquiring unless we know what we're going to
learn if we continue. But if we knew, we
wouldn't have to search or inquire. Uncertainty
introduces a radical indeterminacy into the process of economizing, whether on time or anything else.

higher prices for sellers, how can they simultaneously obtain better buys for purchasers, as the last paragraph asserts? Something is wrong with the argument.

Don't criticize the realtors' association too harshly. The plight of middlemen forced to explain their function is not an easy one, because most people don't see that *information is a scarce good* or what this fact implies. If you want to sell your house for as much as you can get, the appropriate buyer is the one person in the world willing to pay the highest price. That seems obvious. What isn't obvious is how you find that person. You presumably are not omniscient, so you will never even discover the existence of many potential purchasers. It is almost a certainty, therefore, that when you finally do sell, you will not have found that one buyer willing to pay the very top price. Does this imply that you should keep searching indefinitely?

Information is a scarce good with its own costs of production, including all the costs of postponing action. It simply does not pay to go on acquiring information forever before acting. A sensible seller will continue acquiring information, therefore, only as long as the anticipated marginal gain from doing so is greater than the anticipated marginal cost. A sensible buyer will behave in the same way. The reason that both can gain from using the services of a realtor is that the realtor enables each to obtain additional information at low cost. When you think about it, this seems in fact to be the primary function of middlemen: they promote efficiency and hence increase wealth by acting as low-cost producers of valuable information. Real estate agents provide sellers and buyers with better opportunities than they would otherwise have by putting them in possession of additional information. That is a valuable service. Although it's true that only the seller actually "hires" the agent, the fact that buyers go to them and make use of their multiple-listing services shows that real estate agents provide a service to buyers, too.

REDUCING SEARCH COSTS

Suppose you own ten shares of General Electric stock and want to sell. You could go around to your friends and try to peddle it or you could put an ad in the newspaper. But it is very likely that you would obtain a higher net price by using the services of a middleman, in this case a stockbroker. No doubt if you advertised long enough you could find a buyer willing to pay the price the stockbroker obtained for you. But it is most improbable that the cost of your search would be less than the broker's fee.

"Getting it wholesale" is a popular pastime for many people who think that they're economizing. Perhaps they are. If they enjoy searching for bargains (and many people do), then they may well gain from their activities. But for most people, retailers are an important low-cost source of valuable information. The retailer's inventory reveals something of the range of opportunities available, information that is often difficult to obtain in any other fashion. How many times have you gone shopping without knowing what you were looking for, hoping to discover what you want by finding out what retailers have for sale?

Much the same is true of job-placement agencies. People frequently resent the fee charged by private agencies for finding them a job. Unless they had expected the information obtained through the agency to be worth more than the fee, they presumably would not have used the agency's services. But as soon as they have established contact with a suitable employer, the agency seems useless—as it now is, of course—and its fee begins to look like an unwarranted imposition.

A large part of the middleman's bad press stems from our habit of comparing actual situations with better but nonexistent ones. The exchanges we make are rarely as advantageous as the exchanges we could make if we knew everything. So we conclude that the middleman takes advantage of our ignorance. But why look at it that way? Using the same argument, you could say that doctors take advantage of your illnesses, and that they should receive no return for their services because they would be unable to obtain a return if you were always healthy. That is both true and irrelevant. We are neither always healthy nor omniscient. Physicians and middlemen are consequently both producers of real wealth. Other prestigious persons performing similar services are lawyers, teachers, and corporation executives.

MARKETS CREATE INFORMATION

One of the continuing themes of this book is that supply and demand, or the market process of competing bids and offers, creates indexes of value for decisionmakers by placing price tags on available resources. The capacity of the market to generate high-quality information at low cost is one of its most important but least appreciated virtues. Middlemen are important participants in this process.

But what, you may ask, is "the market"? That's a good question and not an easy one to answer. The market is clearly not a place, though it may sometimes be closely identified with a particular place. Nor is it anything one can observe in the usual sense of observation. It is finally just a set of interrelationships, or what we have called a "process of competing bids and offers."

Markets are not peculiar to capitalism. They also exist in the most thoroughly socialist of societies. They aren't uniquely associated with business firms or the "private sector" either. Interrelationships characterized by competing bids and offers are also, as we shall see in Chapter 14, important characteristics of the political process and of government organizations. Nor must money change hands for markets to function, even though the use of money enormously facilitates their working. Rush-hour drivers who look for space, fill it up, and thereby continuously shift the relative value of the options that they all perceive exemplify a market. College students looking for courses to take and departments thinking of courses to offer are participating in a market process, too.

Some markets, like stock markets and commodity markets, are "well organized," which means that the bids and offers of prospective buyers and sellers are rather comprehensively assembled, so that a single price for a fairly uniform good tends to be established for all transactions over a wide geographic area. Other markets, like the market that even the least practiced eye can see operating in a singles bar, are much less well organized: The precise good to be exchanged and the terms of the exchange have to be negotiated for each separate transaction and transaction costs are consequently very high. The market for used furniture is relatively unorganized: transactions take place at prices that vary greatly, because buyers and sellers are not in extensive contact. The market for retail groceries, on the other hand, is far along toward the well-organized end of the spectrum, so that hamburger prices will vary much less over a given area than will used furniture prices.

It is sometimes said that stock markets and commodity markets are more nearly "perfect" than retail grocery markets and used furniture markets. This is a misleading way to describe the difference, because it implies that the latter markets ought to be changed (perfection is better than imperfection). Such a recommendation makes sense, however, only if the costs of improving the markets are less than the gains from more efficient exchange made possible by the improvement. It is often the case, however, that we simply don't know of any way to improve a particular market except at transaction costs too high to make it worthwhile. Morcover, some efforts to "improve" markets through government action look suspiciously like efforts to promote special interests.

But in every case the relationships between buyers and sellers, whether constant and extensive or sporadic and scattered, generate prices of some sort: terms of trade. Each such price is a piece of potentially valuable information to other people about available opportunities. The more such prices there are, the more clearly and precisely they are stated, and the more widely they are known, the greater will be the range of opportunities available to people in the society. The greater will be their wealth, in short. Is that not what we finally mean by an increase in wealth? It is a wider range of available opportunities, the ability to do more of whatever it is we want to do.

Middlemen, brokers, and professional traders are specialists in the organization of markets and hence in the creation of valuable information. They presumably specialize in this way because they think they have a comparative advantage in information production. Whatever their motives, however, they provide services on which we all depend.

That is one side of the coin. The other side is that we don't realize how important these functions are, largely because we have trouble seeing that information really is scarce. This blind spot frequently leads us to impose legal restrictions on traders. Speculators are frequent victims of just this kind of public misunderstanding.

VARIETIES OF SPECULATION

The dictionary defines speculation as "trading in the hope of profit from changes in the market price." That's too narrow a definition, but it will do to get us started. The most celebrated (or more accurately, the most vilified) speculator is the "bear" of Wall Street, who "sells short"—that is, sells for future delivery shares of stock not actually owned at the time of sale. This speculator believes that the stock will go down in price, so that when the time comes for delivery of the shares, they can be purchased at a low price and sold at the previously agreed-upon higher price.

A more important speculator is the commodity speculator, who may trade in such items as wheat, soybeans, hogs, lumber, sugar, cocoa, or copper. This kind of speculator buys and sells "futures." These are agreements to deliver or to accept, at some specified date in the future, amounts of a commodity at a price determined now.

A less-publicized speculator is you yourself. You are buying education now, partly in the hope that it will increase the value of the labor services you'll be selling in the future. But the future price of your services could turn out to be too low to justify your present investment.

Another familiar speculator is the consumer who reads that the price of sugar is expected to rise and responds by loading the pantry with a two-year supply. If the price of sugar rises far enough, these sugar hoarders gain. If it does not, they lose. Their wealth has been tied up in sugar, cluttering the pantry shelves and blocking the opportunity to purchase more valuable assets—an interest-bearing savings account, for example.

The motorist who fills the gas tank at the sight of a sign advertising gasoline at two cents a gallon less than the usual price is speculating; the price may be four cents lower two blocks ahead. The motorist who drives on an almost empty tank in hope of lower prices up ahead is a notorious speculator. And the motorists who continually "top" their tanks when gasoline supplies are rumored to be short are surely speculators.

But many people, while failing to notice that they themselves are often speculators, heap blame on the "profiteers" who allegedly "take advantage" of special situations and innocent people in pursuit of their own unprincipled profit. Are speculators really the enemies of the people they are so often alleged to be?

CONSEQUENCES OF SPECULATION

It is often said that speculators exploit natural disasters by driving up prices before the disaster occurs. And sometimes the expected disaster never even materializes. That is true. But it is only one small and misleading part of the truth. Suppose evidence begins to accumulate in early summer that corn-leaf blight is spreading to major corn-producing areas of the Midwest. A significant percentage of the year's corn crop could be wiped out as a result. People who think this is likely to occur will consequently expect a higher price for corn next year. This expectation will induce some people to pull some corn away from current consumption in order to carry it over into the next crop period when, they believe, the price will be higher. That is speculation.

Many different parties engage in such speculation: farmers substitute other livestock feed for corn in order to maintain their corn stocks at a higher level, either to avoid having to buy corn next year at a higher price or to sell it then at the higher price; industrial users increase their inventories now while the price is relatively low; and traders who might not know a bushel of corn from a peck of soybeans try to make a profit from buying cheap now and selling dear later. There are well-organized commodity markets to facilitate this kind of transaction, in which people can buy or sell "futures"—contracts for future delivery of commodities at prices agreed upon now. The effect of all these activities is to reduce the current supply of corn; the price consequently rises. And just as the critic protested, it rises before the disaster occurs.

But that is only a part of the picture. These speculative activities cause corn to be transported *over time* from a period of relative abundance to one of greater scarcity. The price next year, when the blight is expected to have its effects, will therefore be lower than it otherwise would be. Speculators thus even out the flow of commodities into consumption and diminish price fluctuations over time. Since price fluctuations create risks for those who grow or use corn, speculators are actually reducing risk to others. More accurately, they are purchasing risk, in hope of a profit, from others less willing to take risk and willing to pay something in the form of reduced expected returns to avoid it. (Those who choose to sell risk are called *hedgers.*)

PROPHETS AND LOSSES

All this assumes, however, that the speculators are correct in their anticipations. What if an unusually large crop appears instead? Then the speculators are transporting corn from a period of lesser to a period of greater abundance and thereby magnifying price fluctuations. This is clearly a misallocation of resources, involving as it does the giving up now of some high-priced corn for the sake of obtaining later an equal amount of low-priced corn. That doesn't help other people.

But neither is it profitable for the speculators! They will sustain losses where they had hoped for gains. We should not expect them, consequently, to behave in this fashion *except as a result of ignorance.* Are speculators likely to be ignorant?

Speculators do make mistakes. (Why would they otherwise be called speculators?) But living as we do in an uncertain world, we have no option but to act in the presence of uncertainty. We can't escape uncertainty and the consequences of ignorance by refusing to act or to think about the future. And if we think we know more than the speculators, we can counter them at a profit by betting against them. It is revealing to note that those who criticize speculators for misreading the future rarely give effective expression to their own supposedly greater insight by entering the market against them. Hindsight, of course, is always in copious supply—and the price is appropriately low.

Speculators provide information. Their offers to buy and sell express their judgments concerning the future in relation to the present. The prices generated by their activities are, like all prices, indexes of value: information for decisionmakers on present and future opportunity costs. This information is at least as important to conservatives as it is to gamblers. It is true that the information they provide is "bad" information whenever the speculators are wrong. But harping on this is again a case of comparing one situation with a better but unattainable situation. If we think we can read the future better than the speculators, we are free to express our convictions with money, profit from our insight, and benefit other people in the process.

Meanwhile, those whose ordinary business activities involve them in the use of commodities that are speculatively traded do make effective use of the information generated by the speculators. Farmers consult the prices predicted in the commodity exchanges and so do industrial users. And those who use goods not ordinarily thought of as speculative commodities also take advantage of the information generated by speculators. For we all use prices as information, and prices reflect competing bids and offers inevitably based to a large extent on a (speculative!) reading of the future.

Natural disasters such as droughts, crop diseases, and unseasonable frosts have surprisingly small effects on the price and availability of grain, fruit, and vegetables in the United States. The credit for that must go to speculators, whose foresight acts as an effective buffer between the vagaries of nature and the sturdy dependability of grocers. (An appendix to this chapter discusses in more detail the functions of commodity speculators and the futures markets.)

THE COMPLEX QUESTION OF "INSIDER TRADING"

A substantial part of the public's distrust and dislike of speculators is probably grounded in a suspicion that speculators take advantage of information from which they have no right to profit. The problems created by scarce information and consequent uncertainty are often complicated by this sort of disagreement about specific rights and obligations. What do buyers have a right to know? What do suppliers have an obligation to reveal? What constitutes an unfair advantage with respect to information? And who ought to be responsible for acquiring and disseminating important information about products?

The questions are difficult. Lawyers and ethicists were already arguing in the Middle Ages about the obligations of sellers to reveal to buyers everything they knew when that knowledge might lower prices. If a merchant brought grain to a starving city, was he morally or legally bound to tell his customers that additional grain shipments were on the way? Or could he legitimately keep this knowledge to himself and watch hungry customers bid up the price of his grain?

If you think the merchant had at least a moral obligation in such a case to reveal what he knew (*not* the universal conclusion of medieval ethicists, by the way), would you also say that someone selling corporate stock has an obligation to reveal any unfavorable information he has about the corporation's prospects before he sells? What is the difference between the two cases that might make us decide them differently? Is it the impersonal character of the stock transaction, the fact that sellers don't know who is buying what they sell? Is it the high cost of disseminating information to all prospective buyers? Or is it a lingering uncertainty about the accuracy, reliability, and relevance of the unfavorable information?

While "full disclosure" has an ethically attractive ring, the concept doesn't hold up too well under examination. Sometimes the information people have is wrong; if they have an obligation to reveal what they think they know, do they also have an obligation to compensate people who relied to their detriment on mistaken information? Moreover, information is not a simple matter of words. Telling people doesn't necessarily inform them. They can fail to understand, not believe, not be listening, not care, or not remember. In addressing any large group you will always find that some have forgotten what you said before others have understood, and that some still won't care enough to listen when others have stopped listening out of boredom. Moreover, what is valuable information to one person will often be mere noise to another, and if you try to tell everybody what they want to know, you may generate so much static that no one learns anything from your communication. If you try to avoid deceiving some, you will in the process fail to provide others with information *ε* they wanted to have.

The most serious objection to any full-disclosure requirement is that requiring people to reveal everything they know prior to any transaction would destroy much of the incentive to acquire costly but socially valuable information. We don't require inventors or writers to give away their ideas. Why should we require those who discover, sometimes at considerable cost, valuable information that cannot be patented or copyrighted to make that information freely available to others? While it is surely important that a society's rules of the game endorse honesty and integrity, it is also important that they encourage the search for new knowledge and the willingness to take risks when that knowledge is far from certain.

A high percentage of the "insider trading" cases prominently prosecuted in recent years by the Securities and Exchange Commission involved a violation of what the law calls *fiduciary obligations,* moral and legal duties taken on by contract. When "insider trading" flows from the violation of fiduciary obligations, it can be unambiguously condemned. Suppose the employees of a brokerage or law firm that has been hired to assist in a corporate takeover use the knowledge acquired in the course of their employment to purchase the stock of the target firm before the takeover attempt is announced. Because their actions will raise the price of the target firm and make the takeover more costly, they betray the interests of the firm that hired them. The situation is analogous to that of a county council member who uses his official knowledge to tip off friends about the location of a new highway so they can buy up the land. He would be increasing the cost of the highway project to his constituents, the taxpayers of the county, and his friends' purchases would be properly condemned as "insider trading" because they traded on the basis of information given to them in violation of a fiduciary obligation.

It would be absurd to define illegal "insider trading" as all trading that takes place on the basis of information not available to everyone else. Such a definition would implicitly assert that information is not a scarce good and that markets should function like roulette wheels. We clearly do want to prohibit all trading that violates fiduciary obligations. But what about trading that violates no fiduciary obligations yet does take advantage of "insider information"?

Suppose you are a scientist employed by a leading pharmaceutical firm, and you come to the conclusion that the line of research you are pursuing is likely to be very successful: Your efforts are going to produce an anti-cancer drug, let's suppose, that is likely to produce huge profits for your employer. It would make good sense for you to purchase stock in the company under these circumstances. If you did so, however, you would clearly be trading on the basis of information not available to others, information only available to persons who are "on the inside" of your research work. Would your purchase be illegal?

The law on such cases is not clear at the present time. You might want to ask yourself why a scientist should be prevented from investing in her own work? Whom does she harm? The people who sold her the stock, ignorant of the impending discovery that may *(or may not!)* send the stock price higher? Suppose the scientist already owned a large block of her company's stock, was planning to sell it, and changed her mind because her research on the anti-cancer drug suddenly began to look promising. Should she be accused of *nontrading* on the basis of inside information? The people she hurts now are the people who would have benefited from acquiring stock that was going to rise sharply in value. In either case, why do these people deserve special protection? What rights of theirs were violated by the scientist's decision to buy (or not to sell)?

Hostility to "insider trading" is grounded in the sound conviction that no one should have an unfair advantage. The problem lies in the difficulty of deciding what constitutes an *unfair* advantage. It won't do at all to conclude that *every* advantage is unfair. If we are going to acknowledge that information is an inescapably scarce good, we shall have to wrestle continually with the question of when and why particular inside information confers an unfair advantage.

THE LIABILITY QUESTION

What should be done about transactions that don't turn out as expected? New appliances that don't work properly, medicines that produce undesired side effects, or airplanes that crash? Who should be held liable for the damages?

One good answer is: Whoever agreed in advance to accept the liability. While it is almost impossible to assign liability in a fair and effective way after the fact, it is usually quite easy to do so prior to the transaction. If buyers want warranties against defects or the promise of monetary compensation in the event of an accident, they can refuse to purchase unless they get the contracts for which they are looking. Sellers will only offer such guarantees when they expect the benefits in additional sales to exceed the expected costs. Sellers will presumably start accepting responsibility for mishaps that they are in a good position to control, while buyers will accept the liabilities that they can bear more cheaply than they can persuade sellers to shoulder them. Sellers and buyers alike will have incentives to search for and use all information which they have a comparative advantage in gathering.

Our courts in recent years have been moving *away from* this approach to the problem of liability, apparently influenced by the belief that some parties have the power to negotiate and enforce unfair contracts. Ordinary consumers are too ignorant, from this perspective, to defend themselves against large corporations or expert professionals who know how to write contracts that will let them behave irresponsibly and get away with it. So the courts have been throwing out prior agreements negotiated by the parties and allowing juries to determine liability—after the fact, of course. Juries are drawn from that same population of ordinary consumers who were previously judged incapable of looking out after their own interests. Asked to resolve complex technical questions, they often fall back on the "deep-pocket" principle: "We don't know who is at fault, but these poor people were hurt and those other parties are rich enough to compensate them."

The fairness of that approach to liability must certainly be questioned. Its long-run consequences are equally disturbing. When liability is arbitrarily assigned to the deepest pocket in the neighborhood, possessors of deep pockets will leave the neighborhood. Many products and services whose use entails substantial risk will not be supplied, regardless of the benefits. Cities will close public parks rather than accept liability for the consequences of every foolish act performed on playground equipment; pharmaceutical manufacturers will no longer produce life-saving vaccines if they must pay enormous sums to the tiny fraction of users who suffer adverse side effects; life will become less safe as firms refuse to introduce new and safer technology because the potential liability costs are too high.

Caveat emptor means: Let the buyer beware. It is a legal principle, once widely accepted by the courts, which holds that sellers can be liable only for those qualities of a product that they specifically guarantee. Beyond that, the buyer must pay the consequences of a mistaken purchase. That doctrine has now been almost totally eclipsed by *caveat venditor,* let the seller beware, on the assumption that sellers are always in a better position to anticipate and prevent mistakes and to provide compensation when mistakes occur. Buyers increasingly are receiving the legal right to demand compensation from sellers for any deficiency in the product, including deficiencies of which the seller could not be aware and even some deficiencies created by improper buyer use of the product. The buyer of a rotary lawnmower who cuts off a finger by pulling grass from the mower while it is running may be able to extract financial compensation from the manufacturer by arguing that there wasn't an adequate warning, or that the mower should have been designed so that its user couldn't do such a foolish thing.

People respond to the costs that they expect to bear. If sellers must pay for foolish actions by buyers, they will attempt to prevent foolish actions. How? By selling only foolproof products. Should we applaud? The trouble is that foolproof products will be very expensive products. When mattress manufacturers sell only mattresses that cannot be ignited by a lighted cigarette, everyone who buys a new mattress must pay for a quality that is useful only to the small minority that falls asleep while holding lit cigarettes. That helps a few, but harms many more.

Sellers have a cost advantage in the generation of a great deal of information about products and in the creation of many product safeguards; but with other kinds of information and safeguards the comparative advantage will lie with buyers. If *caveat emptor* once compelled buyers to take high-cost actions to protect themselves, *caveat venditor* is now compelling sellers to take some precautions for which buyers could undoubtedly find much less costly substitutes.

PHYSICIANS AND MALPRACTICE SUITS

The furor over malpractice suits against physicians and the rise in the cost of malpractice insurance raises similar questions. Malpractice once meant negligent or improper action by a physician that resulted in death or injury to the patient. Increasingly today it means making a mistake, any mistake at all that results in harm to the patient, even if the physician's diagnosis and treatment satisfied the highest standards of currently acceptable medical procedures. Where will this take us?

If physicians are held liable for malpractice whenever they make a mistake, they will try even harder to avoid making mistakes. Isn't that what we want? Not altogether. We actually *want* physicians to accept the risk of making mistakes when the cost to the patient of avoiding mistakes becomes greater than the cost of committing them. Forget about money costs, which tend to introduce irrelevant emotions into the discussion, and simply set pain against pain and death against death. How many tests should a physician perform before settling on a diagnosis? Each additional test reduces the probability of pain or death from a particular disease but also entails pain and risk of its own. Would you want to submit to a spinal tap to be certain you don't have an obscure but fatal disease never yet found outside the island of Madura in the Java Sea?

The common contention that even the smallest risk of death is too great to accept simply makes no sense. It might make sense if risk could always be avoided without incurring new risks. That isn't the case, however. It only appears to be the case to those who concentrate on just one risk at a time. The harsh-sounding truth is that some ways of prolonging life are not worth the cost. The apparent harshness of that statement disappears when we recall that resources used in one way to reduce the number of probable deaths are not available for use in other ways that could possibly prevent an even larger number of premature deaths. It's always a good idea to ask, "What will we do instead?" We might, for example, prevent a few airplane crashes if we prohibited all takeoffs in inclement weather; but we would thereby cause far more travelers to die in accidents. Many people, prevented by the safety regulation from taking a commercial airline flight, would substitute a much more dangerous automobile trip.

It also helps to remember that we're dealing with probabilities and uncertainty. If the highway department uses the rest of its budget to straighten out Deadman's Curve, where five people die each year, and consequently leaves uncorrected the Lake Road grade crossing, where three people die each year, the department does *not* thereby "sentence three people to death." No particular persons must die because of the highway department's decision. And any driver who wants to get through that crossing safely has the option to stop, look, and listen. It may in fact be much more productive of "saved lives" in this case to take dollars out of highway improvements and put them into warning signs, thereby increasing the responsibility of buyers (drivers) for their own safety and reducing the responsibility of suppliers (highway builders).

Safety is a complex and multifaceted good that can be produced in an endless variety of ways. It tends to be produced most satisfactorily in a society where the rules of the game are clear and stable and people are encouraged to negotiate the arrangements they prefer.

An Appendix: COMMODITY SPECULATORS AND FUTURES MARKETS

Adam Smith once compared those who speculate on the future price of grain to the prudent captain of a sailing ship, who puts the crew on short rations the moment he discovers there is not enough food on board to last through the voyage. Grain speculators, Smith argued, reduce the suffering that poor harvests cause by inducing consumers to start economizing early. That is still one of the most important achievements of professional commodity speculators. We can see just how it works by looking at speculation on crude oil futures.

The New York Mercantile Exchange maintains a market in futures contracts for *light sweet,* the most popular grade of crude petroleum. Each contract calls for the delivery or acceptance in a specified future month of 1000 barrels of crude oil at a price agreed upon now. This market is used both by oil producers who want to insure themselves against the consequences of a possible future decline in the price of their product and by oil consumers who want to insure themselves against the adverse consequences of a rise in the price of oil.

For example, airline officials looking forward to a booming summer business might start worrying in May about a summer increase in fuel costs that could wipe out all the profits they are hoping to make. The airlines can take out insurance against that eventuality by purchasing, in May, crude oil futures for each of the coming summer months. If the airline buys August futures in May for $19.50, the price at which they are trading in May, it *hedges* against any August increases in fuel costs. A 10 percent increase in the price of jet fuel, caused by an increase in oil prices, will cut into the airline's profits by raising its operating costs. But this reduction in profits will be offset by a 10 percent increase in the price of the August contracts that the airline purchased in May, because the price of the futures contracts will change to match the price of the actual commodity as the date approaches for which the contracts have been made. It all works out *as if* the seller of the futures contract delivers oil to the buyer in August at the agreed-upon price of $19.50, and the buyer of the contract then sells that oil at the August price of $21.45, a price 10 percent higher than the price that had been generally anticipated in May.

Hedging reduces risk. The airline gives up the extra profits it could make if the price of petroleum products fell in order to avoid the loss it would sustain if the price of petroleum products rose. Oil producers, on the other hand, would hedge in May by selling August futures. The producers thereby lock in the May price of August futures for as many barrels as their contracts cover. They are insuring against a fall in price just as the airlines were insuring against a rise in price. If the producers sell August futures in May for $19.50 and the price in August turns out to be 10 percent higher than anticipated, they will make more profit than they had expected on all the oil they sell in August; but part of this will be offset by the loss sustained on those futures contracts, which will have risen to $21.45, requiring them (in effect) to buy oil at $21.45 a barrel and resell it at the contracted price of $19.50. The goal of the hedging operation, of course, was for the producers to insure against the losses they would sustain if the price of the product fell between May and August. They forgo the profit that results from a price increase in order to insure against the loss they would suffer from a price decline.

What is the role of the professional speculator in all this? Speculators widen the market, to begin with. They make sure that those who want to buy or sell futures can find people on the other side of the market ready to do business with them. Suppose lots of oil consumers begin worrying about a future increase in oil prices and consequently try to buy oil futures. There is no reason to believe that oil producers will be willing to sell all the contracts that consumers wish to purchase. But when a shortage of sellers develops, the price of the contracts starts to rise, and that attracts the professional speculators. These are people who have specialized in acquiring information about the commodity whose futures they agree to trade. They step in and deliberately take on risk because they believe that their special knowledge enables them to predict the future course of prices better than others.

Speculators do much more, however, than just help out hedgers. Professional oil speculators have a keen eye for anything that might affect the supply of or demand for oil and thereby alter its price, such as new discoveries, military hostilities, revolutions, conflict among the members of the Organization of Petroleum Exporting Countries, newfound harmony among the members of OPEC, severe storms in offshore oil-producing areas, political changes that might affect governments' energy policies, shifts in attitudes toward the environment—anything at all. When they believe that oil is going to become more scarce, they buy oil futures. That begins to raise the price of futures. As other people notice that futures prices are rising, they conclude that those who are in the best position to know have put their money on a higher price in the future and they adjust their own actions accordingly. That helps all the rest of us.

Those who are holding large inventories of crude oil, for example, will reduce their current sales in order to have more for future sale, when the price is expected to be higher. Those who plan to buy in the future will try to accelerate their purchases in order to beat the predicted price increases. The result of this current reduction in supply and current increase in demand—triggered, remember, by the increase in the price of futures that the speculators caused—will be a *current* increase in the price of oil. The predicted future increase will become an increase right now. And that price increase will enlist everyone who uses petroleum products in the cause of conservation, including the millions of people who don't even know where to find futures prices in the daily newspaper. The final users of petroleum products will respond to the increase in the current price by beginning now to economize on consumption.

Is that good or bad? Suppose that the speculators' actions were based on predictions of military hostilities in the Middle East that will seriously disrupt the flow of oil into world markets. Which is better? That we have no advance warning, do nothing to prepare, and make all our adjustments when the disruption actually occurs? Or that we receive advance warning, start economizing now, and have more oil on hand to tide us over when the disruption hits?

It is hard to see how the first scenario could be better than the second. Unless, of course, the speculators are wrong—which is certainly possible. If they are wrong, then their actions will cause the price of oil and its products to rise in anticipation of a disaster that never occurs. We will have economized when there was no reason to do so. And the petroleum products we saved through our efforts will be on hand to drive future prices down below what they would otherwise have been. Speculators who are wrong cause price fluctuations by themselves disrupting the balance of supply and demand.

But they are correct far more often than they're wrong. It's their business to be correct, and they won't be in the business for long if they are often wrong. Moreover, when they *are* wrong, they are quick to learn and to alter their behavior. They are not like people who don't have to pay the price of their own mistakes and so can go on holding stubbornly to a prediction after every sensible and impartial person can see that it has been refuted.

Speculators are our distant early warning system. They enable us to avoid crises by giving us better information and the incentive to act on it. Their buying and selling of futures contracts provides us with continuously adjusted predictions of what prices will be in the future, thereby enabling all of us to make better decisions in the present. Speculators are a valuable resource. If political hostility sometimes threatens to turn them into an endangered species, better understanding of futures markets and the functions of speculators can help to preserve them.

ONCE OVER LIGHTLY

An opportunity of which you're unaware is not a real opportunity. Information is therefore a valuable resource, whose possession enables people to increase their wealth.

Information is a scarce good whose production usually entails costs. The efficient decisionmaker accumulates additional information only as long as the anticipated marginal benefit is greater than the marginal cost.

A great deal of economic activity is best understood as a response to the fact that information is a scarce good. The much-abused "middleman" is in large part a specialist in information production. Just as the real estate broker enables prospective buyers and sellers to locate one another, so the typical retailer provides customers with knowledge of the goods sellers are offering and brings sellers into contact with those who want the sellers' offerings.

The common habit of viewing the middleman as an unproductive bandit on the highway of trade stems from the erroneous assumption that information is a free good.

Everyone who makes a decision in the absence of complete information about the future consequences of all available opportunities is a speculator. So everyone is a speculator.

People who think they know more than others about the relationship between present and future scarcities will want to buy in one time period for sale in the other. If they are correct, they make a profit on their superior insight and also transport goods through time from periods of lesser to greater scarcity. If they're wrong in their predictions, they perversely move goods from periods of greater to lesser scarcity and suffer the penalty of a personal loss on their transactions.

Because prices are summary indicators of scarcity, they are valuable information. Those whose buying and selling activities create prices are generating information that is useful to others. They lower transaction costs for everyone.

A person who is able to shift the full cost of mistakes onto others has little incentive to gather information before acting. A person who is compelled to bear the full cost of mistakes committed by others will attempt to keep them from committing mistakes. Avoiding mistakes is also costly, but people will tend to slight the costs that they themselves don't have to bear.

The cost of producing information is not the same for everyone. If a system of appropriate incentives is allowed to evolve, people will specialize in the production of those kinds of information in which they have comparative advantage.

QUESTIONS FOR DISCUSSION

1. Students frequently complain about the low prices the campus bookstore pays for used texts. Why then do they sell to the bookstore? Is it true that they cannot find a buyer on their own? Or is it more true that they are unwilling to go to the trouble (incur the cost) of finding a buyer on their own? What useful service does the college bookstore perform in handling used texts? Can you be sure it's a genuine service and not just a "rip-off"?

2. Evaluate the following paragraph from a newspaper article:

   One sure way to save money on groceries is to eliminate the middleman by buying directly from farmers and other suppliers. This is what a group of socially motivated and normally hungry people have decided to do by forming a grocery cooperative.

   If it really is possible to save money on groceries by "buying directly," why do so few people do it?

3. If you found that you could reduce your bills for new clothing 10 percent by buying exclusively from catalogs, would you do it? Why would some people be unwilling to take advantage of this "saving"? What do people do when they go "shopping"? How often have you discovered what you were looking for by seeing what sellers were offering?

4. Would you expect prices for goods of similar quality offered in garage sales to vary more than prices for goods offered in regular retail outlets? Why? Do the differences in prices mean that someone is being cheated, or that someone is taking unfair advantage of someone else?

5. A man approaches you in a busy airport terminal, shows you a handsome wristwatch, which he says is worth $135, and offers to let you have it for $25. Would you buy it? Would you be more willing to buy it if you had better information? What do you "know" when you buy a watch from an established local jeweler that you do not know in this situation?

6. Have you ever tested your butcher's scales to be sure they are accurate? How do you know you aren't being consistently short-weighted?

7. Why does a new car lose so much of its value in the first year? Is it because Americans have an irrational attachment to cars that are new rather than used?

   (a) Which year-old car is more likely to be on the used-car market: one that performed handsomely for its owner or one that had to be taken in regularly for repairs during its first year?

   (b) Which set of vehicles being offered for sale will contain a larger percentage of vehicles with defects known to the seller but unknown to the buyer: new cars or year-old cars?

   (c) What does all this imply about the prices sellers are willing to accept and that buyers are willing to offer for year-old cars, relative to what they would be if all buyers and sellers had complete information?

   (d) Why do used-car dealers sometimes provide warranties with the cars they sell and at other times advertise "As Is—No Warranties, All Sales Final"?

8. You find out in late December that you can probably make $1000 on a business deal if you can gain the goodwill of a client by getting him two tickets to the Super Bowl game. You manage to buy two well-located seats from a scalper for $250. Were you cheated by the scalper? Or are you glad that scalpers exist? Why do so many people intensely dislike scalpers?

9. The spring graduation exercises at Boston University in 1989 featured both U.S. President George Bush and French President François Mitterand. Each of the 5600 graduates was given four free tickets. An active market for tickets developed, and some were reportedly sold for $100.

   (a) Do you think the students who sold their tickets were behaving unethically? (The transactions were *not* illegal.)

   (b) Were the people who paid $100 for "free" tickets exploited?

10. The Augusta National golf club sells badges that function as tickets to the four-day Masters golf tournament for $90. The event has been a sellout for almost 20 years, and a 5000-name waiting list has been closed since 1978. Augusta National requires badge purchasers to sign a pledge that they will not resell their tickets. *The Wall Street Journal* sports commentator Frederick C. Klein found the going rate for Masters badges in 1989 to be $1500.

    (a) Why doesn't Augusta National raise the price of the badges?

    (b) Why does the golf club want to prevent reselling of badges?

11. Suppose that you are leaving tomorrow for a two-week combined business and vacation trip to a distant location. You'll be traveling by plane.

    (a) In what way are you speculating as you pack your suitcase?

    (b) On which side would you be more inclined to err—taking too many clothes and having to haul heavy suitcases around, or taking too few and finding yourself without an item you want?

(c) Would your answer to the previous question differ according to whether you were planning to be in a large city or a remote resort?

(d) Suppose you take only a single pair of dress shoes and accidentally spill ink on one of them just before an important business meeting. You dash out quickly and buy a new pair of shoes. Explain how the shoe seller's willingness to take a risk reduced your risk in taking only a single pair of dress shoes.

12. The June 18, 1979, issue of *Time* magazine contained an article on hoarding in the United States in which a number of social scientists were quoted. A sociologist said that gasoline hoarding was not rational but rather a result of Americans' emotional stake in their cars. A historian said hoarding was an absolutely typical American trait. Some attributed hoarding to a "shortage psychosis," and others spoke of "panic buying." Another sociologist said that strong leadership was required to stop such "competitive behavior."

(a) How could we decide whether hoarding is irrational, psychotic, a national character trait, a product of emotion and panic, *or* an intelligent response to uncertainty?

(b) What is the difference between hoarding and maintaining an appropriate level of inventory?

(c) Why do both business firms and households maintain inventories? How do they decide on the proper level of inventories for particular goods?

13. Are you speculating when you buy fire insurance on your home? Could you save money by getting together with your friends to form an insurance cooperative, thereby eliminating the necessity of paying something to a middleman (the insurance company)? What kinds of useful information do insurance companies provide?

14. A survey some years ago asked consumers to compare the time they spent selecting a doctor, buying a new car, finding the least-expensive supermarket, and bargain shopping for clothes. Thirty-four percent said they spent the most time researching supermarkets, 23 percent spent the most time bargain shopping for clothes, only 16 percent spent the most time selecting a doctor, and 15 percent said they spent the most time buying a new car. Why would these figures, released by the American Board of Family Practice, probably *not* indicate the relative importance people assign to getting good value when looking for food, clothing, physicians, and automobiles?

15. Suppose you are in your car trying to make a left turn across heavy traffic on a busy highway. You plan to turn as soon as the large truck coming toward you has passed. But then you notice that there is a long line of cars following the truck. You make an instant decision and turn in front of the truck.

Assume you saved 2 minutes by turning at that time rather than waiting for the whole line of traffic to clear, that you value your time at $6 an hour, and that there was a probability of .0001 your car would stall and the truck would be unable to stop so that you would be killed. What was the implicit value that you placed on avoiding the collision when you decided to turn? Would it be correct to say that this is the implicit maximum value you assign to your own life?

16. A letter to the editor of an urban newspaper, criticizing as "foolhardy" a fatal attempt by a Japanese mountain climber to make a solo ascent of Mt. McKinley in the winter, concluded with this sentence: "Safe mountaineering is and always should be the bottom line." What is "safe mountaineering"?

17. My neighbor is an orthopedic surgeon who enjoys building things out of wood. He purchased a power saw to reduce the time he had to spend cutting lumber. But he subsequently decided that he didn't want to risk an accident and sold the saw to me. Since he is a more careful worker than I am, the probability that he would have severed a finger using the saw is less than the probability that I will do so. Nonetheless, I am willing to take the risk while he is not. Use the concept of opportunity cost to explain the difference in our attitudes toward the hazards of using power saws.

18. When a manufacturing firm cuts costs in an overseas plant by adopting occupational safety standards that are more lax than the standards governing its domestic operations, is it exploiting its foreign employees? Why might potential workers in a very poor country be willing, even eager, to accept workplace hazards that workers would not accept in a wealthier country? Who is harmed and therefore most likely to protest the adoption of less-strict workplace safety standards in the operation of overseas plants?

19. Does a policy of protecting people against losses due to their own mistakes make those mistakes more frequent and the losses consequently greater?

    (a) Will insured houses have more fires than uninsured houses, other things being equal? Why?

    (b) Would people take more effective precautions against theft of their automobiles if insurance companies stopped selling policies that offered compensation for losses due to theft?

    (c) Why is it so much easier to purchase insurance against loss due to fire than against loss due to being laid off or discharged from one's job?

    (d) People who work in jobs covered by unemployment compensation do have some of the benefits of insurance against job loss. Do you think this causes people to be laid off or discharged more often?

20. If the Food and Drug Administration prolongs the testing period for new drugs in order to protect consumers against threats to their life and

health from the premature introduction of drugs with unknown but dangerous side effects, will it actually succeed in protecting consumers? What is the threat to life and health that the FDA thereby increases?

21. A commissioner of the Food and Drug Administration said that, although he was willing to weigh health risks against health benefits in formulating commission rulings, he was absolutely opposed to weighing health risks against economic factors. Evaluate this statement.

22. We can reduce the probability that children will die from accidentally swallowing large quantities of drugs by requiring drug dispensers to provide containers with child-resistant caps *on request*. Can we further reduce that probability by *prohibiting* the dispensation of drugs except in containers with child-resistant caps? What will drug purchasers do who have difficulty opening these caps, such as people with arthritis, if they are not allowed to purchase prescription drugs in containers with caps that are easy to open?

23. Economists Richard McKenzie and John Warner have estimated that highway deaths would rise by about 150 per year if tighter safety regulations increased air fares by 10 percent. Through what processes would this occur? (McKenzie and Warner conservatively assume that the price elasticity of demand for air travel is only 0.1, and that only 40 percent of those who don't fly because of the higher fares will choose to make their planned trip by car.) The average number of major airline fatalities per year has been *less than* 150 since airline deregulation in 1978. What does this indicate about the desirability of imposing tighter safety regulations on commercial airlines? If new discoveries enable the airlines to increase safety at no cost or a trivial cost, will the airlines adopt the innovations without being legally required to do so? (Data are from a *Wall Street Journal* article of March 7, 1989.)

24. In the autumn of 1981, authorities in the Soviet Union raised the price of vodka in an attempt to reduce alcoholism. Two years later, they lowered the price again, reportedly in order to stop the increase in the incidence of alcohol poisoning. What general rule is illustrated by this case, the case of the child-resistant medicine caps, and the case of overly safe airplane travel?

25. A bill introduced in Congress in 1989 would prohibit federal employees from receiving reimbursement if they stayed at hotels that did not have both sprinklers and smoke detectors. The purpose, of course, was to put pressure on hotels to install these safety devices; the round-about method was chosen because the Constitution doesn't grant this regulatory authority to the federal government. Do you think the benefit in enhanced safety is likely to be large enough to justify the cost of installing sprinkler systems in hotels that do not currently have them? Would you agree that the cost is justified even if it saves only one life?

26. In 1977 Seattle passed an ordinance requiring that new multilevel parking garages have barriers at least 18 inches high to stop automobiles from going through the walls. The ordinance was not made retroactive.

In 1987 a car broke through a fifth-floor wall in a parking garage that did not have the 18-inch barriers because it had been constructed prior to the ordinance. Three people were killed. A local newspaper editorialized as follows:

> It was a freak, as well as tragic, accident. The odds against a similar occurrence are high. Yet certainly it is possible. The City Council therefore must not hesitate in ordering that all multilevel garages in the city be brought into compliance with what are now ten-year-old safety standards.

(a) What is the flaw in the editorial's argument?

(b) Why does it often make sense to apply more stringent safety standards only to new construction while exempting existing structures? Consider, for example, a proposal to make all housing "earthquake proof."

27. The text asserts that the issue of insider trading is a complex one. You might be able to convince yourself of this by trying to answer the following questions.

(a) An art expert spots a drawing in an antique store that looks to her like a Pablo Picasso. If it is a genuine Picasso, it is worth thousands of dollars. The price tag says $35. Should she say nothing and buy it? Tell the store owner that she suspects the drawing is by Picasso? Buy it and share her profit with the antique store owner if it turns out in fact to be by Picasso? Can she be confident the store owner will in turn share *his* profit with the person who sold it to him?

(b) A print shop employee deduces the identity of a corporation that is about to become a takeover target from documents he is preparing for the corporation planning the takeover. Should he be permitted to use this information to purchase stock in the target company?

(c) An oil company is about to announce that it has discovered a huge new oil field in Brazil. Should employees of the company who already know the good news be permitted to purchase their company's stock prior to the public announcement?

(d) A stockbroker with a long list of clients to whom he gives investment advice learns from a disgruntled employee that a seemingly profitable insurance firm has been fraudulently managed and is about to declare bankruptcy. Should he be permitted to advise his clients to sell their stock in the insurance company before news of its plight gets out? Or must he make the information he has acquired public before he may legally advise his clients to sell?

(e) The chief executive of a corporation believes she has put together an extremely competent management team that is going to produce much larger profits for the company than it has been accustomed to earning. Should she be permitted to buy large amounts of the company's stock without first publicizing her belief?

(f) Should people selling their homes be morally obligated to tell potential buyers about all the hidden defects? A basement that floods
after extremely heavy rains? Neighbors who have loud all-night
parties outdoors in the summer? Squirrels that like to nest in the
attic?

28. Does advertising communicate valuable information? Does it inform,
persuade, manipulate, or misinform? Consider each of the following instances of advertising.

(a) The telephone company's Yellow Pages.
(b) Newspaper want-ads.
(c) Grocery-store advertisements of "specials" in the newspaper's food
section.
(d) A television commercial showing rich and handsome people getting
in and out of the advertiser's automobile.

29. Much advertising conveys little information beyond the name of the
product. Is there any way that such advertising could benefit consumers?
Does the fact that a seller is willing to spend money publicizing the name
of a product indicate anything about the seller's confidence in that product's quality?

30. Walter Wriston, former chairman of Citicorp, argued in an address to the
American Society of Newspaper Editors that the government was sup-
pressing information or censoring the news when it tried to prohibit
firms from posting higher prices. He argued that firms don't so much
raise prices as announce that prices have gone up. In what sense are
price controls a form of censorship?

31. Since the Bill of Rights in the U.S. Constitution prohibits government
from censoring the promises of political candidates, however absurd or
irresponsible, why doesn't it afford the same protection to commercial
advertisements? Is it because deceptive commercial claims do more
damage to the society and its members than do deceptive political
claims? Is it because citizens can more easily and effectively evaluate political claims on their own, but need considerable protection against deceptive claims for commercial products? If neither of these seems an adequate explanation for the difference, what explanation would you
suggest?

32. The news media report that a severe frost has done extensive damage to
the Florida orange crop and that frozen orange juice will soon be in very
short supply. How would you evaluate each of the following actions?
Choose one of the options: completely fair, probably fair, probably unfair, totally unfair.

(a) Local grocer raises the price on all frozen orange juice in the store as
soon as she hears the news.
(b) Homemaker rushes to the store and buys a three-month supply of
frozen orange juice as soon as she hears the news.

(c) Orange grower whose crop was not touched by the frost raises the price for all his oranges as soon as he hears the news.

(d) Orange grower whose crop was severely damaged raises the price for all of her remaining oranges as soon as she hears the news.

(e) Orange juice processors rush to purchase as many oranges as they can as soon as they hear the news.

Are all your answers consistent?

33. You decide in May that the coming summer's corn crop will be much larger and the fall corn price consequently much lower than most people expect.

(a) To act on your beliefs, should you buy or should you sell December corn futures? (*Futures* are contracts to buy or sell at a future date at a price established now.)

(b) If a substantial number of knowledgeable people come to share your opinion about the size of this summer's crop, what will happen to the price of December corn futures?

(c) What information will this change in the price of corn futures convey to current holders and users of corn?

(d) How will this information affect their decisions about holding corn for future sale or use?

(e) How will these decisions, based on the information provided by the change in the price of December corn futures, affect June consumption?

(f) Can speculators carry a bumper crop *backward in time* from a period of lesser to a period of greater scarcity?

34. A construction company signs a contract in January with a developer calling for the completion of 100 houses by the end of October at a price fixed in the contract. The construction company wants to protect itself against the possibility of sizable increases in the price of lumber that could wipe out any profit on the transaction. The Chicago Mercantile Exchange offers an opportunity to buy or sell lumber futures, which are contracts calling for the delivery in specified future months of about 150,000 board feet of spruce, pine, or fir at a price agreed upon now. A lumber futures contract is available that calls for July delivery.

(a) Would the construction company want to buy or to sell July lumber futures when it signs the construction contract in January?

(b) Suppose that July lumber futures are trading in January at $200 per 1000 board feet. When July arrives, construction lumber has risen in price to $220 per 1000 board feet. As a result, the construction company will have to pay 10 percent more for lumber than it expected to pay. How will it use its futures contracts to offset this loss?

(c) Suppose the price of lumber had fallen to $180 instead of rising to $220. Why will this not result in an unexpectedly large profit for the construction company on its contract with the developer?

35. *The Wall Street Journal* published two articles in the winter of 1985 on food and famine in Sudan and Ethiopia. One was titled "The Tragedy of Sudan's Spreading Starvation Is That It's Caused by Man's Errors, Not Nature's" (January 22, 1985); the other was headed "Getting Excess U.S. Food to World's Hungry Is Complicated by Politics and Bureaucracy" (March 14, 1985).

   (a) The former article said that the government in Sudan "has had to impose credit restrictions to stop banks from financing speculators hoping to profit from the misery." It also quoted a relief specialist working in the Sudan who claimed that assistance always came too late and who called for " a system of advance warning and standby funds." Don't speculators provide a system of advance warning? Do speculators who "profit from . . . misery" create the misery from which they profit or add to it? Or do they alleviate the misery from which they profit?

   (b) The article also described wasteful crosshauling of food: trucks taking food from A to B passed other trucks hauling food from B to A. It also said that the United States stopped selling food and began giving it away when British charitable organizations protested that the policy of selling the food was depriving those who needed it most. A U.S. official said that the selling policy was instituted at the urging of local governments "who didn't want local markets disrupted," but the United States agreed nonetheless to change the policy. Do you see a connection between disruption of local markets and wasteful crosshauling or other delays in getting contributed food from dockside to hungry mouths?

   (c) Suppose that the U.S. government and all other contributors to famine relief were to distribute among the starving people the money that had been contributed, and let these people purchase food for themselves. Do you think food would more quickly and surely get into the hands of hungry people under such a system than under one in which Western relief organizations try to handle the distribution of the food itself?

   (d) Those who condemn shopkeepers and other middlemen as worthless, wasteful, and wicked seem to be saying that the physical distribution of valuable goods is not a difficult social problem to handle once the goods have been produced. The African nations that have instituted capital punishment for those who speculate in food supplies seem to be saying the same thing. The two articles cited suggest otherwise. But would you want to be a merchant participating in a food distribution system when a charge of speculating or profiteering could result in the death penalty?

36. In December 1991, the United Nations Food and Agriculture Organization and the Worldwatch Institute predicted an increased scarcity of grain worldwide in the coming year. The forecasts particularly emphasized impending shortages of wheat. On the day these forecasts were

published, No. 2 hard Kansas City wheat (a standard and major grade of wheat) was selling for about $4.05 per bushel. On that same day, 1992 wheat futures were selling for the following prices: March, $3.87; May, $3.64; July, $3.33; September, $3.39; and December, $3.51.

(a) Did the professional wheat speculators agree with the forecasts of the FAO and the Worldwatch Institute?

(b) In whose forecasts would you have more confidence? Why?

PRICE SETTING AND THE QUESTION OF MONOPOLY

The term *administered prices* was first introduced to public discussion in the 1930s in order to make a distinction between prices that were set by supply and demand and prices supposedly set unilaterally by sellers. Since that time, the term has been widely used, especially by those who believe that the U.S. economic system is dominated by large corporations. Some critics have accused professional economists of ignoring the role of administered prices in the American economy, and of pretending that prices are all set by supply and demand. According to most of these critics, the American economy is today largely controlled by monopolists and oligopolists, who pay no attention to supply and demand, but instead use their market power to manipulate prices according to their own selfish and narrow interests.

It is impossible to evaluate any of these claims without first obtaining a clearer notion of what is meant by such terms as *administered prices* and *monopolist*. We have consciously steered around these issues as much as we could in the preceding chapters. The tactic that usually enabled us to do so was the implicit assumption that there were so many buyers and sellers in any market at which we were looking that none of them had any power to affect the price through individual action. It is now time to look more closely at issues that have been bypassed.

WHO QUALIFIES AS A MONOPOLIST

We begin with the word *monopoly,* the product of two Greek words meaning "one seller." Are there any monopolists in that strict sense of the word? Try to think of something that is sold exclusively by one seller.

Local telephone service suggests itself as a good example. But is it an accurate example? There were many independent sellers of telephone service in the United States, as a matter of fact, even before the breakup of AT&T in 1984. Still, that may be beside the point. For any given buyer there is typically one seller, since telephone companies usually enjoy exclusive selling privileges in particular areas. On the other hand, buyers don't have to live in a given area; they can move to another franchise area if they prefer the product there. Back comes a justifiably impatient snort: "That's irrelevant." But it's not completely irrelevant. Moving your residence may be a prohibitively expensive way to shift your telephone patronage, and it's hard to imagine people actually moving just because they resent the local phone company. But that *is* a way of obtaining a substitute product. And by its absurdity, our example calls attention to the crux of the problem: the availability of substitutes.

Suppose we redefine the commodity sold by telephone companies and call it "communication services." There would be nothing intrinsically misleading about that. After all, that is why anyone wants a telephone: to obtain communication services. But if this is the product being sold, the telephone company is clearly *not* a monopolist, but rather a seller in competition with Western Union, the post office, various messenger and delivery services, loud shouting, fast running, and all sorts of computer communication techniques. The point of all this is simply that, if we define the commodity broadly enough, not a single commodity in the country is sold by a monopolist.

Now let's look at the other side of the coin. Suppose we define the commodity very narrowly. If telegrams are not the same thing as telephone calls, neither is a gallon of milk at the little store next door the same thing as a gallon of milk three blocks away at the supermarket. If you have no car, are rocking a screaming baby who won't stop until fed, and have no one to leave the baby with, the milk three blocks away is a vividly different commodity from the milk at the store next door. Ask any parent of a small baby. Thus, we are forced to conclude that, when the commodity is defined narrowly enough, every seller is a monopolist, since no two sellers will ever be offering completely identical products.

We're trying to convince you that the word *monopoly* is extraordinarily ambiguous. For everyone or no one is a sole seller depending on how we define the commodity being sold. Furthermore, there is no satisfactory way to decide in all cases just how broadly or narrowly the concept of a commodity ought to be defined. The Supreme Court of the United States has sometimes listened to persuasive arguments on both sides of a contested definition and then divided in its decision. Take cellophane, for example. Is it a separate commodity or should it be put in the category "flexible wrapping materials"? The answer given in cases such as this may determine whether a manufacturer is convicted under federal antimonopoly laws.

ALTERNATIVES, ELASTICITY, AND MARKET POWER

So let's try another approach. What would be so bad about a single seller if we found one? The telephone company hints at the answer when it advertises: "We may be the only phone company in town, but we try not to act like it." If we find a case where there really is only one seller, the customer will have no alternatives. No one wants to be without alternatives. The poorer our alternatives, the weaker our position and the more easily we can be taken advantage of.

But we learned in Chapter 2 that there are always some alternatives. There is a substitute for anything, even the services of the local telephone company. After all, no one "needs" a telephone. On the other hand, a phone is a valued convenience for many families and business firms. The concept from economics that suggests itself is price elasticity of demand.

No seller is a monopolist in the strictest sense of the word because there is no such thing as a *perfectly* inelastic demand. No seller has any buyer totally over the barrel. On the other hand, very few sellers of anything face perfectly elastic demand curves. Anything less than complete elasticity means that sellers will retain some business when they raise their price, which in turn implies that sellers have at least a morsel of market power. Where is the line between a morsel and monopoly?

There is no clear line of demarcation unless we decide to draw one arbitrarily. Elasticities of demand reflect the availability of substitutes; other things remaining equal, the more good substitutes there are for anything, the more elastic will be the demand for it. Market power is thus seen to be a matter of degree and to be inversely related to elasticity of de-

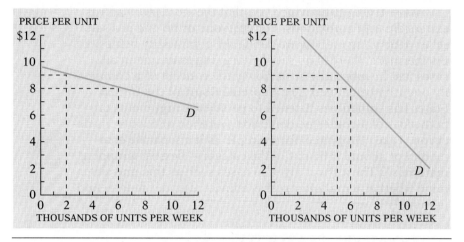

FIGURE 8A   Demand elasticity and "monopoly"
    If the selling firm facing the demand curve on the left in Figure 8A raises its price from $8 to $9, it will lose two-thirds of its sales (in physical units–not in dollar receipts). The demand is highly elastic between $8 and $9. The coefficient of demand elasticity is 8.5. (The formula for obtaining this precise result is discussed in question 36 of Chapter 2.)
    If the firm facing the demand curve on the right raises its price by the same amount, its sales volume (in physical units) will decline by only one-sixth. The demand elasticity is 1.545.
    A seller facing a completely elastic demand curve (a horizontal line) could not raise its price without losing all its sales.
    A monopoly seller in the strict sense would face a completely inelastic demand curve (a vertical line), which would imply that there are no substitutes whatsoever for the good being sold—it is a "necessity" for all its users. Such a seller would be under no competitive constraint to keep down its prices. Do not expect to find any sellers who face completely inelastic demand curves.

mand. Defined in this way, the term *market power* has a meaning that we can talk about and use. But we have not yet found a useful definition for the word *monopoly*.

PRIVILEGES AND RESTRICTIONS

Let's try another approach. In the early nineteenth century there was often no distinction made in the United States between a monopoly and a corporation. The reason was that corporations had always been created by special governmental acts. They received, whether from Crown and Parliament before the Revolution or from state and national legislatures afterward, special "patents," as they were called: official documents granting rights and privileges not available to others. Corporate charters were therefore called "grants of monopoly," since they gave to one party a power that was withheld from others. The East India Company was such a "monopoly," and the special privilege of selling tea in the colonies, given to it in 1773, helped bring on the American Revolution.

Here is another and quite different meaning of monopoly, one related to acts of the state. If the state allows some to engage in an activity but prosecutes others for doing so, or if it taxes or restricts some sellers but not others, or if it grants protection or assistance to some while compelling others to make their own way unaided, the state is creating exclusive privileges. This meaning for the word *monopoly* has contemporary relevance as well as historical significance.

Many business organizations operate with monopoly grants of this kind. In the name of all sorts of commendable-sounding goals—public safety, fair competition, stability, national security, efficiency—governments at all levels have imposed restrictions on entry into various industries or trades. The beneficiaries of these restrictions always include the parties who can escape them. These parties will rarely admit that they enjoy a grant of monopoly power. But the effect of the restrictions nonetheless is to prevent some from competing who would otherwise do so.

We are not saying that restrictions on entry into a market are always to be condemned, or that the businesses which benefit necessarily behave badly afterward, or that consumers can never be better off as a consequence of restrictions on competition. We are only concerned that the restrictions be noted so that their consequences can be evaluated. They will often turn out to be different from what most people assume. We could, if we wished, use the word *monopolist* to describe any individual or organization operating with the advantage of special privileges granted by the government. The trouble is that most people no longer use the word in this way. By such a definition, the postal service is a monopolist, as are most public utilities, many liquor stores, morticians, and crop dusters; the American Medical Association, state bar associations, and labor unions; farmers with acreage allotments, licensed barbers, and most taxicab firms. The list is long indeed.

And so we are going to take the heroic step of dropping the word *monopoly* from our working vocabulary. Its meanings are too many and too vague. "'When I use a word,' Humpty Dumpty said in a rather scornful tone, 'it means just what I choose it to mean—neither more nor less.'" *Monopoly* is a favorite of contemporary Humpty Dumpties. And that's why we are not going to employ it. We shall try to use alternative terms that are more likely to communicate the precise situation we have in mind.

PRICE TAKERS AND PRICE SEARCHERS

Let's go back now to the phrase with which this chapter began: administered prices. Is there a distinction between administered prices and prices that are set by supply and demand?

It's a free country, as they say, and businesses are usually free to set their own prices. The USX Corporation (formerly United States Steel) has substantial discretion when it prints its price lists, and a wheat farmer from Kansas can feel quite safe from the threat of prosecution if he decides to offer his crop at $5.00 per bushel. But there is obviously an important difference that helps to explain why USX hires people to decide what its prices should be and wheat farmers do not. The difference, we shall nonetheless insist, is a difference of degree, not kind.

Take the case of the wheat farmer first. If he consults the financial pages of his newspaper or tunes in for the noonday market reports, he will find that number 2 ordinary hard Kansas City wheat opened at $3.43 ¾ a bushel. That news may disappoint or delight him, but there is almost nothing he can do to change it. If he decides that the price is an excellent one and sells his entire crop for immediate delivery, the market will feel scarcely a ripple. Even if he is one of the biggest wheat farmers in the state, he is still such a small part of the total number of those offering to buy or sell wheat that he cannot affect the price. The difference between what the closing price will be if he sells all his crop and what it will be if he sells only half of it will not be as much as ¼ cent.

Economists therefore call the wheat farmer a *price taker*. He cannot affect the price by his own actions. The price at the local grain elevator is determined by the actions of many buyers and sellers all over the country. If the farmer exercises his legal right to put a price tag on his wheat 2 cents higher than the market decrees, he will sell no wheat. And since he can sell all the wheat he has at the going price, he has no incentive to offer to sell any wheat at less than the going price. Price takers face perfectly elastic demand curves, or what for all practical purposes amount to perfectly elastic demand curves. The demand curves are horizontal at the going price.

Most sellers are not in this position. They can raise their prices if they choose, without losing all their sales. And, unlike the farmer, they can't always sell everything they're capable of producing without lowering their prices. At higher prices they will sell less; at lower prices they will be able to sell more. They must choose a price or set of prices. Economists therefore call them *price searchers*. Torn between the desire for higher prices and the desire for larger sales, they must search out the price or set of prices most advantageous to them.

Price searchers include USX, the trustees of a private university weighing a tuition increase, the proprietor of a local grocery store, and the little boy selling lemonade on a hot afternoon. There is a long tradition in economics of referring to all price searchers as monopolists. But this is a technical use of the word that is confusing to everyone except professional economists. Since the little boy selling lemonade does not face a perfectly elastic demand curve, he is not a price taker but a price searcher. It seems silly to anyone not steeped in the history of economics to call him a monopolist. So we shall not do it. The term *price searcher* captures the situation in which we're interested. Price searchers all have some market power, but it is a matter of degree inversely related to the elasticity of the demand the seller faces.

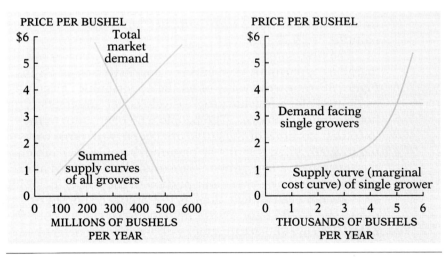

FIGURE 8B   Supply and demand curves for wheat for the total market and for a single grower

In Figure 8B the total demand for wheat intersects the total supply at a price of $3.50 on the left-hand graph. Individual wheat growers cannot sell any wheat at a price higher than this, and can sell all they want to sell without lowering their price below $3.50. They are price takers, "taking" in this case the price of $3.50 per bushel and responding to it as best they can. A grower with the marginal cost curve shown on the right would want to supply 5,000 bushels. (Do you see why he would not want to supply either less or more?)

PRICE TAKERS' MARKETS AND "OPTIMAL" RESOURCE ALLOCATION

Economists applied the disapproving term *monopolist* to what we shall call *price searcher* in large part because they wanted to emphasize the different consequences of these two types of price setting. Markets in which all buyers and sellers were price takers were graced with the approving term *competitive markets*. We want to point out the advantages they saw in price takers' markets without adopting the misleading monopolistic-competitive distinction, which erroneously implies that price searchers face no competition. To do so we shall use the graph of Figure 8C, which shows the demand and supply curves for house painters during a particular summer in the town of Pratte Falls.

The number of house-painting hours that will be demanded and supplied depends on the price per hour of house painters' services. Since people's skills in this area differ considerably, we shall simplify our exposition by assuming that each hour of service shown on the horizontal axis has been adjusted for quality. If Freddie Fumblefingers is only 40 percent as productive in an hour as the average Pratte Falls painter, he will take 2 ½ hours to supply "one hour" of the good shown on the graph. Betsy Brightbrush, who is three times as good as the average, supplies "one hour" of house painting every 20 minutes.

The first point to remember is that supply curves are marginal opportunity-cost curves. The curve labeled SS in Figure 8C shows the value of all the opportunities given up as Pratte Fallers provide progressively larger amounts of house-painting services. The people who contribute to the lower-left portions of the curve are people with large comparative advantages in house painting, because they are either extremely adept painters or extraordinarily inept at everything else. The upper-right portion of the curve, including sections not even shown, depicts the supply responses of those who would have to give up a lucrative law practice to paint, who are subject to attacks of dizziness at heights above seven feet, or who for any other reason must sacrifice a highly valued opportunity in order to supply an hour of house painting. Keep in mind that the marginal-cost curve of any single individual will also eventually slope upward to the right. The value of the opportunities forgone as one devotes more and more time to any particular activity is bound to increase as that activity crowds out alternative activities, simply because people sacrifice their least-valued opportunities first and give up more highly valued opportunities only in response to a stronger inducement.[1]

If the price now settles down at $6 an hour, so that 6000 hours of the good are exchanged over the summer, the heart of many economists will leap with a special kind of joy. Why? Because at the price of $6, given the demand and supply curves, no unit of the good is being produced whose marginal opportunity cost, as represented by the supply curve, exceeds its marginal benefit, as represented by the demand curve. Moreover, every unit of the good whose marginal benefit exceeds its marginal cost is being produced. And how could we do better than that? Economists have traditionally gone so far as to call such an arrangement an *optimal allocation of resources. Optimal* means best, which is surely excessive praise; but let's look a little more closely to see exactly what's happening here.

Suppose that the people supplying those 6000 hours at $6 an hour decide that they deserve larger incomes and somehow persuade the town council to pass a law setting $10 an hour as the minimum price for an hour of house-painting services. We'll suppose further that the law is effectively enforced. What will happen? Only 4000 hours will now be demanded. And since that's all that can be sold, that's all that will *actually* be supplied, even though, as the graph shows, painters will *want* to supply about twice that amount at a price of $10.

Establishment and enforcement of the $10 price will make some people better off and others worse off. Note that some of those who are worse off may be former house painters forced into less desirable occupations by the legislated price increase. Economists have no satisfactory way of balancing one person's gain against another person's loss to decide whether net social well-being will go up or down as the result of such a change. About all they can really do is point out that the Pratte Falls law prevents mutually advantageous exchange. The area under the demand curve between 4000

---

[1]This hypothetical example also illustrates the fundamental similarity of supply and demand. The people who are willing to pay up to $20 per hour to have someone else paint their houses, and who thereby create that portion of the demand curve below $20, may well be among the people who create the supply curve at prices above $20. Example: "I'll pay up to $20 per hour to get my house painted this summer. But if I have to pay more than that, I'll do it myself." Such a person, who stops demanding and starts supplying to himself at some high enough price may, at an even higher price, also begin supplying to others.

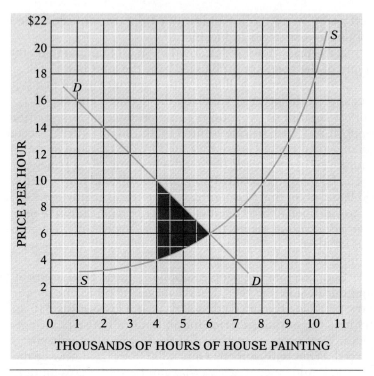

FIGURE 8C   Demand and supply curves for house painting in Pratte Falls

and 6000 hours represents the dollar value of what demanders are willing to give up to obtain those units of the good. The area under the supply curve represents the dollar value of what suppliers are willing to give up to provide those units of service. The difference between the two areas, shaded in Figure 8C, is a potential gain from trade that the ordinance effectively removes by prohibiting any exchanges at less than $10 an hour.

What does all this have to do with price takers' markets and their superiority, in traditional economic analysis, over price searchers' markets? It comes to this: Prices that are fixed above marginal cost rule out some mutually advantageous exchange opportunities. In price takers' markets, sellers don't have the power to set and keep the price above marginal cost. In price searchers' markets, they do.

How serious that problem is and how high the costs of correcting it might be are two of the questions that will run through Chapters 9 and 10.

ADMINISTERED PRICES ONCE AGAIN

It would seem then that price searchers set their own prices, whereas price takers accept what the market sets. Is this the distinction between administered prices and those prices that are set by supply and demand? Not if one thinks about it carefully. Every seller in the last analysis sets the final price, though some sellers can do so with little or no real searching, because they in effect accept the prevailing price (price takers). A more serious objection is that price searchers are by no means free from the constraints imposed by supply and demand.

"Big oil" is a favorite target of those who decry administered prices, but whatever the faults or failings of corporations in the oil industry, their decisions are surely conditioned by supply and demand. Supply depends on cost, and cost is taken into account if price searchers hope to find what they are looking for, which is presumably the most profitable price to set. Firms in the oil industry may have excessive market power. Whether or not they do, or which ones do and which ones do not, or how much market power any firm has—all these questions can best be investigated by looking at marginal-cost curves and demand curves and how they change over time in response to the pressures of competition. We will discover nothing useful if we pretend that there are firms that "administer" prices *in total disregard of supply and demand.*

So we end up with no usable meaning for the term *administered prices* either. *All* prices are administered and *all* prices are set by supply and demand. The term *administered prices* consequently will not be used in subsequent chapters. An examination of its history would reveal that it has more often been used as a polite "bad word" than as a concept to aid analysis or critical discussion. Economic problems are sufficiently complex without complicating them further by using terms that generate much heat and no light.

One other term appeared in the introductory paragraph: *oligopolist.* The dictionary suggests that an oligopolist is "one of a few sellers." The Big Three in automobiles and the major cigarette manufacturers are commonly cited as examples of oligopoly situations. But what about the daily newspapers in a large city? Or do they compete with other newspapers that can be trucked or flown in, with news magazines, billboards, television, the Yellow Pages? What is the commodity that allegedly has only a few sellers? Should it be broadly or narrowly defined? What about gasoline stations? Hardware

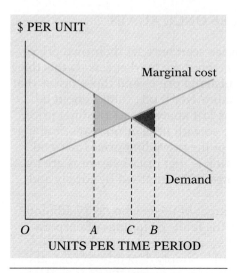

FIGURE 8D   Demand and marginal-cost curves

The demand curve in Figure 8D shows how much money people are willing to give up to obtain additional quantities of the good. The marginal-cost curve shows how much money people must be offered to give up alternative opportunities and supply additional quantities of the good. It follows that, when the quantity exchanged increases from OA to OC, the gain to demanders, measured in money, exceeds the cost to suppliers, also measured in money. The net gain is the triangle containing the gold shading. If the quantity exchanged increases from OC to OB, this, by the same reasoning, would entail a net loss equal to the triangle containing the gray shading.

It does not follow that OC is therefore the "correct" or socially ideal quantity per time period, because the costs and benefits accrue to different people. A $1000 benefit to one set of people is not necessarily of greater value than a cost or a benefit forgone by another set of people totaling $800. However, the $200 net gain does give the prospective beneficiaries the means and the incentive to share their benefits with those who will have to bear the costs, as a way of securing their cooperation. This is what drives the supply-and-demand process.

stores? Automobile dealers? Shops that restring tennis rackets? How few is few? We don't have to multiply examples to discover that all the problems associated with defining a monopolist as a single seller return to haunt us when we define an oligopolist as one of a few sellers.

There is a special market situation to which many economists have chosen to apply the term *oligopoly*. We'll examine and analyze that situation in Chapter 10. But we shall not use the word *oligopoly*, on the grounds that, like administered prices and monopoly, it creates confusion rather than clarity and understanding.

ONCE OVER LIGHTLY

The word *monopoly* means literally one seller. But whether any seller is the only seller depends on how narrowly or broadly we define the product. Under a sufficiently broad definition, there are innumerable sellers of every product. Under a sufficiently narrow definition, however, every seller's product differs from every other's, and all sellers are monopolists. The word *monopoly* is therefore inherently ambiguous and will not be used in subsequent chapters.

The antisocial connotations of the word *monopoly* stem from the belief that the customers of a sole seller have no alternatives and are therefore at the mercy of the seller. Since there are in fact alternatives to every course of action and substitutes for every good, no seller ever has unlimited power over buyers. Market power is always a matter of degree.

The concept of price elasticity of demand provides a useful way of thinking and talking about the degree of market power. Demand elasticities, which can vary between zero and infinity, reflect the availability of substitutes. The more good alternatives buyers have, the more elastic are the demand curves sellers face and the more limited is the power of sellers to establish terms of sale strongly advantageous to themselves.

In the early years of the United States, a monopoly usually meant an organization to which the government had granted some exclusive privilege. The monopolist was often the only legal seller. Although this meaning of the term is no longer common, it does have contemporary relevance since federal, state, and local governments are extensively involved in the granting of special privileges that restrict competition.

A useful distinction to make in trying to understand how prices are established is the distinction between *price takers* and *price searchers*. Price takers must accept the price decreed by the market. Buyers have such excellent substitutes for the product that any attempt to raise the price or otherwise shift the terms of sale will leave the seller with no customers at all. The price searcher, on the other hand, can sell different quantities at different prices and must therefore search for the most advantageous price.

When price is greater than marginal cost, some goods are not going to be produced and sold despite the fact that the monetary value buyers place on acquiring them is higher than the monetary cost to suppliers of making them available. Competition tends to push production in price takers' markets to the point where price and marginal cost are equal.

The concept of *administered prices* is misleading inasmuch as almost all prices are "administered" by sellers—within the constraints imposed by their situation. The important question is whether competition imposes adequate constraints in particular circumstances.

The word *oligopoly* is at least as ambiguous as *monopoly;* whether there are just a few or very many sellers depends on how we choose to define the product. And so the word *oligopoly* will also be discarded in favor of terms that are more precisely descriptive.

QUESTIONS FOR DISCUSSION

1. List some commodities or services that are sold by only one seller. Then list some of the close substitutes for these goods. How much market power is possessed by the single sellers you listed?

2. Does a firm have a monopoly if it publishes the only morning newspaper in a particular city? If it publishes the only daily newspaper, morning or afternoon? If it publishes the only daily newspaper and owns the only television channel in the city? What are the various goods that a daily newspaper supplies? With what other goods do they compete?

3. Electric utilities are usually given exclusive franchises by the government to sell electricity in a particular area. Are they in competition with sellers of anything else? Do they compete for sales in any way with electric-utility companies franchised to operate in other areas?

4. Is the U.S. Postal Service a monopoly?

   (a) With whom does the Postal Service compete in its first-class mail service (for correspondence)? Its second-class mail service (for publishers of newspapers and magazines)? Its third-class mail service (for advertisers)? Its parcel service? Its express mail service (guaranteed next-day delivery)?

(b) If the Postal Service has the power to set its prices without regard to supply and demand, why does it usually operate at a loss? Why doesn't it raise its prices and eliminate those troublesome losses?

(c) When the Postal Service raised the first-class postage rate by about 15 percent recently (from 25 to 29), do you think its revenue from first-class mail also rose by 15 percent? What would a 15 percent increase in revenue have implied about the elasticity of demand for first-class mail service?

5. Is AMTRAK a monopolist? If you want to travel by train between cities in the United States, you are likely to find that AMTRAK provides the only such service. Why is it nonetheless misleading to refer to AMTRAK as a monopolist? Is "intercity rail passenger service" a commodity for which there are no good substitutes?

6. The good that the public school systems in American cities supply is one that many persons are required by law to consume. Moreover, competing suppliers, because they are denied the right to finance their activities through taxation, must ordinarily charge much higher prices than the public schools charge. Are public school systems monopolists?

7. It is illegal to market certain agricultural commodities, such as tobacco, unless the product was grown on land that the federal government has licensed for the growing of these commodities. Does this mean tobacco farmers are monopolists? Are they price takers or are they price searchers?

8. If monopolies are undesirable, as almost everyone seems to assume, why do governments so often try to protect particular sellers against the competition that additional entrants to the industry would provide?

(a) Why does the U.S. government prohibit people from competing with the Postal Service in the delivery of first-class mail?

(b) Why do cities almost always impose stringent restrictions on those who would like to provide a transportation service to compete directly with the city-owned or -licensed urban bus service?

9. It has been argued by some that we can measure the extent to which "monopolists and oligopolists" control the U.S. economy by looking at *concentration ratios* in various industries. These ratios, calculated by the Bureau of the Census, show the percentage of the total shipments in various industries that are accounted for by the 4 largest, 8 largest, 20 largest, and 50 largest companies in each industry. Table 8-1 shows the ratios for selected industries as calculated from the 1987 Census of Manufacturers, the most current data available at this time.

(a) Why does the concentration ratio in motor vehicles and car bodies provide a seriously exaggerated indication of the market power of U.S. automobile manufacturers?

TABLE 8-1   Share of Value of Shipments Accounted for by Large
Manufacturing Companies in the United States, Selected Industries

Industry	4 Largest	8 Largest	20 Largest	50 Largest
1. Petroleum refining	32%	52%	78%	95%
2. Motor vehicles and car bodies	90	95	99	99+
3. Blast furnaces and steel mills	44	63	81	94
4. Aircraft	72	92	99	99+
5. Meatpacking plants	32	50	66	80
6. Fluid milk	21	32	48	67
7. Newspapers	25	39	55	71
8. Sawmills and planing mills	15	21	31	44
9. Plastic materials and resins	20	33	61	89
10. Soap and other detergents	65	76	84	89

(b) The concentration ratios in meatpacking plants and fluid milk are similar. It is much more costly, however, to ship fluid milk long distances than it is to ship processed meat. What difference does this make if we're trying to infer the degree of market power from an industry's concentration ratio?

(c) Why is the similarity of the concentration ratio in newspapers to that in fluid milk probably not very significant?

(d) Do the progressively higher concentration ratios in lumber, plastics, and then soap (the 8th, 9th, and 10th industries listed) indicate a progressively greater degree of market power? How large geographically are the markets for the lumber, plastics, or soap shipped from a particular manufacturing plant?

(e) Petroleum refining is more highly concentrated than petroleum production or distribution. Do the data suggest that the oil companies can set whatever prices they choose?

10. One often reads that there are "only three firms in the industry" (or five firms, or eight firms), and that this is too few for competition to be effective. How would you define an industry? Do firms in different industries (however defined) compete with one another? Are all the firms within a single industry (however defined) in competition with one another?

11. Do steel girders for bridge construction produced in Utah compete at all with girders produced in Maryland? (The phrase "at all" will usually

make a statement true.) Can you think of ways in which wood products compete with steel girders?

12. Is the college you're attending a price searcher? How much freedom does it have in setting the tuition rate you will pay? Might a just-en-rolled freshman answer the above differently from an about-to-gradu-ate senior? Does your college enjoy any special grants of legal privi-lege?

13. Those who use the term *administered prices* do not include in this classifi-cation the prices charged by grocery stores. Nonetheless, grocers plug-ging prices into their scanners seem clearly to be "administering" prices. Can you suggest criteria that would enable us to distinguish "adminis-tered" from "nonadministered" prices?

14. Adam Smith wrote the following in *The Wealth of Nations:* "The price of monopoly is upon every occasion the highest which can be got . . . the highest which can be squeezed out of the buyers, or which, it is sup-posed, they will consent to give." Does this assertion have any clear and defensible meaning, or must we conclude that even the founder of eco-nomics sometimes reasoned carelessly?

15. It has been argued that the development of the railroad in the middle of the nineteenth century substantially reduced the market power of many American manufacturing firms. Explain.

16. The graph on the left in Figure 8E portrays the market demand for U.S.-grown wheat *(D)* and the aggregated marginal cost curves of U.S. wheat growers *(S)* in a given year.

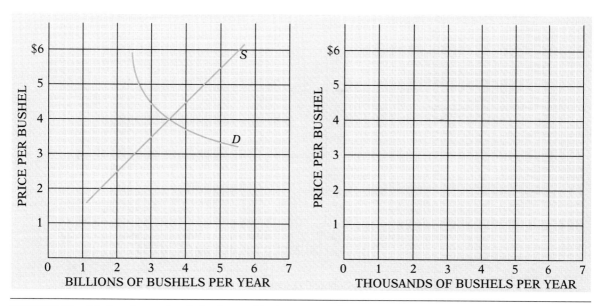

FIGURE 8E   **Market demand and the demand facing one producer**

(a) Draw the demand for the wheat of Ferdinand Elizer, a South Dakota wheat farmer, on the right-hand graph.

(b) How would the demand curve faced by Ferd Elizer shift if the government offered all wheat farmers a subsidy of $1.50 per bushel?

(c) What would Ferd Elizer's demand curve look like if the government imposed a tax on wheat, requiring farmers to remit $1 for every bushel they sell?

17. The number of moorage sites for houseboats in Seattle has been limited by law to 440 since the city adopted a Shoreline Management Plan in 1975. All sites are currently occupied by houseboats. Some houseboat owners who do not own their moorage sites asked the city to impose controls on the rents that owners could legally charge. They claimed that, with the vacancy rate at zero, owners had acquired a monopoly and could consequently set rents as high as they pleased.

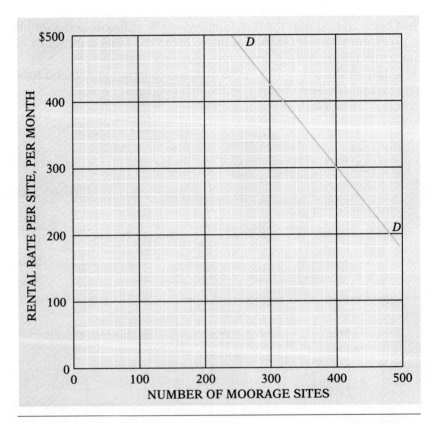

FIGURE 8F   Hypothetical demand and supply curves for houseboat moorage sites in Seattle

(a) The graph in Figure 8F shows an imaginary demand curve for moorage sites, labeled *DD*. Construct the supply curve from the data provided above. [Assume throughout this problem, until part (i), that the sites are owned by 440 different people.]

(b) What will happen if owners set the rental rate at $275 per month?

(c) What will happen if owners set the rental rate at $225 per month?

(d) Is it true that a zero vacancy rate enables owners to set any rental rate they please? What does a low vacancy rate in residential or office space usually indicate?

(e) What effect on the rental rate would you predict if houseboat living became much more popular in Seattle? What would happen if houseboat living declined in popularity? What are some factors that might cause such an increase or decrease in the demand for houseboat living?

(f) What would be the effect on the rental rate if 40 additional moorage sites became available through a modification of the Shoreline Management Plan?

(g) What would be the effect on rental rates of a $50-per-month increase in the property tax that site owners must pay? Demonstrate your result graphically.

(h) What would be the effect of a $50-per-month tax on houseboat occupants? Use the graph to answer.

(i) Does a zero vacancy rate indicate monopoly power? Suppose all 440 moorage sites were acquired by one party who consequently became the only supplier of moorage sites for houseboats in Seattle. Would this owner now be able to set rents as high as she pleased? What do you think would happen to the vacancy rate if one party became the only seller of moorage space?

(j) Why do you suppose the houseboat owners chose to use the word *monopoly* in asking the city council to regulate rental rates?

18. Market power is not the only kind of power that business firms might have and exercise. Neither market power nor any of these other types of power is necessarily correlated closely with the size of business firms. You might want to think about the nature, sources, and consequences of some of the powers listed below and how they are linked (or not linked) with market power. Power:

(a) As capability, the ability to achieve desired results.

(b) To influence the outcome of elections.

(c) To influence legislation.

(d) To influence regulatory agencies of government.

(e) To manipulate people through advertising.

(f) To pollute the environment; to reduce pollution.

(g) To pursue sexist and racist hiring policies; to institute affirmative action programs.

(h) To intervene in the affairs of other nations.

(i) To shape the basic attitudes and beliefs of people.

What about the power that we sometimes assume others must have simply because we ourselves feel power*less*? Is it true that someone always has power to cause or to prevent undesirable events?

19. Congress has authorized the Federal Communications Commission to monitor the content of radio and television broadcasts and to revoke the licenses of stations that do not adequately serve the public interest. No member of Congress would seriously contemplate exercising such supervision over newspapers, especially in view of the clear prohibition contained in the U.S. Constitution's Bill of Rights. Two justifications are usually offered whenever anyone questions this control over broadcasters' freedom of expression. One is that Congress may regulate radio and television stations because the airwaves belong to the public. The other is that broadcasting frequencies are naturally scarce, and that broadcasters must be prevented from abusing the power given to them by control of a scarce natural resource.

(a) Why do the airwaves belong to the public? Can you think of a fair and effective way for the public to relinquish its ownership, so that Congress would no longer be obliged to control broadcast content?

(b) There are over 1500 television stations and more than 10,000 radio stations currently broadcasting in the United States. More than 95 percent of U.S. households receive at least five television signals, and cable has enormously expanded these options. Dozens of radio stations are available in major urban areas, and where they are not, it is not because of any scarcity of spectrum space. How much power does the natural scarcity of broadcasting frequencies actually give to broadcasters?

PRICE SEARCHING

How do price searchers find what they're looking for, and what happens when they find it? We're going to argue in this chapter that price searchers estimate marginal costs and marginal revenues and then try to set prices that will enable them to sell all those units of their product—and only those units—for which marginal revenue is expected to be greater than marginal cost. Does that sound complicated? It's just the logic of the process for maximizing net revenue, or total revenue minus total cost. But is it the procedure business firms actually use? It sounds much too theoretical, like something an economist might dream up but few real-world sellers would even recognize.

THE POPULAR THEORY OF PRICE SETTING

It certainly is not the way most people assume that prices get set. The everyday explanation is a simple cost-plus-markup theory: business firms calculate their unit costs and add on a percentage markup. A large number of price searchers will themselves describe their price-setting practices in terms of the cost-plus-markup theory. Their testimony deserves to be taken seriously, but it isn't conclusive evidence. A lot of people cannot correctly describe a process in which they themselves regularly and successfully engage. Most people who ride bicycles, for example, don't know how they keep the bicycle balanced. And if asked to think about it, they'll conclude that they keep the bicycle from tipping by leaning or shifting their weight slightly each time the bicycle inclines in one direction. If that were the way they actually balanced, they wouldn't make it to the end of the block. In reality, they balance by steering, not leaning; they turn the front wheel imperceptibly and allow centrifugal force to counter any tendency to tip. The fact that they don't know what they're doing doesn't keep them from doing it. Although they can balance successfully only by winding along a series of curves whose precise curvature will be inversely proportional to the square of the speed at which they're proceeding, many mathematical illiterates are skillful cyclists.

There are excellent reasons for doubting cost-plus-markup theory. One is that it tells us nothing about the size of the markup. Why choose a 25 rather than a 50 percent markup? Why do different firms mark up their prices by different percentages? Why will the same firm vary its percentage markup at different times, on different products, and even when selling to different people? Why do sellers sometimes set their prices *below* their average unit cost?

Moreover, if firms can always mark up their prices proportionately when their costs rise, why don't they raise their prices *before* their costs rise? Why are they satisfied with a smaller net revenue when they could be earning more? That doesn't square with the perennial complaints of many price setters that they aren't making adequate profits. We all know, too, that firms are sometimes forced out of business by rising costs. That couldn't happen if every firm were able to mark up its prices to cover any increase in costs.

The popular cost-plus-markup theory is obviously inadequate. It just doesn't explain the phenomena with which we're all familiar. We'll return to the question of why so many people, including price searchers themselves, nevertheless hold to the theory. But we can't do that until we've gone through the economist's explanation of the price-searching process.

INTRODUCING ED SIKE

Simple cases are best for illuminating basic principles. We're going to examine the imaginary case of Ed Sike, a sophomore who is supporting himself at Ivy College by working as special-events manager for the College Student Association. One of Ed's tasks is to run a Friday night feature-film series that is open to the college community, and a large part of that job is setting ticket prices.

Let's suppose that Ed has to pay the following bills each time he shows a movie:

Film rental	$1800
Auditorium rental	250
Operator	50
Ticket takers	100
Total:	$2200

Ed's budget receives all the revenue from ticket sales. The auditorium seats 700 people. And Ed has somehow discovered the precise demand for the films he shows. (We'll relax

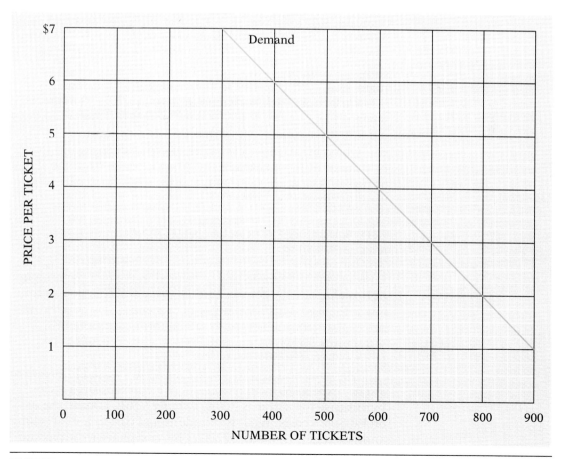

FIGURE 9A   Weekly demand for tickets to films

that heroic assumption later on.) The demand, which (quite remarkably) doesn't change from film to film, is graphed in Figure 9A. Given this information, what will Ed want to charge for tickets?

We can't answer that question until we know Ed's objectives. If his aim is to fill all the seats without having to turn anyone away, $3 would be the best price to set. That's the price at which the quantity of tickets demanded would equal the number of seats available in the auditorium. One possible objection to a $3 price, however, is that each film showing would lose money. Total costs would be $2200, but total revenue would be only $2100.

That isn't necessarily a compelling objection. The student association may be willing to subsidize the films, perhaps because someone thinks movies make an important contribution to liberal education. If Ed doesn't have to cover costs out of ticket revenue, all sorts of possibilities open up. For example, he might set the price at $2.50. That would cause the quantity demanded to exceed the quantity supplied, but it might also make Ed a very popular man on campus—someone who can get you tickets to a Friday night film even though the film is already "sold out."

We'll come back to that possibility in a later chapter when we look more closely at how "nonprofit" institutions work. Let's assume for now that Ed not only has to get enough revenue from ticket sales to cover all costs, but that he's under orders to earn as much *net* revenue from the series as he can. Under these circumstances, what price will Ed want to charge for a ticket?

THE BASIC RULE FOR MAXIMIZING NET REVENUE

Look again at the basic rule presented in the first paragraph of this chapter, the rule we said all price searchers try to follow if their goal is to maximize net revenue: Set the price or prices that will enable you to sell all those units and only those units for which marginal revenue is expected to be greater than marginal cost.

Marginal cost you've met before. That's the additional cost a seller expects to incur as a result of a contemplated action. In this case the action is *selling another ticket*. Look at the data on Ed Sike's costs. What is the additional cost to him of selling another ticket? Since all $2200 of his costs have to be paid no matter how many tickets he sells, the marginal cost of selling another ticket is zero, under the assumptions we've adopted. If you wanted to draw the marginal cost curve on Figure 9A, it would be a horizontal line running across the graph at $0.

THE CONCEPT OF MARGINAL REVENUE

But what's marginal revenue? *Marginal revenue is the additional revenue expected from an action under consideration.* For Ed Sike, marginal revenue is the extra revenue received from selling one more ticket.

If you look at the demand curve in Figure 9A, you can see at a glance that Ed Sike's net revenue is going to depend on the price he decides to set. At $3 total revenue would be $2100, and so net revenue would be *minus* $100. At $6 net revenue would be $200: $2400 in total revenue minus $2200 in costs. It would also be $200 if the ticket price was set at $4. At what price would net revenue be maximized, given the data with which we're working?

The answer is $5. If the price is set at $5, then 500 tickets will be sold. Total revenue will be $2500, and net revenue will be $300. Ed can't do any better than that.

How do we know? One way to find the answer is to try out every possible price. A better way, because it clarifies the logic of the process we're trying to explain, is to locate the quantity at which marginal revenue equals marginal cost and then find the price at which exactly that quantity can be sold.

The logic is simple. Each of the first 500 tickets that Ed sells adds more to his revenue than it adds to his costs. (Remember that in this particular case it adds *nothing* to his costs; marginal cost is zero no matter how many tickets are being sold.) But each ticket sold beyond 500 adds more to costs than to revenue. It adds nothing to costs, but it adds *less than nothing* to total revenue, because marginal revenue becomes negative after 500 tickets have been sold.

WHY MARGINAL REVENUE IS LESS THAN PRICE

It seems at first that this can't be correct. Since Ed is still taking in money for each ticket he sells beyond 500, the additional revenue from selling another ticket, or marginal revenue, looks as if it ought to be positive. But that appearance is in fact false. It ignores something very important. In order to sell additional tickets, Ed has to lower the price. And when he does so, he lowers the price not only to the additional customers he's trying to capture with the price decrease, but also

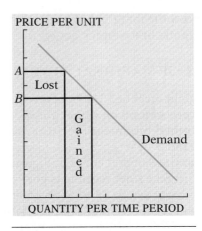

PRICE PER UNIT

A

Lost

B

G
a
i
n
e
d

Demand

QUANTITY PER TIME PERIOD

FIGURE 9B   Revenue lost and revenue gained through a change in price
    Lowering the price from A to B gains some revenue from additional sales. It also results in some lost revenue, however, because all buyers now pay the lower price.

to all those customers who would have purchased tickets at the higher price. The additional revenue he gains from the new customers is offset by revenue lost, or given up, from the old customers. After he has sold 500 tickets, the revenue lost becomes greater than the revenue gained, and so marginal revenue becomes negative.

Let's check it out by looking carefully at the graph. Suppose Ed set the price at $5. At that price he would sell 500 tickets, and total revenue would be $2500.

What would happen if he decided to sell 550 tickets? To do so, he would have to lower the price to $4.50. That would bring him an additional $4.50 from each of the 50 "new" customers, for a total of $225 extra. But it would cost him 50 cents *not* paid now by each of the 500 "old" customers who were willing to pay $5 until Ed offered to sell them tickets at $4.50: 500 times 50 cents is $250. That more than offsets the $225 gained. Ed Sike actually reduced his total revenue by $25 when he decided to expand his ticket sales from 500 to 550. Marginal revenue is *negative* over this range.

We can be even more precise. Since the additional revenue from the 50 additional tickets sold is minus $25, we can say that marginal revenue per ticket is minus 50 cents when Ed tries to expand sales from 500 to 550. If we want to show that on Figure 9A, we can plot marginal revenue as minus 50 cents at 525 tickets, the midpoint between 500 and 550.

Check your understanding of the basic idea by asking what happens when Ed expands his sales from 450 to 500 tickets. The demand curve shows he could sell 450 tickets for $5.50 each. To sell 500 tickets, he must lower the price to $5. So his total revenue will be $2475 when he sells 450 tickets, and $2500 when he sells 500 tickets. The additional or marginal revenue is 50 cents per extra ticket sold when Ed expands his sales from 450 to 500 tickets. We would therefore plot plus 50 cents as the marginal revenue at 475 tickets.

If we connected these two points with a straight line, the resulting marginal-revenue curve would intersect the marginal-cost curve at precisely 500 tickets. Consequently, we can say that if Ed is content to sell fewer than 500 tickets, he sacrifices potential net revenue by failing to sell some tickets for which marginal revenue is greater than marginal cost. If he sells more than 500 tickets, Ed sacrifices potential net revenue by selling some tickets for which marginal revenue is less than marginal cost. He therefore maximizes net revenue by selling exactly 500 tickets: the quantity at which marginal revenue equals marginal cost. And the de-

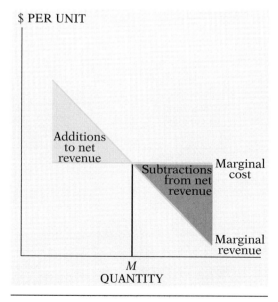

FIGURE 9C   Maximization of net revenue
    Net revenue is maximized by selling the quantity M, because this includes all units that add more to revenue than to cost and no units that add more to cost than to revenue.

mand curve tells us that 500 tickets can be sold by setting the ticket price at $5.

SETTING MARGINAL REVENUE TO EQUAL MARGINAL COST

You can be sure you've grasped the idea if you're able to figure out what would happen if the film distributor changed the rental fee from a flat $1800 to $800 plus $2 for every ticket sold.

The key difference is that Ed's marginal costs would now rise from zero to $2. Each additional ticket sold would now add $2 to total cost; the marginal-cost curve is a horizontal line at $2. Since to maximize net revenue, Ed must sell all those tickets for which marginal revenue is greater than marginal cost, and no tickets for which marginal cost is greater than marginal revenue, Ed wants to find the price and quantity at which marginal revenue will exactly equal $2.

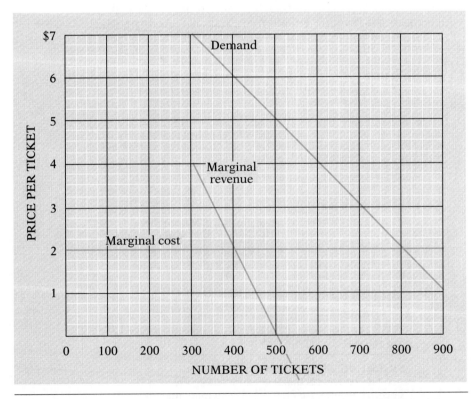

FIGURE 9D   Weekly demand for tickets to films and marginal cost of selling tickets

The marginal-revenue curve has been drawn in Figure 9D. This curve shows by how much the sale of one additional ticket increases total revenue at the various volumes possible. Marginal revenue is $4 when 300 tickets are being sold and falls rapidly as sales increase, becoming negative after 500 tickets are sold. We now see at once that, given the film distributor's new policy, Ed will want to sell 400 tickets. This is the quantity that equates marginal revenue and marginal cost. To sell 400 tickets, Ed should set the price at $6. It turns out that Ed does somewhat better under the film distributor's new policy than he did under the old one. Total revenue is now $2400 and total cost is $2000, for a net revenue of $400.

WHAT ABOUT THOSE EMPTY SEATS?

Under both the old and the new policy, seats were "going to waste." That phrase is in quotation marks because waste, you should recall from Chapter 6, is an evaluative concept. What constitutes waste from the point of view of moviegoers may be efficiency from the point of view of exhibitors like Ed. Still, there does seem to be something wasteful about this situation from everyone's perspective. There are people who want to see the movies, who are willing to pay Ed an amount greater than his marginal cost if he will let them in, but to whom Ed nonetheless denies admission. Movie fans are missing an opportunity for which they're willing to pay the marginal cost; and Ed isn't getting any revenue from those empty seats for which people are willing to pay more than his marginal cost. There seems to be a substantial gain from exchange that isn't being realized. (The situation matches the case of the house painters under a legal minimum wage, as discussed in Chapter 8; it's not an "optimal" arrangement of resources.)

Situations like this are extremely common, of course. At almost every major-league baseball game there will be empty seats inside the stadium, and people outside the stadium who would be happy to pay the team owner for the chance to sit in them. Since letting in another spectator adds nothing to the cost of playing the game, the owner would gain extra net revenue from each additional fan admitted at any ticket price greater than zero. But this will be the case only if the owner can reduce the ticket price to the "new" customers without also reducing the price to those who are willing to pay more to see the game.

THE PRICE DISCRIMINATOR'S DILEMMA

There's the catch. It is in fact efficient (from his point of view) for Ed to leave 200 or 300 seats empty, as long as the cost of discriminating among potential ticket buyers is greater than the additional revenue that can be gained through discrimination. Let's see what this means.

Suppose Ed is paying a flat $1800 rental fee, charging $5, selling 500 tickets, and earning $300 per week. One Friday night he looks over the house and says to himself: "I could increase my net revenue by filling those 200 empty seats. All I'd have to do is lower the price to $3, but *only* for those who won't attend if I charge them more than that. I'd get an extra $600 each week, and 200 additional people could enjoy these fine movies."

A brilliant idea? The following week Ed hangs up a new sign at the campus ticket outlet: "$5 per ticket," it says; and then it adds in smaller print: "$3 for those unwilling to pay more." What's going to happen? Almost all the ticket buyers will pay $3, of course, because they're all "unwilling to pay more" if they can get their tickets for $3. Ed will end up with only $2100 in revenue and a loss of $100 from that week's program. It wasn't such a brilliant idea after all.

The flaw, however, was more in the execution than in the idea itself. What Ed must do if he wants to eliminate the "waste" of empty seats and lost revenue is find a sufficiently low-cost procedure for distinguishing among potential buyers. He has to be able to offer low prices to those who otherwise won't buy, without making those low prices available to customers who are willing to purchase tickets at higher prices. Ed might be able to pick up a few hints from the Ivy College administration.

THE COLLEGE AS PRICE SEARCHER

College administrators often talk about the high costs of providing an education and the need for charitable contributions to make up that 50 percent or so of the cost not covered by tuition. Have you ever wondered why it is, then, that privately owned colleges grant tuition scholarships to needy students? If colleges are so poor that they must ask for charity, why do they simultaneously *dispense* charity? The answer is that they probably don't. Tuition scholarships for needy students may be a partially successful attempt to do what Ed Sike failed to do.

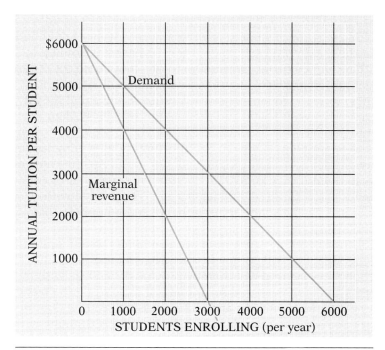

FIGURE 9E   Demand curve for enrollment at Ivy College
    Note: There is a simple gimmick you can use to obtain quickly
the marginal-revenue curve corresponding to any straight-line demand curve. Draw perpendiculars to the price axis from the demand
curve; bisect the perpendiculars; extend a straight line through these
midpoints. The marginal revenue corresponding to any point on the
demand curve will then be the point on this line (the marginal-revenue curve) directly below the point on the demand curve in which
you're interested. Thus the marginal revenue is zero when the price
is $3000. A better way to put it: at the quantity 3000, the marginal
revenue is zero and the price is $3000.

    Figure 9E is the demand for admission to Ivy College as
estimated by the college administration. We shall assume
that the marginal cost of enrolling another student is zero.
That isn't accurate, but it's realistic enough for our purposes
and it doesn't affect the logic of the argument in any event.
Ivy College wants to find the tuition rate that will maximize
its receipts.
    If Ivy restricts itself to a uniform price for all, it will set
the tuition at $3000 per year, enroll 3000 students (the enroll-
ment at which marginal revenue equals marginal cost), and
gross $9,000,000. But some students whom it would be prof-
itable to enroll are excluded by this tuition rate, and some
students who would have been willing to pay more are admit-

ted for only $3000. Ivy's administrators wish they could charge what each student is willing to pay. If they could find out the maximum each student (or the parents) would pay rather than be denied admission to Ivy, they could set the annual tuition at $6000 and then give scholarships (price rebates) to each student. The scholarship would equal the difference between $6000 and the maximum each student is willing to pay.

The problem is how to get information on willingness to pay. Students or their parents will not reveal the full value of Ivy to them if they know that candor will cause them to pay a higher price. But if willingness to pay is correlated with wealth, a partial solution lies at hand. Ivy announces that scholarships are available to needy students. Need must be established by filling out a statement on family wealth and income. Families will complete the forms in order to qualify for scholarship aid and will thereby provide the college with information it can use to discriminate. If the correlation were perfect between income and willingness to pay, and if families filled out the forms honestly, Ivy could discriminate with precision and increase its gross receipts to $18,000,000 (the area under the entire demand curve). Marginal revenue would be equal to price despite the fact that Ivy is a price searcher.

Be careful about condemning Ivy College! Notice some of the consequences of this discriminatory pricing policy. First of all, Ivy earns more income. If you approve of Ivy, why begrudge it a larger income from tuition? Is it better for philanthropists and taxpayers to cover Ivy's annual deficit than for students (or their parents) to do so through being charged the maximum they're willing to pay? Notice, too, that under a perfectly discriminating system of tuition charges, 3000 students who would otherwise be turned away are enabled to enroll at Ivy. They aren't complaining.

SOME STRATEGIES FOR PRICE DISCRIMINATION

Sellers have developed a wide variety of strategies for doing what Ivy College does through its tuition scholarship program. The goal is to find low-cost techniques for distinguishing high-price from low-price buyers and then to offer reduced prices exclusively to those who otherwise won't purchase the product.

For example, grocery stores often offer discounts to customers who present special coupons clipped from newspaper advertisements. Why do they do this? The discounts are de-signed to attract bargain-hunting shoppers who otherwise wouldn't patronize the store. Customers who fail to present coupons at the checkout counter thereby identify themselves as people who aren't price-conscious bargain-seekers. So they pay higher prices.

If airlines lower their ticket prices, they can fill some empty seats with vacation travelers who would otherwise go by car. But the airlines don't want to lower their prices for business travelers who are willing to pay high fares to save time, and for whom the cost of travel is a tax-deductible ex-pense anyway. How can the airlines distinguish these two classes of travelers and give discounts only to those who won't fly without them? One way is to confine the discount prices to those who buy round-trip tickets far in advance and stay more than a week or over a weekend. Business travelers usually can't afford to stay away that long and frequently have to travel on short notice. It's far from an infallible way to dis-criminate, but it's a low-cost system and it works surpris-ingly well.

Discount prices are commonly offered for all kinds of en-tertainment events to children, students, and senior citizens. Is this an act of generosity on the part of those who sponsor the events? It's more likely that they want to attract some ad-ditional business from groups that are more sensitive to prices, but without lowering the price to everyone. Potential customers with more elastic demands for the good are prime targets for special price reductions, *if* the seller has a low-cost way to identify the people with more elastic demand curves *and* can prevent them from reselling to people with less elas-tic demand curves.

ED SIKE FINDS A WAY

Let's return to the case of Ed Sike. Suppose his data on the de-mand for tickets enable him to distinguish the student demand from the staff and faculty demand. In Figure 9F we've drawn two demand curves to show these separate student and staff-faculty demands for tickets to the Friday film series. (If you add the curves together—summing the quantities demanded by each group at various prices—you'll get the demand curve presented in Figure 9A.) Our question is: Can Ed, knowing these separate demand curves, increase his net revenue by set-ting different prices for students and for staff or faculty?

Intuition suggests it might work. The typical student doesn't have a lot of income and so tends to pay attention to

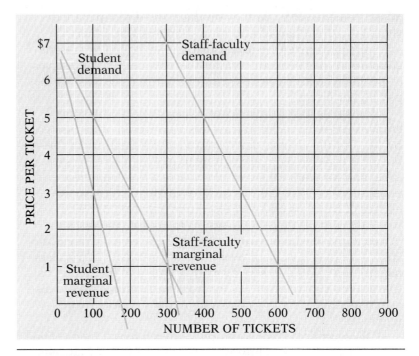

FIGURE 9F   Weekly demand for tickets to films

prices. Staff and faculty members who want to see the films are less likely to change their minds because of a modest price increase. It might be that Ed could do better by lowering the price he charges students and raising the price to staff and faculty.

Recall that when marginal cost was zero, Ed maximized net revenue by charging $5 per ticket and selling 500 tickets. Now he wants to set marginal revenue equal to marginal cost *for each group separately.*

Marginal revenue from sales to the students equals zero (marginal cost) at 175 tickets. To sell 175 tickets to students, Ed should charge them $3.50.

Marginal revenue from sales to staff and faculty equals zero at 325 tickets. To sell that number to staff and faculty, Ed should charge them $6.50.

He'll still be selling 500 tickets. But his total revenue will now be $2725 rather than $2500, and his net revenue will increase from $300 to $525.

Why did it work? It worked because the student demand for tickets was much more elastic than was the staff and faculty demand at the common price of $5. By lowering the price to the students, who are more responsive to price changes, and raising the price to staff and faculty members, who are less responsive, Ed does a more effective job of extracting from each group what it's willing to pay.

Note carefully, however, that the entire scheme is crucially dependent on Ed's ability to identify members of each group and prevent them from reselling tickets. It won't do to let students buy tickets for $3.50 and then sell them to members of the staff or faculty. Ed's price-discrimination system would probably work because he could, at low cost, print the tickets in different colors and require that official college I.D. cards be shown when the tickets are presented at the door.

RESENTMENT AND RATIONALE

Of course, Ed would also have to justify his "exploitation" of staff and faculty. That's not likely to be a problem in this case. He could say that $6.50 is what each ticket "really" costs and that the $3.50 price to students is the result of a special subsidy to promote liberal education. Don't underestimate the importance of "justification." Price discrimination of this type increases Ed's net revenue and doesn't compel anyone to pay more than they're willing to pay. But it can arouse fierce indignation on the part of those who aren't offered the discount prices.

As an example, consider the bitter complaints of all those cross-country air travelers who found a few years ago that they had to pay more per mile than people flying between Los Angeles and New York. Why should a round-trip ticket from Chicago to New York, for example, cost more than a similar ticket from Los Angeles to New York, especially when Chicago is so much closer to New York? The explanation was the fierce competition among the numerous carriers operating between the nation's two largest cities. This competition created excellent substitutes for any one airline's tickets, made the demand curve that each airline faced very elastic, and kept prices close to marginal cost. To Chicago-New York travelers, however, it looked as if they were subsidizing Los Angeles–New York passengers, and they didn't like it.

LUNCH AND DINNER PRICES

Everything we've been talking about is nicely illustrated in the common restaurant practice of charging more for the same food in the evening than at lunch.

Why do restaurants catering to both a luncheon and a dinner trade mark up their prices so much more on dinners than on lunches? The theory we've presented looks for the answer in different elasticities of demand. Lunch customers as a class are much more responsive to price increases or decreases than are dinner customers. A 10 percent increase in the price of a luncheon entrée will often lose the restaurant more customers than would a 30 percent increase in the price of the same item on the dinner menu. There are several reasons for this.

One is the fact that lunch customers eat out so much more frequently. People who buy lunch five times a week have many opportunities to gather information on relative prices. And because 50 cents less or more adds up over the course of a month, they have a strong incentive to shop around for the best deal, to stick to it when they think they've found it, and to shift when something better comes along. A dinner out, by contrast, is a much more rare event for most people; they have, as a consequence, less opportunity and less incentive to gather information on relative prices.

Another major reason for the lower price elasticity of demand among dinner patrons is the fact that what they pay for their food is typically only a fraction of what they are paying for the entire event or experience of "dinner out." A couple going out for dinner may pay $10 for a babysitter, $3 for parking, and $15 for cocktails or wine. If they pay $14 each for their dinners, the food is only half of their costs for the evening. And so a 40 percent hike in the menu price comes through to them as only a 20 percent increase in the cost of their evening out.

We should therefore expect to see restaurant managers following low-markup policies at lunch and high-markup policies at dinner. To reduce the chance of indignation and resentment, they will do a little more than merely raise the price of the London broil from $8 at lunch to $14 at dinner. They will also offer the dinner patron both soup *and* salad (the luncheon customers must choose one or the other) and perhaps include coffee in the price of the dinner (but not the lunch). A $6 increase is thus "justified" by an increase in marginal food cost of perhaps 40 cents. The real reason for the different markups, however, is found in the different elasticities of demand characteristic of luncheon and dinner patrons.

Those who automatically condemn all instances of price discrimination might want to take a broader look at the practice. Successful discrimination increases the wealth of sellers, of course; that's why they do it. But it also increases the wealth or well-being of those buyers who can obtain, as a result of price discrimination, goods that would not otherwise be available to them. Price discrimination eliminates some of the "waste" that occurs when A and B cannot arrange a transaction despite the fact that A wants what B has to offer and is more than willing to pay B's cost of supplying it.

You can legitimately view price discrimination as a form of cooperation between sellers and buyers, cooperation that only occurs, of course, when the transaction costs are sufficiently low. In the case of price discrimination, those costs are principally the costs of distinguishing among different demanders, preventing them from exchanging among themselves, and controlling any resentment that might prompt potential buyers to take their business somewhere else. If it were not for transaction costs, we would observe far more price discrimination than we actually do.

COST PLUS MARKUP RECONSIDERED

So how do price searchers find what they're looking for? By (1) estimating the marginal cost and marginal revenue, (2) determining the level of output that will enable them to sell all those units of output and only those units for which marginal revenue is greater than marginal cost, and (3) setting their price or prices so that they can just manage to sell the output produced. That sounds complicated, and it is. The logic is simple enough. But the estimates of marginal cost and especially the estimates of demand and marginal revenue are hard to make accurately. That's why price searchers are called "searchers." And why they could sometimes be called price "gropers."

The complexity and uncertainty of the price searcher's task help explain the popularity of the cost-plus-markup theory. Every search has to begin somewhere. Why not begin with the wholesale cost of an item plus a percentage markup adequate to cover overhead costs and yield a reasonable profit? If costs increase, why not assume that competitors' costs have also increased and try passing the higher cost on to customers? Why not begin with the assumption that the future will be like the past and that the procedures which have previously yielded good results will continue to do so? In that case, one would try to increase prices roughly in proportion to any cost increases experienced, and one would expect eventually to be forced by competition to lower one's prices roughly in proportion to any lowering of costs.

The cost-plus-markup procedure is in general a rule of thumb for price searchers, offering a place from which to begin looking, a first approximation in the continuing search for an elusive and shifting target. But price searchers engage in cost-plus-markup pricing only as a search technique and only until they discover they are making a mistake. The marginal-cost/marginal-revenue analysis of this chapter explains how price searchers recognize mistakes and what criteria they use in moving from rules of thumb and first approximations toward the most profitable pricing policy.

ONCE OVER LIGHTLY

Price searchers are looking for pricing structures that will enable them to sell all units for which marginal revenue exceeds marginal cost.

The popularity of the cost-plus-markup theory of pricing rests on its usefulness as a search technique and the fact that people often cannot correctly explain processes in which they regularly and successfully engage.

A crucial factor for the price searcher is the ability or inability to discriminate: to charge high prices for units that are in high demand and low prices for units that would not otherwise be purchased, without allowing the sales at lower prices to "spoil the market" for high-price sales.

A rule for successful price searching often quoted by economists is: Set marginal revenue equal to marginal cost. This means: Continue selling as long as the additional revenue from a sale exceeds the additional cost. Skillful price searchers are people who know this rule (even when they don't fully realize they're using it) and who also have a knack for distinguishing the relevant marginal possibilities. The possibilities are endless, which helps to make price theory a fascinating exploration for people with a penchant for puzzle solving.

Sellers in the real world don't have precisely defined demand curves from which they can derive marginal-revenue curves to compare with marginal-cost curves. Working with such curves is nonetheless good exercise for a student who wants to begin thinking systematically about the ways in which competition affects the choices people make and the choices they confront.

QUESTIONS FOR DISCUSSION

1. The rule for maximizing net revenue (total revenue minus total cost) is: Take any action if, but only if, the expected marginal revenue exceeds the expected marginal cost. What is marginal revenue? How is it related to

demand? You can test your grasp of this key concept by examining the case of Maureen Supplize, who runs a yacht dealership. She has five potential customers, and she knows how much each would be willing to pay for one of her yachts.

J.P. Morgan	$13 million
J.D. Rockefeller	11 million
J.R. Ewing	9 million
J.C. Penney	7 million
J.P. Kennedy	5 million

(a) Fill in the blanks in the second column on the next page to complete the demand schedule implied by these data.

(b) Fill in the blanks in the third column to show Maureen's total receipts from yacht sales at the various prices listed.

(c) Fill in the blanks in the fourth column to show the extra revenue obtained by Maureen from each additional yacht she manages to sell when she lowers her selling price.

(d) How many yachts will she want to sell if her goal is to maximize *total* revenue? (Don't start thinking yet about selling to different people at different prices. We'll take that up later. Assume for now that she can't get away with charging one buyer more than another.) What price will she want to set?

(e) Now assume that her goal is to maximize *net* revenue and that the marginal cost to her of selling a yacht is $6 million. In other words, each additional yacht she sells adds $6 million to her total costs. How many yachts will she now want to sell? What price will she want to set?

(f) If you have proceeded correctly, you should now be able to experience something of Maureen's frustration. Ewing and Penney are both willing to pay more for a yacht than it costs Maureen to sell one to them. Yet she can't sell to either without reducing her net revenue. Why?

(g) Suppose now that none of her customers is acquainted with any of the others and that she can consequently get away with charging each one the maximum he is willing to pay. Under such an arrangement, which we shall call "perfect" price discrimination, what is Maureen's marginal-revenue schedule? Fill in the blanks in the fifth column.

(h) How many yachts will Maureen now want to sell?

(i) Fill in her *total* revenue schedule under "perfect" price discrimination.

2. "A price searcher should set marginal revenue as far above marginal cost as possible." Explain why this statement is wrong. What is being erro-

Price of Yacht	Quantity Demanded	Total Revenue	Marginal Revenue	Under Perfect Price Discrimination	
				Marginal Revenue	Total Revenue
$13 million	___	$ ___	$ ___	$ ___	$ ___
11	___	___	___	___	___
9	___	___	___	___	___
7	___	___	___	___	___
5	___	___	___	___	___

neously assumed by someone who thinks that net receipts will be zero at an output where marginal revenue equals marginal cost?

3. Locate the most profitable uniform price for sellers to set in each of the situations graphed in Figure 9G and the quantity they will want to produce and sell. Then shade the area that represents the net income from that pricing policy. What will happen to net income in each case if the price is raised? If it's lowered? (Caution: What happens if a seller whose marginal-revenue curve is the same as the demand curve raises the price?)

4. The marginal-cost curves of the Anchorage Aardvark Breeding Company and the Houston Aardvark Breeding Company are identical, but the demand curves they face differ, as shown in Figure 9H.

   (a) What price will each firm want to set?
   (b) Suppose something happens to raise marginal cost for each firm to $20 while nothing else changes. What price will each now set?

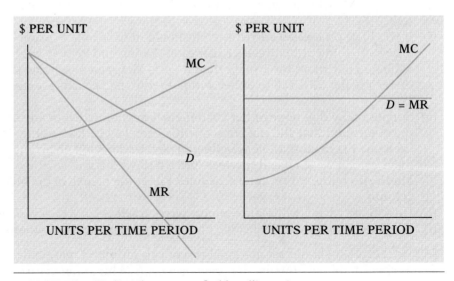

FIGURE 9G   Finding the most profitable selling price

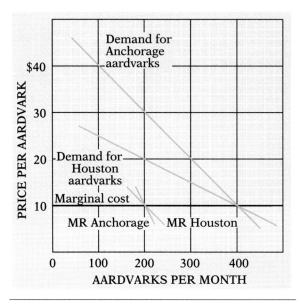

FIGURE 9H   Marginal cost and demand curves for two companies

(c) What is the relationship between clasticity of demand and the profit-maximizing percentage markup?

5. Have you ever wondered why otherwise identical books usually sell for so much more in hardcover than in softcover editions?

   (a) Is it because publishers must pay so much more to produce books with hardcovers?

   (b) Some potential buyers will have a strong preference for a hardcover edition. They include libraries, purchasers who intend to use the book intensively, and people looking for gift items. Would you expect the price elasticity of demand at any particular price to be greater or less for the hardcover than for the softcover edition?

   (c) Figure 9I shows the marginal cost to a publisher of producing and selling hardcover and softcover editions of a particular book and the demand curve for each edition. What prices will the publisher want to set? How much of this reflects cost differences?

6. The graph in Figure 9J presents the daily demand for round-trip tickets on Transcontinental Airlines' flights between St. Louis and New York City and between Los Angeles and New York City. Assume that the cost to Transcontinental of carrying an additional passenger is $25 one way, for a round-trip marginal cost of $50.

   (a) What specific expenses would enter into Transcontinental's marginal cost (of selling an additional round-trip ticket)?

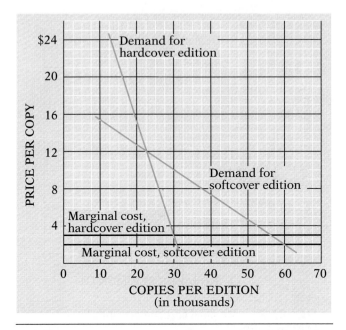

FIGURE 9I   **Marginal cost and demand curves for a book publisher**

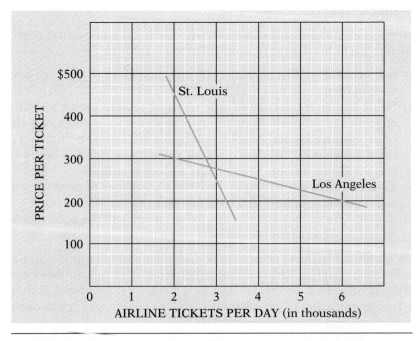

FIGURE 9J   **Airline tickets between St. Louis–NYC and Los Angeles–NYC**

(b) Construct the marginal-revenue curves that correspond to each of the demand curves shown, using the technique described in Figure 9E.

(c) How many tickets of each kind would Transcontinental want to sell to maximize its net revenue?

(d) What price would it want to set on each route?

(e) Are St. Louis customers subsidizing Los Angeles customers? What price would Transcontinental want to set for its St. Louis flights if it terminated its Los Angeles operation? For its Los Angeles flights if it terminated its St. Louis operation? Are St. Louis prices higher *because* Los Angeles prices are lower?

(f) Are St. Louis prices perhaps *lower* because of Transcontinental's Los Angeles operation? Since Transcontinental is adding to its net revenue by flying Los Angeles passengers, it could well be the case that the Los Angeles operation is enabling it to stay in business. How would this contribute to lower prices for St. Louis customers?

7. Many firms use a technique called *target pricing* in trying to decide what prices to set for new products they're introducing. The target price is a price that enables the firm to recover a certain percentage of the product's development and production costs. What, in addition to costs, must the seller know in order to calculate the return a particular price will yield? If earnings from the sale of the product turn out to fall short of the target, should the firm raise the price? If earnings exceed the firm's expectations, should it lower the price?

8. How should the British and French manufacturers of the Concorde supersonic commercial airliner take account of the plane's development costs in determining the prices to charge airline companies? Should they suspend production if they can't obtain a price that will cover development costs?

9. When the university's athletic director announces that football ticket prices are being raised for next year, he is likely to say this unfortunate step has been made necessary by rising costs—perhaps the rising cost of the women's sports program. How does the cost of the women's sports program affect the marginal cost of selling a football ticket? If you are unable to think of any answer to that question, ask yourself how the prospect of a winning season affects the cost of selling a football ticket. Which plays a larger role in determining the most profitable price at which to sell football tickets: the athletic department's budget for women's sports or an excellent team?

10. On the day of home football games, the University of Washington raises the price of parking on some of its lots from $1.50 to $10 per vehicle. This is done, according to the Committee on Transportation, so that regular parking users do not subsidize the cost of providing parking for football fans. Would regular users be subsidizing football parkers if the rate stayed at $1.50 on football Saturdays?

11. Are advertising costs capable of affecting the net-revenue-maximizing price for the product advertised?

   (a) Do beer drinkers have to pay more for the beer they drink because the brewery pays a huge sum of money to advertise it on national television?
   (b) When a breakfast-food company pays a celebrity athlete a million dollars for the right to put his picture on the cereal box, will this lead to an increase in the price of the cereal?

12. Can an oil company raise the price of its gasoline to cover the costs of a huge oil spill for which it is liable? What would happen if Exxon, for example, raised the refinery price of gasoline at a time when other refiners were not raising their prices?

13. Do small convenience stores charge higher prices (on average) than large supermarkets charge because the small stores have higher overhead costs per unit of sales? How can a seller induce customers to pay a higher price for a product than they would have to pay elsewhere?

14. Can hog owners raise the prices at which they sell when feed costs go up?

   (a) A rise in the price of hog feed increases the cost to hog farmers of continuing to feed the hogs they have. What is the alternative to continuing to feed and fatten hogs? Why might an increase in the price of hog feed lead to a short-run decline in the price of hogs?
   (b) By what process will an increase in the price of hog feed eventually produce an increase in the price of hogs?

15. In 1985 Missouri began assessing commercial property for tax purposes at a higher percentage of "fair market value" than residential property. For purposes of this reassessment, apartment buildings of 5 or more units were classified as commercial property; property taxes on such buildings increased sharply, while taxes on apartment buildings with 4 units or fewer did not change.

   (a) Would you expect this change to increase the rents paid by people living in large apartment buildings relative to the rents paid by tenants in buildings with fewer than 5 units? Does the tax increase affect either the marginal cost to the landlord of renting or the demand for apartments on the part of tenants?
   (b) What effect do you think this tax change will have on the average size of apartment units in existing buildings? What effect will it have on the average size of apartment buildings constructed in the future?
   (c) What effect would you predict from this change in assessment methods on the demand for units in buildings of fewer than 5 units and hence on the rental rates tenants will pay for such units?

(d) The president of the St. Louis Apartment Association was quoted as saying that no apartment owners would pay those tax increases, but rather would pass them along in the form of rent increases. If owners can raise rents in this fashion after property taxes rise, why don't they raise them *before* the taxes rise and increase their income? If owners can pass on tax increases, why did some Missouri apartment owners go to the expense of filing a suit to overturn the reassessment?

16. One store sells Wilson Championship extra-duty felt optic-yellow tennis balls at $2.49 for a can of three. Another store in the same shopping center sells Wilson Championship extra-duty felt optic-yellow tennis balls at $1.99 for a can of three. How is this possible? Why would anyone buy balls from the first store? Why do you think we repeated the long description in the second sentence instead of just saying "identical tennis balls"?

17. Why do camera retailers so often sell the cameras themselves at prices very close to their own wholesale cost, while marking up the price of accessories (carrying cases, lens cleaner, filters, and so on) by 100 percent or more?

18. Some Manhattan restaurants have experimented with using two breakfast menus. One, with higher printed prices, is handed to entering customers who look like tourists. The other menu, with lower prices, is given to customers in business clothing who look like people on their way to work. How might this two-menu policy raise net revenue for the restaurants using it?

19. A *Wall Street Journal* story (July 25, 1980) reports that tourists in China are charged more than double the price that Chinese pay for movies, taxicabs, and airline or train tickets, and that many manufactured items offered for sale in "friendship" stores can actually be purchased for half as much in retail stores in Hong Kong. Can you explain this?

    The Chinese also charge foreign diplomats very high prices for apartments, but often charge lower "friendship" rents to representatives from poor Third World nations. Do the lower rents charged Third World diplomats represent a foreign-policy decision or an attempt to maximize net revenue?

20. Professional sports teams used to sponsor "Ladies' Days," occasions on which women were admitted at reduced prices. Was this a case of discrimination against males, since the teams never had a "Gentlemen's Day"? How would you explain "Ladies' Day"?

21. In a city where most movie theaters charge $5 or more for admission, a few movie theaters, called discount movie houses, may charge as little as $1 or $2 for admission. The discount theaters will often show the same movies as the more expensive theaters, but a few months later.

    (a) Do the first-run movie houses have higher costs that necessitate their higher prices?

(b) The studios that provide the movies often charge as much as 90% of the box-office revenue in the first week or two after a major movie has been released, but the percentage then drops steadily. The studio take may be as low as 35% by the time a movie reaches discount houses. Can this fact account for the difference in ticket prices?

(c) Why are the studios able to extract 90% of the gross ticket revenue from first-run movie houses but willing to let discount houses show their films for only 35% of gross?

(d) Movie theaters usually net about 75 cents out of every dollar spent on refreshments. How does this help explain why theaters are willing to give up 90% of their ticket revenue to obtain a first-run showing of a "blockbuster"? (Does this fact make you at all skeptical about signs that prohibit movie goers from bringing food or drink in from outside "for the safety and comfort of our patrons"?)

(e) If studios raise the price they charge discount houses to $1 per ticket or 35% of ticket revenue, whichever is greater, by how much would you expect a discount house currently charging $1 to raise its price?

22. Some theaters presenting live drama have begun experimenting with "Pay-What-You-Can" pricing for certain performances. A theater in San Diego adopted this policy for one Saturday matinee per production. Normal ticket prices run from $18 to $28. Payments for the special matinees ranged from 25 cents to $18.

(a) How do these theaters prevent *everyone* from taking advantage of the lower prices?

(b) Why would anyone pay $18 for a ticket that they could have purchased for 25 cents?

(c) Do you believe that people will really pay what they *can* under such a system? Do you think that wealthier people will on average pay more than poorer people?

(d) Many theaters sell steeply discounted tickets on the day of the performance. How do they keep all their patrons from waiting until the day of the performance to purchase tickets?

23. New York City has an ordinance requiring retailers to post prices for items they sell. In 1988 the Department of Consumer Affairs began to enforce the ordinance against art galleries. Many gallery owners protested vehemently. Why?

24. An August 1981 newspaper story reported what it called "a mystery." Representatives of the manufacturer and the regional distributor of Head skis tried to buy the entire stock of their own skis being offered for sale at very low prices by a chain of discount stores. At one store the purchasers immediately went outside and broke all the skis in the store parking lot. Can you explain this mystery?

Does the following information provide any clues? The manager of a sporting goods store that regularly carries Head skis said the action was an attempt by the distributor to get defective skis off the market. An executive with the discount store said the skis were not defective but were a standard production model originally destined for shipment out of the country. What were the manufacturer and distributor trying to do and what went wrong?

25. Advice columnist Ann Landers has several times attacked in her column a practice engaged in by some clothing retailers. They will slash or tear items they have been unable to sell and throw them away rather than give them to employees or low-income people. Ann was puzzled by this behavior. The only plausible explanation she could think of was one suggested by a Nebraska reader: Stores are trying to protect themselves against people who will obtain such merchandise at no charge and then bring it back to the store for credit. Can you give her a much more plausible explanation?

26. Would telephone companies earn larger or smaller net revenues if they charged for local service on the basis of the number of calls made? Draw the demand curve of a "typical" customer and compare the possibilities. How well could the phone company do by setting the net-revenue-maximizing price for individual calls? How well could it do by charging the maximum amount a customer is willing to pay rather than do without phone service and then giving customers an unlimited number of "free" local calls? Why is it, do you suppose, that local calls are typically "free" for residential customers while they must pay extra for each long-distance call?

27. The National Collegiate Athletic Association has a rule that sponsors of post-season "bowl" games must pay a minimum of $500,000 to the colleges supplying the football teams. Sometimes the bowl bid will be contingent on the college's willingness to purchase a large number of tickets to the bowl game.

(a) How much is a college actually being paid for a bowl appearance if it receives $500,000 but obtains the invitation on the condition that it purchase 10,000 twenty-dollar tickets?

(b) Will a college consent to such an arrangement if it knows it cannot hope to sell more than a hundred or so of the tickets to its fans?

28. The discussion of lunch and dinner prices at the end of the chapter may be leaving out something important. Dinner patrons almost always take more time to eat than do lunch patrons. Doesn't this raise the cost of providing dinner? Under what circumstances would it *not* raise the cost? If lingering over a meal is costly to restaurants, they will presumably try to prevent or limit it. How might they do this without irritating customers? Will restaurants ever want to *encourage* lingering? How might they do this?

29. In 1980 Heublein Inc. raised the price of its Popov brand vodka by 8 percent in what it called a move to "reposition" the brand. Sales fell only 1 percent in response to the 8 percent price increase.

   (a) Since vodka is colorless, odorless, and tasteless, why do you suppose consumers are willing to pay substantially more for some brands of vodka?
   (b) What do you suppose Heublein was trying to do when it "repositioned" its Popov brand?
   (c) Marketing people refer to certain goods that are kept on display as "ego-sensitive" merchandise and point out that consumers show a preference for higher prices when it comes to ego-sensitive goods. Does that mean that sellers of such goods can always earn more by raising prices?

30. Suppose you're willing to pay 60 cents for one doughnut with your morning coffee and 30 cents for a second doughnut. The owner of the doughnut shop knows this and also knows that his cost of selling an additional doughnut is 20 cents. Should he charge you 60 cents or 30 cents if he wants to maximize his net revenue? How about 60 cents and two for 90 cents?

31. Why will sellers make offers like this one? "Buy two giant pizzas at regular price and get a third one for only a dollar."

32. If a surgeon charges $1500 to remove the gallbladder of a wealthy patient and $500 to remove another patient's gallbladder, is she exploiting the first patient or giving a discount to the second? How does she prevent the second patient from buying several operations at the lower price and re-selling them for a profit to wealthy patients?

33. You want to sell at auction an antique dining-room suite. There are three people who want it, and they're willing to pay $8000, $6000, and $4000, respectively. Your reservation price (the price above which the bidding must go before you sell) is $5000. No one in the room has any information about the value of the suite to anyone else.

   (a) At about what price will the suite be sold?
   (b) Suppose you run a Dutch auction. The auctioneer announces a price well above what anyone would be willing to pay and then gradually lowers the price until a bid is received. At about what price will the suite be sold?
   (c) Why do stores sometimes add to their advertisements: "Available only while supplies last"?

34. You and your fiancé are shopping for wedding rings. After showing you a sample of his wares, the jeweler asks, "What price did you have in mind?"

   (a) Why does he ask this question?

(b) If you tell him you don't plan to spend more than $200 on each ring, are you helping him find the rings to sell you or the price to charge for the rings you prefer?

(c) What might be a good technique for finding out the lowest price at which the jeweler is willing to sell the rings you like?

35. Let the graph in Figure 9K portray the demand for tickets to a college football game. Your task is to construct on the graph the corresponding marginal-revenue curve, using the assumption that all tickets have to be sold at the same price.

(a) Before beginning: What would the marginal-revenue curve look like if the athletic department could get away with selling to each fan at the top price each one is willing to pay?

(b) Here we go. What would total revenue be if the price was set at $32? At $28? How many *additional* tickets would be sold by lowering the price from $32 to $28? So how much additional revenue is gained per extra ticket sold by lowering the price from $32 to $28? Call this "marginal revenue" and plot it at 25,000: the additional revenue per ticket as sales expand from 20,000 to 30,000. Run through the same process between $24 and $20. What is total revenue at $24? At $20? What is the additional revenue per ticket sold between 40,000 and 50,000? Plot this value at 45,000.

(c) Now connect these two points with a straight line and you will have constructed the marginal-revenue curve corresponding to the de-mand–when we assume that all tickets must be sold at a single price.

(d) That was time consuming. Take a close look at Figure 9E in the text and use this gimmick to construct the marginal-revenue curve. If you don't get an identical result, you made a mistake somewhere.

36. Use the graph on which you worked in Discussion Question 35 to do some price searching.

(a) The marginal cost of selling addditional tickets is for all practical purposes zero. (Do you see why? None of the costs of putting on the game are affected by a decision to sell more tickets.) So what price should the college set if it wants to maximize net revenue? How many tickets will be sold?

(b) Suppose the Town Council levies a tax of $4 on each ticket sold, to cover congestion costs. What price will the college now want to set? How many tickets will be sold?

(c) Assume the stadium seats 65,000. How many empty seats will there be at the game if there is no tax? If the tax of $4 is imposed?

(d) Suppose the college knows that all the fans willing to pay $12 or more are nonstudents. It also knows that the demand of the students would be shown by a straight line running from zero tickets de-manded at $12 to 30,000 demanded at a zero price. How might the

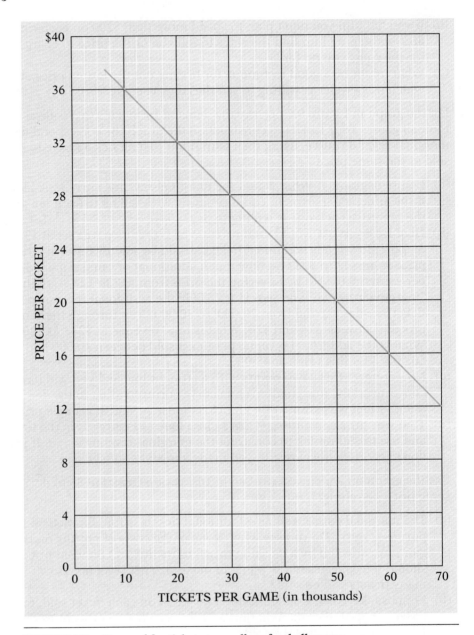

FIGURE 9K   Demand for tickets to a college football game

college fill those empty seats and make everyone happy? Draw the student demand curve and the corresponding marginal-revenue curve. Assuming that the college can costlessly distinguish students from nonstudents, what prices will it want to set for each group? How many tickets will it sell to each group?

COMPETITION AND GOVERNMENT POLICY

Will economic competition disappear unless the government has an active program to preserve it? Or does competition preserve itself, sometimes in the face of diligent efforts by the government to restrict it?

Is the government promoting competition when it prevents larger, more efficient, or perhaps more unscrupulous firms from driving other firms out of business? Or does the protection of competitors entail the suppression of competition?

When the government prohibits mergers, is it preventing competitors from eliminating rivals? Or is it stifling the development of more competitive and efficient organizational forms?

What do we mean by competition and how are we to decide whether the economy or some sector of it is adequately competitive? Is competition in an industry to be measured by the number of competitors, by the practices in which they engage, or by the behavior of prices, costs, and profits and the industry's record with respect to innovation?

Those questions will not be answered conclusively in this chapter. But we hope that, when you've finished thinking about the sources and consequences of competition as well as the origins and effects of government policies, you will have a better sense of what the issues are.

THE PRESSURES OF COMPETITION

All sellers facing demand curves that are less than perfectly elastic—tilted downward to the right rather than horizontal—will maximize net revenue by restricting sales or output and keeping the selling price above marginal cost. (Unless they can practice "perfect" price discrimination.) How and why that occurs was the theme of the preceding chapter.

One problem from the seller's viewpoint with prices higher than marginal cost is that they are a standing invitation to competition. If a piece of apple pie that costs the cafeteria owner 30 cents is selling for 90 cents, the owner is likely to insist that the 60-cent difference isn't profit; it's only a contribution toward meeting all the other costs of running the cafeteria: labor, taxes, rent, equipment maintenance, breakage, theft, and so on. That may be completely true. Nonetheless, each additional piece of pie that is sold for 90 cents contributes a net 60 cents toward the owner's wealth. If the same is true for all the other cafés and cafeterias in town, each owner will be earnestly wishing that more hungry people would abandon the other eating places and buy their apple pie from him.

Wishes like this often prompt action. Pie prices might be slightly reduced after 3 P.M. to induce some afternoon coffee-break customers to allow themselves a little treat. Or a sign could be put up after 3 P.M. announcing free coffee with pie purchases. There are dangers inherent in this strategy. Some lunch customers may simply postpone their dessert at noon and have it at three when it's cheaper. And competing restaurants may undermine the promotional effort by offering their own inducements, so that instead of capturing additional customers each owner ends up selling only as much pie as previously but at lower prices.

We assumed in the last chapter that Ed Sike and some of the other sellers whose policies we were examining somehow knew exactly what the demand was for their product. That assumption was useful in enabling us to present the logic of the simple price-searching process. In reality, of course, sellers must usually probe for information on the demand for their product and try to stimulate and maintain it by advertising and by offering reliable service. Moreover, when there are several sellers of a product in the market, each seller's demand curve is going to depend on the policies, including the price policies, of those competing sellers. The demand for Ed Sike's film series will shift downward to the left if neighboring theaters show better movies or cut their prices, or if sororities and fraternities pick Friday night to sponsor parties, or if the college basketball team plays home games on Friday nights and hits a winning streak.

The price that any one cafeteria in the downtown area sets for apple pie will affect the demand (curve or schedule) for apple pie at other restaurants. Since each of the restaurants will be using estimates of its own demand to set prices that will, in turn, affect the demand all other restaurants encounter, we have a situation more closely resembling chess or poker than a technical maximization problem. The best price for anyone to set *next* may depend on the price set *last,* as in a game of chess. The neat little world of Chapter 9, with its clearly defined curves, becomes blurry. Unfortunately from an analytic standpoint, though perhaps fortunately from an aesthetic one, the real world is not as neatly outlined as the pages in a coloring book.

Chapter 8 introduced the word *oligopoly,* meaning "few sellers." We decided there that the concept of a few sellers shared all the ambiguities of the concept of a single seller, ambiguities inherent in the problem of deciding just how broadly or narrowly to define the commodity being sold. Some economists have retained the slippery word oligopoly and have assigned it a very special meaning: a situation in which the demand curve of one seller depends on the reactions of identifiable other sellers, sometimes called *rivals.* Whether or not we choose to call this oligopoly—the usage is certainly misleading—situations of that sort, where the demand curves of different sellers are significantly interdependent, are obviously both common and important. It all adds to the competitive pressures of which sellers so commonly complain.

CONTROLLING COMPETITION

Then why don't sellers agree not to compete, or to compete less, or to share the market among themselves in some mutually satisfactory way? The answer is that they would very much like to do so and often try, but it isn't as easy as it might seem at first. Just as transaction costs often prevent suppliers and demanders from cooperating effectively, so they frequently prevent suppliers from getting together to take advantage of demanders. To begin with, agreements between competing sellers to maintain prices and share markets are usually unenforceable in court and are, moreover, illegal under the laws of many states and under federal law where it is applicable. That fact alone substantially raises the transaction costs of arranging an agreement not to compete. In addition, it's very difficult to devise agreements that everyone will accept, that will cover all the major possibilities, and that can be enforced without the aid of the courts. The incentives to compete are so persistent that soon one or another party will find an excuse to circumvent the agreement or, lacking an acceptable excuse, will circumvent it secretly. On top of all this, successful collusion by the members of a cartel[1] will attract the attention of outsiders, who will begin trying to enter the business in order to enjoy some of the profits that collusion has created.

Cartels consequently reveal a fragility that often surprises people who don't realize on how many margins competition can occur. To be successful in increasing the wealth of its members, a cartel must solve two problems. It must first prevent competition among its own members from dissipating the profits of collusion, whether through a fall in actual selling prices or a rise in selling costs. And then the cartel must find some way to keep new competitors from spoiling the whole operation by trying to enter the act.

That is why price searchers and even price takers yearn so ardently for *legal* restrictions on competition. Sellers are sometimes extraordinarily imaginative in devising reasons why the government ought to outlaw price cutting or prevent new sellers from entering the market. Here are a few actual items culled from a number of newspapers, with identities sometimes altered slightly to protect the guilty. It's a very good idea to ask in each case exactly who stands to gain and who is most likely to lose.

> The Washington, DC, Medical Society launched a major lobbying campaign over the weekend against proposed legislation that would encourage granting of hospital privileges to qualified nurse midwives, psychologists, podiatrists, and other nonphysician health professionals. The medical society envisioned erosion of standards, speculating in its newsletter that "pretty soon a boy scout with a rusty knife will be permitted to perform brain surgery."

> All plumbers must spend a minimum of 140 hours a year for five years learning higher mathematics, physics, hydraulics, and isometric drawing.

> Woolen makers are arguing that since woolen worsted fabric is essential to national defense, the government should impose quotas on imports from abroad.

[1] A cartel is an agreement among a group of sellers to regulate prices or output. There are also buyers' cartels, such as the owners of professional basketball teams mentioned in Chapter 3 who want a single league to keep down the cost of hiring players.

The deregulation of cosmetologists and barbers would put consumers in our state at the mercy of professionally uneducated and governmentally unregulated hairdressers and barbers. This is extremely irresponsible, because hairdressers today utilize extremely hazardous acids and alkalines in the course of their everyday work.

The prominent owner of a local television sales and service center said today that he welcomed the state's investigation of the television repair business and he demanded regulation of the industry. "We must eliminate janitors, firefighters, messengers, and similar amateurs who defraud the public by providing poor-quality service at cut-rate prices," he argued.

The Senate Public Health Committee yesterday rejected a bill to allow use of multiple offices and trade names in the diagnosis of eye problems and fitting glasses. Single-office optometrists contend that optometrists who have private offices are in effect employed by their patients. If optometrists work under a trade name, their boss is their company.

The owner of the Piney Woods Nursing Home and secretary of the State Association of Licensed Nursing Homes accused the state health department last night of approving new nursing-home construction without proper investigation of the need for additional facilities or the qualifications of the applicants. "Unqualified people, including speculators from other parts of the country, are hoping to reap big profits," he said. "A great surplus of beds will bring about cutthroat competition, which means nursing homes will have to curtail many needed services, resulting in lower standards detrimental to patients and the community."

Some state officials are so adamant that dogs' teeth should be cleaned only by licensed veterinarians that they sent in an undercover pooch a couple of months ago to break up what they considered an illegal dog-tooth-cleaning operation. The executive director of the state's Board of Examiners in Veterinary Medicine said that groomers who invade a dog's gums are practicing medicine and might cause the dog unnecessary pain. [Do you think people with their hand in a dog's mouth are likely to cause the dog unnecessary pain?]

THE AMBIVALENCE OF GOVERNMENT POLICIES

An old proverb wisely asserts that the wolf should not be sent to guard the sheep. Should the government be relied on to preserve competition in the economy? The history of government intervention in economic life reveals a pattern of concern for the special interests of competitors at least as strong as concern for competition. And the two are not identical, even though our rhetoric so often and easily uses them interchangeably.

The cases cited above show government taking or being urged to take a variety of actions designed to prevent potential sellers from offering more favorable terms or more attractive opportunities to buyers. These actions constitute restrictions on competition, regardless of the arguments used to defend them. The ultimate effect of a particular restriction on competition might be to preserve competition, by protecting a substantial number of competitors who would otherwise be forced out of business. But whether or not that is the long-term effect in certain cases, it is important to begin any evaluation of government policy toward competition by acknowledging one principle: *A law that restricts competitors restricts competition.*

One extremely common justification for such laws is that they preserve competition by preventing "predatory" practices.

SELLING BELOW COST

Do you agree with the following paragraph?

"In order to preserve our competitive economic system, we need laws that prohibit unfair practices such as sales below cost. Large firms can often afford to sell products below cost until their rivals are driven out of business. If they are not restrained by law, we could easily wind up with an economy dominated by just a few huge corporations."

Most Americans apparently accept this argument. For our laws, at the federal, state, and local level, abound with provisions designed to prevent or inhibit price cutting. Many states have statutes prohibiting sales below cost, statutes that usually go by some such name as Unfair Practices Act. And regulatory commissions, ostensibly created to hold down the prices that may be charged by public utilities, often wind up enforcing minimum rather than maximum rates. This is true, for example, of the grandfather of all such commissions in the United States, the Interstate Commerce Commission (created by Congress in 1887).

It's fairly obvious why some business firms would approve that kind of legislation: They want protection against competition. But why do consumers and the general public go along? The public seems to have accepted the argument that price cutting can create "monopolies" by driving competitors out of business. And monopolies, of course, are Bad Things.

The paragraph with which this section began states the essential argument. How valid is it? Is it possible to construct a defensible case for laws that prohibit "sales below cost"? A lot of questions should immediately arise in your mind.

WHAT IS THE APPROPRIATE COST?

What is the cost below which prices should not be set? Does anyone actually sell below cost? Why would anyone interested in increasing his wealth ever want to?

Case: Matilda Mudge, proprietor of the Thrifty Supermarket, orders 1000 pounds of ripe bananas. She gets them for 5 cents a pound, because the produce distributor is eager to move them before they become too ripe. Mudge advertises a weekend special on bananas: 10 cents a pound. But Monday morning finds her with 500 pounds of bananas, now beginning to turn brown. How low can Mudge cut her price without selling below cost? The answer is *not* 5 cents a pound. That is sunk cost and hence no cost at all. If Mudge will have to pay someone to haul the unsold bananas away on Tuesday morning, her cost on Monday could be less than zero. In that case it might be to her advantage to give the bananas away. If a zero price is to her advantage, how can it be "below cost"? (By the way, did Mudge *buy* the bananas below cost?)

Or suppose Mudge bought a truckload of coffee: 1000 one-pound cans for $750. It was an unknown brand on which a local distributor offered her an attractive price. But it turns out that her customers aren't interested. She cuts the price down to 80 cents a pound, but still can't move it successfully. Four weeks after her purchase she still has 987 cans of coffee cluttering her shelves and storage room. If she now cuts the price below 75 cents, is she selling below cost? She is not. She has no intention of replacing the cans she sells so each sale is that many additional cents in the till and one less can in the way. The relevant cost of a pound of coffee could well be zero. The relevant cost is, of course, the marginal cost.

Let's try a different kind of example and then return to Matilda Mudge. It might make sense to estimate the cost of producing a steer, but does it make any sense to estimate separately the cost of producing hindquarters and forequarters? Should the price of steaks, which come from the hindquarters of a beef carcass, cover the cost of producing the hindquarters, leaving it to pot-roast prices to cover the cost of the forequarters from which they derive? The question is nonsensical.

Unless it is possible to produce hindquarters separately from forequarters, one cannot speak of the cost of producing one and the cost of producing the other. Hindquarters and forequarters, or steaks and pot roasts, are joint products with joint costs. There is no way to determine the specific costs of joint products or to allocate joint costs "correctly."[2]

Back to Matilda Mudge. Can we legitimately segregate the costs of each item sold in her grocery store? Think of her frozen-food items, for example. How much of the cost of owning and operating the freezer case should be allocated to vegetables, how much to Chinese dinners, and how much to orange juice? It's true that she could not carry frozen cauliflower without a freezer case. But if she finds it profitable to own and operate a freezer case just for the sake of the frozen juices she can sell, and if she then has some extra room in which she decides to display boxes of frozen cauliflower, it might make sense for her to assign *none* of the freezer cost to the cauliflower.

A successful businesswoman (or businessman) is not concerned with questions of cost allocation that have no relevance to decisionmaking. She knows that production—and a merchant is a producer just as certainly as is a manufacturer—is usually a process with joint products and joint costs. The businesswoman is interested in the additional costs associated with a decision and the additional revenue to be expected from it, not in such meaningless problems as the allocation of joint costs to particular items for sale. If there is room for a magazine rack near the checkout counter, the question is: How much will its installation *add* to total costs and how much will it *add* to total revenue? If the latter is larger, the rack makes sense; and the magazines sold need not have a price that covers utilities, rent, depreciation on cash registers, *or even the wholesale prices of the magazines.*

Mark well the italicized phrase. It may be profitable to sell a morning newspaper for 35 cents even if it costs 40 cents to obtain it from the distributor. Why? Because availability of the newspaper may bring in new customers who add to net revenue through the purchases of other items. Matilda Mudge is interested not in the net revenue on any one item she sells but in the difference between total revenue and total costs. Hardware stores that sell odd-lot bolts, screws, and nuts lose

---

[2]If there are techniques for growing steers with relatively larger hindquarters than forequarters, or vice versa, then it may be possible partially to distinguish the costs under appropriate circumstances.

money on each sale but (or so their owners hope) more than make it up through the goodwill they thereby create.

"PREDATORS" AND COMPETITION

There would be little point in stressing all this were it not for the popular mythology of "selling below cost." Our argument suggests that many allegations of sales below cost are based on an arbitrary assignment of sunk costs or joint costs. Business firms often complain about below-cost sales, of course; but that is because they dislike competition and want government to protect them from its rigors by prohibiting price cutting.

But aren't there dangers to competition in allowing firms to cut prices as low as they wish? It is odd, but not really surprising, how often people identify the protection of competitors with the preservation of competition. In reality they are more like opposites. Competitors are usually protected by laws inhibiting competition, laws that benefit privileged producers by restricting consumers and nonprivileged producers. The hobgoblin hauled out to justify this is "predatory price cutting" backed up by a "long purse."

Predatory price cutting means reducing prices below cost in order to drive a rival out of business or prevent new rivals from emerging *with the intention of raising prices afterward to recoup all losses.* It is supposedly a favorite tactic of larger firms that can stand prolonged losses, or temporary losses on some lines, because of their larger financial resources—the so-called "long purse." Economic theory does not deny the possibility of predatory price cutting. But it does raise a long list of skeptical questions, headed by all the questions we have been discussing regarding the proper definition of an item's cost.

How long will it take for such a policy to accomplish its end? The longer it takes, the larger will be the short-run losses accepted by the predator firm and, consequently, the larger must be the long-term benefits if the policy is to justify itself.

What will happen to the physical assets and human resources of the firms forced out of business? That's an important question, because if those assets remain in existence, what is to prevent someone from bringing them back into production when the predator firm raises its prices to reap the rewards of its villainy? And if this occurs, how can the firm hope to benefit from its predatory policy? On the other hand, the human resources may scatter into alternative employments and be costly to reassemble.

Is it likely that the predatory firm will be able to destroy enough of its rivals to secure the degree of market power that it must have to make the long-run profits justify the short-run losses? Charges of predatory pricing have most frequently been leveled against large discount houses, drug chains, and grocery supermarkets. But these sellers are not pitted exclusively against small independent competitors: they must tangle with other large discount houses, other drug chains, and other supermarkets. Perhaps a grocery chain could cut its prices far enough and keep them low long enough to drive Matilda Mudge out of business, but that wouldn't work on other chains. And it isn't Matilda Mudge who keeps grocery chain executives awake at night.

We are not denying the possibility of predatory pricing in business. Well-documented examples are hard to find, but it is surely possible. Minimum-price laws, however, offer the *certainty* of higher prices in order to eliminate the *possibility* of higher prices: a case of accepting a known and certain evil as a way of avoiding an uncertain evil of unknown dimensions. That may or may not be a good social bargain. But since it is so often advocated by business firms that clearly stand to gain from it, we should at least approach their arguments skeptically.

"ANTITRUST" POLICY

We shall see in Chapter 14 why it is that governments so often intervene in ways that harm consumers by *reducing* competition, despite the fact that consumers and competition always win easily in the rhetorical battles. But local and state governments and especially the federal government also have adopted specific policies to *promote* competition, policies that are ordinarily justified on the ground that competition is an effective coordinator of economic activity but requires some government maintenance if it is to be adequately preserved. The assessment of these laws, their applications, and their consequences forms an interesting study in history and judicial interpretation as well as economic analysis. All we shall try to do here, however, is raise a few fundamental questions.

The most important such law is the Sherman Act, often called the Sherman Antitrust Act, enacted by Congress with almost no debate or opposition in 1890. (The name reflects the attempts of nineteenth-century businessmen to use legal trusteeships as a device to prevent competition.) Its sweeping language has caused some to call it the constitution of the competitive system. It forbids all contracts, combinations, or conspiracies in restraint of interstate trade and all attempts to monopolize any part of interstate trade. The language is so sweeping, in fact, that it was bound to be qualified in its application. After all, any two partners entering into business together could be deemed to have combined with the intention of making trade more difficult for their competitors and thus gaining an ever-larger share of trade for themselves. The federal courts consequently came to hold that combinations or other attempts to monopolize had to be "unreasonable" or major threats to public welfare before they could be prohibited under the Sherman Act.

INTERPRETATIONS AND APPLICATIONS

To help the courts in their efforts to apply the policies of the Sherman Act, Congress has passed additional legislation such as the Clayton Act and the Federal Trade Commission Act, both of which became law in 1914. The latter act created the Federal Trade Commission as a supposedly expert body and authorized it to promote competition by prohibiting a wide range of "unfair" practices. A principal provision of the Clayton Act (and subsequent amendments) aims specifically at the question of mergers, prohibiting all mergers that might "substantially" lessen competition. But difficult and important questions remain unresolved.

When does a merger substantially lessen competition? And do mergers ever increase competition? Suppose two steel firms want to merge. This is usually referred to as a *horizontal merger.* At first glance we would be inclined to say that the merger will substantially lessen competition in an industry already made up of a relatively few very large firms. But suppose they sell in different geographic areas? Suppose they each specialize in a different line of steel products? Suppose each is on the edge of failure and that the merger will lead to economies that may enable both to survive?

A great deal of dispute has arisen in recent years regarding so-called *conglomerate mergers:* mergers between firms producing widely divergent goods. Does the acquisition of a car-rental firm by an electrical-machinery manufacturer enable the rental firm to compete more effectively against Hertz and Avis? Does it lead to special arrangements between the machinery manufacturer, its suppliers, and the rental firm that tie up a portion of the car-rental business and thus reduce competition? Do conglomerate mergers lead to concentrations of financial power that are dangerous and undesirable regardless of their effects on competition?

What about *vertical mergers,* mergers between firms that previously existed in a supplier–buyer relationship, as when a supermarket chain acquires a food processor? Is this more likely to increase efficiency or to reduce competition by depriving other food processors of opportunities to sell?

What constitutes an illegally unfair trade practice? Is it unfair for a large firm to demand discounts from its suppliers? Is it unfair for suppliers to offer discounts to some purchasers but not to others? What about the whole question of advertising? Do large firms have unfair advantages in advertising, advantages that advertising increases? Must advertising be truthful in order to be fair? Of course it must, almost by definition. But what is the truth, the whole truth, and nothing but the truth? Anyone who thinks about this issue seriously or for very long is forced to admit that the regulation of "deceptive" advertising by the Federal Trade Commission inevitably involves the commission in complex questions of purpose and effect and in a large number of judgments that appear quite arbitrary.

And always we return to the root problem: Restrictions on competitors will reduce their ability to compete. Competition is essentially the offering of additional opportunities, and additional opportunities mean a wider range of choices and hence greater wealth. But the manner in which a firm expands the set of opportunities it offers may diminish, over a short or a longer period, the set of opportunities other firms are able to offer. Under what circumstances do we want the government to restrict one firm's competitive efforts for the sake of the larger or long-run competitive situation? It is important to remember that many of the most effective pressures on government policies stem not from consumer but from producer interests. And those policies will too often be shaped by the desire of producers to protect themselves against the rigors of the competitive life.

VERTICAL RESTRAINTS: COMPETITIVE OR ANTICOMPETITIVE?

Current controversies over vertical restraints on competition illustrate many of the opposing arguments and conflicting interests that complicate antitrust policy. From 1937 to 1976, federal legislation exempted from the Sherman Act state-endorsed price-fixing agreements between manufacturers and retailers. Congress had no sooner rescinded this exemption, making such agreements automatically illegal once again, than the courts started to carve out exceptions to the principle that manufacturers may not try to control competition at the retail level. Congress subsequently responded by trying to prohibit altogether what it had once encouraged. Legislation has been introduced in both the House and the Senate in recent years that would sharply curtail the power of manufacturers to control the behavior of those who distribute their products.

Is there any way that consumers could benefit from a manufacturer's refusal to sell to a retailer who reduced the resale price below some recommended minimum, or from a decision to limit the number of retail outlets that will be allowed to carry the manufacturer's product in a given geographic area? It would seem that such actions could only produce higher prices and poorer quality service for consumers. That conclusion becomes much less certain, however, when we ask why any manufacturer might want to prevent price discounting by retailers or hold down the number of stores carrying its product.

Manufacturers sometimes conclude that they will be unable to market their product successfully unless consumers are provided with a substantial range of pre- and post-sale services, such as information on ways the product can be utilized profitably, continuing instruction on operating procedures, or fast and dependable maintenance service. Retailers will only want to supply these services if they can increase their own net revenue by doing so, that is, if supplying these services will increase their sales by more than enough to cover the cost of the services.

Such services will not be supplied, and hence the manufacturer's product cannot be successfully marketed, whenever retailers are able to "free ride" on the services provided by other retailers. Consider the case of personal computers. These products could not have been introduced into offices and homes as quickly as they were if selling effort had not been accompanied by a whole lot of instructional effort. Instructional effort *was* selling effort, perhaps the most effective kind of selling effort. But did it produce sales for the party providing the instruction? There's the catch. Retailers who incurred the cost of teaching people how to make effective use of one type of personal computer could easily be undermined by competing retailers who provided no instructional services but catered to the demand that others had created.

Manufacturers who set minimum resale prices or limit the number of outlets in an area may be trying to protect co-operating distributors from free-riding distributors. Their interest would be in marketing their product effectively, not in reducing competition. Of course, the manufacturer's actions *would* limit competition. But in the absence of such actions there might be even less competition, as the product could not be effectively marketed at all.

Should manufacturers be allowed to restrict competition at the retail level, then, as part of a reasonable effort to market their product? The courts have been allowing such activities in recent years, on a case-by-case basis, looking at the context, intent, and probable effects of the "vertical" restrictions. That hasn't made everyone happy. Distributors who were cut off or otherwise disciplined by manufacturers have complained to Congress and some members of Congress have responded with bills that would severely limit the rights of manufacturers in this area. Proponents of such bills argue that they want to enhance competition. Opponents reply that the effect will be to reduce competition by seriously curtailing the power of manufacturers and distributors to devise and agree upon effective marketing procedures.

THE RANGE OF OPINION

Is the whole body of "antitrust" law perhaps more of a hindrance than a help to competition? There are some who come to that conclusion. There are others—heavily concentrated, it often seems, in the economics profession— who would retain the Sherman Act and the antimerger provisions of the Clayton Act and junk the rest. Some of these defenders claim that the Sherman and Clayton acts have made important contributions to the maintenance of a competitive economy. Others claim that they could make a much larger contribution if they were seriously enforced. But still others view them at best as harmless rhetoric, at worst as weapons that, in the hands of ignorant political appointees, may do a lot of damage to the economy.

The author is firmly convinced that he doesn't know who is right. "Antitrust" policy is certainly full of contradictions, of cases where the right hand is doing what the left hand is undoing. State laws rarely promote competition; more often they promote the interests of the competitor protectors rather than the competition protectors. Federal enforcement of the Sherman Act and the antimerger provisions of the Clayton Act often seems to strain at gnats while swallowing camels. Firms unable to compete effectively by offering their customers lower prices and better quality sometimes file complaints under the antitrust laws to see if they can persuade the courts to raise the prices or reduce the quality of their competitors' offerings. On the other hand, the existence of the

Sherman Act, with its ringing denunciation of price-fixing conspiracies, may have retarded the development in this country of the cartel arrangements that have so often appeared in western Europe and Japan. The economist George Stigler once suggested that "the ghost of Senator Sherman is an ex officio member of the board of directors of every large company." While that statement will never meet the minimum criteria for empirical scientific truths, good history is still a long way from being a pure science.

TOWARD EVALUATION

The conclusions that we shall offer at the end are far more modest than the questions with which we began. They are only two in number.

Restrictions on potential competitors reduce the range and diminish the availability of substitute goods and allow sellers more room to increase their own wealth by denying opportunities to others. Competition is a process, not a state of affairs. To put it another way, competition can be recognized only in motion pictures, not in still photographs. The fact, for example, that the price of some good is exactly the same, no matter from which seller you buy, establishes absolutely nothing about whether the industry producing that good is adequately competitive. The important question is how those prices all came to be identical. It happens with surprising frequency that even public figures, who ought to know better, will infer an absence of competition from the uniformity of price. The quickest antidote to this error is the recollection that wheat farmers all charge the same price.

The other observation is that an inadequate situation must be compared with more desirable situations that are actually attainable. It is a mistake to contrast a less-than-ideal situation with an ideal-but-unattainable situation. There are costs involved in changed market structures, such as the cost of an investigation, prosecution, court order, and compliance under antitrust statutes. Only if these marginal costs are less than the marginal benefits can one maintain that we would be "better off" if we took legal action to reduce the market power of price searchers, to prevent business mergers, or to prohibit practices that might eventually lessen competition.

ONCE OVER LIGHTLY

A gap between the price of a good and the marginal cost of making it available is a source of potential advantage to someone. Competition occurs in the economy as people locate such differentials and try to exploit them by filling that gap with additional goods.

Competition takes more forms than we can list and usually more forms than competitors can anticipate and head off.

Because competition tends to transfer the gains from providing a good to purchasers and to other suppliers, firms frequently try to obtain government assistance in excluding competitors, often displaying remarkable ingenuity and stunning sophistry.

Firms often charge that their competitors, whether domestic or foreign, are "selling below cost" and call for the government to prevent such "predatory" practices. Most such charges make sense only if they include some expenses in per-unit cost that are irrelevant to the particular decisions under attack. They make a different kind of sense when we remember that sellers characteristically prefer less competition.

The notion that government is the Defender of Competition Against Rapacious Monopolists is probably more a hope than a reality. Federal, state, and local governments have created and preserved numerous positions of special privilege whose effect is to restrict competition and reduce the options available to consumers.

An adequate and balanced evaluation of the substantial body of statutes, commission decrees, and judicial holdings that makes up federal antitrust policy has not yet been published.

Competition is a process in which competitors engage. We obviously cannot have competition without competitors. It does not seem as obvious to people that we also cannot have competition if we prohibit competitors from taking actions intended to increase their share of the market.

QUESTIONS FOR DISCUSSION

1. A few years ago a major airline began asking in-flight passengers to complete a lengthy "Passenger Survey." A cover note from the Senior Vice President for Marketing said that passengers who completed the survey would be helping the airline provide "the best possible service." Questions were asked about the purpose of this trip, frequency of flying, type of fare paid, what would have been done had no discount fare been available, how the ticket was purchased, and income of the traveler. What was the airline trying to do?
2. How would you account for the fact that although some observers claim competition is declining in the American economy, every business firm insists that it faces strenuous competition?

3. Consult the technical definition of *oligopoly* presented in the text. Are commercial airlines oligopolists by that definition? Are the owners of the gasoline stations in a small town oligopolists? Name some other sellers who are and are not oligopolists by that definition.

4. If a commercial airline reduces its prices in September, at the end of the vacation season, for tickets purchased two weeks in advance with a stay over a Saturday night, what will happen to the number of tickets it sells? Does it matter whether other airlines match its price cuts? Suppose the airline knows that changes in its fares *will* be matched by all its major competitors. If it nonetheless decides to reduce its fares, will it be causing a change in the demand for its tickets or only a change in the quantity demanded?

5. The attempt by sellers to make their product more attractive to consumers is sometimes called *product differentiation.*

   (a) Is product differentiation a wasteful process, imposing costs on sellers that are greater than the benefits conferred on buyers? Think of cases where it probably is wasteful in this sense and other cases where it is not.

   (b) Evaluate the following argument: "New practices initiated by sellers to differentiate their products are liable to be wasteful from the social point of view because they are liable to entail high marginal costs and low marginal benefits. But this only means that producers have already made use of the low-cost/high-benefit techniques of product differentiation; it does not show that the whole process of product differentiation is wasteful."

6. A 1982 survey by a New York advertising agency found that many consumers thought there were too many different brands available for sale in several product categories. For example, 72 percent of the consumers surveyed thought there were too many brands of dry cereal, and 60 percent thought there were too many brands of bar soap. How many is "too many" from your point of view if you know exactly what you want? How many is "too few" if you can't find what you're looking for? (The survey, by Batten, Barton, Durstine, and Osborn, was described in the April 22, 1982, issue of *The Wall Street Journal.*)

7. Why must an effective price-fixing agreement between sellers include such restrictions on sales as output limitations or geographic divisions of sales territory?

8. This problem is designed to help you appreciate the joys and tribulations of cartels.

   Let D in Figure 10A be the demand for oil and MC the sum of the marginal cost curves of all oil producers. (Ignore the line labeled H for now.)

   (a) If oil producers are price takers because there are thousands of them and they have no effective cartel, why will the price of oil move to-

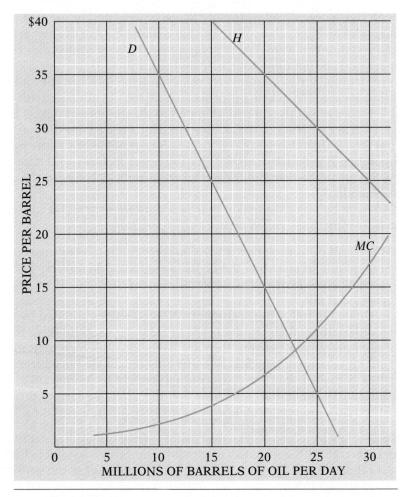

FIGURE 10A   Market demand for oil and combined marginal cost curves of producers

ward $9 per barrel? What will occur if the price is much above or below $9?

(b) Now assume that one party acquires control over all producing oil wells and hence the power to control the price by controlling output. How many millions of barrels per day (mb/d) will be produced if the goal is to maximize net revenue? What price will be set?

(c) Change the above assumption slightly. The oil wells remain under the ownership and control of the thousands of original owners, but each owner agrees to sell only at the price determined by the Organizer of Prices to Exploit Consumers (OPEC). This is an agent hired by the oil producers to determine and announce the price for oil that will be most advantageous to oil producers collectively. OPEC announces that the price shall be $29 per barrel. What must occur if this price is to hold?

(d) Why will the individual oil producers want to sell individually a quantity of oil that sums in aggregate to far more than 13 mb/d?

(e) How can OPEC prevent output from expanding way beyond 13 mb/d and thereby bringing down the price of oil? If OPEC assigns production quotas to each individual oil producer, how can it make sure that all the producers will be satisfied that their quotas are "fair"? How can it make sure that individual producers don't exceed their quotas?

(f) Is the demand curve for oil that obtains when oil has long been selling at $9 per barrel and is expected to remain at about that level likely to remain unchanged when the price of oil rises to $29 per barrel and is expected to stay at that much higher level for a number of years? What sort of developments are likely to *shift the demand* over time? What effect will this have on the oil producers who created OPEC?

(g) A serious threat to the wealth of the OPEC oil producers is likely to come from *new* producers who are attracted into the industry by OPEC's success in raising the price of oil. In the case of the real-world OPEC (Organization of Petroleum Exporting Countries), the 13 member nations saw their sales decline between 1980 and 1985 from over 30 mb/d to fewer than 15 mb/d, with some of the difference reflecting a reduced total demand but most of it a result of increased production by non-OPEC members. Suppose that H had been the demand for OPEC oil in the happy days when the cartel began operating. Compare the price, output, and total revenue of OPEC's members when the demand is H with the price, output, and total revenue when the demand is D—even assuming no "cheating" by cartel members.

9. The analysis in the preceding question raises an interesting issue: Why did the Organization of Petroleum Exporting Countries succeed so well for so long in raising the world price of oil? A major part of any answer is contained in the concept of the marginal cost of producing and selling oil. The cost of extracting oil from an established field can be very low indeed, so low as to be almost negligible. But the relevant marginal cost is the cost of extracting *and selling*. In the 1970s, many respected parties were predicting that, because the demand for petroleum products was highly inelastic and the world's reserves were quickly running out, the price per barrel might rise by the end of the century as high as $1000 a barrel. How do expectations of such dramatically higher future prices affect the opportunity cost of selling oil currently? How would such expectations solve OPEC's "cheating" problem? Why did those extravagant expectations, so common in the 1970s, disappear by the mid-1980s?

10. Some states have established legal minimum prices for liquor sold at retail. Do you think this eliminates competition among retail liquor stores? Why do you think retailers in such states often lend glassware without charge to customers planning parties?

11. All the real estate brokers in an area will generally charge the same fee for selling a house, a certain percentage of the sales price established by some association and adhered to by all real estate agents as a matter of "ethical practice."

    (a) Why would it be unethical if a broker offered to accept 5 rather than 6 percent for selling your house? Toward whom would it be unethical?
    (b) How do real estate agents compete with one another?
    (c) Is an industry likely to become overcrowded if it's successful in fixing a high minimum price for its product? Is the real estate profession overcrowded in your judgment? What evidence might be used to answer this question?

12. A survey reported in the *Harvard Business Review* asked businesspeople to describe the unethical practices in their own industry that they would most like to see eliminated. Of those responding, 62 percent mentioned "unfair pricing," "dishonest advertising," "unfair competitive practices," or "cheating customers." How would you interpret these responses? How would you define the practices they condemn?

13. Examine the paragraph in the text on page 273 recounting the complaint of the nursing-home operator. How many wrong or misleading assertions can you locate in that paragraph?

14. The legislature of a large state recently considered a bill that would require all grocery stores and drugstores selling package liquor to provide separate entrances to their liquor departments. It was maintained by supporters of the bill that this was necessary to prevent minors from entering the liquor department. Who do you think lobbied for this bill? Why?

15. A study several years ago pointed out that 73 percent of the professions licensed by a populous midwestern state required entrants to have "good character." Why? How can good character be determined? Who is best able to determine whether morticians' characters are sufficiently blameless to entitle them to a license?

16. The Seattle City Council stopped setting taxicab rates in May 1979. Soon thereafter efforts began to compel the city to resume regulation. Are you surprised to learn that those efforts were financed and promoted by the owners of taxicabs? Do you believe their statement: "We're doing it to keep people from being ripped off"?

17. A former chief executive officer of AT&T testified in August 1981, in an antitrust suit, that AT&T had tried to forestall competition to the Bell system in order to safeguard its quality of service rather than to protect its profit. Does that claim surprise you? Do you think it's true?

18. A March 10, 1982, letter to *The Wall Street Journal* argued that "continued economic regulation of the motor carrier industry . . . is in the public

interest." The letter, signed by the president of the American Trucking Association, argued that collective rate making and restrictions on entry were necessary to prevent unstable service, industry concentration, loss of service to small communities, predatory pricing, and discrimination against small shippers and small communities. Are you surprised to learn that members of the American Trucking Association *want* to be regulated by government so that they don't act contrary to the public interest?

19. The president of a county medical society in Florida warned doctors there that if they took out even a small ad in the Yellow Pages, they would be "summarily called before the executive committee of the county association to explain their actions." He added his opinion that using boldface type in a standard Yellow Pages listing constituted "unprofessional conduct."

   (a) What kind of doctor is least likely to want to advertise? Which doctors are most likely to want to advertise?
   (b) What is the consumer interest in this matter? Is advertising by physicians likely to lead to better or poorer service for patients?

20. An advocate of state regulation of cosmetologists and barbers in Washington State argued that the state cosmetology agency had taken in $756,805 in revenue in the preceding year while spending only $589,014, thus providing a net benefit to the state. Where would you look to locate some additional costs created by the agency?

21. When the Washington State legislature was debating a bill in 1981 that would allow optometrists to administer certain eyedrops during eye exams, 50 ophthalmologists descended on the Capitol to lobby against the bill. The chairman of the state Academy of Ophthalmology told a reporter: "There is no economic advantage one way or the other." The ophthalmologists' sole concern was that, if the bill became law, "more people will be harmed through inappropriate use of drugs." Do you believe that 50 medical specialists all took a day off from their practices to lobby the legislature exclusively out of concern for the public's health?

22. In 1987 the Washington State Utilities and Transportation Commission began a crackdown on unlicensed movers of household goods.

   (a) The commission's enforcement chief said the crackdown occurred because of consumer complaints about damaged goods and price manipulation and because authorized carriers were complaining about growing competition from unlicensed movers. Which set of complaints do you suppose put the most pressure on the commission? How many consumers do you think know about the existence of the State's Utilities and Transportation Commission? How many licensed movers probably know about the Commission?
   (b) State officials have said that the legislature set strict requirements for entry into the moving industry in the 1930s because legislators were concerned that "unregulated, cutthroat competition would lead to a deterioration in service, safety problems, overly intensive competi-

tion in urban areas and a lack of service in rural areas." Do you agree that these problems are likely to arise in the absence of regulation? Does competition *usually* lead to a deterioration in service? When is competition "cutthroat" and "overly intensive"? If you ask this last question of people already in the moving industry, how are they likely to respond?

(c) There is a "stringent public convenience and necessity test" for any new firm seeking a mover's permit, which places on the applicant firm the burden of proving that its services are needed. Can that be proved?

(d) The transportation director for the state commission is on record as believing that there are currently "more licensed movers than is necessary—as far as service rather than rates are concerned." What is the relationship between high rates and sufficient service?

(e) What does the fact that there are dozens of unlicensed movers operating in the state indicate about the transportation director's claim?

23. In January 1983, a U.S. appeals court rejected a lower-court finding that AT&T had engaged in "predatory pricing" against MCI Communications Inc. by setting rates "below cost" on some of its long-distance services. Go back to question 4 in Chapter 5 and examine AT&T's explanation of what a long-distance call "costs." Would you be willing to argue that any price under 68.9 cents for the initial minute is evidence of below-cost pricing? How would you determine whether particular long-distance rates are above or below cost?

24. The Big Three auto makers in the United States asked the Commerce Department in 1988 to "consult" with Japanese manufacturers about alleged "dumping" of compact pickup trucks in the U.S. market. Under trade law, illegal "dumping" occurs when foreign firms sell in the United States at prices below what they sell for in their domestic market *and* thereby cause the profits or employment of U.S. competitors to fall.

(a) Why would a Japanese firm want to sell pickup trucks in the United States for less than it charges in Japan?

(b) Since the Big Three's truck sales were nearing record levels when the complaint was filed, they could not show a drop in profits or employment. Instead, they argued on the basis of "lost opportunity": 140,000 additional trucks would have been sold had the Japanese not "dumped" vehicles in the United States. If lost opportunity constitutes injury, is there any reason to require a showing of injury to support a dumping complaint?

25. In June 1983, the U.S. Justice Department agreed to drop a consent decree that it had extracted from Safeway 25 years earlier, under which Safeway had been prohibited from selling at prices below its cost of acquiring grocery products or at "unreasonably low prices" that might be

above cost. The decree stemmed from a government suit that had accused Safeway of selling below cost in an effort to monopolize the market for retail food in Texas and New Mexico.

(a) How likely is it that Safeway or anyone else would be able to monopolize the market for retail food in two states?
(b) The alleged attempt to monopolize led Safeway to reduce prices to customers. Who do you suppose complained to the Justice Department about Safeway's behavior?
(c) What is the appropriate way to determine the cost of specific grocery items? Is a retailer selling paper bags below cost when it makes them available to customers at no charge? Is the retailer cross-subsidizing paper bags? [For more on cross-subsidies, see question 28 below, especially part (d).]

26. Which of the following products are being sold below cost? With what other products are they competing? Is the competition "unfair"?

(a) Coffee offered by a bank to its customers without charge.
(b) As many cups of coffee after dinner as the diner in an expensive restaurant requests, at no extra charge.
(c) Commercial television programs.
(d) Soft drinks on an airline flight.
(e) A roll of film given to each adult customer during a pizza shop's first week of operation.

27. Three elements that must be present for a firm to be engaged in predatory pricing are pricing (1) below cost, (2) in order to eliminate rivals, and (3) with the intention of raising prices afterward to recoup. What factors would make the last step of the process difficult to complete? Under what kinds of circumstances would it be relatively easy? Can you cite any actual examples?

28. Here is a simplified problem on "predatory pricing" to help you get a clearer grasp of some of the issues.

The demand for the shipping services of the Midwestern Railroad Company is shown as D in Figure 10B. The marginal cost to Midwestern of carrying freight is $1 per ton-mile. In addition to its marginal costs, Midwestern has monthly expenses of $480,000 covering all those costs that are not affected by the amount of freight the railroad carries: property taxes, mortgage payments on equipment, most wages and salaries, and so on.

(a) If Midwestern sets marginal cost equal to marginal revenue to maximize its net revenue from operation of the railroad, what rate will it set per ton-mile? How many ton-miles of freight will it carry per month? What will be its monthly loss?
(b) Now assume that the demand curve above $2.00 is entirely the demand from coal producers, and that the demand below $2.00 comes

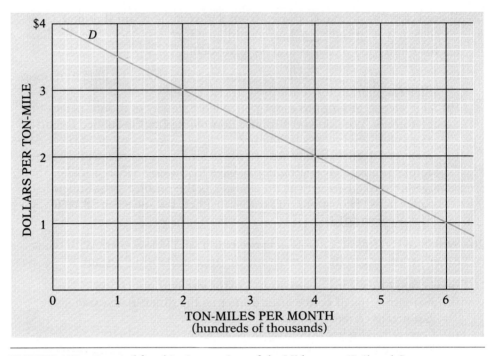

FIGURE 10B   **Demand for shipping services of the Midwestern Railroad Company**

entirely from grain shippers. If Midwestern sets different rates for coal and for grain, what rate will it want to set in each case to maximize net revenue? How many ton-miles of coal and of grain, respectively, will Midwestern carry each month? What will now be its total costs and its total revenue?

(c) Suppose that prior to the institution of a separate and lower price for grain, barge companies on the Ohio, Illinois, and Mississippi rivers had been charging $2.00 per ton-mile to carry grain. Why will they be unhappy about Midwestern's two-price policy? If they want to protest that Midwestern is charging a price "below cost," what evidence can they come up with to support their complaint? What is Midwestern's "total cost" per unit for carrying a ton-mile of freight?

(d) If Midwestern is carrying grain "below cost," is it "cross-subsidizing" by using the "excess profits" earned from "exploiting" coal producers? Or is it also carrying coal "below cost"? How can Midwestern earn a positive net revenue by charging rates "below cost" on all the freight it carries? (To clarify the picture, you might want to plot Midwestern's total cost per unit on the graph, and then note the relationship between price and cost under first a single-price and then a dual-price policy.)

(e) If you were a member of a regulatory commission charged with preventing exploitation of shippers as well as predatory pricing aimed at competitors while also preserving the profits of the railroad, would you approve or disapprove Midwestern's dual-price policy?

29. The Staggers Rail Act of 1980 substantially reduced the power of the Interstate Commerce Commission to control the rates that railroads charge shippers.

(a) The president of the National Coal Association has denounced the system of "letting the railroads charge what the traffic will bear" and has called for renewed rate regulation. Many other shippers, however, applaud the extensive deregulation of the railroads. Why might the coal industry favor rate regulation while most shippers oppose it?

(b) One 1983 study of the price elasticity of demand for rail transport of grain in the Corn Belt states calculated an elasticity coefficient of 3.75. What is the nature of the competition that makes the demand elasticity so high?

(c) If the railroads, barge lines, and trucking firms of this country were allowed to set their rates free from government regulation, what do you think would follow: "gouging of customers" (higher prices) or "ruinous price cutting" (lower prices)? Does this happen in other areas of the economy where prices are not regulated by commissions—for example, in the grocery or automobile industries?

30. What is the difference between reducing prices to attract more customers and reducing prices in order to monopolize?

31. In 1989, an airline coach ticket from Frankfurt, West Germany, to Chicago cost $1313. A coach ticket from Athens to Chicago, with a stop in Frankfurt on the way, cost only $839.

(a) Why would the longer flight cost less?

(b) Travelers flying from Frankfurt to Chicago who learned about this price differential began buying tickets for an Athens-to-Chicago flight. They then boarded in Frankfurt and threw away the Athens-to-Frankfurt portion of the ticket. The airlines countered with a rule that allowed travel agents to sell the bargain tickets only in the country of origin—Greece in this case. The U.S. Transportation Department thereupon issued a formal order objecting to a rule that penalized travelers who buy one-way tickets in this country for travel between two foreign cities, and the airlines backed down (at least temporarily). Do you think the Frankfurt-to-Chicago travelers who used the Athens ticket were behaving unfairly? Was the rule with which the airlines countered unfair? Was it unfair for the Transportation Department to object? (Keep in mind that the Transportation Department has the power to make the life of airlines much more pleasant or unpleasant.) Was it unfair of the airlines to charge less for a flight from Athens in the first place?

(c) What do you think will be the eventual outcome if the Transportation Department continues to prevent the airlines from enforcing their rule on purchasing in the country of origin?

(d) Which would be the more pro-competition policy for the Transportation Department? To allow the airlines to set their own rules on ticket prices and sales, or to prevent them from adopting a rule that makes it difficult for ineligible persons to purchase discount tickets?

32. A federal judge held in November 1988 that commercial airlines may legally refuse to allow discount travel agencies to handle their tickets. These are agencies that sell tickets below the airlines' published prices to travelers who know exactly what ticket they want, by rebating a portion of their commission. Discount travel agencies do not help travelers plan their trips.

(a) How could travelers who need extensive information nonetheless be able to take advantage of the discount prices?

(b) Why might the airlines be interested in protecting the commissions of full-service travel agencies?

33. Suppose Congress decided to prevent manufacturers from controlling "free-riding" behavior among distributors of their products by branding all such efforts as an illegal conspiracy in restraint of trade.

(a) What option would remain open to manufacturers? (Hint: Can a firm conspire with itself?)

(b) How might government efforts to preserve the independence of distributors in their business relations with manufacturers threaten the continued existence of the distributors?

34. Is it legitimate for government to prevent independent business firms from agreeing among themselves not to sell below a certain price? If you have no misgivings about the legitimacy of this legal restraint, ask yourself whether it is also acceptable for government to prevent business firms from agreeing among themselves not to purchase above a certain price? What about extending the prohibition to customers? Why should it be legal for customers to do what business firms may not do? What about employees who agree not to work below a certain wage? Can you reconcile what appears to be legislative discrimination against business firms with the principle that all citizens ought to be equal before the law?

35. Prior to the deregulation of the commercial airlines, Republic and Northwest Airlines were required by the Civil Aeronautics Board to charge the same fares. After deregulation, they were prohibited from getting together to agree on a common fare schedule. After the two airlines merged, they were free to set fares as their interests dictated. If one of these makes sense, how can the others be defended?

36. In 1984 Congress passed the Cable Communications Policy Act and substantially deregulated the cable-TV industry. Since that time the industry
has fought to preserve its unregulated status, generally by claiming that
any legal restraints on its behavior will deny American viewers some of
the programs they want. The industry has simultaneously tried to persuade cities and the federal government not to allow electrical utilities or
telephone companies to build competing systems. They say this will lead
to overbuilding and price cutting. Would you conclude from all this that
the cable-TV industry is in favor of competition or opposed to it?

37. The Federal Trade Commission staff sought (unsuccessfully) in 1980 to
secure approval for "no-fault" antitrust cases. The government would not
have to prove, under this approach, that a large firm had acted anticom-
petitively, only that the firm in fact commands a dominant share of the
market. Would this promote or retard competition?

38. Think about this assertion put forward by the economist M. A. Adelman:
"A useful if not very precise index of the strength of competition . . . is
the resentment of unsuccessful competitors." How would you evaluate
the argument by other firms in the computer software industry that Mi-
crosoft engages in unfair competition?

PROFIT

Perhaps no term or concept in economic discussion is used with a more bewildering variety of well-established meanings than *profit.*" That sentence was written more than sixty years ago by Frank Knight, a distinguished student of the subject, to introduce an encyclopedia article on profit. The situation has not changed greatly since then. A few years ago *The Wall Street Journal* ran a feature article entitled "Some Plain Truth About Profit." The author listed no fewer than seven distinct definitions of the word *profit* that have been employed by "economic experts," decided none of them was very helpful, and then offered his own. A month later the *Journal* published seven letters of response from its readers; their verdicts on the new definition and accompanying exposition ran from excellent through misleading to ridiculous.

So what shall we do? We shall take the coward's course and assert that *there is no correct definition of profit.* The meaning of any word depends, after all, on the way people use it; and it is an incontrovertible fact that people (including economists) use *profit* in many different senses. We certainly don't want to quibble about mere definitions. But attitudes toward profit and such closely related concepts as cost of production and interest affect economic legislation, and those attitudes depend in large part on what people have in mind when they use the terms. So we're going to expend an unusual amount of effort in this chapter trying to decide what things ought to be called, but only insofar as we must do so to avoid both misleading distinctions and misleading identifications. We don't want to ignore important realities. But neither do we want to be misled by language into seeing things that don't exist.

PROFIT AS "TOTAL REVENUE MINUS TOTAL COST"

The most common definition of profit is simply *total revenue minus total cost*. That's almost everyone's intuitive definition of the term and that's how we've used it until now. A synonym would be *net revenue*. When a business firm has paid all its costs, what it has left over is profit, or net revenue. But before we can agree on the size of profits, defined in this way, we have to agree on what counts as costs.

WHAT SHOULD BE INCLUDED IN COSTS?

Monetary outlays are not the same as costs, at least not from the opportunity-cost perspective. This is clear in the case of an owner-operated business: part of the cost of doing business is the owner's own labor, even though owners may not figure their salaries as part of their regular costs and write no weekly payroll check to themselves. If owners pay rent for the building they use, they'll count the rental payments as part of their costs; but they may fail to do so if they themselves own the building. They ought to do so, however, because they're losing the amount that could be obtained from renting the building to someone else. There is a genuine cost in not having the building available for alternative uses.

Business proprietors may also be using equipment that they bought and now own. If they bought the equipment with a bank loan, they will include the interest on their bank payments in their costs. But suppose they bought the equipment out of previously accumulated savings? Then they gave up interest income that they could have obtained from letting someone else use their savings, and this is certainly part of the opportunity cost of doing business. But they may or may not decide to include the forgone income in their costs. The point is that they should. The income forgone represents a genuine cost for the business.

Corporate profits have a legal definition because corporations must pay taxes on their profits. But the legal definition is unsatisfactory from an opportunity-cost point of view. It begins with the commonsense definition of profit as revenue minus costs. But it excludes from cost the dividend payments made to stockholders of the corporation while including the interest payments made to bondholders. Are these payments

that different? Both seem to be payments for the use of borrowed funds. The principal difference is that payments to
bondholders are a contractual obligation of a fixed amount,
whereas the dividends paid to stockholders are a kind of
residual that may vary from year to year or quarter to quarter. Still, the funds loaned by the stockholders are funds not
earning income somewhere else, and those funds were loaned
only because the stockholders expected to receive a return at
least equal in value to their next-best opportunity. Surely
some portion of the dividends paid by corporations represents a cost of doing business, no matter how dividends are
regarded for purposes of taxation.

WHY IS INTEREST PAID?

But why is interest paid in the first place? For what is it a payment?

The notion that interest is a payment for the use of
money, the way that a Hertz or Avis fee is a payment for the
use of a car, is quite mistaken. My employer offers me money
in return for my services; I hand that money over to grocers,
utility companies, and others to secure goods that they supply
and I want; they in turn use the money I provide them to pay
their employees, and so on. None of us pays any interest for
the use of the money that changes hands in this way. Moreover, if I choose to put a pair of $20 bills into my sugar bowl
for a rainy day and it doesn't rain for several years, the Federal Reserve Bank that issued those bills doesn't charge me
for their use during this period. Contrast that with the probable reaction of Hertz or Avis if I stored one of their cars in my
garage for a rainy day.

The usual way to obtain money is to earn it by selling a
service to someone. We only pay interest when we *borrow*
money. Borrowing is a matter of obtaining money that we
have not earned—*yet*. Borrowers want money *now* though
they currently have no valuable service to offer in exchange
for it. They persuade lenders to give them money now by
promising to pay later. The ratio between what is given back
later and what is obtained now determines the interest rate.

*Interest is thus the price that people pay to obtain resources
now rather than wait* until they have earned the money with
which to buy the resources. The best way to think about interest is to view it as *the premium paid to obtain current command of resources.*

To explain why interest is paid, then, we must explain
why present resources are generally more valuable than future resources. That isn't too hard to understand. Having re-

sources now expands one's opportunities. Present command of resources will often enable us to do things that cause our earning capacity to increase over time, so that we will have more resources at some future date than we would otherwise have had. When we see such a prospect, we want to borrow. And we are willing to pay, if we have to, a premium—interest—as long as the interest is less than what we expect to gain as a result of borrowing.

Suppose that Robinson Crusoe, long a useful character in economists' arguments, keeps himself alive from day to day by digging for clams with his fingernails. Five clams a day is the most he can obtain by digging with his hands during every available hour. And five clams per day is just enough to keep body and soul together, so that Robinson is living on the edge of bare subsistence. If he had a shovel, however, he could triple his daily output to fifteen clams. Unfortunately for Robinson, it would require a month's work to manufacture a suitable shovel, during which time he could not dig for clams and would consequently starve.

How many clams would Robinson Crusoe be willing to give up later in return for 150 clams now, or more accurately, in return for five clams a day on each of the next thirty days while he is all tied up in shovel making? He could *afford* to give up as many as 300 clams at the end of the second month and each month thereafter, because that is how much the loan of 150 clams now would increase his productivity in future months. Presumably he would be *willing* to give up any amount less than that if he had no other way of obtaining a shovel.

Clams now are worth more than clams later if, as in this case, present command of clams enables one to increase the future production of clams. The rate of exchange between present and future clams would be the rate of interest in Robinson Crusoe's world. And it would have no relationship at all to money.

There are very few tasks that cannot be performed more effectively with the appropriate tools, which is to say, with the assistance of *capital.* Capital in economics means *produced goods used to increase the production of future goods.* Examples include Crusoe's shovel, cash registers in retail stores, drill presses in a sheet-metal fabricating shop, the card catalogue in libraries, and all the skills embodied in human beings that enable them to produce more goods than they could produce before they acquired those skills. As long as people believe that they can increase their future productivity by acquiring present command of resources and creating capital

from them, they will be willing to pay a premium to obtain resources now rather than wait until they have "earned" them.

Interest is consequently not something unique to capitalist economies, much less a result of the avarice and power of
bankers and other moneylenders. Above all, it is not something that could be eliminated just by making more money
available. Interest rates are generally talked about as if they
were the cost of borrowing money simply because money is
the usual means by which people acquire possession of present goods. But interest would exist in an economy that functioned without money, since it's fundamentally the difference
in value between present and future goods.

We don't want to leave the impression that it's only the
productivity of capital that makes resources now generally
more valuable than resources at some future date. Consumers
also seem to display what the economist calls *a positive rate of
time preference;* that is, people tend to place a higher subjective value on consumption in the near future than on consumption in the more distant future.

You are probably one of those people. Here is a little test
you might use to find out whether you are indeed among that
overwhelming majority with a positive rate of time preference. Imagine that you have responded to one of those innumerable promotions that come in the mail with large and
gaudy announcements on the envelope stating that YOU MAY
ALREADY HAVE WON A BRAND NEW $45,000 SPORTS
CAR. And to your own utter astonishment, you find out that
you have actually won the grand prize! You are very happy, of
course. Then you learn that the car won't be delivered to you
until about one year from now. You are still happy; but you
are probably a lot less happy than you were when you imagined yourself driving that sports car already next week. In
fact, you would most likely be willing to pay a substantial
sum of money to get the car now rather than having to wait a
year. If all this describes you, then you have a positive rate of
time preference.

Some critics have interpreted positive time preference as
evidence of shortsightedness, or of inability to imagine the
distant future with as much vividness and force as one con-
templates the immediate future, or of an innate human tendency to view the future through rose-tinted glasses. Each of
these interpretations casts suspicion on the ultimate "rationality" of time preference. Given the facts of human mortal-
ity, however, and all the contingencies of life, it isn't necessarily irrational or shortsighted to prefer a bird in the hand to
two in the bush. Moreover, if people have reason to believe

that their income will increase over time, they could very logically conclude that giving up something now entails a larger subjective sacrifice than giving up quite a bit more of the same thing at a future date when they expect their income to be larger.

Whatever the relative importance of each factor, it is clear that people's beliefs about the productivity of capital goods and their preferences for consuming sooner rather than later have combined to produce a premium on present goods over future goods and thus a positive rate of interest in every known society. Interest is paid, then—to answer the question with which we began this section—to induce people to give up present command of resources. It is a payment for the value of the opportunity that lenders forgo, a payment that borrowers are willing to make because of the opportunities that borrowing opens up for them.

THE RISK FACTOR IN INTEREST RATES

The rates charged by banks to corporate borrowers, by department stores to customers with revolving charge accounts, or by individuals lending to savings-and-loan institutions all reflect the net rate of time preference in a particular society. But they also include risk premiums of various sizes plus differences in the cost of negotiating loans. It will ordinarily cost you more per dollar to borrow from a commercial bank than it will cost a large and successful corporation. This doesn't really mean that you're paying a higher rate of interest, however. You are paying for the costs incurred by the bank in investigating your credit standing and doing the bookkeeping entailed by your loan, as well as a kind of insurance premium that the bank collects from the borrower in anticipation of losses through costs of collection and defaults. If the bank could not charge this premium, it would not find it advantageous to make loans to customers in higher-risk categories. So when legislators impose ceilings on the "annual interest" that lenders may legally charge, they don't reduce interest rates so much as they exclude certain categories of borrowers from contracting for loans. Since the borrowers wouldn't contract for the loans unless they deemed them advantageous, it's difficult to discover in what way maximum interest-rate laws benefit low-income borrowers.

This is an important point, and not only because it corrects certain popular but mistaken notions about interest-rate legislation. The return that any lender will demand as a condition of lending depends on what the lender could obtain by lending to a different borrower *plus* the risk assigned to that particular loan. Commercial lenders aren't unique in that respect. Imagine the bonds of two corporations, one of them Procter & Gamble and the other a commercial airline teetering on the edge of bankruptcy. Both sets of bonds have a maturity value of $1000 and are scheduled to mature one year from now. At what prices will these bonds be bought and sold on the market?

Suppose the P&G issue sells at $917. That $917 now will be worth $1000 at maturity (in one year) at a 9 percent rate of interest. The $917 price would mean, in effect, that people are willing to hold P&G bonds if they anticipate a 9 percent annual return, because $917 times 1.09, the principal plus the interest, is $1000.

But the bonds of the shaky airline would sell for far less even if they were bought by the same people who purchased the P&G bonds. The probability of default is so much higher in the second case that buyers could be persuaded to take the risk only if they were offered the possibility of a very high return. If the second issue sold for $714, buyers would be demanding the possibility of a 40 percent annual return.

If all works out well, they'll receive $203 more than they would have earned from holding a P&G bond. But that outcome is highly uncertain, and there is also the possibility they'll lose most or all of the principal. The higher "interest rate" on the latter bonds should therefore be interpreted as a risk premium, rather than as pure interest. Perhaps when legislators contemplate interest-rate ceilings, they should ask themselves whether they have ever purchased bonds at a heavy discount.

REAL AND NOMINAL INTEREST RATES

Interest rates include one other component that has been especially important since the mid-1960s. They include, as we have seen, the greater value that present command of resources has over future command of identical resources and a premium to cover both the lender's cost of negotiating the loan and the risk of default by the borrower. They also incorporate an additional amount to compensate the lender for any expected decrease in the purchasing power of money.

In 1981, the U.S. government was agreeing to pay almost 14 percent interest per year in order to borrow money for the next five years. The risk that the federal government will default is negligible, in large part because the federal government can manufacture money to meet its obligations. There are such well-developed markets for these loans that the cost of negotiating loans to the U.S. Treasury is also negligible. Why then was the rate of interest 14 percent? Was the command of resources in 1981 worth 14 percent more than command of those resources in 1982? Not at all. It meant that lenders in 1981 expected serious inflation over the next five years. Because the price level had been rising at the rate of about 10 percent per year, lenders assumed they would be paid back in dollars that continued to lose about 10 percent of their value every year. And so they added 10 percent to the interest rate they wanted from lenders. Lenders were willing to pay that much because they, too, expected dollars to lose about 10 percent of their value each year, which meant that dollars would become about 10 percent easier to earn each year. The market rate of interest, the rate actually quoted and published in the newspapers, is thus the "real" rate *plus* the expected rate of inflation.

Economists sometimes refer to the market rate as the *nominal* rate (the rate in name only), to express the fact that additional interest paid to compensate for inflation is not really interest. Since 1970, the average rate on high-grade corporate bonds (like those of Procter & Gamble) over the course of the year has varied between 7.21 percent (in 1972) and 14.17 percent (in 1981). This variation results primarily from differences in expected rates of inflation. The same is true for home mortgage rates. Borrowers who paid more than 15 percent to obtain mortgages in 1982, when rates on new-home mortgages averaged 15.14 percent, were not paying anything close to that rate to obtain present command of living space. The real rate they were paying was about 3 percent. Perhaps 2 percent was for loan arrangement costs and the risk of default. The rest reflected the high rate of inflation generally expected at the beginning of the 1980s.

UNCERTAINTY: A NECESSARY CONDITION FOR PROFIT

Let's summarize the argument to this point. Total cost is opportunity cost, and so it includes not only a firm's payments to others for commodities and services used, but also the implicit payments for use of any goods—labor, land, capital—that the firm itself supplies. Interest payments are part of the firm's costs, including the portion of its dividends that is about equal to the interest return its shareholders could have received by lending their money elsewhere. When we include all these opportunity costs in our calculations of total costs, there seems to be no reason why any firm would have to earn revenues in excess of costs. Firms could make zero profits and continue in business. They could even be considered successful firms and be able to borrow new funds for expansion—as long as their revenues were adequate to cover all their costs.

In fact, if there were some way for a firm to get into a line of business that *guaranteed* more in revenue than it entailed in cost, wouldn't so many people move into that line of business that competition would reduce the difference between revenue and cost to zero? Remember that cost means all costs, including an actual or implicit payment for getting the business organized and keeping it in operation. The certainty of a return greater than this would surely attract new business firms. Their entry would increase output, reduce the price of the product consistently with the law of demand, and thus reduce the gap between total revenue and total cost. The gap might simultaneously be reduced from the other direction as the new entrants increased the demand and raised the cost for the inputs used in turning out the product. Only when the gap between total revenue and total cost had disappeared, or when profits had been reduced to zero, would there no longer be any incentive for new firms to enter.

In the actual, continually changing, and always uncertain world, it doesn't work that way. People see profits being made in particular lines of business but they aren't sure how to go about cutting themselves in on the profits. In a world of scarce information, the existence of such profits might not even be widely known. And so *profits do exist and continue to exist* without being reduced to zero by competition. But this happens *because of uncertainty,* in the absence of which everything relevant to profit making would be generally known, all opportunities for profit making fully exploited, and profits everywhere consequently equal to zero.

The same argument applies to losses. No one would embark on a business enterprise knowing that the total revenue was going to fall short of the total cost. But the future is uncertain; events don't always work out as investors hope; decisions are made and actions taken that prove to be mistakes; and so losses do occur.

Since there would be no profits or losses in a world without uncertainty, we conclude that profit (or loss) is the consequence of uncertainty. Profit is thus not a payment that has to be made to obtain some resource or another. It is a residual;

it is what's left over out of revenue when costs have all been met; it is the result of predicting the future more accurately than most others have predicted it.

THE PURSUIT OF PROFIT

Let's consider a simple example. Suppose you read an advertisement urging you to invest in Florida real estate because its value increases by 30 percent each year. A 30 percent annual return is more than you can expect to receive from alternative investments, so you sink $30,000 into an undeveloped lot near Orlando. You plan to sell it in a year for $39,000. But you will probably be disappointed.

If Florida real estate really can be expected to increase in value by 30 percent per year, many people will be eager to buy Florida lots. Their eagerness to purchase will bid up the price of the lots, until the lots are no longer better buys than other available investment opportunities. If there happen to be many investors who uncritically accept the claims of the advertisement, their eagerness to benefit from the promised appreciation in real estate prices could even bid the present price of lots so high that price decreases—rather than increases—will subsequently occur.

No one can make a profit by putting money into an asset or an operation that is *generally expected* to return more than the going rate of interest. For that would be a "good deal." And the demand for a "good deal" bids up the cost of getting in on it, until it's no longer a better deal than other assets or opportunities.

Every investor knows this. The time to buy Xerox or Polaroid was before the word got around. Those who bought stock in these companies after it became widely known that they were going to earn large net revenues from their new products received no profits. About the best they could hope for was the going rate of interest as a return on their investment. The market price of Xerox and Polaroid stock was bid up by people eager to share in those companies' future earnings, until the earnings relative to what had to be paid to share in them were no more attractive than earnings generally available in the market.

The common notion that one can accumulate wealth by investing in profitable companies is therefore seriously misleading. Intel is rightly regarded as a highly profitable corporation, because it has consistently earned large returns for many years on its original investment. But the market value of Intel stock long ago increased to take full account of its expected high future earnings. Consequently, Intel stock is not necessarily a better buy than the stock of many companies with dismal earning records.

The way to accumulate a fortune is to supply something that can be sold for much more than it costs to produce, or to invest in someone else's enterprises that are going to generate huge net revenues by doing this. But it's essential that this outcome be uncertain. And there's the rub. You must know more than others—or be able to read the uncertain future more accurately—if you hope to make large profits. Or else you rely solely on luck. But if you rely on luck, you have an equal probability of being unlucky and sustaining a large loss. The significant thing about pure luck is that it's pure. Any investors who consistently make profits, defined as net income *beyond the common rate of return from readily available investment opportunities,* must be predicting the uncertain future more successfully than others.

THE ENTREPRENEUR

The argument of the preceding section may have left the impression that people make profits simply by forecasting better than others, so that profits are nothing but the consequences of successful speculation. That would be highly misleading. The far more important part of profit making is its active and creative side. People don't just sit around and bet on the outcome of other people's activity. They try—or at least some of them do—to organize things differently. Their incentive is the belief that a particular reorganization will return revenues greater than its costs. The term for such people is *entrepreneur.*

The English equivalent is *undertaker,* a nicely descriptive term whose use we have unfortunately lost by surrendering it completely to undertakers of funerals. Entrepreneurs are people who undertake to reorganize a segment of the social world. What makes them the undertakers or entrepreneurs rather than mere participants is that they accept responsibility for the outcome. They say in effect to all the others whose cooperation is required for their project: "I'll pay you an agreed-upon amount if you will perform an agreed-upon service. If my project fails, you won't lose: I'll take the loss. If it succeeds, you will still get only the agreed-upon amount: I'll take the profit." Entrepreneurs claim the residual, what is left over after all prior agreements have been honored. They choose to put themselves in this position because they think they can "pull it off." They have confidence in their own insight, foresight, and organizational ability. What Adam Smith called a commercial society and what most people rather misleadingly call a capitalist society is also sometimes referred to as an enterprise society. Those who choose to call it by that name are emphasizing the crucial role of the entrepreneur.

A good way to understand the role of the entrepreneur and the function of residual claimancy is by asking, "Who gets to be boss?" How do the many people whose cooperation is essential to the production of particular goods manage to agree on who is in charge of each particular operation? Those are important issues to settle, because the opinions and the interests of people are bound to conflict at many points. Down at the gizmo plant on East Industrial Avenue, Achilles maintains that six rivets are more than enough, while Hector insists that anything fewer than nine means shabby work. Nine rivets would make a sturdier gizmo, but also one that's more costly to manufacture. A sturdier gizmo will attract more customers, but a higher price to cover the higher marginal cost will repel some customers. Hector believes that he should be allowed to decide because he has an engineering degree, but Achilles has contempt for college degrees and points to his own many years of experience. Their disagreement could be a completely honest difference of opinion, but it might also be colored by the fact that Hector is the riveter and hopes for overtime, or that Achilles is the riveter and wants to reduce his work load. Who makes the final decision? More to the point, who decides who gets to make the final decision?

The basic answer is *the residual claimant*. If you want to be boss, you must become the residual claimant. You do that essentially by purchasing the consent of everyone else on the team. You make a deal with them. "What are your terms?" The entrepreneur promises to meet those terms. That promise must be believed, of course. To persuade others to give up their next best opportunities and to suppress their misgivings, disagreements, or dislikes and go along with what the entrepreneur decides, the entrepreneur must offer credible guarantees.

WHERE DOES THE BUCK STOP?

Suppose Achilles and Hector actually like each other and decide to open an art gallery together. Achilles knows a lot about marketing and Hector knows a lot about art, so they figure they will make a perfect partnership. Each invests $10,000 and agrees to work 40 hours a week. Then they discover that they can't agree on how to price their artists' work. Hector says he should be allowed to make the final decision because Achilles knows nothing about art. Achilles says the final decision should be his because Hector knows nothing about marketing. If they cannot resolve their disagreements through discussion, an alternative to dissolving the partnership is for one of them to become the (sole) entrepreneur.

"Let me make the pricing decisions," Hector says. "I'll guarantee you $15 an hour for whatever time you put in plus a 10 percent annual return on the money you've invested." If Achilles is willing to work in the gallery for $15 an hour and willing to keep his money invested for a 10 percent return, and if he believes Hector can and will make good on his commitment, he may say: "All right. I still think you're wrong. But it's your funeral if it doesn't work out." Achilles thereby makes Hector the boss. Hector has contracted for Achilles's services and become the residual claimant. He will now take the entire loss if his judgment turns out to be wrong and will reap the entire profit if it turns out to be correct.

Here is another example of a different sort. When you were browsing the other day in a clothing store downtown, you saw some attractive sweaters on sale at a very low price, and you bought one that especially caught your eye. When you got it home, however, you found it was just a little too small. So you returned it to the store, only to discover that you had overlooked something. The huge sign right next to the sweaters says: "ALL SALES FINAL. NO REFUNDS, NO EXCHANGES."

The clerk is very sorry, but she can't exchange it or give you a refund. You are quite upset and point out that you spend a lot of money in this store. The clerk is even sorrier, but she just isn't allowed to do it. When you persist and become a little testy, she says, "I'll let you speak to my supervisor."

The supervisor is extremely apologetic, too, but tells you that the prices were set so low because the store wanted to clear these sweaters out; that's why they put up the big sign stating that all sales were final, and it's a store policy to allow no returns on items sold at super-discount prices. You are now quite angry, and when you say that you spend hundreds of dollars in this store every year, the supervisor relents; she says she will allow you to exchange the sweater for a larger one. Unfortunately, there are no larger sweaters left except for two in a ghastly color. The supervisor smiles weakly and says there is simply no way she can give you a refund except by taking it out of her own pocket because the computer won't allow refunds on super-discount sales. "It's store policy, and I can't do anything about it," she says in a pleading tone.

"It's a rotten policy," you respond. "Let me talk to the owner." Why do you want to talk to the owner? Because that is where the buck stops. It doesn't stop with "store policy," because someone *sets* store policies. If this policy is just part of a larger policy, someone set that larger policy. You want the policy altered. That means you have to reach the person ultimately responsible. You want to argue that the few dollars the store will make by refusing you a refund are not worth all the dollars the store will lose by sending you home infuriated. The person with whom you want to argue is the person with an incentive to take account of *all* costs and *all* benefits. That will be the residual claimant.

"Let me talk to the owner" constitutes an appeal from partial perspectives to the overall perspective. You want to speak with the person who has an incentive to consider *everything* relevant to the business, predict *all* future effects, and construct a balance of *overall* gains and losses, and who has the authority to *decide*. Only the residual claimant matches that description.

NONPROFIT INSTITUTIONS

Residual claimants are crucial actors in any society characterized by extensive specialization and exchange. Institutions that do not have residual claimants do not, by and large, function as effectively as institutions that do. Consider buyers' queues, for example. Standing in line to buy, as we pointed out in Chapter 4, is a deadweight cost, because it's a burden on the buyer that is not also a benefit to the seller. Because that burden is a real cost to the buyer, it reduces the quantity demanded. (How many times have you turned away and gone somewhere else because the line was too long?) Why then doesn't the seller take steps to reduce the length of the line? It might be because the marginal cost of shortening the line exceeds the marginal revenue to the enterprise. But it also might be because there is no residual claimant on the scene. There is no one with the incentive to estimate all costs and all benefits and the authority to act appropriately.

That is why we *expect* long lines at the post office but not at the grocery store. It's not that no one at the post office cares. Postal employees are probably just as caring or noncaring on average as the checkout people in grocery stores. The difference arises from the fact that policies are set for the grocery store by a residual claimant, someone with an incentive to estimate the costs to the enterprise of long lines and the costs to the enterprise of a reserve supply of checkers and the authority to act as those comparative costs decree. There is no residual claimant in the post office branch or in the postal service as a whole.

Nonprofit institutions by definition have no residual claimants. That is why they so often behave in such clumsy ways. If you want an example, try the college or university you are attending. Colleges and universities do a lot of "stupid" things because there is no one with the incentive to compare the cost of continuing current policies with the cost of eliminating them plus the authority to act appropriately. The word *stupid* has to go in quotation marks because the policies of colleges and universities are not really the product of stupidity. They are the product of social institutions without residual claimants and therefore without intelligent command centers.

A standard example of "stupidity," one familiar to almost everyone who has ever worked in a nonprofit institution, is the rush by each department manager to spend every dime in the budget before the budget period ends. Why not? "If we don't spend it, we'll lose it." A department that ends the budget year with $1000 still left in the travel account loses an opportunity to send two people on a round-trip junket. The recapture of that money by the institution makes an additional $1000 available to purchase essential supplies in another department. But the value of the junket to the head of the first department, while small, is still greater than the value *to that manager* of the extra supplies now available to another department in whose welfare the manager of the first department has not the slightest interest.

Who has the incentive and authority in such a case to estimate the relative benefits to the institution as a whole of the junket and the extra supplies and to allocate that $1000 accordingly? College and university administrators know that waste is occurring, just as do administrators in other nonprofit institutions, including the gigantic institutions of government. But in the absence of a residual claimant, incentives to change these situations do not confront people who have the authority to change them. The buck stops nowhere.

THE TRANSITION FROM SOCIALISM

That has been a major reason for the failure of central economic planning, a failure that economists have been predicting on theoretical grounds for almost a century, but that became too obvious to be ignored only at the end of the 1980s. The history of central planning is full of tales about useless goods produced at enormous cost in alternative opportunities forgone. Machines produced without the spare parts that would enable them to keep operating. Poor agricultural harvests that result from failure to coordinate decisions on planting and cultivation. Cost savings that eventuate in goods of such low quality that they have to be discarded. The mythical nail factory that produced only tiny nails when the central planners set its quota in *number* of nails and that produced just one huge nail per year when the planners responded by setting the quota in *weight*.

The correct assortment of nails is the assortment that results from taking account of *all* the benefits and *all* the costs of alternative production strategies. The correct assortment will only be ordered if incentives and authority are brought together appropriately. A system based on residual claimancy brings them together.

Any society that officially condemns profit as mere surplus value extracted from exploited labor will prevent a system of residual claimancy from evolving. It will prevent people from taking on the entrepreneurial function by banning the contractual agreements that enable them to become entrepreneurs. It will not allow Hector to strike his deal with Achilles because that would make Hector a "capitalist" and turn Achilles into an exploited laborer. What turns out to be far worse in its consequences, such a society will not permit the development of the institutions that facilitate the negotiation and enforcement of such contractual agreements.

It is the absence of such institutions that is today hobbling the evolution toward a market system of the former socialist societies in central and eastern Europe and the former U.S.S.R. These countries do not have many of the key institutions that keep transaction costs low in "capitalist" societies and so enable people to work out cooperative arrangements that are often stunning in their complexity. Browse through any issue of *The Wall Street Journal,* especially the section titled "Money and Investing," to see how extraordinarily complex such arrangements have become. They are complex not because of experts who want to keep all us lay people in the dark, but because institutions evolve into complex forms over time as the members of commercial societies search for low-cost ways to make and monitor agreements. Banks, insurance companies, credit-rating organizations, brokers in endless varieties, organized exchanges, bonding companies, consulting agencies, accounting firms, leasing companies, testing specialists . . . the list is endless. Undergirding all these institutions are the accepted property rights of the society, the extensive body of statutes and judicial precedents that make up "the law of the land," and the widely respected customs and moral principles that fill out and firm up "the rules of the game."

A successful transition from "socialism" to "capitalism" will take no less time than is required for these institutions to evolve, will be no less difficult than the successful development of these institutions, and will fail if public patience is exhausted before a sufficient number of these institutions have taken form.

To summarize: Entrepreneurs are society's agents of change. They are the people who perceive gaps between what is and what might be and opportunities to profit from closing those gaps. They acquire control over the resources they must employ to close the gaps by hiring the resources from their owners. The owners surrender control over the resources they own in return for the entrepreneur's payment. The sum of these payments is the entrepreneur's costs. The difference between these costs and the total revenue from the entrepreneur's project is the entrepreneur's profit—or loss, if the entrepreneur's perception was mistaken.

EVERYONE IS DOING IT

We ought to pause a moment to clear the concept of profit (and loss) from the narrow connotations that it may have acquired in the course of this discussion. Profits and losses appear everywhere, for everyone, and not just for business firms or those who invest in financial assets.

Consider the sad case of Giuseppe Vibrato, who attends a music conservatory for three years, planning on a career in opera. At about the time of Vibrato's graduation, the public abandons all interest in opera. So Vibrato sustains a loss. We mustn't exaggerate the loss, for Vibrato may receive a generous return on his educational investment in the form of many years of listening to himself sing Verdi and Wagner. (Education can prepare people to enjoy life as well as provide them with marketable skills.) But to the extent that Vibrato paid tuition and sacrificed earnings for three years in order to earn an income in opera, the unexpected change in public tastes caused him to sustain a loss. Vibrato took the loss because he was the entrepreneur. The music conservatory received all the tuition agreed upon.

In the same way aerospace engineers suffer losses when the federal government cuts back on the space program, college professors receive profits when the federal government decides to spend huge sums on higher education, authors make a profit when they hit on a book that captivates the public, and highly trained astrologers took a loss when people abandoned the belief that the stars shape individual destiny. (But note also that in the last case some of their intellectual descendants have recently made profits from an unexpected return to older persuasions.) Engineers, professors, authors, and astrologers all become entrepreneurs when they undertake reorganizational projects, including projects to reorganize their own knowledge and skills.

All these examples involve monetary income. But profits and losses don't have to entail changes in monetary wealth. The skier who undertakes a trip to the slopes and then finds rain incurs a loss. If he heads for the lodge to drown his sorrows and there meets his future wife, he makes a profit. If she turns out after several years of marriage to be even more pleasant and intelligent than he had thought, his profit increases. And the profit from that rain-drenched ski trip becomes almost exorbitant if they jointly produce a cherubic child who fills their days with cheer. These examples remind us that undeserved profits occur in all aspects of life and—equally important—that they also depend most of the time on the exercise of foresight and discretion. This last point has considerable political importance.

"WINDFALL" PROFITS AND LOSSES

One term that's often used to describe these differences between expected and realized outcomes is *windfalls.* Because the differences can be positive or negative, we should speak of *windfall profits* and *windfall losses.* We don't often encounter the term *windfall losses,* however, and it's worthwhile to think about why we don't. The word *windfall* originally referred to fruit that was blown down from a tree. The fruit was not earned through the effort of climbing and picking but was a gift of the wind, which blows unpredictably and beyond anyone's control. The term *windfall profit* implies an origin in luck rather than merit. Windfall profits are thus undeserved profits, because no one *deserves* good luck.

Of course, no one deserves bad luck either. So why don't we speak of windfall losses? The reason would appear to be that people don't go about claiming a *right* to losses, or insisting that society is violating their rights in compensating them for losses sustained. The adjective *windfall* is only attached to *profit* because only in the case of profit do people frequently want to counter the claim that the recipient earned or otherwise deserved what happened.

When we talk about what people do or do not deserve, we're talking about ethics rather than economics. Ethics is such a difficult subject that we would much prefer to go around it. But economists are once again beginning to discover (Adam Smith was fully aware of it two centuries ago!) that supply curves and demand curves—the most basic building blocks of economic analysis—depend on convictions and commitments that are fundamentally ethical in nature.

The heart of the matter from the standpoint of the economic analyst is that the decisions people make in any economic system depend in a crucial way on the property rights that are established and accepted in that society. The term *property rights*—as we use it in this book—has a much broader connotation than what is usually conjured up in people's minds. Perhaps when you hear the term you picture a rancher with a shotgun saying, "Git off my land," or someone indignantly announcing, "It belongs to me and I can do what I want with it!" We must enlarge the concept far beyond those images if it's to help us understand how economic systems function, how income is distributed, why pollution occurs, or what we can reasonably expect from government. When economists speak of property rights, they have in mind something closely akin to what we have called "the rules of the game." *Property rights are rights to control the way in which particular resources will be used and to assign the resulting costs and benefits.* It is property rights—or what people believe to be the relevant rules of the game—that determine how the processes of supply and demand will work themselves out in a society. The notion of "windfall" profits and losses provides some excellent illustrations.

HOW SHALL WE TREAT "WINDFALLS"?

Oil refiners maintain sizable inventories of crude oil in order to assure a smooth and continuous operation of the refinery. If forces beyond their control increase the demand for or reduce the supply of crude petroleum, its price will rise. The value of the refiners' inventories will therefore rise, too. An increase in the value of a firm's inventories is an addition to its wealth, and additions to wealth are what we call income. Any income of business firms in excess of costs we call profit. So oil refiners, in this case, receive a profit from the occurrence of events beyond their control. Almost everyone will (and did) call that a windfall profit. Some go further and argue that it ought to be taxed away, because the refiners have no right to receive windfall profits. They belong by right to . . . whom?

This case illustrates the dependence of actions on expectations and of expectations on established property rights, as well as the significance of ethical convictions in the shaping or reshaping of property rights. The managers of a refinery accumulate inventories in the first place because they expect to be able to use them when and how they please. (That's not quite accurate; the managers know that they would not be allowed to use the inventories as they pleased if it pleased them to pump some onto the city's sidewalks for the fun of seeing pedestrians slip and slide. But they did expect to be allowed to use the inventories for accepted business purposes.) This expectation reflects existing property rights. Under a different set of rights, the managers of the refinery might have chosen to accumulate less inventory or even none at all. They would have chosen to accumulate very little if, according to the accepted rules of the society, anyone who wants some crude is entitled to draw freely on the inventories of anyone else who happens to have some in stock. The refinery managers would also have chosen to carry smaller levels of inventory had they thought that the taxing authorities would appropriate any increase in inventory value due to price increases, without compensating the firm for losses due to price declines and a consequent fall in the value of inventory. People don't normally accept wagers of the form, "Heads I break even, tails I lose." The accepted rules of the society—customs and moral principles as well as laws—affect people's behavior by defining their property rights.

EXPECTATIONS AND ACTIONS

We're focusing on property rights related to the oil inventories of refiners. But you should notice that everything else associated with the operation of the refineries, including the actions of employees, stockholders, motorists, or legislators, can also be viewed as a response to prevailing property rights. People act as they do because of the expectations created by existing property rights. Employees show up for work because they confidently expect to claim a paycheck on Friday. Stockholders purchase and retain shares because they expect to be cut in, as a matter of legal right, for a percentage of the firm's earnings proportionate to the number of shares they own. Motorists buy automobiles because they expect to be able to obtain suitable fuel at acceptable prices. And legislators draft laws that may alter the expectations of everyone else because they themselves expect to be able to win reelection by doing so.

Expectations are always much more complex than any of the capsule summaries above suggest. Oil refiners don't accumulate inventories exclusively in order to smooth the flow of production or to fulfill their contracts with customers. They also look ahead, try to anticipate changes in supply or demand, add to inventories if they predict higher prices in the future, and reduce inventories to some minimum level if they expect prices to fall. To some degree, in short, the inventory managers of an oil refinery function like the speculators described in Chapter 7. *They cannot choose not to speculate,* since both holding and not holding large inventories are speculative decisions, either of which could lead to a substantial gain or loss. Which of these eventually appears will depend on the relationship between what the managers expect to happen and what actually happens.

The windfalls that result from the inventory decisions of oil-refinery managers turn out now to be not altogether windfalls after all. Windfalls are, by definition, the product of pure luck. It follows that managers who obtain them for their firms by predicting the future a little bit or a whole lot better than others are not really obtaining windfalls. They *are* obtaining increased profits—of that much we can be sure. The source of these profits is the fact that the managers' decisions predicted the future more accurately than did the predictions of others. That's also clear. Were the profits deserved? That is not as clear. It's at least in part an ethical question, and one on which opinions differ sharply.

Although economic analysis cannot by itself resolve such ethical issues, it can contribute to a resolution of the debate by clarifying the consequences of alternative answers. If people expect to have the profits from correct decisions taken away from them, on the grounds that such profits are undeserved, and if they also expect that the losses that accrue from incorrect decisions will not be fully subsidized, they will attempt to minimize risk. Decisions will converge toward the average. Only short-range projects will be undertaken. Fewer resources will be invested in research. Innovative projects will be explored less often. Problems that could have been avoided through better foresight will be encountered more frequently. Coordination failures will occur more often as individuals try to reduce their private risks.

If both the profits and the losses that arise from the inescapable necessity of making decisions in the presence of uncertainty are removed from those who made the decisions and shared by everyone in society, less care will be invested in the making of decisions. Taking care is costly whenever it means, as it usually does, the forgoing of valuable opportunities. That is why people behave "care-lessly" when they themselves have nothing to gain or lose. It is also why students usually read more "care-fully" in a course taken for grade credit than in one they're only auditing. And it explains why people without theft insurance on their automobiles more often take the trouble to roll up all the windows and lock the doors.

The significance of these consequences can, of course, be debated. To what extent do progress, achievement, creativity, wealth, harmony, happiness, or any other of these hard-to-define goods depend on the willingness to take risks or to take care? But the consequences themselves could be denied only by someone who was prepared to argue that superior knowledge of a legitimate kind does not exist, that everyone is equally well informed or equally ignorant—except insofar as some have unfair advantages. That, too, could probably be argued. All advantages become unfair advantages if one begins with the assumption that no one *ought* to have any kind of advantage over another. But does anyone seriously maintain this? Are we prepared to restrict the game of basketball to people who are 5 feet 9 inches tall and require Van Cliburn to wear mittens while playing the piano? The issue of merit, of what people deserve, does without question influence our convictions about the rights that people ought to have. But the rights that people believe themselves to have also entail consequences. In order to secure certain consequences that we want, we may be required to concede rights to people without regard to their personal merit. To take an extreme example: If rewards to criminal informants produce very large benefits for the rest of us, then probably such rewards ought to be paid, even though the informants obviously don't deserve them in any moral sense.

The term *windfall profit* is dangerous, because it suggests that such profits ought to be taxed or otherwise taken away. The difficulty with this is that no one knows how to distinguish the profits that are produced by astute entrepreneurial actions from those profits that are purely the product of luck. Moreover, the potential of profit is an important, perhaps indispensable stimulus to action. The potential of a profit prompts entrepreneurs to search for more efficient ways of combining resources, new products for which there may be a demand, and organizational innovations that promise to increase effectiveness. The potential of profit often persuades people to take pains when they would otherwise prefer not to and to take chances in which the possible benefits to others are associated with the possibility of substantial losses for the one taking the chance. The potential of profit persuades some people (the unusually courageous, or foolhardy, or adventurous, or greedy, or perceptive, or knowledgeable, or public-spirited—who among us is competent to judge?) to increase the security of others by accepting risks themselves.

RESTRICTIONS ON COMPETITION

Something important seems to be missing from this analysis of profit. If profit is always the consequence of uncertainty, what were all those special-interest groups pursuing in the preceding chapter? When associations of physicians, plumbers, farmers, airline pilots, nursing home operators, or automobile manufacturers urge the government to restrict competition in their trade, what are they after? They surely aren't pursuing uncertainty. On the contrary, they are trying to reduce uncertainty, at least for themselves, by preventing price cutting and keeping out competitors. If they succeed in their efforts, don't they secure for themselves something close to a guaranteed profit? And a guarantee is at the opposite pole from uncertainty.

As we said at the beginning of this chapter, there is little to be gained by arguing about definitions. We do want to take a closer look, however, to see whether restrictions on the ability to compete really do give rise to something we can call a guaranteed profit.

Suppose that you accidentally—with no investment of time, effort, or other resources—discover the way to build a better mousetrap. You snagged the blueprints, let's say, while out fishing. Recognizing the value of your find, you immediately obtain a patent from the government and make plans to go into production. Since the world will beat a path to the door of anyone who builds a better mousetrap, and since the patent prohibits any competitor from duplicating your product for 17 years, you are going to become rich. It's a virtual certainty. And the first year's results confirm your happy prediction: net revenue is $100,000. You can confidently expect another $100,000 for each of the next 16 years. It looks like an annual *and fairly certain* profit of $100,000. But let's pursue the story further.

What is the source of this "profit"? It's your patent, of course, which prevents competition from eroding the difference between your total revenue and your total costs. But have you accurately calculated the cost of producing these superior mousetraps?

COMPETITION ON OTHER FRONTS

If ownership of the patent generates a virtually certain $100,000 per year for you in net revenue, wouldn't its ownership generate just as much income for somebody else? In fact, wouldn't the patent be even more valuable—generate more than $100,000 annually—in the hands of someone who had specialized in mousetraps and knew more than you about their production and distribution? So some of those who beat a path to your door when you build a better mousetrap are going to be established mousetrap manufacturers who want to purchase or rent your patent. You will consequently discover that the cost to you of continuing as the exclusive producer of these superior mousetraps has gone up by the value of the opportunity you spurn if you decline to sell or lease your patent.

Suppose a long-established maker of mousetraps offers to buy your patent for $1.5 million. How might the firm arrive at such a figure? It could estimate that your patent will produce at least a $200,000 annual increase in its net revenue. If the going rate of return on relatively risk-free investments, such as U.S. government bonds, is currently 10 percent, your patent is a good investment at a purchase price of $1.5 million; it promises to yield more than 13 percent per year. Of course, the firm would prefer to get that patent for less. At a price of $1.2 million, $200,000 becomes a 16.5 percent annual return on investment. But there are other mousetrap manufacturers; 16.5 percent is too good a deal for them to pass by, and so the winning bid rises to $1.5 million. That's the process by which the market price of your patent would be determined.

What does all this do to your annual "profit" of $100,000? It wipes it out entirely and turns your "profit" into an actual loss. Do you see why and how? When competition among mousetrap makers sets a price of $1.5 million on your patent, the cost to you of continuing to manufacture mousetraps increases by about $150,000 per year, which is the income you will forgo if you decide not to sell your patent and invest the proceeds in government bonds. What has happened is this: When the word got out that ownership of your patent was a virtual guarantee of profit—an annual revenue greater than cost—potential owners began bidding for the patent. Their bids transformed your "profit" into a cost of production: the value of the opportunity you forgo by not selling.

What about the firm that buys your patent? Will it make a profit afterwards? It might. If events turn out as the firm had hoped and its net revenue does increase by $200,000 a year, acquisition of the patent will prove to have been a smart move. Of course, $150,000 of that $200,000 will be a cost of production: the income forgone by investing $1.5 million in the patent rather than in government bonds. The remaining $50,000 could be viewed as a genuine profit, the result of prior uncertainty about the actual value of the patent to the acquiring firm, a return to the firm's entrepreneurial initiatives in obtaining and employing your patent.

Notice, though, that the process of competition just described will resume once the $50,000 becomes relatively "certain." Other firms might renew the bidding for the patent, raising its price above $1.5 million. Should the patent be worth more than $1.5 million *only to this firm,* that would suggest this firm controls some unique complementary resources—a marketing manager, perhaps, with a special talent for designing ads that arouse the fear of mice. In that case, the price of the complementary resources will be bid up as other firms discover what's going on and try to obtain these "profitable" resources for their own use. If the firm is forced to pay the marketing manager a higher salary to retain his services, a part of the "profit" will turn into an addition to its wage and salary costs.

You can watch this happening in all sorts of places once you have learned where to look.

COMPETITION FOR THE KEY RESOURCE

When the government tries to increase the income of wheat farmers by guaranteeing them a higher price for their product, land suitable for wheat production becomes more valuable and so its price rises. Tenant farmers subsequently have to pay more for the land they rent and farmers who try to buy land must pay more to get it. The increased "profit" for wheat farmers at which the government policy was aimed generates, as soon as the policy becomes known, an increase in the cost of producing wheat, through a rise in the cost of using land. The beneficiaries will be those who owned land suitable for growing wheat before it became generally known that the government was going to raise the support price of wheat. The profits from the increase in the support price for wheat will go to those lucky enough or foresighted enough to have the relevant property rights at the appropriate time.

When taxicab operators secure legislation restricting the number of cabs that are licensed to operate in a city, ownership of a license becomes more valuable. Competition for the licenses then bids up their price until the cost of operating a cab—including the opportunity cost of acquiring or of retaining ownership of the license—is equal to the revenue from its operation. That doesn't mean taxicab operators don't get any benefit from their lobbying campaign. Those who owned licenses before the legal restrictions were generally anticipated benefit from an increase in the value of their licenses. That increase is their profit, and it's what they were hoping for when they launched their lobbying efforts, when they became political entrepreneurs. But after the lobbying efforts have succeeded it will cost more to operate a cab, because each cab operator will now have to own a costly license in order to do so.

The right to broadcast on a VHF television channel in a large city is a very valuable property right. If the Federal Communications Commission were to assign these rights to the highest bidder, the government would receive a tidy sum and the "profit" from use of the channel would become a cost of doing business to the broadcaster. In fact, however, the FCC has always assigned the right to use a particular channel, without charge, on the basis of obscure criteria having to do with the merit of competing applicants and the promises they make regarding future public service. As a result, applicants compete by hiring lawyers, accountants, and assorted public-relations specialists to influence the FCC's assignment. In this case the critical resource that creates a "profit" is the FCC's decision, and competition among entrepreneurs consequently aims at acquiring control of that decision. The "profit" from receipt of the channel is transformed along the way into the cost of exerting political influence.

COMPETITION AND PROPERTY RIGHTS

Profits and losses arise from uncertainty and cannot exist in the absence of uncertainty. Where everything relevant to the making of a profit is known for certain, competition to obtain the profit will eliminate it, either by reducing revenue or by raising cost. There's nothing very surprising about that conclusion; it follows logically from the way we have defined cost and profit. What matters, and what this chapter was intended to clarify, are the forms that competition and entrepreneurial activity take in response to the lure of a possible profit and the social consequences that emerge.

Will the pursuit of profit lead people to produce better mousetraps or to prevent others from selling better mouse-traps in their territory? Will it yield more wheat or higher-priced wheat land? Better taxi service or an increase in the cost of licenses? Lower prices for consumers or higher incomes for the owners of critical resources? Exploration or retrenchment? Innovations in technology or in social organization? A wider range of choices or more restrictions on choice? The answers will depend on the rules of the game and the system of property rights that they create.

An Appendix: DISCOUNTING AND PRESENT VALUES

If the prevailing annual interest rate reflects the greater value that people assign to goods now over goods one year from now, it follows that the value of goods expected to be received a year from now must be discounted by the rate of interest to determine their *present value*. The process of discounting to determine the present value of future goods plays a large part in economic decisionmaking. Mastering this process will equip you better to understand the analysis of subsequent chapters and will acquaint you with procedures widely employed in the business and financial world.

Suppose that Ivy College, that well-managed institution of higher learning introduced in Chapter 9, offers the parents of entering students a Tuition Stabilization Plan. Tuition, currently at $2000, is almost sure to rise each year, they point out, because of continuing inflation. Ivy even announces in advance its intention to increase the annual tuition charge by $200 in each of the next three years. But parents who subscribe to the TSP receive a special deal. They pay $8000 in September of the first year and nothing thereafter. In effect, says Ivy's multicolored brochure, parents who sign up for TSP save $1200 on the cost of their child's education. Ivy may go so far as to call it a 15 percent saving.

But is $8000 paid now really less than $2000 now plus $2200 one year from now, $2400 two years from now, and $2600 three years from now? The last three amounts are amounts due in the future, and future dollars, like any other future goods, must be discounted if we want to assess their present value. What interest rate should we use? The best answer is provided by the opportunity cost to the parents of lending money to Ivy College, since that is in effect what they are doing. They are lending Ivy money by paying the tuition before it is due. Thus $2000 of the sophomore year tuition is lent for one year, $2000 of the junior year tuition is lent for two years, and $2000 of the senior year tuition is lent for three years. What's the alternative opportunity for those amounts?

WHAT A PRESENT AMOUNT GROWS TO

Suppose the parents sell stock to obtain the money, and their stock investments ordinarily earn an annual return, in dividends plus increased market price, of 12 percent a year. Then the opportunity cost of lending $2000 to Ivy College for one year is $240. That's $240 expended to avoid $200 in increased tuition—not an attractive arrangement. The junior-year loan is an even poorer investment: $2000 grows in two years, at 12 percent per year, to $2000 × 1.12 × 1.12 or $2508.80. The phenomenon of compound interest is at work, and it makes the three-year loan still less appealing. To avoid the $600 in additional tuition due for the senior year, the parents give up $809.86 that they might otherwise have earned from the ownership of stock, since $2000 × 1.12^3 is $2809.86.

PRESENT VALUE OF FUTURE AMOUNTS

We've assessed Ivy's proposal by calculating what a dollar now will grow to, at the appropriate rate of return, in one year, two years, and three years, and comparing those amounts with the tuition that would ordinarily be due in one year, in two years, and in three years. We can reach the same conclusion by working in the other direction. What is the *present value* of the $2200 that will be due in one year? That amounts to asking: What present sum would grow to exactly $2200 in one year if invested at 12 percent? The answer is $2200 divided by 1.12, or $1964.29, which means that in prepaying the sophomore year tuition the parents give up $2000 now to save $36 less than that in present value. The $2400 that would be due in two years has a present value of $2400 divided by (1.12 × 1.12), or $1913.27, which is $87 less than what the parents actually pay. The $2600, when divided by 1.12^3, turns out to have a present value of only $1850.63.

People who make these computations in the course of their everyday business decisions use tables that enable them to calculate quickly the sum to which a present amount will grow or the present value of future amounts. Three such ta-

TABLE 11-1   Amount to Which $1 Will Grow in the Designated Number of Years When Compounded Annually at Various Interest Rates

Year	1%	2%	3%	4%	6%	9%	12%	15%	24%	36%
1	1.010	1.020	1.030	1.040	1.060	1.090	1.120	1.150	1.240	1.360
2	1.020	1.040	1.061	1.082	1.124	1.188	1.254	1.322	1.538	1.850
3	1.030	1.061	1.093	1.125	1.191	1.295	1.405	1.521	1.907	2.515
4	1.041	1.082	1.126	1.170	1.262	1.412	1.574	1.749	2.364	3.421
5	1.051	1.104	1.159	1.217	1.338	1.539	1.762	2.011	2.932	4.653
6	1.062	1.126	1.194	1.265	1.419	1.677	1.974	2.313	3.635	6.328
7	1.072	1.149	1.230	1.316	1.504	1.828	2.211	2.660	4.508	8.605
8	1.083	1.172	1.267	1.369	1.594	1.993	2.476	3.059	5.590	11.703
9	1.094	1.195	1.305	1.423	1.689	2.172	2.773	3.518	6.931	15.917
10	1.105	1.219	1.344	1.480	1.791	2.367	3.106	4.046	8.594	21.647
11	1.116	1.243	1.384	1.539	1.898	2.580	3.479	4.652	10.657	29.439
12	1.127	1.268	1.426	1.601	2.012	2.813	3.896	5.350	13.215	40.037
13	1.138	1.294	1.469	1.665	2.133	3.066	4.363	6.153	16.386	54.451
14	1.149	1.319	1.513	1.732	2.261	3.342	4.887	7.076	20.319	74.053
15	1.161	1.346	1.558	1.801	2.397	3.642	5.474	8.137	25.196	10.71
16	1.173	1.373	1.605	1.873	2.540	3.970	6.130	9.358	31.243	136.97
17	1.184	1.400	1.653	1.948	2.693	4.328	6.866	10.761	38.741	186.28
18	1.196	1.428	1.702	2.026	2.854	4.717	7.690	12.375	48.039	253.34
19	1.208	1.457	1.754	2.107	3.026	5.142	8.613	14.232	59.568	344.54
20	1.200	1.486	1.806	2.191	3.207	5.604	9.646	16.367	73.864	468.57
25	1.282	1.641	2.094	2.666	4.292	8.623	17.000	32.919	216.54	2180.1
30	1.348	1.811	2.427	3.243	5.743	13.268	29.960	66.212	634.82	10143
40	1.489	2.208	3.262	4.801	10.286	31.409	93.051	267.86	5455.9	..
50	1.645	2.692	4.384	7.107	18.420	74.358	289.00	1083.7	46890	..
60	1.817	3.281	5.892	10.520	32.988	176.03	897.60	4384.0	..	..
70	2.007	4.000	7.918	15.572	59.076	416.73	2787.8	17736	..	..
80	2.217	4.875	10.641	23.050	105.80	986.55	8658.5	71751	..	..
90	2.449	5.943	14.300	34.119	189.46	2335.5	26892	..	..	..
100	2.705	7.245	19.219	50.505	339.30	5529.0	83522	..	..	..

bles are provided on the succeeding pages. You can use the first two, Tables 11-1 and 11-2, to check the conclusions just presented, which is a subtle way of suggesting that you practice with the tables until you're able to obtain the above results. One more problem will be presented to introduce you to the third table, Table 11-3.

PRESENT VALUE OF ANNUITIES

What should a maker of mousetraps be willing to pay for a patent that is expected to produce an additional $200,000 per year for the next 17 years? It is certainly less than 17 times $200,000 or $3.4 million.

TABLE 11-2   Present Value of $1 at the End of the Designated Number of Years When Discounted at Various Interest Rates

Year	1%	2%	3%	4%	6%	9%	12%	15%	24%	36%
1	0.990	0.980	0.971	0.962	0.943	0.917	0.893	0.870	0.806	0.735
2	0.980	0.961	0.943	0.925	0.890	0.842	0.797	0.756	0.650	0.541
3	0.971	0.942	0.915	0.889	0.840	0.772	0.712	0.658	0.524	0.398
4	0.961	0.924	0.888	0.855	0.792	0.708	0.636	0.572	0.423	0.292
5	0.951	0.906	0.863	0.822	0.747	0.650	0.567	0.497	0.341	0.215
6	0.942	0.888	0.837	0.790	0.705	0.596	0.507	0.432	0.275	0.158
7	0.933	0.871	0.813	0.760	0.665	0.547	0.452	0.376	0.222	0.116
8	0.923	0.853	0.789	0.731	0.627	0.502	0.404	0.327	0.179	0.085
9	0.914	0.837	0.766	0.703	0.592	0.460	0.361	0.284	0.144	0.063
10	0.905	0.820	0.744	0.676	0.558	0.422	0.322	0.247	0.116	0.046
11	0.896	0.804	0.722	0.650	0.527	0.388	0.287	0.215	0.094	0.034
12	0.887	0.788	0.701	0.625	0.497	0.356	0.257	0.187	0.076	0.025
13	0.879	0.773	0.681	0.601	0.469	0.326	0.229	0.163	0.061	0.018
14	0.870	0.758	0.661	0.577	0.442	0.299	0.205	0.141	0.049	0.014
15	0.861	0.743	0.642	0.555	0.417	0.275	0.183	0.123	0.040	0.010
16	0.853	0.728	0.623	0.534	0.394	0.252	0.163	0.107	0.032	0.007
17	0.844	0.714	0.605	0.513	0.371	0.231	0.146	0.093	0.026	0.005
18	0.836	0.700	0.587	0.494	0.350	0.212	0.130	0.081	0.021	0.004
19	0.828	0.686	0.570	0.475	0.331	0.194	0.116	0.070	0.017	0.003
20	0.820	0.673	0.554	0.456	0.312	0.178	0.104	0.061	0.014	0.002
25	0.780	0.610	0.478	0.375	0.233	0.116	0.059	0.030	0.005	0.000
30	0.742	0.552	0.412	0.308	0.174	0.075	0.033	0.015	0.002	0.000
40	0.672	0.453	0.307	0.208	0.097	0.032	0.011	0.004	0.000	0.000
50	0.608	0.372	0.228	0.141	0.054	0.013	0.003	0.001	0.000	0.000
60	0.550	0.305	0.170	0.095	0.030	0.006	0.001	0.000	0.000	0.000
70	0.498	0.250	0.126	0.064	0.017	0.002	0.000	0.000	0.000	0.000
80	0.451	0.205	0.094	0.043	0.009	0.001	0.000	0.000	0.000	0.000
90	0.408	0.168	0.070	0.029	0.005	0.000	0.000	0.000	0.000	0.000
100	0.370	0.138	0.052	0.020	0.003	0.000	0.000	0.000	0.000	0.000

If U.S. government bonds are available that pay 10 percent per year, $3.4 million invested in them will yield $340,000 a year, which is considerably more than $200,000 a year. Moreover, that $340,000 will continue indefinitely, while the $200,000 will end after 17 years. So the mousetrap maker clearly won't be willing to pay $3.4 million for the patent.

The maximum that the firm will be willing to pay is the present value of $200,000 to be received at the end of each of the next 17 years. (We assume that all the income becomes available at the end of the year to simplify our calculations.) We could calculate that by summing the first 17 amounts in the appropriate column of Table 11-2 and multiplying by

TABLE 11-3   Annuity Table: Present Value of $1 Received at the End of Each Year for the Designated Number of Years When Discounted at Various Interest Rates

Year	1%	2%	3%	4%	6%	95%	12%	15%	24%	36%
1	0.990	0.980	0.971	0.962	0.943	0.917	0.893	0.870	0.806	0.735
2	1.970	1.942	1.913	1.886	1.833	1.759	1.690	1.626	1.457	1.276
3	2.941	2.884	2.829	2.775	2.673	2.531	2.402	2.283	1.981	1.673
4	3.902	3.808	3.717	3.630	3.465	3.240	3.037	2.855	2.404	1.966
5	4.853	4.713	4.580	4.452	4.212	3.890	3.605	3.352	2.745	2.181
6	5.795	5.601	5.417	5.242	4.917	4.486	4.111	3.784	3.020	2.339
7	6.728	6.472	6.230	6.002	5.582	5.033	4.564	4.160	3.242	2.455
8	7.652	7.325	7.020	6.733	6.210	5.535	4.968	4.487	3.421	2.540
9	8.566	8.162	7.786	7.435	6.802	5.995	5.328	4.772	3.566	2.603
10	9.471	8.983	8.530	8.111	7.360	6.418	5.650	5.019	3.682	2.649
11	10.368	9.787	9.253	8.760	7.887	6.805	5.938	5.234	3.776	2.683
12	11.255	10.575	9.954	9.385	8.384	7.161	68.194	5.421	3.851	2.708
13	12.134	11.348	10.635	9.986	8.853	7.487	6.424	5.583	3.912	2.727
14	13.004	12.106	11.296	10.563	9.295	7.786	6.628	5.724	3.962	2.740
15	13.865	12.849	11.938	11.118	9.712	8.061	6.811	5.847	4.001	2.750
16	14.718	13.578	12.561	11.652	10.106	8.313	6.974	5.954	4.033	2.757
17	15.562	14.292	13.166	12.166	10.477	8.544	7.120	6.047	4.059	2.763
18	16.398	14.992	13.754	12.659	10.828	8.756	7.250	6.128	4.080	2.767
19	17.226	15.678	14.324	13.134	11.158	8.950	7.366	6.198	4.097	2.770
20	18.046	16.351	14.877	13.590	11.470	9.129	7.469	6.259	4.110	2.772
25	22.023	19.523	17.413	15.622	12.783	9.823	7.843	6.464	4.147	2.777
30	25.808	22.396	19.600	17.292	13.765	10.274	8.055	6.566	4.160	2.778
40	32.835	27.355	23.115	19.793	15.046	10.757	8.244	6.642	4.166	2.778
50	39.196	31.424	25.730	21.482	15.762	10.962	8.304	6.661	4.167	2.778
60	44.955	34.761	27.676	22.623	16.161	11.048	8.324	6.665	4.167	2.778
70	50.169	37.499	29.123	23.395	16.385	11.084	8.330	6.666	4.167	2.778
80	54.888	39.745	30.201	23.915	16.509	11.100	8.332	6.667	4.167	2.778
90	59.161	41.587	31.002	24.267	16.579	11.106	8.333	6.667	4.167	2.778
100	63.029	43.098	31.599	24.505	16.618	11.109	8.333	6.667	4.167	2.778

$200,000. Table 11-3 saves us that effort. The row for 17 years shows the present value of $1 received at the end of *each* of the next 17 years at various interest rates.

But what interest rate should we choose? If a less risky investment, like government bonds, pays 10 percent, then we wouldn't want to choose a rate lower than 10 percent. On the other hand, that 10 percent rate on government bonds is the return on a *fixed dollar* amount. It is therefore a nominal, not a real, rate of return: a return expressed in dollars that can change in value rather than a return expressed in real purchasing power. If the value of the dollar were to fall 4 percent each year, which is to say, if inflation occurred at a 4 percent annual rate, then the real return from a nominal interest rate of 10 percent would be only 6 percent.

The net revenue from manufacturing mousetraps can reasonably be expected to vary right along with the rate of inflation. If the price of everything doubles, the net revenue from mousetrap manufacturing ought to double, too—if other things are equal, as we're assuming. In that case, we would be taking account twice of the effects of inflation if we discounted the expected net revenue from acquiring the patent at a rate of interest incorporating expectations of inflation. We should therefore ignore the potential effects of inflation upon future income and discount at a rate of 6 percent or even 4 percent.

Let's try 4 percent. What is the present value of $200,000 to be received at the end of each of the next 17 years when discounted at 4 percent? Table 11-3 says that $1 for 17 years has a present value of $12.166. The present value of $200,000 annuity (an annuity is an annual amount) is therefore $2,433,200.

That's a good bit higher than the $1.5 million estimated in the chapter. Unless that $200,000 is highly certain, however, it's surely too much to offer for the patent. If the mousetrap manufacturer plays it safe and offers only $2,095,400, it would be discounting the expected future income at 6 percent.

At a discount rate of 9 percent, $200,000 a year for each of the next 17 years has a present value of $1,708,800.

Use Table 11-3 to check these results for yourself. The appropriate interest rate will be one that takes account of the patent purchaser's subjective estimate of the risks entailed in the purchase. Will the patent stand up to legal challenges? Will someone else invent an even better mousetrap? Will new technologies for the eradication of mice turn mousetraps into museum relics? The more uncertain the expected income whose present value we want to determine, the higher the interest rate at which we will want to discount it.

One last question: What happens to the present value of the patent if we assume it can be renewed upon expiration for an additional 13 years? If we discount at 9 percent, $200,000 for each of the next 30 years is $2,054,800. Notice that this is only $346,000 more than the value of a 17-year income stream. That shouldn't surprise you. A dollar that isn't due until 18 years from now has a present value of only 21 cents when discounted at 9 percent. And a dollar in 30 years has a present value of only 7½ cents.

ONCE OVER LIGHTLY

Profit is a term with many meanings. The meanings must be sorted out if we want to understand the way in which economic systems function.

Profit can be usefully defined as total revenue minus total cost if we include all opportunity costs in our calculation of total cost.

Interest, which is often confused with profit, is a cost for anyone who pays it. It is the cost of obtaining present command of resources, or the difference in value between present and future goods. It is usually attached to money loans simply because money represents general command over present or future goods.

Quoted interest rates also incorporate the costs of arranging and insuring the loan plus the expected rate of inflation. The real interest rate is the nominal rate minus the expected rate of inflation.

The rate of interest in a society is typically positive because people generally find present goods more valuable than future goods.

Profit arises from uncertainty. In the absence of uncertainty, any differences between total revenue and total cost would be competed away and profits would become zero.

The possibility of a profit encourages entrepreneurial activity. Entrepreneurs undertake to reorganize some part of the social world in the belief that the reorganization will create benefits greater than its costs. The entrepreneur's profit is the residual: whatever is left over after paying all those whose cooperation had to be secured in order to complete the entrepreneur's project.

The system of residual claimancy facilitates social cooperation by enabling people to agree among themselves on who will take responsibility for each aspect of a common project.

The entrepreneur's profits disappear when "the truth gets out." Once the entrepreneur's activity has shown how a profit can be made, the revenue available to the entrepreneur or any imitator will decline. If scarcity of a key resource prevents others from imitating the entrepreneur, competition for that resource will raise its price until cost equals revenue.

The forms that competition takes in any society are determined by the relevant rules of the game, or by the property rights that assign the ability to allocate resources and to appropriate the benefits from their use.

QUESTIONS FOR DISCUSSION

1. Chuck Waggin owns and operates a small tax-accounting firm, which he runs out of the basement of his home.

    (a) The basement was just wasted space until Chuck turned it into an office for his business. He says his firm is more profitable than most tax-accounting businesses because he doesn't have to pay any rent. Do you agree that rent is not a cost of production for Chuck?

    (b) Chuck recently turned down an offer to go to work for a larger firm at a salary of $45,000 a year. Chuck's net income from his business runs about $35,000 a year. Would you say that Chuck's firm is profitable?

    (c) Chuck says he likes being his own boss, and that he would be willing to sacrifice at least $25,000 a year in income to avoid working for someone else. Does that information change your answer to part (b)?

    (d) Chuck recently invested $10,000 of his savings in an office computer. How would you include the effects of this investment in his costs?

    (e) Chuck could have earned 12 percent per year on his savings had he not used them to buy the personal computer. If he had not had these savings, he still would have bought the computer, using a loan from the bank at 18 percent annual interest to finance the purchase. Is the opportunity cost of owning the computer really less for Chuck because he had savings of his own from which to buy it? If Chuck had been required to pay 18 percent interest to the bank rather than giving up 12 percent interest, for what would the additional 6 percent have been a payment? Does Chuck reduce his costs by financing the computer purchase himself?

2. Here are the first three sentences from a booklet titled "The Arithmetic of Interest Rates," published by the Federal Reserve Bank of New York: "Everything has a price. And money is no exception. Its price—the interest rate—is determined in the marketplace where money is borrowed and lent." Is it correct to speak of interest as the price of money?

    (a) If interest is the price of money in the same way in which 35 cents is the price of an orange, then we should expect an increase in the quantity of money to lead to lower interest rates just as an increase in the quantity of oranges leads to a reduced price for oranges. Why then are interest rates very high in nations that allow their money supplies to increase very rapidly?

    (b) A large increase in the supply of money will indeed have an effect on "the price of money" similar to the effect of a large increase in the supply of oranges on the price of oranges —*if* by "price" we mean value relative to other goods. The term we use to describe a fall in the value of money relative to other goods is *inflation*. If an increase in the supply of money creates expectations of inflation, what will happen to interest rates?

(c) Interest is the price of something, but not of money. What is the good whose price has gone up when the interest rate rises?

(d) The law of demand says that a higher price for a good causes less of that good to be demanded. What is the good for which the quantity demanded declines when the interest rate rises?

3. What form would the rate of interest take in a society that used no money but depended entirely on barter for the exchange of goods?

4. You purchase for $900 a $1000 government bond maturing one year from the date of purchase. Will you make a profit if you hold the bond to maturity? Will you make a profit if there is a sharp, general increase in prevailing interest rates a week after your purchase? What effect will this have on the price you can obtain from selling your bond in the market?

5. Humbert and Ambler are very different personalities. Humbert likes to eat, drink, be merry, and let the future care for itself. He suspects that the world is going to disintegrate in a few years anyway. Ambler is only 21 but is already planning conscientiously for her retirement years. What would you predict about their respective rates of time preference? How do people of Humbert's type benefit from the existence of people like Ambler, and vice versa?

6. What effect would you expect the rate of technological innovation in a society to have on the level of interest rates? Why?

7. "When lenders extend credit to high-risk borrowers, they must raise the interest rates they charge low-risk borrowers in order to cover their losses from defaults." Do you agree?

8. Suppose that Congress imposes a 10 percent ceiling on the interest rate that may be charged for federally guaranteed mortgages. Lending institutions, meanwhile, find themselves able to obtain all the mortgage business they want at 12 percent interest. Will they lend at 10 percent? How might the interest ceiling be circumvented? If you wanted to purchase a house and were eligible for a federally guaranteed mortgage, would you want Congress to set an interest-rate ceiling on such loans?

9. "A wealthy society has little difficulty paying interest. But in a poor country with almost no capital, economic planners cannot afford to take interest charges into account in their calculations." What's wrong with that argument?

10. If a district-court judge enters a $300-million judgment against a corporation for violation of antitrust statutes, do the owners of that corporation sustain a loss? What form will it take? If you believe that the judge was in error and that his decision will eventually be reversed on appeal, how could you profit from your knowledge?

11. You buy shares of common stock in two corporations. Over the next six months, the price of one falls and the price of the other rises. Which was a better buy? Which would be the better one to sell if you want cash?

12. In March 1980, 157 farmers filed a suit against the federal government asking for $18 million in damages incurred as a result of an erroneous prediction by the Bureau of Reclamation. The Bureau had estimated that water for irrigation in 1977 would be only 6 percent of normal because of a severe drought the previous winter. As a result, the 157 suing farmers had dug expensive wells, planted less valuable crops, and in some cases had planted no crops at all. The actual runoff proved to be much higher than the Bureau's predictions, but the truth came too late to do these farmers any good. What caused the farmers' loss? How do they want that loss to be allocated? Do you think they had a legitimate case? Should a carnival operator be able to sue the weather bureau if almost no one comes to the carnival on a fine, sunny day because the weather forecast erroneously predicted thunder-showers?

13. In the spring of 1963, Fidel Castro announced a sugar-production goal for 1970 of 10 million tons. As the target date approached and it began to appear that this much-publicized target might not be attained, the Cuban government transferred labor and other resources in large amounts from the production of alternative goods into the production of sugar. The goal was still missed by a large margin. How do you suppose the consequent loss was distributed? How would the profit have been distributed had this decision turned out better than anticipated?

14. Oil producers immediately objected when President Carter proposed in 1979 that the decontrol of oil prices be accompanied by a "windfall-profits" tax.

   (a) The oil producers claimed that the tax would reduce companies' incentives for new exploration and drilling. The press secretary for the late Senator Henry Jackson, then chairman of the Senate Energy Committee, denied this claim in the following words: "As far as increased production is concerned, the oil companies have an enormous cash flow right now. The incentives are already there." Do profits earned in the past (or current cash flow) provide incentives to explore and drill for oil?

   (b) The reported net income after taxes in 1978 of 94 leading companies in the petroleum production and refining industry was $14,971 million. Is $15 billion enough money to finance extensive exploration and drilling for new oil? Were those $15 billion an incentive to explore and drill?

   (c) The nine largest manufacturers of tobacco products in the United States earned a net income after taxes of $1,313 million in 1978. Would $1.3 billion pay for much oil exploration? Under what circumstances might the profits earned in the tobacco industry be used to explore for oil?

(d) Much of the exploration and drilling for oil that occurred in the United States in the past was financed by borrowing, not out of the net income from previous production or refining. Under what circumstances can money be borrowed to finance the search for new oil?

(e) Why would any firm in the business of producing or refining oil choose to invest some of its profits in shopping-center development (or anything else) rather than in exploration for oil?

(f) Does the news that the 94 largest firms in the petroleum production and refining industry earned $15 billion in 1978 make *you* eager to (1) explore and drill for oil, or (2) buy stock in oil companies?

(g) What difference would it make to your answers in the preceding part of this question to know any of the following (which all happen to be true)? (1) Oil industry profits rose 12 percent from 1977 to 1978. (2) The average return on stockholders' equity in the oil industry in 1978 was 14.3 percent compared with 14.0 percent in 1977. (3) The average percentage return of leading manufacturing corporations in 1978 was 15.9 percent; it was 14.9 percent in 1977.

(h) Suppose the government imposes a windfall-profits tax on all net income received from the sale of oil already discovered and flowing, but exempts from the tax all oil that is found after the tax is imposed. Will this maintain incentives to explore and drill for oil?

(i) Why do critics of the oil industry rarely distinguish between producers (who bring oil out of the ground) and refiners (who turn it into useful products)?

(j) Senator Jackson popularized the term "obscene profits" in discussing the profits of the oil industry during and immediately after the original OPEC price increases of 1973–74. Assuming that he intended *obscene* to mean repulsive or disgusting, rather than lewd or sexually exciting, explain the circumstances under which one might reasonably describe profits as obscene.

15. Some people consider the spring herring run near Sitka, Alaska, the most profitable fishing opportunity in the world. Fishing boats have occasionally netted $500,000 worth of herring in a three-hour season. It is not the herring so much as their eggs, called roe, that the fishermen are after, because of the enormous Japanese demand. The basic question: Is it really possible to earn enormous profits by fishing for a few hours in the ocean off Sitka?

(a) In order to protect the spawning herring from overexploitation, the state limits the season to a few hours and a small area and allows only licensed boats to participate. The number of permits has been 52 since 1978. Anyone who wants to participate must purchase a license from a current holder. The price is about $300,000. Why? What determines the going price of a license? How does this affect the profitability of herring fishing?

(b) Boat captains hire airplane spotters to increase the likelihood that they will catch some herring during the three-hour season. Spotting is a dangerous occupation with several dozen planes crisscrossing a small area, and pilots can sometimes command $30,000 as herring spotters. Why are boat captains willing to pay such an extraordinary fee?

(c) If a licensed boat's fishing gear malfunctions, the captain may rent a bystander's boat for as much as $100,000. Why would anyone pay such an exorbitant rental fee? Why would there be any bystanders in the area in the first place?

(d) A licensed boat may catch as much as $500,000 worth of herring. Or it may catch nothing. Estimate the annual loss of a licensed captain whose boat catches nothing.

(e) The crew's wages depend on their boat's success. Are they entrepreneurs? Are their wages really wages? Or are they profits (or losses!)?

(f) If a captain who has agreed to pay each of five crewmen 10 percent of the catch and to pay his airplane spotter 20 percent hauls in $100,000 worth of herring, has he earned a profit?

(This question is based on a *Wall Street Journal* feature of May 15, 1987.)

16. The text argues that if an activity is known to be profitable, more people will go into that activity and the profits will disappear. Does that apply to the selling of cocaine?

   (a) The costs of selling cocaine include the risk of being arrested and imprisoned. Why is a ten-year sentence not twice as strong a deterrent as a five-year sentence? Why does one chance in five of being imprisoned for ten years translate into *less* than two years' imprisonment? Is a cocaine seller likely to use a high or a low discount rate in deciding on the subjective cost of possible imprisonment? Why is the threat of imprisonment more effective in deterring some people than others?

   (b) Another cost of selling is the risk of being killed by competitors. This cost will be much lower for some people than for others. Characterize a person for whom this cost will be relatively low.

   (c) For whom is the selling of cocaine profitable?

17. About half of all new restaurants fail within a year, and 85 percent close within five years. What do these figures indicate about the profitability of the restaurant business? Why do so many entrepreneurs nonetheless start up new restaurants every year?

18. In June 1979, the provincial legislature of Quebec gave final approval to legislation authorizing the expropriation of Asbestos Corporation, a mining concern with headquarters in Montreal. Asbestos Corporation was at the time a 55 percent-owned subsidiary of General Dynamics Corporation.

(a) General Dynamics had repeatedly insisted that it did not want to sell to the province of Quebec. What do the officers of a corporation usually mean when they say they do not want to sell a subsidiary?

(b) In a voluntary sale the price is set by mutual agreement. In a forced sale some other method must be used to determine the price or compensation to be received for the expropriated property. A study commissioned by the province put the value of Asbestos Corporation at about $42 a share. A valuation done for General Dynamics set the value at almost $100 a share. If you were the arbitrator asked to decide on the *true value*, what data would you consult to find the answer?

(c) Suppose someone suggests that the fair value of the corporation be determined by the going market price of Asbestos Corporation stock. If the stock were widely held by the public, investors would determine the value of a share by what they were willing to pay to own it or had to be paid to surrender ownership. What is the flaw in this proposal? What determines the price of a corporation's stock when that corporation faces imminent nationalization?

(d) Could General Dynamics benefit from nationalization if the compensation received was less than the sum of what was originally paid to purchase the assets of Asbestos Corporation, plus the cost of all subsequent additions and improvements to those assets?

(e) General Dynamics finally agreed to sell in late 1981, under the threat of expropriation. Soon thereafter, mounting concern over the health effects of exposure to asbestos particles led to a massive decline in the demand for asbestos, and the government-owned firm began to incur losses. By 1985, the stock had fallen to $4.50 a share from $37 a share just prior to its acquisition by the Quebec government. Did General Dynamics profit from the nationalization?

19. Everybody knows that laborers receive wages and capitalists receive profits. But is it true?

(a) If employees agree to continue working for an employer who is currently unable to pay them, because they don't want the firm to fail, are they working for wages or for profits?

(b) If you agree to loan your lawnmower to someone who wants to start a lawn-care business, on condition that he pay you $2 each time he borrows it, are you a capitalist? Is your $2 properly called profit? Would your answers differ if he agreed to pay you 20 percent of his gross receipts?

20. A dedicated high school principal has lost all patience with meddlesome school boards, bureaucratic school superintendents, uncooperative teachers, whining parents, and lazy students. She wants to run her school "the way a high school ought to be run."

(a) Explain why she should be called an entrepreneur, or at least a would-be entrepreneur.

(b) What will she have to do to get her wish? Who are the people to whom she will have to provide credible guarantees?

(c) Is her residual claim likely to be positive, i.e., is she likely to make a profit?

21. Are entrepreneurs necessarily capitalists?

(a) The text defines the entrepreneur as the one who assumes responsibility by guaranteeing all others a fixed amount for their cooperation. When and why do others trust the entrepreneur's guarantee? If this question seems abstract, ask yourself whether you will work hard for someone when you don't expect to see your first paycheck until you have worked three weeks. When and why will you not trust an employer in this way?

(b) Who besides employees typically receives guarantees from the entrepreneur that they must trust if they are to do business with the entrepreneur? What is the basis for their confidence in the entrepreneur's promises?

(c) Why do employees ever agree to let the employer have all the profits?

(d) Why do employers ever agree to guarantee the employee a certain wage, no matter how badly things turn out?

22. You ask your college for permission to set up a lemonade stand at the annual spring commencement, and the college grants permission. After paying your bills for materials (lemons, sugar, cups, and so forth), you clear $250 for an afternoon's work.

(a) Did you make a $250 profit?

(b) Are you likely to be given the lemonade concession again next year? What difference does it make whether or not word gets around about how much you cleared?

(c) If the college next year auctions off the franchise, how much would you be willing to bid? Who will then get the profit from the lemonade stand?

23. Prior to 1980, the Interstate Commerce Commission rarely granted new permits to trucking firms to haul goods interstate, and operating rights were often extremely valuable. They were listed as assets on the books of trucking companies and made up a significant part of the purchase price whenever such companies were sold.

(a) What factors established the market value of such operating rights?

(b) When the Motor Carrier Act of 1980 took effect, allowing much easier entry into interstate trucking, the market value of operating rights fell. Why?

(c) Was this fall a loss?

(d) Losses as well as profits are the consequence of uncertainty. What was the uncertainty that produced this loss for trucking companies in 1980?

(e) What would have happened to the value of operating rights in the 1970s if everyone had known 10 years in advance that Congress was going to ease restrictions on entry into interstate trucking after 1980?

(f) The Motor Carrier Act of 1980 was a change in the rules of the game. Which were the principal property rights affected, and with what consequences?

24. In June 1985, the U.S. Department of Agriculture announced its decision to end controls on hops production. In 1966, each hops grower in business at the time had been assigned a share of the total amount of hops that could be sold. Ever since, new hops farmers have had to purchase or lease allotments from existing growers, at a considerable price. The Agriculture Department, in announcing its decision to terminate the system, objected to the fact that new growers had to pay for an allotment that had been given to the original growers at no charge. Does the Agriculture Department's objection make any sense? If the allotments had *not* acquired any value after 1966, what would this imply about the original decision to restrict hops production?

25. The following paragraph is condensed from a long letter to the editor of a metropolitan newspaper:

> If you want to make money real fast, buy a mobile home park. You can raise the rents to your heart's content, because the tenants usually can't afford to move. And even if they could, there is usually no place to go, since there aren't enough mobile home parks to take care of all the people who own mobile homes.

(a) If the situation is as dire for owners of mobile homes as the letter writer says, what will already have happened to the purchase price of mobile home parks? Do owners of such parks make huge profits from renting space to mobile home owners?

(b) If existing mobile home parks can be operated very profitably or sold for very high prices, why don't entrepreneurs create more such parks?

(c) If the city responds to the complaint of this letter writer and others by putting price controls on the rental rates mobile home parks may charge, what will happen to the price of mobile homes currently occupying rent-controlled sites?

26. Can those who own the stock of a large business corporation prevent the managers from pursuing their own interests rather than the interests of the shareholders? How can they effectively monitor the managers' behavior and persuade the corporation's board of directors to discharge execu-

tives whose goal is power, privileges, and "perks" for themselves rather than net revenue for the owners? Can't the managers generally use their positions and the corporation's resources to nominate and secure the election of directors who will be partial to management rather than guardians of the shareholders' interests? (The question that follows continues this line of inquiry, but in a different direction.)

27. Can those who own the stock of a large business corporation prevent the managers from pursuing their own interests rather than the interests of the shareholders?

    (a) What happens to the price of a corporation's stock when it is managed for the benefit of the managers rather than the shareholders?
    (b) What would happen to the stock price if some individual or group gained voting control over the board of directors and replaced the management with people willing and able to pursue maximum net revenue for shareholders?
    (c) How do these facts create incentives for some people to invest resources in monitoring managers' behavior?
    (d) How does the prospect of what managers like to call "a hostile takeover" restrain the behavior of managers? Toward whom is a hostile takeover hostile? Toward whom is it friendly?
    (e) Are those who specialize in corporate takeovers entrepreneurs?

28. Marxists often used to argue that the owners of capital were not entitled to any income from that ownership because labor produced all value. Today they are more likely to admit that capital contributes to the production of value, but they still deny the right of capitalists to receive a profit on the grounds that the *ownership* of capital is not productive.

    (a) Would you be willing to argue that those who own capital *have a right* to whatever income they can obtain from that capital? Is this the same as arguing that they *deserve* the income? Is it the same as saying that they *ought to be allowed* to receive the income?
    (b) Does the productivity of resources depend at all on those who manage those resources, or are all individuals and all organizations equally good at managing resources efficiently? Does the ownership of resources have anything to do with who manages those resources? Is it true that the ownership of capital is not productive?

29. Are the profits of entrepreneurs obtained through coercion or through persuasion? (Definition of terms: *coercion*—inducing people to cooperate by threatening to reduce their options; *persuasion*—inducing people to cooperate by promising to expand their options.) If you don't know how to answer the question, try thinking about the adequacy in this context of the proposed definitions for coercion and persuasion.

30. An increased demand for walnut furniture has greatly increased the price of black walnut lumber, prompting some people to plant black walnut trees on their property. If mature walnut trees are worth $500 apiece and

take 50 years to grow to a harvestable size, what is the present value of a black walnut tree that has just been planted? Defend your choice of a discount rate. How low will the cost of planting have to be to induce substantial planting at this time? How will substantial planting at this time affect the probable harvest value of the trees? Do you see why it's difficult to profit from planting valuable trees?

31. A *Wall Street Journal* article on fire safety in high-rise buildings contained this argument: "Sprinklers can save on insurance rates by providing added protection. By one estimate the savings over 30 years would pay for the system, but high-rise buildings are often built by speculators who plan to sell them far sooner than that."

   (a) Why is the fact that builders typically sell high-rise buildings within a few years irrelevant to the decision about installing sprinkler systems?
   (b) If you don't see that it's irrelevant, ask yourself why contractors who build homes that they plan to sell within a year often put on roofing material with a fifteen-year warranty.
   (c) Suppose a sprinkler system costs $30,000 to install and produces savings in insurance premiums of $1000 per year. How many years of such savings would be required to justify the expenditure if the interest rate is 1 percent per year? 2 percent? Are you surprised that builders aren't impressed by savings on insurance that takes 30 years to equal the amount spent to obtain those savings?

32. The Army Corps of Engineers estimates that a canal between Tussle and Big Stone would save shippers $500,000 per year. The canal would cost $20 million to construct and $200,000 per year to maintain.

   (a) Is it correct to say that the canal is a good investment in the long run because it will save society a net $300,000 per year and eventually that will come to more than the $20 million construction cost?
   (b) About how low would the interest rate have to be to make the canal a profitable investment? (The canal would not be profitable if the interest payments plus maintenance costs ate up the saving to shippers.)
   (c) "The advantage of having the government build the canal is that government can do things that are in the public interest whereas private enterprise is constrained by narrow considerations of profitability." Evaluate that argument.

33. A company offers retiring employees an option on their pension benefits. They may choose either to receive a designated sum each month for as long as they live or a lump sum at the time of retirement.

   (a) How could the firm go about determining the present value of a certain amount each month for life?
   (b) How will a rise in interest rates affect the size of the lump-sum option?

(c) What is the present value of a $10,000 annual pension to be received at the end of each of the next 15 years when discounted at 9 percent? When discounted at 12 percent?

(d) Does a rise in interest rates make the lump-sum option less attractive to retiring employees?

34. Many mortgage contracts on residences include a due-on-sale clause, which says that the full amount of the unpaid balance falls due when the residence is sold. This prevents the new buyer from taking over or "assuming" the mortgage of the seller.

(a) If in 1985 the seller still owed $20,000 on a 30-year mortgage taken out in 1965 at 6 percent interest, and current mortgage rates are 12 percent, why will the lending institution *not* want the buyer to assume the existing mortgage?

(b) If the buyer assumes the existing mortgage, she will have to make monthly payments of about $225 to pay off the $20,000 still due to the lending institution. If the buyer has to secure a new loan at 12 percent, the monthly payments would come to about $295 if the $20,000 balance is to be paid off in 10 years. By assuming the mortgage, the borrower is able to save about $840 a year for 10 years. How will the seller be able to capture that saving for himself?

(c) In recent years some state legislatures and occasionally even state courts have decided that due-on-sale clauses in mortgage contracts should not be enforced. This was a change in the rules of the game. How did it affect property rights, and with what consequences for these parties: lending institutions; sellers of houses with low-rate mortgages containing due-on-sale clauses; buyers of such houses; sellers of houses without low-rate mortgages?

35. The state lottery claims that its grand prize is $1 million. The lucky winner will receive $50,000 upon presentation of the winning ticket plus $50,000 at the end of each of the next 19 years. Is that really a $1 million prize? What is it actually worth? Will you want to use a real or a nominal interest rate to discount these future amounts? Why? Suppose the 19 future payments were all to be adjusted for any intervening changes in the value of money. What interest rate would you use then to calculate the present value of the "$1 million" prize? What effect does the decision to "index" future payments to changes in the value of money have on the present value of the prize?

36. "Save it," somebody says. "Don't sell it. It's not worth much now, but in 20 years it will probably be worth five times as much." Should you save it or sell it? What will $1 now be worth in 20 years if invested at the rate of interest currently obtainable from relatively risk-free loans?

37. What is the present value of each of the following when discounted at interest rates of 4 and 15 percent?

(a) A $10,000 prize in a limerick-writing contest, to be received one year from now.

(b) A $10,000 cash legacy from your Aunt Mehitabel, to be received when you reach your 25th birthday. (If you have already passed it, choose some other birthday.)

(c) $10,000 per year for each of the next ten years, beginning one year from now, as first prize for telling in 25 words or less why you like a detergent.

(d) Ownership of an office building from which you expect to receive an annual net income of $10,000 per year for each of the next 30 years, at the end of which time you expect to sell the building and land for $100,000. Assume the annual amounts are all received at the end of each year.

(e) $10,000 in additional income per year from age 25 to age 65 if you're willing to go to school for an extra 5 years when you reach the age of 20.

38. If a gallon of gasoline currently costs $1, and if the price increases in future years at exactly the rate of inflation, what will be the price of gasoline five years, ten years, and twenty years from now if inflation occurs at an annual rate of 2 percent? If it occurs at a 6 percent annual rate? If it occurs at a 12 percent annual rate?

39. The U.S. Constitution prohibits government from taking private property for public use "without just compensation."

(a) In what manner do rent controls "take" private property?

(b) If a city were required to compensate owners for any losses they incurred as a result of rent controls, would cities be less likely to impose such controls?

(c) If a city *abolishes* rent controls that have been in effect for many years, does it "take" property from anyone?

40. When the government takes over privately owned land for a highway and pays compensation to the owners, should that compensation be based on its value in its present use, on its value in the use to which the government will put it, or on the value of the adjoining land that will increase (or decrease) in value because of the highway? What is unfair about each option?

41. Suppose it costs $100,000 a year just to maintain a large, old church building on Manhattan Island in New York City. Membership has declined to about 100, and so the congregation discusses whether it can afford to keep the church open any longer.

(a) What is it costing per member to continue using the building as a church? What major cost component have you left out if your answer is $1000?

(b) If a developer offers $2 million for the site (not an unreasonable price in Manhattan), what is the annual cost to the congregation of continuing to use the building?

(c) If the congregation had 400 members and was quite capable of meeting the regular maintenance costs, could it afford to ignore the developer's offer of $2 million? What would be the real cost, as distinct from the nominal or money cost, of rejecting the offer?

(d) In 1977, a Manhattan synagogue with declining membership sold its building to a Seventh-Day Adventist congregation for $400,000. The rabbi said he was "happy to get rid of it" because of dwindling attendance and high operating costs. But the new owners soon encountered the same problems. When they then put the building up for sale, it was purchased for $2.4 million. Who, if anyone, made a profit from these transactions?

(e) The people who live near an old, attractive church building would usually much prefer to see the building remain than to have it torn down and replaced by an office tower or condominium complex. In New York City, neighbors have sometimes been able to lobby the Landmarks Preservation Commission and have the building officially declared a "landmark." Once that occurs, the building cannot be torn down or substantially altered. Are such neighbors entrepreneurs? How does such an official landmark designation alter property rights? Would a congregation that wants to sell its building profit from removal of a landmark designation?

(f) The executive director of the NYC landmarks commission, when asked to comment on a suit filed by a congregation whose church building had been declared a landmark, said that "a church should be forever." Do you think this is or should be part of the established rules of the game in society: that church buildings are forever?

(g) A former director for the arts of the National Council of Churches commented as follows on the demolition of church buildings in favor of commercial structures: "I don't give a damn what others think. It's a perversion that property is more important than beauty." Has he accurately described the issue in depicting it as a choice between "property" and "beauty"? (This entire question draws extensively upon a *Wall Street Journal* article of September 27, 1982, written by Luis Ubinas.)

THE DISTRIBUTION OF INCOME

Have you ever reflected on the fact that we all obtain our incomes by inducing other people to provide them? We also produce some goods for ourselves directly, of course, and there may even be a few hermits in the country who never use money and never have to depend on other people's cooperation. Except for counterfeiters, however, we all get our money incomes from other people.

We persuade them to hire us, to buy from us, to lend to us, or simply to recognize that our status entitles us to income. That last technique is the one employed by children to extract income from their parents, by retired people to get social security benefits, by people who qualify for unemployment compensation, and by the lucky holders of winning lottery tickets, to mention just a few. Another way to put it is that we supply what other people are willing to pay for. In short, the distribution of income results from supply and demand.

SUPPLIERS AND DEMANDERS

We took this roundabout route to get to that very orthodox conclusion in order to underline the fact that income isn't really distributed—regardless of what the title of this chapter asserts. No one actually distributes income in our society in the sense of parceling it out. People's incomes are the outcome of many interacting decisions, decisions ultimately made by different individuals on the basis of the benefits and the costs they expect from their decisions.

Individuals aren't free to decide just anything they please, of course. Few of us can decide to obtain $300,000 per year by getting others to watch us play basketball. People make *constrained* choices. But they do choose. Income is not a fact of nature. Unlike height and (natural) hair color, choice can change it. Income may be more like place of residence. Although few of us can choose to live anywhere, most of us have substantial discretion about where we're going to live, whether Iowa or California, city or suburb, apartment or house. The decisions of other people, from relatives through employers to housing developers, interact with our own preferences to determine the relative costs and advantages of living in one place or another. Places of residence, like incomes, are the outcome of millions of interrelated decisions.

Those decisions, it should be noted, can even be unfair—and often are. Racial prejudices limit people's options with respect both to choosing residence and to securing money income. Suppliers and demanders sometimes perpetrate frauds. People are the victims of poor schooling or destructive environments that limit their options in later life. Sometimes what matters is who you know rather than what you can do. Thus, the claim that income accrues to people as a result of supply and demand is not an endorsement of existing income patterns but a way of thinking about the subject.

Economic theory explains the distribution of income as the product of the supply of and demand for *productive services.* The word *productive* means no more than *demanded;* an activity is productive if it enables people to obtain something for which they're willing to pay. All sorts of thoroughly disreputable persons (you may provide your own list) are thus suppliers of productive services. Nor does the word *service* necessarily mean that effort has been expended. A man who lives entirely on his inheritance is supplying a productive service, in our sense of the term, by giving up some command over current resources. No one would dream of commending him for effort, since he makes none. But a playboy heir who lives off dividends still contributes to current production by the activity of not consuming his capital. The relevant fact for economic analysis is not the merit of the playboy but the demand for the resources whose ownership provides him with regular income.

The demand for productive services will generate no income for a person who owns no resources capable of supplying those services. The distribution of income among individuals or families depends fundamentally, therefore, on the ownership of productive resources.

Sometimes this is expressed by saying that the distribution of income depends on the prior distribution of wealth. That's an acceptable restatement, as long as we don't define wealth too narrowly. The trouble is that most empirical studies of personal wealthholdings, as well as the ordinary connotation of the word, restrict wealth to such assets as cash, stocks, bonds, and real estate. However, most of the income that Americans receive annually does not derive from ownership of wealth in these forms but rather from the ownership of *human capital.*

CAPITAL AND HUMAN RESOURCES

We defined the term *capital* in Chapter 11. As economists use the word, it means *produced means of production,* or *goods that can be used to produce future goods.* Machinery is capital, as are industrial and commercial buildings. But so are the knowledge and skills that people accumulate through education, training, or experience and that enable them to supply valuable productive services to others. Only when we include human capital in our definition of wealth is it at all adequate to say that the distribution of income depends on the distribution of wealth.

Total employee compensation, for example, regularly dwarfs corporate profits in the government's annual calculations of the national income. During the 1980s, "compensation of employees" came to about 15 times the total of dividends plus retained corporation earnings.

This does not mean that factory operatives and office workers take home the bulk of the nation's income. The human services that produce most of the nation's income include the services of physicians, corporate executives, athletes, actors, and rock stars as well as teachers, typists, and technicians. The point is that, contrary to popular belief, inequality in the distribution of income in the United States today arises primarily from unequal abilities to supply valuable human services. Human capital has to be included in our definition of wealth, because most income is earned in the United States by supplying the services of human resources.

HUMAN CAPITAL AND INVESTMENT

Is it misleading, though, to refer to these resources as *capital?* Capital means *produced resources.* To what extent are the abilities that enable people to command high incomes *pro-*

duced rather than inherited or just stumbled upon? It seems impossible to generalize safely or usefully in response to this question. Perhaps the word *capabilities* would therefore be a more neutral and consequently more satisfactory term.

On the other hand, the implication that these capabilities are *produced* does call attention to a fact of some importance. People can and do choose to acquire additional capabilities in the expectation of earning additional income. They invest in themselves by going to school, acquiring special job training, practicing certain skills, or otherwise adding to the value of the services they can supply to others. It makes sense to refer to such investments in oneself as the acquisition of human capital.

We must once again beware of confusing the question of function with the question of merit, a confusion to which we referred earlier in discussing profits—and that seems to crop up in conjunction with any issue of income distribution. The value of a tax accountant's services doesn't depend on the extent to which his or her skills were acquired rather than inherited. But it does depend on the level of those skills, and that level can usually be raised through diligent effort. The expectation of an increased income from the sale of their services induces tax accountants to pore over tedious tax-court rulings when they would rather be playing golf. Pride and a sense of craftsmanship may also be at work. But the prospect of a greater income exercises a constant and steady pressure on people to acquire capabilities that will permit them to supply more valuable services to others. That's a useful social function, even if we were to decide that all differences between people are ultimately matters of good or evil fortune, so that people are never authorized to say that they *deserve* the incomes they receive.

PROPERTY RIGHTS AND INCOME

Who then owns productive resources? They're owned by many different people, individually and jointly, through partnerships, corporations, and informal arrangements. The owners acquired these resources by many different means, most of which we can never hope to untangle in retrospect. The resources themselves have an enormous variety of forms, running all the way from ideas and skills to turret lathes and fertile fields. Do not assume, however, that the people who own productive resources are the ones who happen to have possession or who have the title deed in their safe-deposit box. Property rights depend on the reigning rules of the game, not on mere physical facts.

Suppose you "own" your driveway but are unable to prevent people from parking on the street in a way that blocks your entrance. Since you can't expect to park in it yourself or to receive income from renting the space to others, you don't have an effective property right and consequently don't own a parking space. Perhaps what you own is a shuffleboard court or a splendid place to play hopscotch.

Consider the case of a woman who has been expertly trained as a physician but can't obtain a license to practice because she was educated in a foreign country. She owns a human resource of limited value; the only services she can supply will be to her own family and friends.

The owner of an apartment building under rent controls may be unable to set rents high enough to cover taxes and maintenance. In that case, he doesn't actually own the units. The services that the units provide are appropriated by the tenants occupying the apartments, who are thus the effective owners. The proof of the nominal owner's actual non-ownership in such a case would be his inability to sell the units at any price and his willingness simply to abandon them by surrendering legal ownership to the taxing authorities.

Federal law says that the airwaves belong to the public. But the Federal Communications Commission allows the owners of television stations to use assigned channels at no charge. Since the owners of the stations can appropriate the income from supplying television services, they are the actual owners of the channels. A proof of this will be their ability to sell the physical plant and facilities at a price many times greater than the cost of the facilities' reproduction—*if* the purchaser can expect to obtain, along with the station, the right to use the assigned channel.

The mayor of a city doesn't legally own any of the city's facilities. But if she can expect to enjoy the benefits supplied by a spacious office, a large staff, motorcycle escorts for her limousine, and a place at the head table for just about any banquet she chooses to attend, her wealth is much greater than it seems. She cannot sell these property rights, it's true; so they're limited in that respect. But *all* property rights are limited in one respect or another. The ability to sell is an important part of property rights; but it is only one stick in a larger bundle, and its absence limits but doesn't eliminate property rights.

ACTUAL, LEGAL, AND MORAL RIGHTS

A useful distinction that can often help us agree on what we're talking about is the distinction between actual, legal, and moral property rights. It is people's actual rights that govern their expectations and consequently determine how they will behave. If the city council decrees that dog owners must keep their pets on a leash while they are in city parks and clean up all mementoes that the dogs leave behind, the council thereby grants city residents the *legal* right to stroll barefoot through the parks without fear or trembling. If the police cannot enforce the ordinance, however, and many dog owners simply ignore it, resident's *actual* rights will diverge from their legal rights. What park users see as their actual rights will determine whether or not they take off their shoes. If they leave their shoes on while indignantly insisting that they "have a right" to a park free of dog feces, they are asserting a *moral* right, a right that they believe they *ought* to enjoy.

Because rights are social facts, they depend on acceptance by others of the appropriate obligations. Until dog owners accept the obligation to monitor their pets' behavior—either to avoid legal penalties or to show consideration for others—park users will not enjoy the actual right to frolic fearlessly and will consequently keep their shoes on while strolling in the park.

EXPECTATIONS AND INVESTMENT

Every decision about the use of resources is based finally on the expectations of the decisionmaker. Families and individuals decide whether to consume or to invest their income by assessing the relative values of the benefits they expect to receive from each option. And they choose among alternative investments by considering not only the expected rates of return, but also the confidence with which those returns can be expected. People who fear confiscation of their investments will opt for investments that are difficult to confiscate, even though they promise a lower return than more vulnerable investment projects. Dictators who suspect their control is slipping shift into Swiss bank accounts, and ethnic minorities encountering native hostility invest in jewelry or other readily portable wealth. The most readily portable form of wealth is human capital, which may explain why prospering ethnic minorities have so often obtained unusually high levels of education. Of course, even human capital *can* be confiscated;

people who are barred from practicing a profession for which they were trained have effectively been deprived of the human resource which that training created.

When you reflect on the fact that the returns from investment decisions are *future* returns, you realize that a person's rate of time preference also affects consumption or investment decisions. Someone who discounts future events at a high rate will be present-oriented, will prefer consumption to investment, and will thereby choose in effect to receive a lower income in future years. On the other hand, people who discount at a low rate of interest will be more willing to give up present consumption for the sake of greater consumption in the future and will consequently invest more heavily while they're young, thereby securing for themselves a higher expected income in later years. The interesting implication of all this is that people choose, to some extent, their lifetime income profiles.

A further implication is that we can't always tell from a simple comparison of two people's current incomes which of them has the higher income. A promising student in the last year of medical school probably has a large *negative* income. But would we really want to say that he or she is poorer than someone the same age who is earning $10,000 a year from a semiskilled job? The relevant comparison is *lifetime* incomes. That was the comparison relevant to the medical student's decision to become a physician, and it's probably the more relevant comparison for anyone who wants to evaluate the equity of a particular income distribution.

Data on lifetime incomes are hard to obtain, of course, except long after the fact. That's probably why we continue to exaggerate the poverty of many people who are students and the wealth of many who were students long ago. The two errors don't necessarily cancel out, however. If public policy responds to these opposite exaggerations by transferring income from the older to the younger group, it lowers the expected rate of return and hence the amount of investment that will occur during people's younger years.

THE LAW OF DEMAND
AND PRODUCTIVE SERVICES

The demand for the services of productive resources is like all other demand curves: It slopes downward to the right. Other things remaining equal, a larger quantity will be demanded at lower prices and a smaller quantity at higher prices. In the case of productive resources, this relationship may be so well disguised that people won't see it or will refuse to believe it. But the relationship will hold whether it's recognized or not.

The best example is probably the case of labor services demanded by an employer. Employers purchase labor services after estimating the probable contribution those services will make toward the creation of income. They hire when they expect the additional revenue from a hiring decision to be greater than the additional cost which the decision entails. They use the simple rule of Chapter 9: Take those actions and only those actions whose expected marginal revenue is greater than their expected marginal cost. The higher the wage rate, the higher the marginal cost of purchasing labor services. Other things remaining equal, therefore, a smaller quantity of labor services will be demanded as the price that must be paid to obtain them goes up.

Why is this so widely and frequently denied? It's denied, for example, by those who insist that opposition to legal minimum wages is evidence of indifference toward the plight of the poor. But do poor people really benefit from legislated increases in the minimum wage? If the legal minimum is no higher than what employers are already paying, it has no effect. It will have an impact only if some covered employers are paying less than the legal minimum. But won't these employers lay some workers off if they're compelled to pay a higher wage, or at least not replace workers who quit?

"They wouldn't have to" isn't a good answer. It's a common answer, because so many people believe that employers pay wages "out of profits" and can therefore refrain from laying workers off when wage rates rise, as long as profits are adequate to cover the increased wages. This seems to imply that the quantity of labor services demanded is a constant, dictated perhaps by technology, so that the only options before employers are either to pay the higher wage rates or to close down the operation. But the demand for labor services is not perfectly inelastic and will at times be highly elastic, because employers can almost always find substitutes, within some range, for labor services of any particular type.

What we have here is a clear example of the Popular Perspective described in Chapter 4. Most voters seem to reason about the minimum wage as if both the number of unskilled persons willing to work and the number of unskilled workers that employers want to hire are constants. Below some low minimum wage ($3 an hour?), no one will be willing to work. Above some maximum ($7 or $8 an hour?), employers who rely on unskilled labor will have to close their doors. Between these limits, the demand curve for unskilled labor is completely inelastic. Under these circumstances, whoever has the most clout is going to determine the wage for unskilled labor. Why leave that clout in the hands of employers? When the law steps in and decrees a minimum, employers are compelled to pay at least a decent wage. A modest amount of wealth is thereby transferred from employers (and their customers if employers raise prices in response to the higher legal minimum wage) into the hands of some of the neediest members of society. From the Popular Perspective, the only issue is how we want income to be distributed.

The traditional (some would say notorious) hostility of most economists to a high legal minimum wage is rooted in their conviction that supply curves slope upward to the right and demand curves slope downward. The number of unskilled persons willing to supply their labor services is not a constant but increases when the wage rate rises, so that more people will be competing for the available jobs when the prevailing wage is higher. And at higher wages, employers of unskilled workers find all sorts of ways to economize on the help they "need."

Consider what the owners of a fast-food franchise might do if an increase in the legal minimum wage forced them to pay a 25 percent higher hourly wage to the teenagers they employ. It simply is not true that it takes a fixed number of workers to operate the franchise; there are many margins on which adjustments might be made that would reduce the number of employees. One is hours of operation; at a low wage rate, it might be profitable to open during less busy times of the day, but not at a higher wage rate. Another is quality of service; quick service can be offered at peak times by having surplus employees during slack times; when wage rates rise, economies can be achieved by reducing that surplus and making customers wait a bit longer during peak periods. Of course, that will raise the effective price to customers and so turn some away; but no sensible business firm wants to serve customers regardless of the cost of doing so. There are all sorts of ways to economize on labor of a particular kind, ways that an outsider won't be able to think of. Some of them will be ways to economize that the owners didn't think of either, until a rise in their labor costs gave them a strong incentive to think harder and longer.

It's true but largely irrelevant that the present federal legal minimum wage won't provide a weekly income sufficient to support a family at the level to which most Americans are accustomed. For one thing, many wage earners don't have

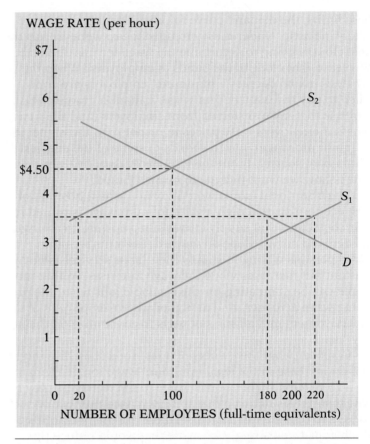

WAGE RATE (per hour)

NUMBER OF EMPLOYEES (full-time equivalents)

FIGURE 12A   Supply and demand curves for fast-food employees

Will an increase in the legal minimum wage reduce employment? The answer depends in large part on the supply curve of labor.

Let D in Figure 12A portray the demand for labor on the part of fast-food establishments in some city. If the legal minimum wage is $3.50, employers will want to hire 180 full-time equivalents. If the supply curve of labor to fast-food establishments is S_1, 220 people would like to work at that wage. However, we would not want to say that the $3.50 minimum wage causes 40 people to be unemployed, because if there were no minimum wage, competition would reduce the hourly rate to $3.25. And only 200 people would be willing to work for $3.25 an hour.

If the supply is S_2, the $3.50 legal minimum has no effect. At $3.50 an hour, employers would want to hire 160 more workers than would be willing to supply their services at this wage. Competition will bid the wage rate up above the legal minimum toward the market-clearing rate of $4.50 an hour.

Which of the two curves shown do you think comes closer to portraying the current supply curve of labor?

families to support or are not the principal source of support for the families to whose incomes they contribute. Nearly one-half of those employed at the minimum wage are members of families with incomes *above* the U.S. average. More crucially, if $150 a week isn't an adequate income, nothing per week is even less adequate. A large increase in the legal minimum wage would produce more income for some, but it would mean less income for a substantial number who could not obtain employment at a significantly higher wage.

It's important to look at the actual numbers when talking about the probable effects of an increase in the legal minimum wage and also at who is exempted. If the minimum is raised to $5.75 an hour at a time when fast-food franchises are offering $6 to starting employees, and if exemptions are written into the law for agricultural workers, employees who receive income from tips, and trainees, the increase would probably have few observable effects. Battles over the minimum wage do sometimes seem to be mostly opportunities for people with different political views to call each other insulting names.

PEOPLE OR MACHINES?

The strange notion that the demand for labor services of any type is completely inelastic with respect to the wage rate also seems to underlie the widespread belief (or fear) that machines "destroy" jobs because they are so much more productive than people. But what could it mean to say that machines are "more productive" than people? Employers aren't interested in mere physical or technical capabilities; they're interested in the relation between marginal revenues and marginal costs. A machine is more efficient than a person and hence will be substituted for a person only if the marginal revenue from the machine's use *relative to its marginal cost* is greater than the same ratio for a person. That implies, among other things, that wage rates play an important part in shaping the speed and direction of technological change in the economy.

Automatic elevators didn't replace elevator operators in the United States in recent years merely because of improvements in technology. Time, money, and energy were spent to develop automatic elevators—and building owners subsequently installed them—because of benefit-cost estimates they made, not because automatic elevators were new and shiny. In some other society where the wage rates (opportunity costs) of elevator operators are quite low, elevators run by trained operators could still be more efficient than automatic elevators.

The fear that our society or any society may run out of jobs is an odd kind of fear. A job, after all, represents an obstacle to be overcome. A society that has run out of jobs for people to do has come very close to overcoming scarcity; and that would be something to cheer, not fear. We're not in any such fortunate situation. Technological innovations release labor resources from some employments to make them available for others. The automatic or self-service elevator made it possible for people who were formerly employed in transporting passengers up and down to do something else, to make some other and additional contribution to our total output of commodities and services.

The reallocation of labor in response to changed circumstances does lead to a loss of wealth for some people. A rising demand for labor attracted some elevator operators into more remunerative employments and pulled up the wages of the rest; automatic elevators were in part a response to this situation. But as they were introduced, some elevator operators found themselves pushed rather than pulled: deprived of their present jobs and compelled to accept less desirable alternatives, rather than attracted away from their present positions by better opportunities. Such people suffered, at least temporarily, a loss of wealth. They were forced to incur the cost of searching for new employment, and they were not guaranteed that the new job would be better than the old. Resistance to technological change and fear of automation are therefore quite understandable. Even college professors have been known to speak harshly about the introduction of such technological innovations as videotaped lectures and teaching machines.

THE DERIVED DEMAND FOR PRODUCTIVE SERVICES

Another factor that may help to conceal the downward-sloping character of the demand curve for productive services is the derived nature of that demand. The demand for productive services is derived from the demand for the goods they produce. When firms announce that they're expanding their hiring or laying some workers off, they almost never attribute the decision to a change in wage rates. Instead, they credit (or blame) the market for their product: "Sales have increased beyond our expectations" or "Inventories of finished goods have grown to unacceptable levels because of disappointing sales." Thus, the quantity of services demanded at any time from carpenters or automobile assemblers will seem to depend on conditions in the housing or automobile market, rather than on the wages of carpenters or automobile assemblers.

But they actually depend on both. The prices of houses and of automobiles and the way they are produced have been influenced by the wage rates that had to be paid to obtain the services of carpenters and of automobile assemblers. In the case of carpenters, fewer new houses are purchased, and hence fewer carpenters are employed, insofar as the cost of obtaining carpenters' services has raised the price of new construction. Moreover, houses are increasingly constructed in ways that economize on carpenters' services, with less elaborate woodwork, for example, and with factory-built cabinets.

DEMAND CREATES INCOME

Our discussion of the demand for productive services has emphasized the demand as a *constraint:* The income that owners of productive resources can obtain by supplying the services of the resources they own is limited by the demand for those services. The corollary also deserves emphasis: The income that resource owners can receive is *created* by the demand for the services of those resources. Any sheik who owns an oil well provides a vivid illustration.

Whether a country which each year produces about a thousand barrels of oil per inhabitant is fabulously wealthy or almost desperately poor depends on the demand for the services of a thick and flammable liquid hydrocarbon that seemed both ugly and useless when it was first discovered. In the absence of that demand, the Organization of Petroleum Exporting Countries (OPEC) would have had less influence over world affairs during the 1970s than the Audubon Society. But given the enormous demand that had developed in this century for the services of petroleum, OPEC became a household word.

WHO COMPETES AGAINST WHOM?

When owners of productive resources form organizations like OPEC in an effort to increase their incomes, they often argue that their association will enable them to compete more effectively against the buyers of whatever service they're supplying. Whether we call this argument confused or devious depends on how we want to assess the motives of those who make it. The plain fact is that buyers don't compete against sellers. Buyers compete against one another to obtain what sellers are supplying. Sellers compete against sellers to obtain the custom of buyers. The competition that OPEC was designed to eliminate was competition among the petroleum-exporting countries. OPEC succeeded insofar as it was able to restrict production.

Buyers may try to play the same game. We can refer at this point to an example used earlier: the agreement among owners of professional sports teams not to compete for the services of athletes. To make this agreement effective, they had to assign the exclusive right to each athlete's services to a single owner. This is the purpose of the "draft," as developed by owners' associations in major professional sports. When buyers present this kind of unified position, organization on the part of sellers may be an effective way of countering their power. But the objective of the sellers' association in such circumstances would be to *reactivate competition* among the buyers or to *reduce competition* among the sellers and could not be described correctly as an attempt to compete more effectively against the buyers.

UNIONS AND COMPETITION

In the case of labor unions, the basic federal statute regulating union organization and collective bargaining makes the mistake of asserting in its preamble that unorganized workers need unions to help them compete against corporations. But workers compete against workers, corporate employers against corporate employers. And this is the competition that affects wage rates.

Employers can't pay their workers whatever wage their callous hearts suggest for the same reason that Exxon was never able to buy oil from Saudi Arabia for whatever price it chose. Workers have alternative opportunities in the form of other employers, and Saudi Arabia always had alternative opportunities in the form of other refiners. The services of workers are valuable to employers, and so they're willing to bid for them, even though that may raise the going wage. The services of crude oil are valuable to refiners, and so they too are willing to bid, raising its price above $3 a barrel in 1972 before OPEC learned how to restrict production, above $30 a barrel when OPEC mastered the art, and keeping it for a while above $20 a barrel even when OPEC began to disintegrate in the 1980s.

Similarly, workers cannot successfully insist on the wage they think they deserve if other workers are willing to supply very similar services at lower wage rates. Workers compete against other workers, and unions are in part attempts to con-

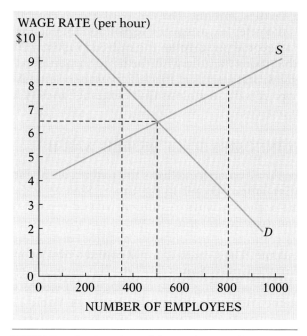

FIGURE 12B   Supply and demand curves for union employees
A union could raise the hourly wage in the case shown in Figure 12B from the market-clearing rate of $6.50 per hour to $8 if it could somehow limit the supply to 350 workers. Alternatively, it could insist, under threat of a strike, upon an hourly wage of $8. At $8 an hour, however, 800 people would be willing to accept employment. The union would have to find some way to make sure the 350 available jobs went to its members.

trol *this* competition. The implication is that unions improve the position of the members they represent by finding ways to restrict competition from those who are not members of the union. They may do this directly, for example, by securing contracts with employers that make union membership a prior condition of employment and then limiting membership. Or they may do it indirectly. Just as a legal minimum wage excludes some people from employment opportunities, so a high wage secured by union contract (perhaps under the threat of a strike or total withdrawal of labor services) excludes those who would be willing to work for less.

The belief that unions arose in the United States to counter the power of large corporations is unsupported by history. Unions first became powerful in this country in industries characterized by small-scale firms: construction, printing, textiles, mining. The railroads are an exception that supports the rule: It was special legislation that enabled unions to become powerful in the railroad industry. The unions that today bargain with the large corporations in steel, automobiles, and electrical machinery were originally missionary projects of the unions that bargained mostly with small employers.

FAMILY INCOMES SINCE WORLD WAR II

What does it all come to? What's the pattern of the income distribution among people in the United States?

There are many ways to summarize and present the data on income distribution that the Bureau of the Census gathers. The most common is the quintile (by fifths) distribution of family income. The Census Bureau counted over 66 million families in the United States in 1990. This includes everyone except individuals living alone or living with persons to whom they were not related by kinship or marriage. Table 12-1 shows the percentage of total family income received in 1990 and in four earlier years by the 20 percent of these families with the lowest incomes, by the second-lowest fifth, and so on up to the 20 percent who received the highest incomes. If family income were equally distributed, each fifth would receive 20 percent of the total. That obviously isn't the case. The percentage received by the highest 5 percent is also shown in the table.

People who encounter these data for the first time are usually quite surprised. The figures seem to indicate that the distribution of income in the United States hasn't changed

TABLE 12-1 Money Income of Families—Percentage of Aggregate Income Received by Each Fifth and Highest 5 Percent

	1950	1960	1970	1980	1990
Lowest fifth	4.5	4.8	5.4	5.1	4.6
Second fifth	12.0	12.2	12.2	11.6	10.8
Middle fifth	17.4	17.8	17.6	17.5	16.6
Fourth fifth	23.4	24.0	23.8	24.3	23.8
Highest fifth	42.7	41.3	40.9	41.6	44.3
Highest 5 percent	17.3	15.9	15.6	15.3	17.4

Source: U.S. Bureau of the Census, *Current Population Reports*, series P-60. No. 174.

significantly since World War II, despite progressive income taxes and vastly expanded government programs for transferring income to low-income families and individuals. The data don't agree with "what everyone knows."

In this case, however, "what everyone knows" may be more accurate than what the percentages seem to show. To begin with, these percentages refer to income before the payment of personal taxes. The data also take no account of *in-kind transfers.* They do reflect *money transfers.* Thus, they include income from private pensions, veterans' benefits, social security benefits, the program of Aid to Families with Dependent Children (AFDC), and all other welfare assistance — *when paid in money.* But they don't include the value of such in-kind transfers as medical assistance, rent subsidies, or food stamps—all of which are income even though they don't involve the exchange of money. Nor are the data adjusted to take account of differing family sizes. The top quintile contains 30 percent more persons than the lowest quintile.[1] When these adjustments are made, the share of lower-income groups rises and that of upper-income groups falls. One careful attempt to make these adjustments for the year 1984 produced the results shown in Table 12-2. The share of the top fifth declines from nine times to five times that of the bottom fifth.

A SPURIOUS RIGIDITY

A more fundamental difficulty with data of this sort is that they don't actually mean what they seem to say. Even the adjusted data of Table 12-2 give a misleading picture of the actual inequality of the U.S. family-income distribution. We're inclined to assume without thinking about it that the families in the second or fourth quintile in a current year are the same families (or an earlier generation of the same families) who occupied those fifths in some preceding year. This isn't necessarily the case. In fact, it's quite unlikely to be the case for one simple reason: The relative income position of a family depends very much on the age of the family's principal earner.

The data of Table 12-3 illustrate what we're talking about. They show the average (mean) income of all households in 1990 by the age of the householder. (Embarrassed by its use of the term *head,* the Bureau has substituted the term *householder,* defined as the owner of the residence or, in the case of

---

[1]It's also important to know that families in the top quintile supply four times as many weeks of work as families in the bottom quintile.

TABLE 12-2   Percentage of Aggregate Family Income Received by Each Fifth of Families in 1984: Census Bureau Data and Adjusted Data

	Money Income as Calculated by Census Bureau	Census Bureau Data Adjusted to Take Account of Taxes, In-kind Transfers, and Family Size
Lowest fifth	4.7%	7.3%
Second fifth	11.0	13.4
Middle fifth	17.0	18.1
Fourth fifth	24.4	24.4
Highest fifth	42.9	36.8

Source: Frank Levy, *Dollars and Dreams* (New York: Norton, 1987) p. 195.

joint ownership, the person whose name appears first on the survey form.) The table demonstrates unmistakably that a substantial amount of the inequality that shows up in a still picture would disappear if we were able to take a moving picture—that is, to compare the incomes of households over the lifetimes of the householders.

When we compare the data of Table 12-3 with the upper limits of the various family-income quintiles in 1990, we find that "an average family" would move in its lifetime from the second fifth through the middle fifth into the fourth fifth and descend to the second fifth again when the householder retires.[2]

ON REDISTRIBUTING INCOME

Interest in issues of this sort usually grows out of a belief that too much inequality in the distribution of income is undesirable. Few people pause to think their way carefully through the questions of why inequality is undesirable, how much inequality is acceptable, or why income inequality should be of so much more concern than inequalities of other kinds.

Regardless of how these important questions are answered, programs to reduce the income inequality among U.S. families and individuals will run up against a fundamental difficulty: Since income isn't really distributed, it can't actually be redistributed. No one is in a position to ap-

[2]The upper limits of the lowest through the fourth fifth in 1990 were, respectively, $16,846; $29,044; $42,040, and $61,490.

TABLE 12-3   Household Money Incomes in 1990

Age of Householder	Mean Income
15 to 24 years	$21,484
25 to 34 years	34,484
35 to 44 years	45,076
45 to 54 years	50,003
55 to 64 years	41,459
65 years and over	24,586

Source: U.S. Bureau of the Census, *Current Population Reports,* series P-60, No. 174.

portion shares of the social product. The most that even government can do is alter the rules of the game in the hope of securing a preferred outcome. What happens next will not be exactly what was intended and may be something altogether different.

The simplest and most direct way to reduce income inequality would appear to be a program of taxes on high incomes and cash transfers to people with low incomes. But nothing about economic systems is ever as simple and direct as it seems at first glance. To raise taxes on high incomes, the government must change the rules that relate taxes owed to particular kinds of income received. When it does so, people don't merely pay the higher taxes; they also try to adjust their behavior to minimize the impact of the new rules. Some of these adjustments will be legal tax avoidance; others may be illegal tax evasion; but they all combine to drive a wedge between what was intended when the rules were rewritten and what actually emerges. The revenue that results from the tax increase will be less, and may be much less, than what was hoped for.

In order to supplement the incomes of poor people, government must write new rules controlling eligibility for grants. These rule revisions will also have undesired effects as people adjust their behavior to fit the new criteria. Once again the adjustments will be both legal and illegal; but their combined effect can be substantial, because there are so many margins along which adjustments can be made. The number of people classified as poor may actually increase as a result of efforts to reduce poverty.

Consider the hypothetical but unfortunately not implausible case of a single-parent family with three small children.

Suppose the mother is currently receiving $400 a month in cash grants, food stamps worth $100 per month, and subsidized medical care for herself and the children worth $50 a month. Then she obtains a job offer promising $1000 per month. Will she take the job and go off welfare? Would she be better off if she did so?

Her income from welfare is not taxed, but she will have to pay social security and income taxes on her earnings. She will also have to secure day care for the children, buy some additional clothing, and incur transportation expenses if she takes the job. Moreover, she will lose her monthly cash grant and her family's eligibility for food stamps and Medicaid. When she adds up all these costs of taking the job, she may find that her earnings are going to be taxed at a marginal rate of 90 percent or more.

Plug in some plausible numbers and check the results for yourself. If the income and social security taxes plus day care, transportation, and clothing expenses take $350 a month from her paycheck, and the loss of welfare reduces her monthly income by $550, she would be giving up $900 in order to earn $1000. That amounts to a 90 percent marginal tax rate, or a 90 percent tax on *additions* to her welfare income— which isn't terribly attractive. No one could accuse a mother in such a situation of laziness or irresponsibility if she decided to turn down the job offer, stay on welfare, and care for her children.

People with yachts are wealthy; people who scrounge through trash barrels and garbage cans are poor. But if we write new rules that obligate every yacht owner to contribute $10,000 a year to a fund for trash and garbage scroungers and grant each scrounger a right to $2000 a year from the fund, the number of recorded yacht owners will rapidly decline and the number of people claiming to be scroungers will show a remarkable increase. That may be an overly dramatic way to summarize the problem, but it makes the essential point. A large society such as the United States cannot allocate tasks and benefits to its citizens the way that loving parents do it in a family: on the basis of abilities and needs. Tasks and benefits will inevitably be allocated in response to people's pursuit of their own interests under the perceived rules of the game. What government can achieve by way of income redistribution is pretty well confined to what can be achieved by changing the rules. That will almost certainly turn out to be something less satisfactory than what was hoped for when the rules were changed.

CHANGING RULES AND
SOCIAL COOPERATION

It might be thought that the solution is to change the rules again when the initial change doesn't yield the desired results, and to keep on modifying the rules until the target has been attained. But who has the knowledge that would be required to choose these fine adjustments? Even if the knowledge were available, would anyone have the power to put them into effect in a democratic society? Most important of all, what happens to the complex cooperative processes on which a highly specialized economic system depends if the society is subjected to continuous changes in the rules of the game?

People invest, make sacrifices, and otherwise commit themselves in the belief that established property rights will be respected, that the rules will *not* be changed "in the middle of the game." A rule that says the rules can be changed at any time would destroy the foundation for most social cooperation. Property rights must be reasonably clear and stable if people are to plan for the future and to take long-run consequences into account.

It's also worth observing that when expectations are regularly frustrated by unanticipated changes in the rules of the game, participants stop playing the ordinary game and shift their attention to the game that matters: making the rules.

ONCE OVER LIGHTLY

The distribution of income is the result of the supply of and demand for productive services.

The production of productive resources is investment, or the creation of capital. One important form of capital is human capital, or productive capabilities embodied in human beings. The production of human capital is an important consideration, because monetary income is primarily earned in the United States, even by the wealthy, through supplying the services of human resources.

The amount and nature of the investment that will occur in a society depend on established and accepted property rights, because property rights determine what people can expect from the actions that are open to them.

Lower rates of time preference encourage investment over consumption. Greater uncertainty about future returns from investment will prompt the discounting of future income at higher rates and consequently will lead to less investment.

The demand for productive services of any kind will not be perfectly inelastic. A greater quantity will be demanded at lower prices and a lesser quantity at higher prices, because there are substitutes for any productive service.

Potential users of productive services decide on the amount they will demand by comparing the marginal-benefit/marginal-cost ratios of alternative procedures for achieving their purposes.

The demand for productive services, and hence their price, is partly dependent on the demand for the goods they produce. But the price of productive services also reacts back on the cost and price of producing particular goods and thus on the quantity that will be produced and sold.

Suppliers of productive services don't compete against buyers of those services. Suppliers compete against other suppliers, buyers against other buyers. The quest for higher incomes produces attempts to suppress competition, because what a seller can obtain and what a buyer must pay will depend on the alternative opportunities that competitors are providing.

Census Bureau data on the distribution of family money incomes exaggerate the inequality of income in the United States by neglecting in-kind transfers, personal taxes, differences in family size, and other important factors. They also give an erroneous impression of rigidity by ignoring the extensive circulation of individual families throughout the overall distribution.

Social cooperation on any extensive scale requires relatively stable property rights because it presupposes the ability to predict the consequences of decisions.

QUESTIONS FOR DISCUSSION

1. *Income* is a flow of receipts per unit of time: $240 per week, or $30,000 a year. *Wealth* is a stock of assets: cash, shares of stock, buildings, tools, and so on. How are income and wealth related?

    (a) If you own an annuity that will pay you a $10,000 income for each of the next 20 years, what is the present value of that annuity? How much does the annuity contribute to your wealth?

    (b) Suppose you own 100 shares of stock in a promising new company that has not yet begun to pay dividends and probably won't do so for several years. The stock is currently exchanging on the New York

Stock Exchange for $50 a share. What is your wealth from ownership of this stock? If you wanted to convert this wealth into income, how could you do so? About how much income could you obtain without reducing the amount of your wealth?

(c) Why would the stock referred to above be bought for $50 a share if the company isn't expected to pay any dividends for several years?

(d) A privately owned automobile is wealth. Does it yield income to its owner? In what form?

(e) What determines the market value of a house and thus its contribution to the wealth of the owner? Do the expected benefits from living in the house (income) determine the value of the house (wealth)? Or does the price of the house determine the income received by living in it? Suppose someone happens to detest the house which he owns and occupies because it has such distracting views of the bay and the mountains from every window. Would this idiosyncratic attitude reduce his income from living in the house? Would it reduce his wealth from owning the house? What behavior would this inconsistency between his income and his wealth probably induce?

(f) Is an engineering degree wealth? What determines the value of such a degree? How could an engineer with a freshly minted degree who is just beginning her first job convert some of her wealth into current income in order to buy furniture for her apartment?

(g) A successful and popular physician decides to retire and "sell his practice." What is he actually selling? What will determine its value to a potential buyer?

(h) Is the expectation of future retirement benefits a part of one's wealth? Is the expectation of social security benefits a major part of the wealth of someone 65 years of age?

2. In a widely publicized 1983 case, the ex-wife of a doctor sued to obtain half the value of his medical degree, on the grounds that she had helped put him through medical school and was entitled to half of everything they owned under California's community property law.

(a) The attorney for the doctor insisted that education was not property and so could not be shared because it had no value at the time it was acquired. If the doctor had dropped dead upon receiving his diploma, his wife would not have gotten one cent, the attorney claimed. Do you agree?

(b) Suppose the couple had owned a house, which burned down at the time of their divorce. What steps do people take to protect themselves against the accidental destruction or other loss of valuable physical assets? What steps do young physicians usually take to assure their families a large income even if the physician drops dead?

(c) The wife's attorneys asked for $250,000 as her share of the value of her ex-husband's medical training. Suppose the medical degree could be conservatively expected to add $30,000 per year for 30 years to what the doctor would have earned without the degree. Since this amount will presumably rise with any inflation that occurs over the period, a real rather than nominal interest rate should be used to calculate its present value. Would you support the ex-wife's attorneys in their estimate of what she was entitled to? What is one-half the present value of a $30,000 annuity for 30 years when discounted at 4 percent?

(d) The doctor said: "I don't think she is entitled to half of my future." His ex-wife said: "I should get a return on my investment in the partnership." The couple separated after ten years of marriage, during which she worked as an accountant while he completed medical school, an internship, and a residency. How would you decide the issue?

3. By investing $20,000 (income forgone and other expenses) for each of the next 5 years in a college education, Jack and Jill can reasonably expect to enhance their earning power by $10,000 per year for the following 25 years.

(a) Use Table 11-3 in Chapter 11 to decide whether this would be a good investment for Jill, who discounts at 3 percent.

(b) Is it a good investment for Jack, who discounts at 9 percent?

(c) How is the wisdom of the investment affected by the fact that both Jack and Jill love learning?

4. Who owns national parks? The government? The people? Park Service officials in the Interior Department? What are the implications of a sign that reads: "U.S. Government Property: No Trespassing"?

5. Your airplane boarding pass assigns you seat A, by the window. When you come to your row, you find a six-year-old child sitting in your seat. His boarding pass says C. You ask him to move, but he says he wants to look out the window and tells you to take his seat on the aisle. Since you also want to look at the scenery, you call the cabin attendant and explain the situation. The cabin attendant says, "Do you *really* want me to make that little child move away from the window?"

At this point, who owns seat A? Sort out the actual, legal, and moral property rights in this case.

6. A Santa Monica apartment owner decided to tear down his six-unit apartment building rather than operate under rent controls. The city refused him permission to tear down the building, however, claiming that its interest in preserving rental housing took precedence over his right to demolish his property. The California Supreme Court sustained Santa Monica's refusal to allow the demolition.

Who owns the building? Sort out the actual, legal, and moral property rights in this case.

7. "Entitlement programs" of the federal government are defined as "programs that provide benefit payments for individuals whose eligibility is

determined by law." Because the criteria for eligibility are established by existing law, expenditures are not controlled by the process of congressional appropriation.

(a) Would you say that the beneficiaries of entitlement programs receive income because of certain property rights?

(b) The criteria for some entitlement programs are outside the range of the beneficiaries' choice: Payments based on age are an example, or veterans' benefits. Other programs use criteria that persons can more or less choose to satisfy. Would you expect the law of demand to affect the rate at which expenditures increase in this second category?

8. Teachers began encountering serious job shortages in the 1970s after many years of rising demand for their services. An intensified interest in unionization followed. What can unionization accomplish for teachers in a highly unfavorable job market? Who is likely to benefit? Who will be harmed?

9. "Farmers complaining that they can't get field hands now that the bracero program has been curtailed aren't sincere," said an official of the United Packinghouse Workers Union. "About one-third of the unemployed in Los Angeles are former farm workers, and the farmers could get them back if they'd make wages and working conditions attractive enough." Do you think farmers are insincere? Could California farmers get enough workers if they tried harder? Explain.

10. Under a closed-shop arrangement, employers may hire only workers who are already union members. Under a union-shop arrangement, employers may hire whomever they please but the employees must then join the union. What different effects would you expect these alternative arrangements to have on wages? On employment? On discrimination by the union against members of minority races? Why?

11. College professors in the United States have never had an effective union. Then why did their average wage rise spectacularly in the 1960s? How might college professors have used unionization to obtain even larger salary increases over this period? Why might some professors be interested in a law that prohibited anyone without an earned doctorate from teaching in colleges? What consequences would you predict if a few states passed such a law?

12. Do the relative salaries of humanities professors and football coaches at major state universities reflect the relative value of football and humanities? Do they reflect the number of years that professors and coaches must spend acquiring an education? The number of hours they work? The difficulty or unpleasantness of their work? Why do the football coaches usually receive salaries that are so much higher?

13. Until the program was abolished in 1987, the government of Holland paid a stipend to artists, based on such factors as marital status and number of children, and took in return a selection of the artists' work deemed equivalent in value. Most of the work so purchased disappeared into warehouses.

(a) Do you think a program like this raises the average income of artists?

(b) How might it actually lower the average income of artists?

14. There has been a growing trend in recent years toward two-tier contracts in wage negotiations between employers and unions. Current employees receive one wage; new employees are hired at a much lower wage rate.

    (a) How might such an arrangement benefit each of the following four parties: employers; current employees; union leaders; new employees?

    (b) For which of the above four groups would such a two-tier contract tend to become less satisfactory as time went by?

15. Do high wage rates in such strongly unionized industries as steel and automobiles pull up the general level of wages in nonunionized, lower-wage industries? If you think they do, what is the process by which this occurs? If contracts that call for high wages reduce employment opportunities in the industries that must pay these wages, where do the excluded workers find employment?

16. A plumbers' local in Fort Lauderdale, Florida, some years ago voluntarily lowered by 45 percent the hourly rate for union workers on low-rise construction projects. The higher rate continued to apply to high-rise construction. The business manager of the union said this was being done to curb inflation and help homeowners. Do you think it might also have been done because nonunion plumbers were available in the area at less than half of union scale? Why do you suppose the union didn't lower the rate on high-rise construction work as well?

17. "If we had no unions with their united strength, we would have unlimited hours of work, low wages, child labor wherever possible, speed-up and unsafe and dangerous working conditions. All these evils of the industrial system have been eliminated by workers united into unions and withholding their labor."

    (a) Do you agree with that statement from a newspaper letter?

    (b) Can you think of a way to test the statement or any part of it?

18. A letter to a magazine wonders "how [we will] cope with the growing number of unemployed put out of work by corporate capital-intensive high technology," and asks: "To what end these corporate methodologies that actually impoverish more than they enrich most of us?"

    (a) Can you help the writer find an answer?

    (b) The percentage of Americans 16 and over and not in the armed forces who were employed through the year averaged 57.4 percent in 1970, 59.2 percent in 1980, and 62.7 percent in 1990. Does this trend support the letter writer's argument?

19. A nationally syndicated columnist, in attacking a proposal to reduce the federal minimum wage for teenagers, stated: "Any employer with an eye

to the bottom line, would prefer to hire help at 85 cents an hour less, given a choice."

    (a) If the minimum wage for teenagers were lowered by 85 cents, why would some employers "with an eye to the bottom line" choose *not* to reduce the wage rate paid their teenage employees?

    (b) Why do so many employers pay teenagers (and others) wages that are far above the legal minimum wage—even in the absence of a union contract or any apparent threat of unionization?

    (c) The same columnist denies that lowering the minimum wage for teenagers would increase the number of jobs available to teenagers. "It takes McDonald's X amount of workers to offer its products to the public and that is probably going to be the amount of help hired, regardless of wages." Do you agree? What do you think would happen if McDonald's had to pay $9.00 an hour to its employees? Would X turn out to be a constant?

20. How would each of the following groups be affected by a large increase in the legal minimum wage?

    (a) Unionized workers.

    (b) Teenagers.

    (c) Unskilled workers.

21. "Comparable worth" is the name of a movement that began in the 1980s to determine the worth of different jobs and then to adjust relative wage rates to the relative worth of those jobs. The movement gains most of its support from the belief that women are unfairly discriminated against in the labor market. The jobs at which most of them work (e.g., secretaries and nurses) are regarded as "women's jobs" and so are allegedly paid less than their "comparable worth." The comparison is with jobs traditionally held by men.

    (a) Can a job have an inherent worth? Can you think of any situation where the worth of a job is not its value to some particular party in a specific situation?

    (b) Imagine a medical clinic with 20 medical doctors, one nurse, and one laboratory technician. Is it plausible to suppose that an additional nurse or lab technician could have more worth to the clinic in such a situation than an additional doctor?

    (c) The worth or value that influences decisions is always *marginal* worth or value. Why is a secretary worth more to the economics department if it employs only one than if it employs eight? Describe a situation in which the worth of a secretary to the economics department would likely be greater than the worth of an economist fully armed with a Ph.D.

    (d) Why will an employer who follows the maximizing rule of Chapter 9—do more if marginal revenue exceeds marginal cost, less if marginal cost exceeds marginal revenue—want to pay each employee a wage equal to his or her marginal worth? What would be implied by the assertion that an employer was paying employees less than their marginal worth?

22. The graph in Figure 12C depicts the marginal value of nurses and of custodians to the Community General Hospital.

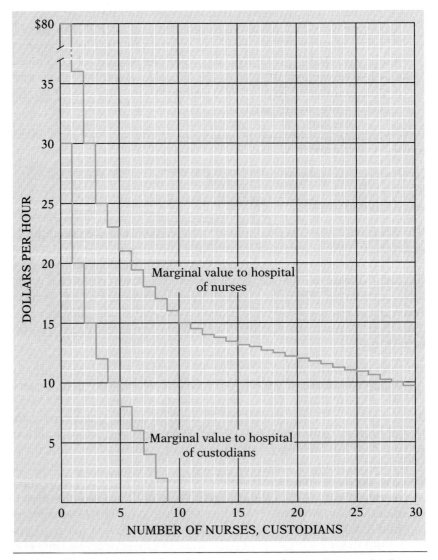

FIGURE 12C   Marginal value of nurses and custodians at Community General Hospital

(a) Why might a nurse be worth as much as $80 an hour to the hospital? Why might a custodian be worth as much as $30 an hour? Do you think a hospital forced to pay $75 an hour for the services of a nurse would ever put the nurse to work emptying bedpans, taking temperatures, or serving meals to patients?

(b) Now suppose that the custodians are unionized and that the hospital must pay its custodians $19 an hour. How many custodians will the hospital hire? What will be the marginal worth of a custodian?

(c) Assume that the nurses are not unionized and that the hospital is able to obtain as many nurses as it wants to hire at an hourly wage of $10. How many nurses would it want to hire? What would be the marginal worth of a nurse?

(d) What would be the relative worth in this situation of a custodian and a nurse? Would their relative worth reflect the intrinsic importance of their work?

(e) Will hospitals use nurses to empty bedpans if it can hire them for $10 an hour? Will it ask nurses or will it ask custodians to empty wastebaskets if custodians must be paid twice as much as nurses? What hospital tasks do you suppose would be performed by custodians if they had to be paid $29 an hour? Would a custodian's services become worth three times as much as a nurse's services?

23. Why would nurses be willing to work for as little as $10 an hour, as in the preceding question?

(a) What factors determine the supply curve of nurses' services?

(b) Until fairly recently, one could become a registered nurse by completing a three-year nurses' training program at a certified hospital. The general rule now is that nurses must acquire a bachelor of science degree and will not be admitted to nursing curricula until they have successfully completed courses in inorganic and organic chemistry, microbiology, mathematics, social science, and language. Do these tougher requirements increase the value of registered nurses to prospective employers? Do they shift the supply curve of nurses? Are they likely to affect the wage rate that must be paid for nurses? Will this affect the marginal worth of nurses?

24. What happens when buyers are not price takers, but price searchers? Suppose you receive $6.25 per 100 for distributing advertising flyers door to door. You have a very large territory so that your business is limited only by your ability to hire help. Your potential help consists exclusively of the teenagers in your neighborhood, each of whom can distribute 100 flyers per hour. They are all willing to work one hour for you, but each insists upon a different minimum wage. Here are their minimum demands:

Alan	$3.00
Betty	3.50
Chuck	4.00
Donna	4.50
Elmer	5.00
Frances	5.50
George	6.00
Hepzibah	6.50

How many of these workers do you want to hire if your goal is to maximize your net revenue and *all employees must be paid at the same wage rate?*

(a) What is your marginal revenue from hiring an additional worker?

(b) What is your marginal cost from hiring an additional worker when you hire Alan? When you hire Betty? When you hire Chuck? Which is the last worker you can hire if you want to keep marginal cost from exceeding marginal revenue?

(c) Suppose a large hospital is in a similar position with respect to nurses. It can hire all the nurses it is likely to want, but it must offer a higher wage to attract additional nurses: Some will work for very little, others for a bit more, and so on up to those who will only work if they can obtain a very high wage. Why might such a hospital find itself facing what it perceives as a chronic shortage of nurses? How might it respond? (Hint: What do *sellers* attempt to do when additional sales would "spoil" their market?)

25. Question 22 above assumed that the custodians' union was able to enforce a wage rate of $19 an hour.

(a) Is this likely, given what you know about supply and demand for custodians' services?

(b) What would the union have to do to maintain the wage rate for custodians at $19 an hour?

(c) Why is it easier for a union of electricians than for a union of custodians to establish a wage of $19 an hour for members?

(d) Why are so few typists and clerical workers organized into unions?

(e) Why have skilled workers, who tend to receive higher wages anyway, generally been more successful in forming unions and raising their wages than unskilled workers?

26. Should high-school history and English teachers be paid as much as science and math teachers?

(a) Suppose that a school district pays all high-school teachers with the same years of experience the same salary, regardless of teaching field, and that this produces a surplus of history and English teachers and a shortage of science and math teachers. Would this create a case for salary differentials?

(b) How could the problem of concurrent surplus and shortage be solved without paying science and math teachers more than history and English teachers?

(c) Why has the policy of identical wages in fact produced shortages of science and math teachers along with surpluses of history and English teachers in many school districts? What factors have contributed on the demand side? On the supply side?

27. According to the American Medical Association, physicians in family practice have experienced a decline in their average incomes in recent years while medical specialists' incomes were rising. Surgical specialists have been doing best of all, and their average incomes are now about twice what generalists earn.

(a) Much of this difference in income arises from long-established differences in the fees paid by insurers for various medical services. The American Society of Internal Medicine claims that insurers' fee schedules are unfair. How would you decide on the validity of such a claim? What is a fair way to determine the relative worth of a successful surgical procedure against that of an accurate diagnosis followed by an effective prescription?

(b) Surgeons justify their higher incomes by claiming that they spend four more years in school than do general practitioners. Do four additional years in school justify higher fees because it's costly to attend school, or because those extra years in school improve knowledge and skill levels?

28. A survey conducted during the 1980 recession revealed that 118,000 households were dissolved in one month.

(a) Why would a recession cause households to disappear? What happens to them?

(b) What happened to average family income as a result?

29. In each of the cases described below, an increase in the family's monetary income puts all members of the original family into families with lower incomes. Explain how this occurs. Does it imply that the individuals involved are worse off? What important questions does it raise about the interpretation of family-income data?

(a) An elderly couple living with their married son receives an increase in social security benefits that permits the couple to obtain their own apartment.

(b) Two married people who fight constantly, and stay together only because they can't afford to maintain two homes, separate with great relief when both receive promotions and raises, each taking one of the children.

(c) The husband of an orthopedic surgeon quits his job to stay home, tend the house, and give the children better care when his wife's practice begins to earn a very large income.

30. How should in-kind transfers be treated in calculating the incomes of people on welfare?

(a) Does it make sense to count the monetary value of food stamps, rent subsidies, and free school lunches in the income of a family on welfare?

(b) How would this lead to an overstatement of their income? (Hint: Would you rather have a shopping cart full of items that someone else selected or the money equivalent of those items?)

(c) Medicare benefits are a major contribution to the well-being of many elderly Americans. If an elderly person receives a $5000 operation, should we calculate that person's income as $5000 higher?

31. We often encounter the phrase "the low-income elderly." How poor are elderly people in the United States?

(a) Why does the figure in Table 12-3 seriously understate the average relative income of people over 65?

(b) In 1982 only 8.5 percent of all elderly persons in families lived below the official poverty line, as compared with 27 percent in 1959. How do you suppose this change came about?

(c) How many benefits can you think of that accrue to people over 65 but don't affect their money incomes?

32. Prior to 1977, the national food stamp program gave each participating household a monthly stamp allotment sufficient to purchase a minimally adequate diet. The allotment varied with family size but not with family income. What varied with income was the price the family had to pay for the stamps. This ranged from nothing for the poorest families to about 85 percent of the stamps' value for the eligible families with the highest incomes. This system was changed in 1977 to one in which allotments did vary with family income but stamps were given away rather than sold. The 1977 reform received strong support from the argument that it was absurd if not downright immoral to make poor people pay for food stamps. Was it absurd? What were the consequences of this policy?

(a) Suppose a family earning $300 a month chooses to spend $150 on housing, $100 on food, and $50 on other goods. Then it is given $100 in food stamps. Why can't we predict how much the family will subsequently spend per month on housing, food, and other goods? What is the range of possibilities?

(b) If government officials want to be sure that the poor family uses its food stamp allotment to double its monthly expenditure on food, how can they constrain the family's choice to the outcome desired by the officials? (Assume that the family does not sell the stamps for money, something that does occur but is illegal.)

(c) Is a family better off if it chooses to use food stamps as a substitute for income previously spent on food, so that it can increase its consumption of other goods? Or should the family be constrained to follow an expenditure pattern dictated by government officials (and presumably based on the recommendations of nutritionists)?

(d) If the government makes large grants to church-owned colleges to support instruction in science but provides no funds to support religious instruction, does the government in reality support science but not religion?

(e) If a donor to a united charity appeal earmarks her contribution for alcoholism counseling, does she thereby increase the funds that will be available for alcoholism counseling in her community?

33. The claim is often made—and also often ridiculed—that taxes on income reduce people's incentives to earn income.

(a) If you were required to pay the government 50 percent of all money income you earn during the summer, would you choose to work more or fewer hours than if your income was not subject to tax? Would you look for ways to raise your income without raising your money income or taxable income?

(b) How does a 50 percent marginal tax rate (additional taxes divided by additional income) affect the cost to a physician of building his own home rather than hiring a contractor?

(c) An unmarried woman with three preschool children has no earned income but is receiving $400 a month in cash welfare assistance, plus food stamps worth $200 a month and government-financed medical care worth $100 a month. She is offered a job that will pay $1000 a month. If she takes the job, she will no longer be eligible for any of the cash or in-kind assistance. What is the marginal tax rate to which her earnings are subject? Would you take the job in her situation?

34. A substantial number of government programs are specifically intended to improve the relative position of lower-income groups. In addition, government economic policies in other areas are often formulated in ways designed to avoid harming lower-income groups. Such policies are usually defended on the grounds that they promote greater justice in the distribution of income.

(a) Can you defend the assertion that the distribution of income that emerges from the interactions of demand and supply is just? Can you defend the assertion that it is unjust?

(b) How would you define a just distribution (or an unjust distribution) of income?

(c) If the preceding question is too difficult, perhaps you can define a *more* just (or less unjust) distribution of income.

(d) Two common but very different ways to define justice are in terms of *rules* and in terms of *results*. We usually define a just (or fair) game of any sort in terms of rules: Were the rules clearly stated, known and accepted in advance, and impartially enforced? We do not use the game's final score as a test of its fairness. On the other hand, we are likely to assess the justice with which food, clothing, and other goods are distributed among children in a family in terms of results: Does each child receive an equal share except in so far as differences among the children clearly call for unequal shares? Few would want to define a just distribution of income among children in terms of impartial rules regarding competition for goods.

Which of these provides better criteria for assessing the justice or injustice of the income distribution in a society such as the United States?

35. Almost everyone at one time or another has used the term *a fair wage*. What does it mean? Evaluate each of the following definitions of a fair wage. What insight does it express? What reality does it overlook?

(a) A wage that reflects the social value of the work.
(b) A wage that reflects the danger, difficulty, and general arduousness of the work.
(c) A wage that adequately compensates the employee for the time and trouble spent learning the trade.
(d) A wage that meets the employee's needs.
(e) A wage sufficient to support a family.
(f) A wage that reflects the profitability of the employer's business.
(g) The customary wage.
(h) The wage established through collective bargaining.
(i) The same wage for everyone.
(j) A wage that the employee considers fair.
(k) A wage of which the employer is not ashamed.
(l) The wage that clears the market.
(m) A wage agreed upon by employer and employee when both are adequately informed.

36. Suppose you have an irrational prejudice against non-Polish pickle packers and refuse to purchase any pickles that haven't been packed by Polish people.

(a) How will this prejudice affect the price you must pay for pickles of a given quality?
(b) How does an employer pay for any decision to discriminate in hiring on the basis of criteria unrelated to job performance?
(c) Do employers in general benefit from employment discrimination directed against nonwhites and women? Who does benefit?

EXTERNALITIES AND CONFLICTING RIGHTS

According to the economic way of thinking, individuals choose their courses of action by weighing the expected marginal benefits of any decision against its expected marginal costs. Benefits and costs for other people will not affect the decision unless the benefits and costs for others *matter to the actor.* That turns out to be extremely important for the understanding of a wide range of social problems.

EXTERNALITIES, NEGATIVE AND POSITIVE

Harry is the very model of a courteous driver, partly because he values his own safety, but mostly because his heart just overflows with kindness and consideration. Yet Harry enters the freeway each weekday morning at about 7:45 with no regard whatsoever for all the drivers whom he slows down by doing so. They don't affect his decision because they don't enter into his calculations. He has actually never thought about them. Traffic engineers can figure out the additional time that each of the motorists who are behind Harry at 7:45 will have to spend on the freeway because Harry added slightly to the congestion; and when they multiply this time delay by the number of motorists on the expressway at that hour, it sums to a significant figure. Harry, the soul of sweetness and consideration, is dumping a lot of cost on his companions in the commute. Because *he does not take this cost into account* in making his decisions, economists call it an external cost of

Harry's action, or a *negative externality*. A less fancy term is *spillover cost*.

Harry would be distressed to find out that he is generating negative externalities but absolutely delighted to learn that he often generates *positive externalities*. These are *benefits from an action that the decision maker does not take into account*. Last summer Harry painted his garage a gleaming magenta, which he himself rather dislikes, because his neighbor loves magenta (and you remember the kind of person Harry is). Harry knows that his neighbor derives benefit from the new paint job—that's why he did it—and so his neighbor's benefit is not an externality. What Harry does *not* know is that many passers-by also derive great joy and laughter from seeing his magenta garage for the first time. This benefit is a positive externality because Harry did not take it into account when deciding what color to paint the garage.

Unfortunately, there are also people in the neighborhood who avert their eyes when passing Harry's place because the sight of that magenta garage turns them faintly ill. Harry's paint job, as it turns out, generates both positive and negative externalities.

Chapter 13 will focus on negative externalities. Some of the interesting problems that positive externalities create will be taken up in Chapter 14.

PERFECTION IS UNATTAINABLE

The beginning of all wisdom on this topic is a clear recognition that negative externalities cannot be eliminated. To see why not, let's consider the case of Rodney, who lives in a pleasant suburban neighborhood and commutes to work on a motorcycle. When he innocently starts up the cycle at 6:30 each weekday morning, he wakes up eight neighbors, who individually curse his cycle and roll over for another hour of sleep. Each of them, if they thought about it, would be willing to pay up to $5 a week to be rid of that 6:30 motorcycle noise. And Rod, if he thought about it, would be willing to push his motorcycle out of earshot before starting it up for a payment as low as $15 a week. In other words, the neighbors would be willing to pay $40 to get rid of the noise and Rod would be willing to accommodate them for $15. But they probably won't make a deal, because the transaction costs are too high.

Transaction costs, you recall from Chapter 4, are the costs of arranging contracts or transaction agreements between demanders and suppliers. Transaction costs rule out a lot of wealth-enhancing exchanges that would otherwise occur. While the neighbors and Rodney would all be better off if each neighbor gave Rodney $3 a week to push his motorcycle out of earshot before cranking it up, the total cost of gathering the required information, collecting the payments, and enforcing the agreement would be larger than the potential benefit. So nothing happens and the externality persists.

It doesn't necessarily take a monetary payment to eliminate an externality. Rodney might hear through the grapevine (grapevines often reduce transaction costs) that his 6:30 departure irritates some of his neighbors and decide on his own to push the cycle to the end of the block before starting it up. He would be deciding that he dislikes offending his neighbors more than he dislikes pushing the motorcycle. But first he has to find out that he is generating an externality. When he finds out, he "internalizes the externality," which means he takes it into account—and then chooses to alter his behavior.

Rodney doesn't have to be such a nice guy. He might push the cycle to the end of the block because some angry neighbor taped an anonymous note on the cycle seat threatening unspecified damage to the cycle if Rodney continued cranking it up before 7:30. That also internalizes the externality.

Another possibility is that someone calls the police, who then inform Rodney that a suburban ordinance prohibits the operation of motorcycles in residential areas prior to 7:30 on weekday mornings. In this case, it's the visit from the police officer that internalizes the externality for Rodney.

In an urban, industrialized society, where people interact daily with thousands of others, negative externalities will multiply rapidly. We learn to ignore most of the negative externalities that others inflict on us, and we try to be sensitive to the unintended costs that our own actions impose on others. The first step toward containing the problem of negative externalities is to cultivate the civic virtues of empathy, courtesy, humility, and tolerance. Civilization will simply be impossible among a people who don't possess substantial amounts of these virtues. If people insist on obtaining absolutely everything to which they think they have a right, civilization will give way to warfare. How to cultivate or renew these virtues where they have withered is a question far beyond the scope of this book. We would do well to remember, however, that all the other procedures that we're going to discuss for dealing with problems created by externalities presuppose these virtues to some extent.

NEGOTIATION

Our everyday garden-variety procedure for minimizing the social problems that negative externalities create is negotiation. We strike bargains with one another. People consent to bear the costs associated with the production of particular goods because other people who want those goods offer compensation that makes it worth their while. That's why baggage handlers don't complain about jet noise or automobile mechanics about the grease on their clothes, and why the owner of a dog kennel will cheerfully let other people's dogs perform the same act that arouses an urban lawn fancier to fury.

"Work it out for yourselves" is sound advice. Because people differ so widely in their tastes, talents, and other circumstances, they will often be able to negotiate an exchange of costs that makes everyone involved better off than before. Moreover, the necessity of working it out for themselves encourages cooperation among those who are in the best position to know the possibilities. When people aren't required to negotiate, they often adopt positions that are costly to others. For example, they demand legislation that would prohibit smoking in restaurants, rather than ask for a table where no smoke will blow. And they point indignantly to minute traces of tobacco smoke in the air, while ignoring the dangerous emissions that they themselves put into the atmosphere by driving to the restaurant.

We would probably have a much greater respect for negotiation as a social procedure for reducing externality problems if we learned to recognize the myriad ways in which we actually use it. People who hate the noise and dirt of the city move to outlying areas. People who detest the culture of suburbia live in small towns. People who despise the isolation of rural life choose to live in the city. The hard-of-hearing get residential real estate bargains under airport approach lanes. Surfboard riders seek out companions and thereby voluntarily segregate themselves from swimmers who hate to dodge surfboards. The afternoon naptaker pays $1.59 for a box of earplugs and thereafter lives in peace with the neighboring teenager's mufflerless motorcycle. Not everyone is completely satisfied. But voluntary exchange does reduce the total of costs imposed on reluctant bystanders.

Negotiation cannot be effective, however, unless property rights are adequately defined. Voluntary exchange of any sort works well only when all involved parties agree on who owns what. In some cases, a clarification of property rights may be all that stands in the way of a mutually satisfactory agreement.

Suppose, for example, that Smith and Brown disagree by two feet on the location of the boundary line dividing their properties. It wouldn't matter much, since both want to plant flowers in the disputed strip, except for the fact that Smith wants to plant zinnias and Brown has his heart set on petunias. Until the question of who has a right to do what is settled, neither one will plant flowers, and both will be living with the inferior alternative of crabgrass.

If they then hire a surveyor who proves that Smith in fact owns the disputed strip, flowers can finally bloom. Nor will the flowers necessarily be zinnias! Once it's clearly established that Smith is the owner and hence has the right to decide what will grow in the boundary strip, Brown may be able to purchase that right. Brown's passion for petunias could be so powerful that he offers Smith $25 a year for the right to grow them between their lots. And if Smith prefers petunias *with* $25 to zinnias without $25, the flowers that bloom will be petunias.

REDUCING EXTERNALITIES THROUGH ADJUDICATION

In introducing the boundary surveyor, we introduced another important social procedure for reducing externality problems: *adjudication,* by which we mean a process for deciding who has which rights. People will not be able to improve their positions through the exchange of rights if they aren't sure what rights anyone has to begin with. Adequately defined property rights are not a sufficient condition for successful negotiations, but they do seem to be a necessary condition.

Property rights that might once have been clearly and adequately defined can become vague and uncertain when surrounding circumstances change. The development of low-cost photocopying techniques, to take one example, created an enormous amount of uncertainty about what copyright holders could realistically expect to sell in view of the new capability that photocopy machines gave to every possessor of a book. When evolving circumstances make previously compatible property rights incompatible, adjudication is one way of settling the conflict.

We are using the term *adjudication* to refer specifically to the kind of resolution that the surveyor provided: a resolution that *discovers* who has which rights. The surveyor answered the question of ownership by investigating, not by choosing. If Smith and Brown had agreed to flip a coin, they would have relied on a procedure that does not discover but rather *creates* property rights. The distinction between the discovery and the creation of property rights is an important one, because *discovery or adjudication aims at maintaining the continuity of expectations.* At the end of Chapter 12 we emphasized the importance of stable expectations in securing effective cooperation among the members of a society. When expectations change radically, supply and demand decisions also change radically. That, in turn, alters in unpredicted ways the relative costs and benefits of all kinds of actions and so induces additional changes in supply and demand. In short, if no one knows what to expect, no one knows what to do or what others will do. The result is chaos. Stable expectations are another of those realities whose importance we haven't learned to recognize, because we don't notice how society is working when it's working well.

THE CASE OF THE COMPLAINING HOMEOWNER

We can use the flights of commercial airliners to bring out the importance of adjudication, or the discovery rather than creation of rights, in resolving disputes over externalities. Polly Sigh, who owns a house ten miles from a major airport but directly under the principal approach route, may decide one morning—when her sleep has been interrupted by commercial jets—that she deserves compensation. The airport or the airlines ought to pay her something, she decides, for depriving her of the opportunity to use her bedroom as a place of rest and renewal. She is the victim of an externality. So she files suit demanding compensation.

    Ought she to get it? Is she *likely* to get it? Assume that Polly bought the house before the airport was even thought about, so that no one can say she knew the situation when she bought and has already received her compensation in the form of a lower purchase price. *Should* she be compensated?

    The trouble is that there are thousands of homeowners with equally valid claims. If one receives compensation, all ought to receive compensation. But if all receive compensation, a heavy cost will be imposed on the airport and the airlines and eventually on airline passengers, either through reduced service or higher prices.

    At first glance, that might seem fair enough. Higher prices will compel airline passengers to pay the costs of the noise that is created as a by-product of their travel. But now a new problem forces itself on our attention. Externalities run throughout society. Shall we correct for them *all?* Shall homeowners receive compensation for the automobile traffic that goes past, the dandelions that their neighbors let go to seed, the passing gifts of dog-walkers and their pets, the noise of the neighborhood children, the sound of power mowers, the spreading chestnut tree next door that blocks their view, or the loss of the shade if their neighbor cuts down the spreading chestnut tree because it blocks *his* view? When we are through with homeowners, we would have to start ordering the compensation of pedestrians, many of whom suffer from the same sorts of uncompensated costs that afflict homeowners. Perhaps we could, in the final stages of our effort to make the world perfect, impose fines on especially dull people in order to compensate those whom they bore.

We just can't do that. There are too many spillovers; the appropriate compensations would be too difficult to determine. Even the direction in which compensation ought to be paid will often be unclear. Wouldn't it be just as much in order, for example, to levy fines on inattentive people to compensate the bores whose sensitivities they offend? Who says bores are worse than boors?

THE IMPORTANCE OF PRECEDENTS

We are ready for the question: *Should* Polly Sigh, the homeowner ten miles from the airport, be compensated by airline passengers for the inconvenience she suffers as a result of the flights from which they benefit? Our answer: It would be extraordinarily difficult and probably impossible to do so in a way that was both practical and fair.

We originally asked *two* questions, however. The second question asked whether homeowners in such circumstances were *likely* to receive compensation. The answer to this question is almost certainly *no.* The courts would attempt to decide the issue by *discovering* what rights the contending parties have, and homeowners would end up with very little to show on their behalf. The ruling consideration would almost surely be this: that homeowners and those in the business of providing airline transportation have proceeded for a long time on the expectation that no such compensation must be paid. *These expectations indicate the respective property rights of homeowners and airlines.*

We could even prove that homeowners ten miles from the airport don't have a legal right to be compensated for the noise, simply by showing that the market price of homes under the approach route would jump sharply if the court decision held in favor of the homeowner. This would be an *unexpected event* that would create profits for homeowners and losses for holders of airline stock. The appearance of these unexpected changes in values would be conclusive evidence that the affected parties did not believe such compensation was owed, and that the court decision had consequently *created* property rights that had not existed previously.

There's a qualification to this conclusion that further establishes the point we're making. If a judge held for the homeowner in such a case, the price of affected houses might rise very little, because prospective home buyers would probably be advised that the judge had erred and was likely to be reversed on appeal. The concept of error is instructive. There can be no error when the decision *creates* the rights. Error is possible only when the decision seeks to *discover* what the rights are that actually prevail and therefore ought to govern the outcome of the case.

Adjudication, or the attempt to resolve conflicting claims by seeking to discover existing rights, always tries to avoid unexpected decisions or outcomes. It tries to settle disagreements over property rights by supporting and reinforcing *the expectations that are most widely and confidently held.* Adjudication is thus an effort to maintain the continuity of expectations in the presence of changing circumstances. And stable expectations, we remind you once more, are the foundation of effective cooperation in any large, complex society.

THE PROBLEM OF RADICAL CHANGE

Adjudication is an evolutionary approach to the problems created by negative externalities. But sometimes changes don't occur at an evolutionary pace. When we're overtaken by events so novel that established principles and practices furnish little guidance in dealing with them, adjudication cannot work very well. Technological innovations often force rapid changes on us in a wide variety of situations. Snowmobiles, pesticides, radar-assisted whaling ships, antibiotics, and nuclear reactors are just a few of the many examples that could be cited from recent years. When technological innovation radically multiplies negative externalities, new rules may be required to resolve the problems.

The demand for new definitions of property rights has also been created by rising incomes. Not too many years ago Americans seemed to have had a working consensus that the social advantages from allowing the atmosphere to be used as an industrial dump were greater than the disadvantages. Our laws and customs decreed that the atmosphere belonged to everyone and therefore to no one, so that factory owners were free to use it unthinkingly as a receptacle for industrial wastes. People could move away from factories, or purchase residential space near the factories at a low price if they preferred that saving to the delights of clean air. Meanwhile, factories held their costs down by discharging wastes into the atmosphere, and this meant a greater availability of the goods that factories produced. But the situation has changed. The goods that factories produce are now available in much larger quantities, and many people have begun to place a lower relative valuation on them. When we begin to place a higher relative value on blue skies and clean air, we start to think of them as our *right*. We start to claim a property right in these environmental goods and demand that others stop putting them to uses that are incompatible with our ability to enjoy them. That requires new rules, not just an application of the old rules to new situations.

REDUCING EXTERNALITIES THROUGH LEGISLATION

We call the creation of new rules *legislation*. The line between adjudication and legislation is not as clear in practice as all this pretends. But the distinction is important in principle, because legislation creates changes in prevailing property rights, and changing the rules of the game always raises the question of fairness and often compels major adjustments in behavior. The challenge for a society is to legislate in ways that avoid gross injustices and that minimize the cost of achieving the objectives. We shall focus on the second of those criteria, not because it's more important, but because economic theory has more to say about minimizing costs than about maximizing justice.

As you have probably noticed by now, many of the social problems that we refer to as "pollution" can be usefully analyzed as the product of negative externalities. People don't dirty the air or water because they prefer to live with dirty air and water, but as an unintended consequence of some other activity in which they want to engage, such as using their car or producing goods for sale. They ignore the spillover costs because they don't seem to matter. Motorists driving back and forth to work do dirty their own air, but not by enough to notice, whereas taking the bus would be (in their judgment) a huge inconvenience. They overlook the fact that they are also dirtying the air of thousands of other people and that a lot of dribbles of dirt too small to make any noticeable difference add up to a huge amount of dirt, which makes a great deal of difference. Nonetheless, each contributor to the problem acts as if his or her own benefit from driving exceeds in value the tiny additional cost that this act imposes on everyone in the community. The final result can be disastrous. The solution, it would seem, is to internalize those externalities through new legislation.

The legislation of physical restrictions is a popular approach to the problem of pollution. "Command and control," it's called. After some date, no one is allowed to discharge more than so many particles of this or that into the air or the water system. This approach will almost certainly fail to minimize the cost per unit of pollution reduction. It ignores the variety of ways in which a given objective can usually be achieved and, therefore, offers few incentives to people to search for and implement the least costly alternative. We're going to use a very simplified example to illustrate some principles of pollution control that deserve to be better understood and more widely appreciated.

Suppose that everything that fouls the air over the city of Springfield comes from three sources: automobiles, utilities, and factories. The following table shows the quantities of polluting material put into the air of Springfield monthly by each source. It also shows the cost to each polluter of eliminating the objectionable emissions. (You will notice that the analysis treats each of the three sources as a *single decision making unit,* to keep the analysis simple enough to be useful.)

	Units of Obnoxious Material Emitted Monthly	Cost of Eliminating Emissions, per Unit
Automobiles	20,000	$5
Utilities	30,000	10
Factories	40,000	20

Now let's suppose that the Environmental Protection Agency (EPA) decides to improve the air quality over Springfield by securing a reduction of monthly emissions from the present total of 90,000 to a tolerable total of 60,000. (We'll pass by the question for now of how the EPA decides that 60,000 is the tolerable level.) There are many ways to reach that objective. The EPA could set 20,000 as the maximum allowable emissions from each source, or require each source to reduce its emissions by 10,000, or order a one-third reduction in emissions by each source. Let's compare the costs of each approach.

Setting a 20,000-unit ceiling on each source would achieve the goal at a total cost of $500,000. Utilities would pay $10 for each of the 10,000 units by which they reduce their emissions, factories would pay $20 for each of the 20,000 units by which they reduce their emissions, and automobiles would escape all costs, because they're already at the target level.

Requiring each source to reduce emissions by 10,000 units would achieve the goal at a total cost of $350,000. Automobiles would pay $50,000, utilities $100,000, and factories $200,000. This is clearly a less costly way to reach the goal.

Ordering a one-third reduction by all sources would result in total costs of $400,000: $33,333 to the automobiles, $100,000 to the utilities, and $266,667 to the factories. From the standpoint of cost minimization, that's better than the first solution but not as good as the second.

There's an even less costly way to go, however. The EPA would minimize the cost of achieving its objective if it ordered a 20,000-unit reduction by automobiles and a 10,000-unit reduction by utilities and left the factories alone. The total cost of getting pollution down from 90,000 to 60,000 units by this method would be $200,000: $100,000 paid by the automobiles and $100,000 paid by the utilities. Would the EPA be likely to choose this approach?

ANOTHER APPROACH: TAXING EMISSIONS

Let's defer that question and examine the problem further. Suppose that the EPA doesn't actually know how much it will cost per unit to reduce pollution from each source. That's much more plausible than our original assumption, for several reasons. The polluters themselves will be in the best position to know the actual costs, but they will also have an incentive to exaggerate their costs in pleadings before the EPA or the public. Moreover, exaggeration will not be wholly dishonest, because one never knows for certain the costs of something that hasn't yet been tried, and it's just ordinary prudence to estimate them high, especially if higher estimates mean the costs are less likely to be imposed. Finally, though costs can usually be reduced through research and experiment, no one can predict the results that research and experiment will produce. What is the least costly solution when the EPA is faced with this kind of information scarcity?

The EPA would gain the applause of many economists if it responded to this situation by imposing a tax per unit of emissions and then allowing each party to respond as it thought best. If you're willing to grant that pollution is a spillover cost, a cost not borne by its producer, placing a tax on polluting activities makes good sense. If the tax per unit of pollutant can somehow be set equal to the spillover cost per unit, the creator and presumed beneficiary of the costs is made to bear them.

If that makes the polluting activity too costly to continue, it will cease, as it should if its costs are greater than its benefits. If the benefits still outweigh the costs when the tax is being paid, then the polluting activity will continue, though at a lesser rate because it's now more costly. But in that case the tax revenue will be available to compensate—to buy the consent of—those on whom the spillover costs are falling.

In the Springfield case, any tax rate between $5 and $10 will reduce pollution by 20,000 units per month. It will induce the automobiles to avoid the tax by choosing the lesser-cost alternative of eliminating their obnoxious emissions. Utilities will choose to avoid the tax when it rises above $10 per unit emitted, so that a tax rate of $11 would reduce emissions by 50,000 units per month, while simultaneously garnering $440,000 in revenue with which to compensate the suffering citizens of Springfield for the obnoxious material the factories are continuing to spew into the air.

As we have set up the problem, there is no tax rate that achieves a reduction to exactly 60,000 units: $9.99 would lower pollution to only 70,000 units, and $10.01 would lower it all the way to 40,000 units. In the real world, costs would not be the same for all levels of emission reduction but would be relatively low for small percentage reductions from each source and extremely high as we approached 100 percent. The pursuit of perfection is almost always prohibitively expensive.

But the inability of *any* tax rate to achieve some particular physical target is not so much a criticism of the tax approach to pollution control as a criticism of physical targets. Why aim at 60,000 units? *Every* unit is a "bad," so why not eliminate them all? The answer, as you know by this time, is that there are costs of eliminating those costs that we call pollution. The task for the EPA is to compare the marginal costs of reducing the emissions with the marginal benefits. The use of taxes enables the EPA to acquire information about these costs and benefits by observing what happens when variously estimated pollution costs are assessed against the polluters. It's an approach that lends itself to learning by experimentation. And obtaining reliable information about costs and benefits is essential to any program of environmental protection that is concerned with human well-being.

LICENSES TO POLLUTE?

Let's go back now to a question that we asked but deferred answering. After comparing the costs of four different ways of reducing Springfield air pollution to 60,000 units per month, we asked whether the EPA was likely in such a situation to choose the least costly approach. We put off answering in order to argue that physical directives of any sort—the command-and-control method—were generally inferior to taxes as a way of controlling pollution. By taxing emissions, we enlist the aid of the price system in solving our problem. But the tax approach isn't popular with the public for a reason that would also make it difficult for the EPA to issue the least costly set of physical directives. Taxes on pollution have acquired the derogatory label of "licenses to pollute," which sounds a lot like official permission to commit crimes.

This begs an important question, however. While we may want to regard some polluting acts as so inherently undesirable that they ought to be prohibited altogether, we clearly do not want to take this attitude toward most of what we now call pollution. The polluting activities in which people engage are commonly activities that generate benefits, sometimes very large benefits, for other people as well as for themselves. To condone these activities is to condone pollution, whether we want to admit it or not.

The very word *pollution* probably misleads us here. Historically the term has had a strong moral connotation, as any good dictionary will point out. In classical literature, a polluting act corrupted the whole community. A "license to pollute" in such a context is like a license to commit immoral or criminal acts. But surely no one wants to say that homeowners who turn on their furnaces and thereby put "pollutants" in the air are behaving in an immoral or criminal manner. Most pollution should be viewed as a cost, not a crime, and should therefore be "licensed" if the cost is less than the properly calculated value of the benefits associated with it.

EFFICIENCY AND FAIRNESS

Some people also object to taxes on pollutants because they regard such taxes as fundamentally unfair. They supposedly place the whole burden of reducing pollution on the poor while allowing the rich to go right on fouling the environment. Choosing the people who must reduce their pollution on the basis of the cost to them of doing so, which is required by the least-cost solution, also seems arbitrary and unjust to many people.

An important part of any reply to those who raise the fairness issue, however, is to show that the *efficient* solution can be achieved while settling the *fairness* issue in different ways. In other words, we don't necessarily commit ourselves to place the costs on any particular parties when we select the most efficient solution. The Springfield case can again provide our illustration.

Suppose that the EPA wants to impose the entire cost of pollution reduction on the factories, whether because the factories can best afford it, because they have long been the heaviest polluters, or because they were the last group to show up in the area. Whatever the reason, all the EPA need do is tell the factories that they will have to pay a tax of $10.05 for each unit of pollution emitted monthly in excess of 60,000, regardless of the pollution's source. The factories will then look for the least costly way to deal with this situation. If they have all the information that we have, they will offer the automobiles $100,000 to eliminate all their pollution and offer the utilities $100,000 to reduce their pollution by 10,000 units.

The factories will thus reduce the level of pollution in Springfield to 60,000 units. They'll do so to avoid a tax of $301,500. But rather than reduce their own emissions by 30,000 units, which would cost the factories $600,000, they'll pay the most efficient pollution reducers in the city $200,000 to do the job for them.

Pollution reduction is a lot like any other useful activity in that some are more efficient at it than others. Just as we gain from having our food, toys, and cosmetics produced by those with a comparative advantage in their production, so we gain by having additional clean air produced by those with the greatest comparative advantage at the job. But comparative advantages are exploited through exchange. That's why the tax approach to pollution reduction is in general superior to an approach that assigns physical restrictions to particular firms. The tax approach tries to alter relative money costs to reflect new decisions about who has which rights. But it then leaves all parties free to trade on the basis of their own comparative advantages and to secure the new social goals in the most efficient manner.

THE BUBBLE CONCEPT

In 1979, the Environmental Protection Agency took a large step in the direction suggested by this analysis when it issued new regulations to permit and encourage trade-offs among air-pollution sources. Rather than set rigid limits on allowable emissions from each smokestack, enforcement agencies would permit factories to exceed the limits at one point if they could make it up at another point. They could pretend that there was a giant bubble over the entire factory (hence the name for this approach—the bubble concept) and control total emissions into the bubble. Under this policy, firms could lower the cost of achieving a target level of air quality by allowing emissions to rise wherever their control was especially costly and making it up where emissions could be reduced at lower cost.

This approach was challenged in court by environmental groups, who claimed that it allowed additional pollution to occur in areas where air quality was already not in compliance with EPA standards. A firm should not be allowed to belch obnoxious substances from smokestack A just because it had reduced the emissions from smokestack B. If the emissions from B could be reduced at low cost, the environmentalists argued, then they should be reduced. But the emissions from A should not be allowed to increase. The environmentalist argument implicitly assumes that there is only one good: clean air.

The Supreme Court rejected this argument in 1984, thereby opening the way for existing plants and factories to expand in areas with air quality problems (without worsening the air quality) and encouraging the EPA to go one step further. If firms and plants were to be allowed to make internal trade-offs in the interest of efficiency, or achieving given goals at the lowest possible cost, why couldn't such trade-offs also be allowed *between* firms? If an electrical utility wanted to build a new generating plant to satisfy its customers' demands, it might be able to do so without worsening air quality by persuading some other firm to reduce its emissions by the amount that the utility was going to expand emissions. In effect, firms would be allowed to buy and sell "rights to pollute."

That did not sit at all well with more ardent environmentalists, who argued that no one owned a "right to pollute" and therefore no one else could buy it. The premise is questionable, however. Firms do in fact have rights to discharge obnoxious substances into the air, as proved by the fact that they do it openly and are not fined. They have both actual and

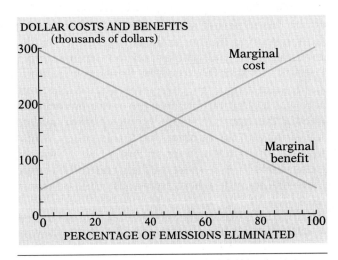

FIGURE 13A   Marginal-cost and marginal-benefit curves for emissions control

Suppose we are able to measure the benefits of a program to improve air quality by the amount of money that people in the affected area would be willing to pay for the improvements. Costs of the program are measured by the dollar value of the opportunities forgone in implementing the program. Under ordinary circumstances, we would expect the marginal benefits to decline and the marginal costs to rise as controls on emissions are tightened. That's because we typically place a lower value on any good, including even clean air, when we have more of it, and because the lower-cost procedures for accomplishing any objective are typically used first.

Figure 13A portrays such a situation. The total benefits and total costs of the program are the sums of the marginal benefits and costs, or the areas lying underneath the marginal curves. The difference between total benefits and total costs is maximized when emissions are reduced by 50 percent.

If the EPA or some other authority ordered a 60 or even an 80 percent reduction in emissions, the total benefits would exceed the total costs; but the net benefits would be less than with a mere 50 percent reduction. Ordering a 100 percent elimination of emissions would (in this case) reduce net benefits to zero.

legal "rights to pollute." By accepting and clarifying those rights, the EPA allowed a market in such rights to evolve, which meant in turn that firms could purchase their pollution control programs from other firms that had a comparative advantage in pollution control. If the EPA allows the purchasing firm to use only some percentage of the rights purchased—to use 100, for example, they have to purchase 130—it can enlist the expanded bubble concept in the service of progressively cleaner air. Note, too, that those who want the air to be even cleaner than the EPA requires may be able, under this system, to buy up "pollution rights" and retire them.

The system won't work, however, unless the rights are clearly defined and can be counted on. No individual or group will be willing to buy up rights in order to retire them if the regulatory authorities can respond by creating new rights to replace the ones retired. Nor will firms be willing to pay money to purchase rights if they believe they can get the same rights from the regulatory authorities with just a little lobbying. And firms are much more likely to invest resources in discovering and devising ways to reduce their emissions below what they are legally entitled to emit if they know that they can sell the results to someone else.

Cleaning up the air is an especially difficult environmental challenge. The sources of air pollution are numerous and hard to monitor. And the costs of cleaning up the air, in benefits forgone, will often be much higher than we are inclined to suppose when we're thinking exclusively about factories (where other people work) and conveniently forgetting about our own chimneys, automobile exhaust pipes, backyard barbecues, and household sprays. The enormous benefits from cleaner air coupled with the high costs of attaining it ought to make us appreciate any system that can give us more of what we want at a lower cost.

RIGHTS AND THE *SOCIAL* PROBLEM OF POLLUTION

We don't want to conclude this chapter with an endorsement of efficiency, because inefficiency is not the fundamental problem. Pollution is a major social and political concern at this time because people disagree about rights. More people are beginning to say: "You are obtaining your benefits by imposing this cost on me (or us), but you have no *moral* right to do that and so should have no *legal* right."

Disagreements of this sort can be extremely difficult to resolve. The economic way of thinking suggests a few principles that might be of considerable help as we embark on the task.

The first is that the demand is never completely inelastic for any good, not even for the good of clean air. We must decide how much we want, preferably with a clear-eyed recognition that more can only be obtained by giving up ever larger amounts of other goods that we also want.

The second is that we should leave people as much freedom as we can to choose their own ways of adapting. If our goal is to reduce the burning of fossil fuels, for example, we want to let people choose the means that reduces the cost to themselves. We should avoid "command and control," which typically raises the cost of achieving any objective and, by raising the cost, also increases resistance to the objective itself. Using the price system lowers costs. Letting people exchange also lowers costs.

Finally, we should keep in mind the importance of stable property rights. When people know what the rules are and can count on them not to be changed arbitrarily, transaction costs go down and effective cooperation increases.

ONCE OVER LIGHTLY

The actions that people take often impose costs on others that the actors do not take into account. Economists call these spillover costs or negative externalities.

Negative externalities multiply rapidly in urban, industrialized societies. Even where the spillover costs of particular actions are greater than the benefits to the actors, transaction costs will frequently prevent people from negotiating more satisfactory arrangements.

Negotiation is the standard procedure used by members of a society to secure the cooperation and consent of others without imposing unwelcome costs on one another. Clearly defined property rights make negotiations easier by lowering transaction costs.

Conflicting claims of right can often be resolved by examining established principles and practices. Adjudication in this manner preserves the continuity of people's expectations. Unexpected changes in property rights make social cooperation more difficult by making it harder for anyone to plan with confidence.

Rapid or radical social change may make it so difficult to resolve conflicting claims of right through adjudication that legislation is called for. Legislation entails the creation of new rules to establish and define what people may do with the resources at their command.

New rules will produce lower-cost resolutions of such negative externality problems as "pollution" if the rules make it easier for people to exchange rights and obligations. Taxes on undesired spillover costs and systems for trading "pollution rights" provide appropriate incentives to polluters and facilitate low-cost arrangements to reduce "pollution." So-called "command and control" approaches, by contrast, pay far less attention than do market-oriented systems to the information and incentive problems that challenge any policy aimed at reducing "pollution."

QUESTIONS FOR DISCUSSION

1. Officials in River Edge, New Jersey, passed an ordinance in 1982 making it illegal for residents to park vehicles with commercial license plates or with signs on the doors in their driveways overnight.

    (a) Were the parkers generating negative externalities?
    (b) Why did those who disliked seeing such vehicles in their neighborhood choose to push for a new ordinance rather than talk directly to the owners of the vehicles?
    (c) The ordinance made some people better off and some worse off. How can we know whether the benefits of the ordinance exceeded its costs?

2. Which of the following actions generate negative externalities *that also create social problems?*

    (a) Tossing peanut shells on the sidewalk.
    (b) Tossing peanut shells on the floor at a major league baseball game.
    (c) Dropping a candy wrapper on the sidewalk.
    (d) Dropping confetti from an office building during a downtown parade.
    (e) Setting off loud firecrackers on Independence Day.
    (f) Producing a fireworks display on Independence Day.

3. Why do people sometimes disturb others by talking during movies? Do the talkers and those whom they disturb agree about the rights one acquires when purchasing a movie ticket? How could the owners of movie theaters resolve this conflict? Why don't they do so?

4. What are the property-rights claims that are in conflict in each of the cases described below? How would you prefer that they be resolved (assuming that you are an impartial observer)?

    (a) Owners of motorcycles want to remove their mufflers to obtain more efficient engine performance, but the law limits the noise that any motorcycle may emit.

(b) A group wants to prohibit billboards along rural highways, but farmers claim they have a right to erect any kind of sign they want on their own property.

(c) A Missouri state legislator introduced a bill in 1984 making it a crime to blow your nose in a loud or offensive manner in a restaurant.

(d) A Connecticut state legislator proposed a bill in 1985 that would ban the throwing of rice at weddings on the grounds that uncooked rice is unhealthful for birds.

(e) Restaurant owners want to exclude people whose dress doesn't satisfy certain standards. (Should this be legal?)

(f) People who never bathe want to use city buses. People who never brush or comb their hair want to sit and stroll in public parks. (Should the unwashed be barred from the buses? The unkempt, from the parks?)

5. "I'd pay almost anything if I could get all my classes scheduled before 11:30 so that I can take this great job I've got lined up for the afternoons." Why will it be difficult for the speaker to get what he wants despite his willingness to pay a high price for it?

6. A large mulberry tree in your neighbor's yard provides you with welcome shade but gives her only a lot of inedible and messy mulberries. She wants to cut the tree down.

(a) Does she have the legal right to do so?

(b) You say to her: "I know you hate those messy mulberries, but not nearly as much as I would hate losing the shade." Can you prove your statement? If you can't prove that you value continued shade more than she values a clean yard, can you induce *her* to place a higher value on *her* benefits from leaving the tree than on *her* benefits from cutting it down? (Hint: How do you induce the sewer cleaner to decide he would rather clear your sewer line on a Sunday afternoon than watch his favorite football team?)

(c) An alternative route for you is to challenge her legal right to cut down the tree. You might try to have the tree declared a historic landmark, or go to court to demand that she file an environmental impact statement before being allowed to remove the tree. What is the danger to you in this tactic? (Hint: If you think you may be prevented in the future from exercising a right you now possess, will you wait to see what becomes of your right or will you exercise it while you still clearly have it?)

7. Two children are quarreling about who gets to choose the program that will be watched on the family's single television set. This is a case of conflicting property rights.

(a) Should the parents tell them to work it out for themselves? Under what circumstances is this likely to produce a satisfactory resolution of the conflict?

(b) How do poorly defined property rights make it more difficult in such a case to achieve a satisfactory resolution through negotiation?

(c) Show how the parents might contribute to a resolution of the conflict first by offering adjudication, then by providing legislation.

8. The sign on the beach says, "$25 fine for littering." A beach user nonetheless tosses his used soda bottles on the sand rather than walk to the distant trash barrel. He knows that the beach patrol has seen him and will issue a citation; but he is very wealthy and so places a very low marginal value on money and a very high marginal value on time. Would you call him a litterer if he is willing to pay the fine? Or has he purchased the right to use the sand as a waste receptacle?

9. Surveys by the Michigan Highway Department showed that beverage-container litter decreased 82 percent and total litter decreased 32 percent when the state adopted a mandatory-deposit law for beer and soft-drink containers. According to one estimate of the effect of the law on prices, Michigan consumers were paying an extra $300 million per year for beer and soft drinks as a result of the law.

(a) If these figures are correct, is this mandatory-deposit law "cost effective" in your judgment? How could you decide?

(b) Suppose we knew that Michigan citizens actually value the reduction in litter at more than $300 million per year. Would this demonstrate the cost effectiveness of the mandatory-deposit law?

(c) How many people could be hired full time to walk around picking up litter for $300 million per year! Assume that litter-lifters receive $5 an hour, which works out to $10,000 a year for 50 weeks of 40 hours each. Do you think such an army of full-time litter-lifters could reduce total litter by considerably more than 32 percent?

10. Bombast City allows motor vehicles to be operated without mufflers if they carry a current noise license, which costs $20 per month. In Tranquil Heights it is illegal to operate a motor vehicle without a muffler, and the fine for violation is $100. Motorists who choose to violate the ordinance are caught and fined about once every 5 months. In other words, Bombast City permits noisy vehicles upon payment of a fee and Tranquil Heights prohibits them and fines violators. The fee and the fine are monetarily equivalent when we multiply the fine by the probability of .2 that it will have to be paid in any month.

(a) Given this monetary equivalence, what is the difference between the approaches of Bombast City and Tranquil Heights to the problem of mufflers and noisy motor vehicles?

(b) It's clear that people who drive without mufflers in Bombast City are licensed to make noise. Do the people who drive without mufflers in Tranquil Heights acquire a license when they pay their fines? Would the legislators of Tranquil Heights agree that payment of the fine authorizes one to drive without a muffler?

(c) One difference between "you may make noise if you pay" and "you may not make noise and you'll pay if you do" is that in the latter case but not the former the party who makes noise does something that the society condemns as *wrong*. Does this fact exercise its own effect on behavior? How do societies usually respond when individuals *persist* in behavior that has been legally condemned as wrong? Does the penalty remain constant, as it does in the case of a fee for permitted behavior?

(d) Does this distinction aid us in understanding what lies behind some of the objections to pollution fees? When people protest that fees based on emissions into the air or water constitute a "license to pollute," are they perhaps objecting to the law's *authorization* of the emissions? Do they want the emitters to bear moral blame as well as higher monetary costs? Why might people who are intensely interested in cleaner air or water want the issue to be a moral one?

(e) When would it be desirable to treat discharges into the air or the water as costs imposed on others that will be allowed upon payment of a fee, and when would it be better to treat them as crimes punishable by fines?

11. History books often lament the destruction of the great herds of bison that roamed the western prairies prior to the arrival of white men.

(a) Why were so many white men willing to shoot these animals and leave their meat and hide to rot? Wasn't this highly wasteful? Why did so many people apparently place such a high value on a moment of sport as to kill these animals for no other reason than the excitement of it?

(b) Who bore the costs when a hunter shot a bison or "buffalo" from the window of a passing train?

(c) Was the near extinction of the buffalo an irreversible act? Or could we bring those huge herds of buffalo back within a few years if the proper incentives existed?

(d) What is the animal that has replaced the buffalo on the western prairies? Why do the numerous vast herds of cattle that cover the country not suffer the fate of the buffalo? What do you think would happen to the relative size of cattle and buffalo herds if Americans lost their taste for beef and acquired an intense love of buffalo meat?

12. What difference does ownership make?

(a) What response would you predict from the Sierra Club if an oil company requested a permit to extract natural gas from a wilderness area owned by the federal government?

(b) What difference do you think it would make to the Sierra Club's decision if the oil company were willing to pay an enormous royalty to the federal government because there was a great deal of natural gas available in that wilderness area?

(c) What difference do you think it would make if the oil company promised to extract the natural gas in ways that had a very small impact on the environment?

(d) What difference do you think it would make if the wilderness area, instead of belonging to the federal government, were the property of the Sierra Club?

(e) Why do you suppose the Audubon Society allows three oil companies to extract natural gas from its 26,800-acre Rainey Wildlife Sanctuary in Louisiana?

(f) The oil companies in the Rainey Sanctuary pay almost a million dollars per year in royalties to the Audubon Society. Do you think this arrangement promotes the purposes of the Audubon Society? Do you think it promotes the well-being of natural-gas consumers? (The instructive story of the Rainey Sanctuary was told by economists John Baden and Richard Stroup in the July 1981 issue of *Reason* magazine.)

(g) Is it rational for the Audubon Society to allow extraction of natural gas from its own land while opposing it elsewhere?

13. Do we need laws to prevent cropland erosion? Does cropland erosion create negative externalities?

(a) How will farming practices that cause soil erosion affect the present value of farmland?

(b) How will an owner of farmland who wants to maximize the present value of the land decide whether or not to adopt particular soil conservation measures?

(c) Why will a tenant farmer ordinarily adopt fewer and less-effective soil conservation techniques?

(d) Why would landowners ever permit farm tenants to reduce the present value of the land through practices that raise current yields but increase the vulnerability of the land to erosion?

(e) What are some of the consequences of soil erosion that impose costs on people other than landowners? Will even an owner–operator take these costs fully into account in making decisions about whether and how to plow and plant land that is particularly subject to wind or water erosion?

(f) Suppose that people who are farming their own land have trouble earning enough income to pay their mortgages and begin to fear that they will lose ownership of the land to lending institutions. How will this fear affect their decisions about the trade-off between increased yields and reduced soil erosion?

(g) A Montana farmer buys hundreds of thousands of acres of grazing land from longtime ranch operators, then plows up the land and plants wheat. Why did the ranchers sell? Why did the purchasing farmer convert the land from livestock to wheat production? If the farmer knew he would be required to compensate residents of the country for the dust storms that will result when the land is shifted from livestock to wheat, might he find raising livestock more profitable than growing wheat?

(h) Should farmers whose practices aggravate the problem of dust storms be required to compensate others for the additional dust they put into the air? How could such a compensation system be administered?

14. Here is a multiple-choice question for you to think about.

The buildings and grounds at Ivy College are far more littered than the buildings and grounds at the Ivyville Shopping Mall because: (1) students are slobs by nature; (2) more people use the Ivy College campus than use the shopping mall; (3) customers at the shopping mall have less opportunity to litter because they don't smoke or purchase take-out food; (4) customers at the mall have less incentive to litter because they are proud to be "Ivyville Mallers" and so take good care of their "campus"; (5) there are people at the mall but not on the Ivy College campus who expect to receive substantial financial benefits from keeping the buildings and grounds litter-free.

15. When you bought your house, only 5 commercial planes passed over it daily, on the average. That number has grown slowly and almost imperceptibly over the intervening years and now numbers 150. Is the change from 5 to 150 a drastic or radical change? Is your situation with 150 planes flying over your house each day more tolerable because the number increased slowly and imperceptibly? Would you be more likely to receive compensation of some sort if the changes had occurred over a very short period of time? Does the fact that we can't tell which straw broke the camel's back mean that the addition of more straw to the camel's burden was not the cause of its broken back?

16. Many large urban airports have established programs for buying out those homeowners most seriously affected by airport noise.

(a) Do people who own houses directly under an approach route and within 5000 feet of the runway deserve compensation for the noise made by planes landing or taking off? If you think they do, ask yourself where you will draw the line. What about people whose homes are 15,000 feet from the beginning of the runway or who live very close to but not quite under the approach route?

(b) If the owner is renting the house out, should it be the owner or the tenants who receive compensation? Why?

(c) Are current owners the appropriate people to compensate? Wasn't a current owner compensated in the purchase price if the house was bought within the past few years?

(d) What difference does it make in your answer to the previous question whether it was generally believed when the house changed hands that the airport would buy out those homeowners most severely affected by the noise?

17. If airlines are required to pay landing fees that are adjusted to take account of the level of particular aircraft's noise emissions, the time of day or night when they land, and the density of the residential population in the vicinity of the airport, how will airlines take steps to reduce the impact of their operations on homeowners who live near airports?

   (a) A government agency in 1977 calculated for each of 23 airports the decline in the annual rental value of surrounding property due to noise and divided this total by the number of takeoffs and landings during the year. The highest average was $196.67 for New York's La Guardia; the lowest was the Portland, Oregon, airport, with a cost of $0.82 per takeoff or landing. This means that each takeoff or landing imposed a combined cost of almost $200 on La Guardia's neighbors, but less than a $1 cost on all those living around the Portland airport. Will airlines find it in their interest to use some airports more than they now do and others less if their landing and takeoff fees are increased by these amounts?

   (b) Will airlines be more likely to install retrofitted noise-control gear or buy new and quieter planes if they must pay higher fees for noisier aircraft? Respond to the argument that "no airline is going to scrap an expensive 707 just to save a few $400 airport surcharges." Is this critic of surcharges thinking marginally?

   (c) How would such a system of surcharges induce airlines to fly their noisier planes to Portland and their quieter ones to New York City, or to use Dulles Airport rather than National when flying into Washington, DC? (Dulles, which is far out in the Virginia countryside, showed a cost of $5.64 per operation in the 1977 study.)

18. Each additional vehicle that enters the freeway during the morning rush hour slows all the other automobiles using the freeway. What are the costs considered by each motorist as he or she decides whether or not to use the freeway? What are the costs created for others by this decision? Why is it true—not a joke—that "cars multiply to congest the expressways constructed to eliminate congestion"?

19. What would be the consequences of making the freeway into a tollway? Why might you, as a regular user of the expressway, prefer a toll during the rush hour to not paying any toll? When is it better for a limited-access highway to be a freeway, and when is it better for it to be a tollway?

20. There are two passenger ferries that can be used to cross the river: a tug (large but slow) and a speedboat (small but fast). Every hour, 15 people want to cross the river. Since there is no charge for using either ferry, passengers choose to minimize the time spent in crossing. The tug can carry 1 passenger or 15 passengers across in 21 minutes. The

crossing time for the speedboat depends upon the number of passengers:

Number of Passengers	Travel Time in Minutes
1	10
2	12
3	14
4	16
5	18
6	20
7	22

(a) How will the 15 passengers distribute themselves each hour between the two ferries?

(b) What kind of fee system would minimize *total travel time?*

(c) What are the negative externalities present in this problem?

(d) Who would gain and who would lose if fees were charged for crossing in the speedboat?

21. Some EPA officials began wondering aloud in 1989 whether it was really worthwhile to control ozone as stringently as the Clean Air Act requires. The ozone standard was set at a level that would prevent any adverse health effects on people who exercise in an area with high ozone concentrations.

(a) Is there any scientific way to decide whether the benefits from a stringent ozone standard are greater than its costs?

(b) According to a *New York Times* article of April 3, 1989, 51 percent of the annual emissions of volatile organic compounds that produce ozone at ground level come from the operation of motor vehicles. So we could protect our health either by prohibiting so much driving or by exercising less in those urban areas where, on a few days in the year, ozone levels exceed the standard. Which is the more efficient way to protect our health?

(c) Industrial solvents create 4 percent of the emissions and household solvents create 5 percent of them. If we pass legislation to reduce the use of solvents, is the legislation more likely to restrict industrial or household use? Would a restriction on industrial use show that people are more important than profits?

22. In 1987 a Tacoma, Washington, electrical utility purchased from a manufacturing firm, for $265,000, the right to add 60 tons of "particulate matter" to the air each year. The manufacturer had reduced its annual emissions by 69 tons a few years earlier through modernizing its plant.

The representative of an environmental organization objected that the practice of selling rights to pollute simply meant that "as soon as one air polluter drops out of the ring, there will be a ready substitute."

(a) What benefits of the system does this criticism ignore?
(b) The utility used the credits to renovate and operate a generating plant that would burn garbage as well as other fuels, thus reducing solid waste disposal problems. Is it better for the environment to bury or to incinerate garbage?

23. Suppose that government environmental agencies decide exactly how much of each kind of industrial pollutant they will allow within a given airshed and sell the rights to discharge these quantities of pollutants to the highest bidder.

(a) Which firms would offer the highest bids?
(b) How could citizens interested in cleaner air than the environmental agency had ordered use this system to obtain what they want?

24. "Taxes can't control pollution. They'll just drive the little firms out of business while the big firms, who can afford to pay, go right on polluting." Do you agree?

25. Assume that the graph in Figure 13B shows how much it costs per year per car to reduce undesirable automobile emissions by various percentages through mandatory exhaust-control devices.

(a) Why does the curve rise slowly at first and increase more rapidly as emission levels decline? Is this a peculiar characteristic of auto-

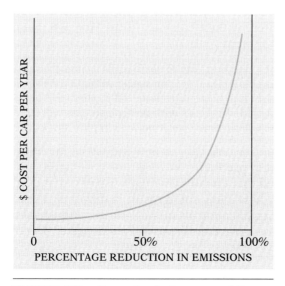

FIGURE 13B   Costs of reducing automobile emissions

mobile exhaust-control systems, or is it a more general relationship?

(b) Does this curve tell us how much emissions ought to be reduced? Does it provide any guidance at all to those who make public policy in this area?

(c) If you think of this curve as the marginal cost of supplying cleaner air, what kind of data would you want in order to construct the demand for cleaner air? What would be the significance of the intersection between these two curves?

(d) Suppose you want to find out how much people in your area value cleaner air. So you commission a survey in which people are asked how much they *would be willing to pay* in order to obtain various levels of reduction in the amount of noxious automobile emissions in their community. Can you generally count on them to tell the truth? Remember that they know they won't be held to their valuation—that is, they won't actually be required to pay what they say they would be willing to pay. What are the major sources of bias in such a survey procedure?

(e) Suppose that your survey is done for the government and that the people whom you ask know they will actually be required to pay an annual tax equal to the amount they say they are willing to pay for whatever level of reductions is finally decided on and enforced. What sort of bias will this introduce into your measurement of the community demand for cleaner air?

(f) "No cost is too great to pay to reduce the smog level." Do you think that people who make such statements expect to be among those who actually pay the costs of reducing the smog level?

26. Here is a paragraph from a letter to *The Wall Street Journal* (September 20, 1982) written by the Chairman of the House Subcommittee on Health and the Environment:

> The cheapest and best way to clean air is to make sure that new industrial facilities are built clean. It is far easier to build a new coke oven or blast furnace clean than to try to retrofit an old facility with pollution controls. Just as replacing old, dirty cars with new, clean cars will lessen automotive pollution, so too will turning over America's capital stock clean the air.

A law that requires new cars or new industrial facilities to be "clean" raises the cost of producing new cars or new facilities and hence their price. How will that encourage longer use of old and "dirty" cars and facilities? Show how a law could result in *dirtier* air by setting excessively stringent and costly controls on new cars or industrial facilities.

27. Where is the best place to dispose of solid waste? The most common answer is NIMBY—Not In My Back Yard.

(a) How does a city discriminate unfairly against some people whenever it chooses a new waste disposal site?

    (b) What makes people willing to let others dispose of solid waste in their "back yard"?

    (c) What would happen if a city "awarded" its new waste disposal site to the community that was most willing to accept it? How might such willingness be obtained and measured?

28. A *Wall Street Journal* article (September 16, 1981) on business attitudes toward regulatory standards under the Reagan administration reported that many corporate executives say that they have adjusted quite well to existing regulations and see no big need for a rollback.

    (a) Why might a company that has been compelled by law to reduce its emission of air pollutants *not* want to see the law relaxed?

    (b) Why is it important that regulations governing air pollution by industry not be changed frequently?

29. Here is a quotation from *A Treatise of Human Nature* by David Hume. The words were written around 1740.

> Our property is nothing but those goods, whose constant possession is established by the laws of society; that is, by the laws of justice. . . .
>
> No one can doubt, that the convention for the distinction of property, and for the stability of possession, is of all circumstances the most necessary to the establishment of human society, and that after the agreement for the fixing and observing of this rule, there remains little or nothing to be done towards settling a perfect harmony and concord.

Has Hume exaggerated the importance of clearly defined and stable property rights?

MARKETS AND GOVERNMENT

What should we leave to the market and what are appropriate tasks for government? It's difficult to answer that question unless we know what we mean by *the market* and by *government*. To choose intelligently, we must know what the options are, and the choice between market and government is by no means as clear as our public-policy debates often make it seem.

PRIVATE VERSUS PUBLIC?

Most of the standard contrasts between the market system and government don't hold up very well under close examination. To begin with, the market is usually characterized as the *private* sector, with government agencies and officials occupying the *public* sector. But what can this possibly mean? It surely doesn't mean that consumers and the managers of business firms pursue private interests, whereas everyone who works for government pursues the public interest. The senator who claims that "the public interest" guides all his decisions is in fact guided by a personal interpretation of the public interest, filtered through all sorts of private interests: reelection, influence with colleagues, relations with the press, popular image, and place in the history books. Senators *may* be less interested than business executives in maximizing their private monetary income, but they're probably more interested on average in acquiring prestige and power.

The same kind of analysis applies to any employee of a

government agency, whether it's a high appointed official on a regulatory commission or someone just starting a job at the lowest civil-service rank. However lofty, noble, or impartial the stated objectives of a government agency, its day-to-day activities will be the consequence of decisions made by ordinary mortals, subject to the pull and push of incentives remarkably similar to those that operate in the private sector. Moreover, in recent years a special devotion to "the public interest" has been claimed for themselves by many executives in leading business corporations, eager to persuade us that the ultimate touchstone for their policies is not the maximization of net revenue but the fulfillment of their social responsibilities. We would be well advised to discount *all* the rhetoric about public versus private interests and to look for the incentives that actually shape the decisions that people make.

COMPETITION AND INDIVIDUALISM

Some other common contrasts between the market and the government also grow more indistinct the longer we look at them. The market sector is often called the *competitive* sector. But there is competition in government, too, as every election year demonstrates. Within any government agency, competition for promotion exists among employees. Competition also occurs between government agencies vying for a larger share of appropriations. The two major political parties are continually competing. The executive branch competes with the legislative, members of Congress compete for committee assignments, even district judges compete with one another in the hope of an eventual appointment to a higher court. Do Supreme Court justices, holding appointments for life at the pinnacle of their profession, compete for reputation among editorial writers and law-school professors?

Sometimes we're told that *individualism* is the distinguishing characteristic of the market sector. But what constitutes "individualism"? Many of those who enter the market sector go to work for large corporations right after leaving school and continue as employees until retirement. Is there any significant difference between working in Baltimore as an employee of the Social Security Administration and working in Hartford as an employee of an insurance company? When Britain experimented after World War II with nationalizing, denationalizing, and renationalizing its steel industry, most of the employees (and lots of other people, too) had trouble discerning any difference. Some of the characters who frequent the halls of Congress seem far more individualistic (or at least more idiosyncratic) than the people who pass through the corridors of business.

ECONOMIC THEORY AND GOVERNMENT ACTION

Economic theory attempts to explain the workings of society on the assumption that all participants want to advance their own interests and try to do so in a rational way. The marginal-cost/marginal-revenue rule that we introduced explicitly in Chapter 9, but have in fact been using throughout the book, is merely a formal expression of these assumptions: the way to advance one's interests is to expand each activity whose marginal revenue exceeds its marginal cost and to contract any activity whose marginal cost is greater than its marginal revenue. The economist does not assume, as we've pointed out before, that money or material goods are the only costs and revenues (or benefits) that consumers and producers care about, or that the interests people pursue are narrow and selfish ones. Economic theory can throw light on the social consequences of every kind of human interest.[1] Why shouldn't that apply to the human purposes and the social processes that control the course of government activities?

Our answer is that it *does* apply. The principles of social interaction that guide production of *Time* or *Newsweek* are not as different from those that guide production of the *Federal Reserve Bulletin* as people commonly suppose. Governments as well as privately owned firms produce commodities and services. Governments, too, can do that only by obtaining productive resources whose opportunity cost is the value of what they would have produced in their next most valuable employment. Governments as well as privately owned firms therefore must bid for the resources they want and offer the owners of those resources adequate incentives. You'll want to note (we'll come back to it) that the government can use negative as well as positive incentives: The threat of imprisonment, for example, may be a major incentive as some people decide what portion of their income to offer the Internal Revenue Service each spring. United Way can't use that inducement. Governments even face the problem of marketing their

---

[1]An interest in chaos might be the one exception. In a society where people did not value rationality, but celebrated instead the rule of caprice, accident, and purposeless action, economic theory would have almost no predictive power. Its predictive power is correspondingly greatest in those areas of social life most marked by foresight and premeditated action.

output and of price searching, though monetary prices play a much smaller role in the distribution of government products. But there can be no doubt that demand curves exist for government-provided goods and that, since these goods are characteristically scarce, they must be rationed by means of some discriminatory criteria. And the people with a demand for government goods will consequently compete to satisfy those criteria, to pay the established price. The main advantage of looking at government in this way is that it counters the tendency to think of government as a deus ex machina: a heaven-sent power that can resolve difficulties as magically as a playwright does in the final act of every farce. It makes our expectations of government more realistic. It encourages us to ask about the conditions that enable government to act effectively in any given circumstance and not just to suppose that government always gets what it wants or catches what it chases. This way of looking at government also reminds us that the immediately preceding sentence was misleading in its suggestion that government is an "it"; for government is *many different people interacting on the basis of prevailing property rights.*

If you're wondering what property rights can possibly have to do with the behavior of government, you may have forgotten momentarily that economists use the concept of property rights to describe the rules of the game. Every participant in the processes of government, from voters through civil-service employees to the president, has certain expectations about what voters or civil servants or the president can and may do. Those expectations reflect *property rights.* Maybe it would help if we substituted for *property rights* the phrase *what people think they can get away with.* Unfortunately, that has connotations of conniving and unethical behavior that we don't intend at all. But the phrase does convey the force of the property-rights concept; the actions that people take will depend on their expectations about the consequences of those actions, on the anticipated marginal benefits and marginal costs to themselves of the decisions they're weighing. That's as true in the Senate Office Building as it is on the floor of the New York Stock Exchange. The key to understanding each of those worlds is a grasp of the very different property rights of senators and of stockbrokers.

THE RIGHT TO USE COERCION

There is one significant difference between government and nongovernment that doesn't grow indistinct or disappear as we inspect it more carefully. *Government possesses a generally conceded and exclusive right to coerce adults.* The right is *generally* conceded, but not universally; thoroughgoing anarchists don't grant it, and neither do those who accept government in principle but reject as illegitimate the authority of the particular government under which they live. It's an *exclusive* right because, as we say, "people don't have the right to take the law into their own hands"; everyone is supposed to appeal to officers of government (police, judges, legislators) when coercion seems called for. And it's the right to coerce *adults* that uniquely distinguishes government, because parents are generally conceded the right to coerce children under certain circumstances.

What does it mean to coerce? We smuggled our definition of coercion into a discussion question in Chapter 11. *To coerce means to induce cooperation by threatening to reduce people's options.* Coercion should be contrasted with the other way of obtaining cooperation from people, which is persuasion. *To persuade means to induce cooperation by promising to expand people's options.*

In a few cases, we may not be able to agree whether particular actions constitute coercion or persuasion. These cases will often turn out to involve real or alleged deception, so that our disagreement turns on the issue of what people actually thought their options were when they were induced by others to cooperate. Or we might be disagreeing about the rights that we think people *ought* to have. But this definition will usually allow us to distinguish coercive from noncoercive efforts to influence the behavior of others. It is only to government that we grant the right to secure cooperation by withdrawing options, reducing people's freedom, taking away some of their rights.

Coercion has a bad reputation, because most of us believe (or think we believe) that people should generally be allowed to do what they want to do. In addition, coercion implies authority, and many of us react with automatic hostility to claims of authority. But the traffic laws that tell us we must drive on the right and stop when the light turns red simultaneously coerce us and expand our freedom. The reason they expand our freedom is that they also coerce others. We all get where we're going faster and more safely, because we accept the coercion of traffic laws. This is the traditional defense of government and its right to coerce: We may all be able to achieve greater freedom and expanded options if we all accept some limitations on our freedom and some reduction in our options.

IS GOVERNMENT NECESSARY?

But do we have to use coercion? Couldn't we get equally good results by relying on voluntary cooperation? We have seen throughout this book that voluntary exchange is the principal mechanism of coordination in our society. Why couldn't voluntary exchange become the *only* means through which we induce cooperation? By asking this question seriously and pushing for an answer, we can gain some additional insights into the capabilities and limitations of the various ways in which we try to get things done.

One way to get at the issue is to ask what would happen if there were no government at all in our society. What problems would arise? Would important tasks cease to be performed? Couldn't people resolve those problems and accomplish those tasks either through individual action or by forming voluntary associations? A good example with which to begin sorting out the issues is the case of police protection. Would there be no police if there were no government? That can't be the case, since private police forces exist at the present time. But these forces supplement a basic, given level of government police protection, providing additional protection for those who want it and are willing to pay for it. Could we obtain that basic protection in the absence of government?

EXCLUDING NONPAYERS

Why not? If there were no government, people who wanted police protection could simply purchase it from private security agencies—much as those people do who aren't satisfied with the service that government provides now. Wouldn't that system even be more fair than the one we actually have? People with lots of property to protect and little time, inclination, or ability to protect it themselves would have to pay for the service. Those who own little property or are in a good position to guard it themselves wouldn't have to pay taxes for police protection that doesn't really benefit them. We make people pay for their own food, rather than providing it out of tax revenues, because we know that people want vastly different quantities and qualities. Why not use the same system for police protection?

The correct answer is *not* that police protection is a "basic necessity"; food is even more basic and necessary. The difference is that food can be supplied exclusively to those who pay for it and denied entirely to those who refuse to pay. And that's not altogether the case with police protection. The patrol officers whom my neighbors hire to guard their houses provide a measure of security also to my house, as a spillover benefit, when they patrol our street. Potential burglars won't realize that I haven't subscribed to the neighborhood security service and that they're consequently safe from apprehension if they break into my house. In fact, the burglars may *not* be altogether safe if they do that. The patrol officers might decide that they can most effectively protect their customers' property by arresting *all* the burglars they discover, regardless of whose property is being burglarized. That gives me protection for which I didn't pay.

In much the same way, firefighters hired to protect my neighbors' houses might choose to put out a grass fire in my yard or a blaze in my attic just to keep it from spreading to their customers' property. And when they extinguish fires on their customers' property, they diminish the chance that the property of adjacent nonsubscribers will catch fire. In both cases, someone who doesn't pay nonetheless acquires a benefit from production of the good. The key feature is the inability of the producers—the police officers or the firefighters—to exclude nonpayers.

THE FREE-RIDER PROBLEM

When people can obtain a good whether they pay for it or not, they have less incentive to pay. They're tempted to become *free riders: people who accept benefits without paying their share of the cost of providing those benefits.* But if no one has an incentive to pay the costs, no one will have an incentive to provide the benefits. As a result, goods won't be produced, despite the fact that everyone values them more than the cost of producing them.

The free-rider concept describes one of the most frustrating problems in the study of social organization. It especially frustrates those who don't understand why the problem exists and who therefore keep insisting that it *ought* to go away:

"We can lick the energy problem if each of us will only. . . ."

"There would be no litter on our highways if each of us would only. . . ."

"If each of us studies the issues and goes to the polls on election day. . . ."

"If every nation would only renounce forever the use of force as a means of resolving international disagreements. . . ."

Those who plead so plaintively in all these and dozens of similar cases recognize correctly that we could all gain "if each of us would only." They are frustrated by the persistent failure of people to do what would clearly and by everyone's admission make them all better off.

The free-rider problem frustrates economists, too, because economists encounter so much resistance when they try to persuade people that each *will not do what is in the interest of all unless it is in the interest of each.* People's actions are guided by the costs they expect to bear and the benefits they expect to receive *as a result of those actions.* If the benefits accruing to Jane Marcet will be exactly the same for all practical purposes whether or not she takes a particular action—but she will incur significant costs by taking it—she will not take the action.

If Jane is noble and generous, she will derive a great deal of benefit from helping others, while thinking lightly of the sacrifices she makes to do so. Consequently, she will take some actions that others will not take. That must be stressed, because the free-rider concept definitely does not assert that people are completely selfish or that altruism plays no part in social life. Quite to the contrary, no society could continue to exist in which people were *completely* selfish. We asserted in Chapter 13—and will remind you again here—that some amount of genuine concern for the well-being of others is essential if any social cooperation at all is to occur. Neither markets nor governments could exist among people with no ability to empathize, to internalize at least some of what others experience.

POSITIVE EXTERNALITIES AND FREE RIDERS

In stressing the significance of the free-rider concept, the economist is insisting only that people have *limited* concepts of self-interest, that they do not by and large entertain the inner feelings of others, especially more distant others, with as much vividness and force as they experience costs and benefits that impinge on them more directly. The economist who calls attention to the free-rider problem is saying that positive externalities exist as well as negative ones, and that these externalities encourage people to behave as free riders. *Positive externalities are benefits that decisionmakers do not take into account when making their decisions.* They raise this question: Will anyone have an adequate incentive to create those benefits, or will everyone wait and hope to receive them as a spillover benefit from the actions of others?

Positive externalities or spillover benefits are probably even more widespread in modern societies than are spillover costs, the negative externalities that give rise to complaints about pollution. Homeowners who maintain beautiful lawns produce spillover benefits for neighbors and passers-by. People with engaging smiles distribute spillover benefits to everyone they encounter. Citizens who take the trouble to inform themselves on community issues improve the quality of public decisions and thereby benefit everyone. Moreover, ordinary producers and sellers regularly and as a matter of course provide benefits to customers considerably greater than what the customers are required to pay for them. Eliminating all spillover benefits would be as absurdly impossible as eliminating all pollution. Nonetheless, spillover benefits and the free-riding tendencies they encourage do create some serious social problems. Coercion through the agency of government is a way of dealing with these problems.

Remember that exchange always entails transaction costs. Demander and supplier must find each other, agree on what they're willing to offer and want to receive, and make reasonably sure that they're actually getting what they expected to get. Sellers in particular must incur transaction costs to be sure that nonpayers don't obtain the goods that they're supplying. Long-established business operations keep down transaction costs by reducing them to routine, thereby enabling all parties to derive larger net benefits from exchange. When transaction costs are so high, however, that they exceed the benefits from exchange, exchange won't occur and the potential benefits will be lost. *Government can be viewed as an institution for reducing transaction costs through the use of coercion.*

LAW AND ORDER

Let's take a look at some traditional functions of government to see how much this approach explains. We begin with the problem of "law and order." We can now summarize the argument of the last few pages: High transaction costs make it difficult to exclude nonpayers from the spillover benefits of police patrols. To prevent free riders from destroying the incentive to supply police protection, government employs coercion. It supplies the service to everyone and pays for it with involuntary contributions called taxes.

A judicial system for resolving disputes that arise between citizens could perhaps be created through voluntary efforts somewhat more easily than a police force, as is suggested by the existence of numerous arbitration systems financed by voluntary efforts. But everyone benefits when the people occupying a common territory are all subject to the same system of laws and judicial rulings. Uniform and consistently enforced rules that are binding on all, whether or not they consent, make it much easier for everyone to plan with confidence. And the ability to plan confidently is what distinguishes a cooperating society from a chaotic mob. Since a system of laws and courts confers substantial benefits on people whether or not they choose to help pay for it and to be bound by it, societies use coercion to create and operate systems of justice.

NATIONAL DEFENSE

National defense is a very traditional function of government, and it provides the classic example of a benefit that can't be provided, except at prohibitive cost, exclusively to those who pay for it. Because free-rider problems would make it practically impossible to rely on voluntary contributions to finance a system of national defense, societies resort to coercion, collecting the funds through taxation.

Note carefully, however, because the point is easily overlooked, that government does not have to rely entirely on coercion to produce the good called national defense. And no government does. The taxes used to finance a military force are coercive levies. But when the funds are used to hire people for the armed forces and to purchase equipment from suppliers, government is relying on persuasion and voluntary cooperation, just as it does in supplying police officers and judges. This raises an interesting question. Why will a government sometimes use coercion to achieve its objectives when it would appear that persuasion would work just as well or even better? Why will a government choose to draft people into the armed forces (and onto juries) rather than rely on volunteers? Most people who work for government are persuaded, not compelled to do so. Why are some coerced? The dangers to which military personnel are subject cannot be the whole answer, since people are attracted into far more dangerous occupations without conscription. We'll suggest an explanation a little further on.

ROADS AND SCHOOLS

What about roads? Would we enjoy an adequate system of streets and highways if we didn't use coercion to finance them? Be careful; an adequate system doesn't necessarily mean the quantity and quality we now have. Roads are oversupplied if the benefits from particular additions are less than the costs of making those additions, and that can surely occur. But is there any reason to expect a systematic undersupply of streets and highways if their provision is left entirely to voluntary efforts? The transaction costs could be rather staggering if all streets and highways were owned and operated by people who had to rely entirely on tolls for the collection of revenue. The benefits, moreover, don't accrue exclusively to those who drive. People who live along a dusty gravel road receive benefits from the paving of that road even if they never drive. The experience of those who have built roads in remote areas or in private developments without using coercion suggests both that it can be done and that the costs of securing cooperation by exclusively voluntary means can be quite high.

What is the case for using coercion to finance education? The argument here is that people will acquire education only up to the point at which the marginal cost to themselves equals the marginal benefit to themselves. But education supposedly generates substantial externalities, benefits that accrue to people other than the person acquiring the education. Thus, everyone in a democracy benefits when citizens learn to read and to think. Because we don't take account of the spillover benefits to others in deciding how much education to obtain, we obtain less than the optimal amount. By using taxes to subsidize education, the government lowers its cost

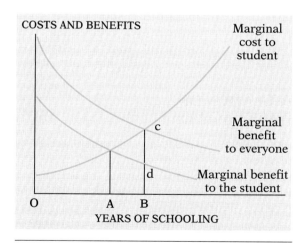

FIGURE 14A   Marginal-cost and marginal-benefit
curves for education
        Students considering only the cost and benefits
to themselves would choose to acquire *OA* years of
schooling. If their costs are subsidized by the amount
cd, they will choose *OB* years of schooling.

to potential students and induces them to acquire more than they otherwise would. The question arises, as it does with roads, whether the use of coercion to prevent undersupply does not lead in practice to oversupply. We'll return to that question.

INCOME REDISTRIBUTION

Another important category of government action is the provision of special benefits—money grants, food stamps, medical care, housing subsidies, and a variety of social services—to impoverished or disabled people. Why does this kind of activity require the use of coercion? Why don't we leave it to voluntary philanthropy, rather than compel people to contribute through the tax system? One part of the answer is that charity is subject to the free-rider problem. Assume that all citizens are charitably disposed and want to see more income made available to especially poor and unfortunate people. Although some citizens derive direct satisfaction from contributing to a charitable cause, most would prefer that problems be solved and suffering be relieved at a minimum cost to themselves. They want to see poor people helped, but they also want to see others do the helping. And so they tend to behave like free riders. They hold back somewhat on their contributions in the hope that others will contribute enough to take care of the problem. But with everyone waiting for others to contribute, contributions fall short of the amount that everyone would prefer to see raised. Under such circumstances taxation can make people want to contribute more by assuring them that others are also doing their share.

THE REGULATION OF VOLUNTARY EXCHANGE

What about the extensive list of government activities that fall under the category of regulation? Why do federal, state, and local governments regulate so many of the activities of citizens, using coercion to control the terms on which people may engage in voluntary exchange? Putting it in just that way—using coercion to control voluntary exchange—may prompt us to think a little harder and longer about all the things that government does in the name of regulation.

Part of the answer is the widely held belief that the powerful and unscrupulous will take unfair advantage of the weak and the innocent unless the government regulates certain kinds of voluntary exchange. This is the parentalistic argument,[2] which no doubt has some merit but which has also often been abused by special interests precisely to take unfair advantage of the weak and the innocent.

Transaction costs provide another part of the answer. It would be very costly for all of us to carry our own scales to check the accuracy of the ones that butchers use and our own gallon cans to be sure the gasoline pumps aren't cheating us. When physicians must be licensed and new drugs approved by the Food and Drug Administration before they can be marketed, buyers are spared the cost of evaluating goods whose quality most of them would be unable to assess for themselves—except at prohibitive costs. By compelling sellers to obtain certification, government agencies can enable us all to make satisfactory exchanges at lower cost. A substantial amount of government regulation can be viewed as coercion designed to reduce the cost of acquiring information.

The glaring flaw in this defense of regulation, however, is that it fails to account for the enthusiasm with which sellers so often support regulation. Those who have studied the matter know very well that the demand for government regulation of sellers more often originates with the sellers than with their customers. We saw in Chapter 10 why this occurs: Sellers are eager to restrict competition, and government regulation in the name of consumer protection is a technique of proved effectiveness for eliminating competition. But why do the victims cooperate? Why does government employ coercion to promote special interests when it's supposed to be the responsibility of government to promote the public interest?

GOVERNMENT AND THE PUBLIC INTEREST

The basic answer suggested by economic theory brings us back in a surprising way to the problem with which we began this chapter. The coercive actions taken by government to compensate for the limitations inherent in purely voluntary cooperation are themselves subject to the same limitations. The reason for this is that coercion itself depends on voluntary cooperation. Persuasion always precedes coercion, because government will not act until particular people have been persuaded to act. Government is not the genie in Aladdin's lamp. Government is people interacting, paying attention to the expected costs and benefits of the alternatives that they perceive. The disconcerting part of all this is that the

---

[2]Most people would say *paternalistic*. But *parentalistic* is a more accurate and less sexist term.

problems created by transaction costs, positive externalities, and free riders are particularly acute in the political life of democracies.

A surprising number of people assume without thinking about it that "government acts in the public interest." But does it really? Does it always do so? Why do we think so? Do citizens become more virtuous when they move from the line in the supermarket to the line at the polling place? Do people's characters change when they give up a post in industry or academia to take a position with the government? Suppose we define the public interest as what everyone would want if everyone were adequately informed and impartial. Does economic theory have anything useful to say about the likelihood that government actions will proceed from adequate information and an impartial viewpoint?

Those whose decisions make up the sum of government actions will pay attention to the information actually available to them and the incentives that actually confront them. Economic theory predicts that this information and these incentives will tend to be both limited and biased.

INFORMATION AND DEMOCRATIC GOVERNMENTS

We can begin with citizen voters. None of us knows enough to cast an adequately intelligent vote. To persuade yourself that this is so, conduct a little mental experiment. Suppose you know that your vote, whether on a candidate or a ballot proposition, would determine the outcome of the election; your vote and your vote alone will decide the question. How much information would you gather before casting that crucial vote? A lot would depend, of course, on the importance of the office or the issue. But you would surely invest far more time and energy in acquiring information than you do when you're just one voter among 50 thousand or 50 million. As it is, most citizens, including intelligent, well-read, and public-spirited citizens, step into the polling place on election day equipped only with a lot of prejudices, a few hunches, some poorly tested bits of information, and vast areas of total ignorance. We do this because it's rational to do so! Given the actual importance of our one vote in 50 thousand or 50 million, it would be an almost unconscionable waste of time for us to learn enough to cast an adequately informed vote. The issue is not simply one of selfishness or lack of dedication to the well-being of society. A voter who wanted to make a personal sacrifice for the good of the commonwealth could do far more per hour, per dollar, or per calorie in social-service volunteer work than by gathering enough information to cast an adequately informed vote.

"But if everybody thought that way," goes the standard objection, "democracy wouldn't work." This objection is another instance of the argument that the free-rider phenomenon doesn't exist because the world would be a more satisfactory place if it did not exist. Those who are committed to democracy had better concern themselves with ways to make it work when citizen voters are uninformed and misinformed, and not pretend that voters have knowledge they obviously don't have.

Some defenders of democracy aren't overly discouraged by the incompetence of citizen voters. They rely on elected representatives to acquire the information that must be available if decisions are to be made in the public interest. Their confidence has a reasonable foundation in reality. Because the vote of each legislator has a far greater probability of affecting the outcome, because legislators can use the information they acquire to influence others in significant ways, because legislators are provided with staff and other information-gathering resources, because many people will have a strong interest in making relevant information available to legislators, because legislators' votes are monitored and must be defended—for all these reasons and more, elected representatives are far more likely to be adequately informed about the issues on which they vote than are ordinary citizens.

THE INTERESTS OF ELECTED OFFICIALS

But even if we can assume that legislators' votes are adequately informed, are we entitled to assume that they will be votes in the public interest? Are elected representatives impartial? Another way of asking the same question is to ask whether they will always vote in the way that the information available to them tells them they ought to vote. Economic theory assumes that people act in their own interest, not that they act in the public interest. Sometimes it will be in a legislator's interest to pursue the public interest. But finding ways to produce such harmony is the major issue in the design of political institutions; we can't simply *assume* this advantageous concord without asking whether the institutions under which we live are likely to produce it. Because an interest in reelection is a common and healthy interest among most elected officials, we'll focus our analysis on this one particular private interest. Is an interest in being reelected likely to lead elected officials to vote and act in the public interest?

Let's begin by noticing how it limits their planning horizons. Elected officials can't afford to look too far ahead. Results must be available by the next election or the incumbent could be replaced by someone who offers better promises. In considering any policy that requires current sacrifices for the sake of future benefits, elected officials will tend to discount heavily the value of all future benefits that aren't expected until after the election. Their interest in reelection will thus keep them from fully using their own superior knowledge about the consequences of particular policies.

In listing some of the reasons why legislators are likely to be well informed, we mentioned two that also explain why legislators will not always vote in the way that their information tells them they ought to vote. These were the last two reasons cited: Many people have a strong interest in making relevant information available to legislators, and legislators' votes are monitored and must be defended. The problem is that the interest in providing information (or lobbying) and in holding legislators accountable for their actions is concentrated in special-interest groups. The positive externalities associated with the political process make this almost inevitable.

Conflict in recent years over deregulation in the transportation industry illustrates the problem and also shows how the special interests can sometimes be defeated. The commercial airlines were essentially deregulated in 1978 and the regulatory authority, the Civil Aeronautics Board, went out of business completely in 1982. This occurred despite the airlines' predictions that service quality would decline, the pilot union's warnings about safety, the objection of smaller cities that they would be deprived of service, and the determined resistance of many members of Congress who knew how to earn political points with the special interests among their constituencies by leaning on the CAB. The interests of passengers in more flights and lower prices were effectively championed in this case by a handful of legislators who seem to have read some economics and who were aided by the tide of disillusionment with government that rose in the 1970s and crested in the 1980s.

The continuing struggle to deregulate the trucking industry shows how special interests can sometimes defeat other special interests. Regulation by the Interstate Commerce Commission over the years had produced wasteful practices and higher prices to shippers that ultimately showed up as higher prices for just about everything we buy. But there were people who benefited from all this. By restricting competition, regulation created privileged positions for the trucking firms that owned operating rights and for members of the Teamsters Union. These groups expected deregulation to reduce their wealth substantially. They were therefore extremely active in lobbying members of Congress, in making campaign contributions, and in threatening retaliation against elected officials who might vote to "throw the trucking industry open to the chaos of competition."

The dollar benefits to the rest of us from lower transportation costs would almost surely be greater in the aggregate than the losses that the trucking firms and the drivers expected to suffer from deregulation. Nonetheless, we did not see any significant amount of lobbying effort, campaign contributions, or demonstrations on the part of ordinary consumers directed at getting Congress to vote for deregulation. The individual interest that each of us has in deregulation is simply not great enough to induce any of us to involve ourselves actively in the fight. The political pressure for deregulation that persuaded Congress came from shippers. Because they stood to gain large benefits from deregulation, shippers organized the political opposition that led to partial deregulation of the motor carrier industry in 1980. They received a powerful assist from the same political tide that helped abolish the CAB.

Similar stories can be told about the railroad industry. The maritime industry, on the other hand, still uses "national security" arguments to retain the benefits of government regulation that has produced absurd wastes but also huge financial benefits for a favored few.

The process is always the same. The few who have much to gain invest vast resources in trying to influence the legislature. The many with more to gain in total but less to gain individually invest nothing. Legislators respond to this sort of pressure, because a substantial number of them find that doing so serves their interest in being reelected. It seems rather futile to fault them for this; an *ex*-legislator with untarnished principles is a less effective public servant than a legislator who has bent a few principles to survive and fight another day. The fault lies with the positive externalities that prompt most of us to behave like free riders, hoping that someone else will assume the costs of lobbying for the measures from which we would all benefit.

POSITIVE EXTERNALITIES AND GOVERNMENT POLICIES

Our conclusion should come as no surprise. Government policies will tend to be dominated by special interests. Government will lean toward actions that harm many people just a little bit, rather than actions that displease a few people very much. Government policies will be guided not so much by the public interest as by an endless succession of extremely partial interests. This is why consumer interests win the oratorical contests, but producer interests control policy. The interests of producers are simply more concentrated, more sharply focused. Producers know that their action or inaction can make a significant difference to their own welfare, and so it's in their interest to act. But no individual consumer can expect more than a small benefit from political action, so none of them has an incentive to accept the costs.

Is this why the use of coercion to prevent an undersupply of roads often leads to an oversupply? The taxpayers' general interest in economy doesn't fare well when it goes head to head with a small group's intense interest in having a road or building a road. The same analysis applies to schooling. Those who produce schooling (the author's own vested interest, let it be noted) can make life difficult for legislators who try to save taxpayers money by reducing expenditures on education or research. Here is an explanation for the otherwise puzzling behavior of legislatures that approve larger and larger expenditures—even when every member favors reduced expenditures. There is no way to cut a budget without cutting specific projects. With every special interest organized to make certain that the cuts occur in someone else's project, expenditures cannot be reduced.

Why did we long have a military draft in this country, and what is the probability that Congress will restore it? Military conscription, as we noted earlier, extends the use of coercion into areas where persuasion is quite capable of securing the cooperation we want (at least in peacetime). The draft probably persisted as long as it did because the military establishment had a strong and sharply focused interest in maintaining a ready flow of personnel for the armed forces, whereas most of those who were adversely affected by the draft had a stronger incentive to find a personal escape route than to attack the whole system. It is interesting to note how many current advocates of reinstating the draft are now talking about *universal* conscription of young people for short-term service of some kind. Will this tactic (assuming that it is a tactic) increase the number of those who are opposed to the draft? Or will it reduce the expected cost to each draftee below that critical point at which he or she would be willing to do political battle to prevent reestablishment of the draft?

What can we say about government actions to relieve poverty? We can predict that legislators will be slow to replace in-kind transfers with money transfers. Farmers benefit from the food-stamp program, the building trades benefit from housing subsidies, the medical-care industry expands with health-care assistance, teachers benefit from educational subsidies for the poor, and social workers know that giving money to the poor will never be as advantageous as hiring more members of the "helping professions." The political influence of these groups makes it easier for legislatures to support in-kind transfers to the poor than to support money transfers. There may be other and better grounds for rejecting money transfers, but this alternative would get more respectful attention in Congress if money were produced and sold by a money industry.

HOW DO PEOPLE IDENTIFY THE PUBLIC INTEREST?

None of this implies that farmers, hospital administrators, or social workers have no regard for the public interest. It implies only that they all have *some* regard for their own interests. And even those who work for government agencies charged specifically to protect the public interest define it with reference to their own special interests.

Consider, for example, a member of the Food and Drug Administration (FDA), responsible for preventing the introduction of new drugs without adequate testing. What is adequate testing? It's testing that makes sure we know all the side effects of a new drug before we allow it on the market. But we can *never* be sure. All we can do is acquire additional information and thus reduce the risk that someone will be killed or seriously harmed by an unanticipated side effect. How far should we reduce the risk? Not *too* far, because there are costs as well as benefits attached to additional testing. A major cost will be the lives lost and the suffering not relieved because the drug isn't available while it's being tested.

How will an FDA commissioner evaluate these two costs: the lives lost through premature introduction and the lives lost through excessive delay in introduction of new drugs? People will blame the FDA if an approved drug turns out to

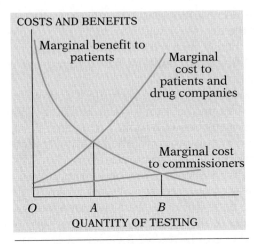

FIGURE 14B   Marginal-cost and marginal-benefit curves for drug testing
    In a situation like the one portrayed, how much testing would FDA commissioners decide to require before agreeing to authorize distribution of a new drug? *OA* **or** *OB?*

have disastrous side effects, and they will applaud the FDA if it refuses to approve a drug that subsequently turns out to have disastrous side effects in other countries. But almost no one condemns the FDA for lives lost while a drug is being tested or applauds the FDA for cutting the testing period short in order to get a new drug on the market. The conclusion is obvious. FDA commissioners will find it in the public interest to test drugs beyond the point at which the marginal benefit equals the marginal cost to patients.

THE PRISONERS' DILEMMA

An interesting concept that illuminates the central feature in many of the problems we've been discussing is The Prisoners' Dilemma (a name that reflects the original exposition of the dilemma through a story about two prisoners and a clever prosecutor).

    Let's suppose that every citizen urgently desires Good Government and would gladly give up two hours of leisure per week to secure it. Those two hours would be spent, let's say, investigating current issues, discussing policy questions with other citizens, and monitoring the actions of legislators. If all or almost all citizens contribute those two hours per week, Good Government is assured. Will we get Good Government? Since, by assumption, every citizen sincerely desires Good Government and is willing to make the required sacrifice to obtain it, it would seem that we ought to. Nonetheless, we probably will not.

Here is the dilemma. Each citizen knows that his or her decision will not affect the outcome. If I spend two hours Doing My Duty but none of my fellow citizens do theirs, my efforts will be wasted. I will be just one informed voice and vote lost in a hundred million uninformed voices and votes. I will have given up two hours of bowling (or whatever is my most valued forgone opportunity) to accomplish exactly nothing. On the other hand, if I decide just to do my own thing while all my fellow citizens are Doing Their Duty, I will get all the advantages of Good Government plus two hours of recreation at the alleys as a bonus. And so my *dominant strategy* is to go bowling. I will always be better off if I bowl than if I Do My Duty, because I cannot through my own decision affect anything except whether my time gets spent in tedious politicking or in joyous bowling.

Unfortunately, choosing recreation over duty will be the dominant strategy for everyone else, too, with the consequence that we will not get Good Government even though everyone wants it and is willing to contribute his or her share of what is required to obtain it.

We can summarize all this in the diagram of Figure 14C. Each citizen follows the dominant strategy in choosing Duty or Recreation, with the results portrayed. The society ends up in the southeast square despite the fact that every single member prefers the northwest square. That's the dilemma.

There are four possible payoffs for each individual who chooses. The one who must give up bowling to Do His Duty will always be better off by choosing Recreation over Duty, because by so doing he obtains the good of Bowling. The choices of others determine whether he gets Good or Bad Government. But each of the others faces the same situation. So all choose Recreation and all end up with Bad Government, despite the fact that all would be willing to give up the equivalent of Bowling to obtain Good Government.

Dilemmas of this sort are fairly common. Everyone in the city wants clean air, for example, and would be willing to reduce their driving to obtain it. But since no *one's* decision can measurably affect the quality of the air, everyone chooses to continue driving, and the city's air becomes unbreatheable.

Here's a different sort of example. Every seller in an industry knows that the entire industry would be better off if

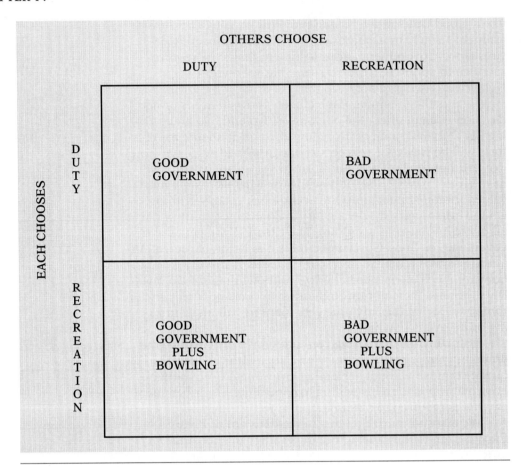

FIGURE 14C   A prisoners' dilemma

each seller restricted output and thereby caused the price to rise. But with many sellers in the industry, it is in the interest of each seller to maintain the old output level while hoping (vainly) that other sellers will restrict output. Everyone behaves like a free rider because everyone is aware that their individual decision has a much larger effect on their own welfare than on the welfare of the group as a whole. And so everyone ends up worse off than they would have been had they been able to overcome the free-rider problem or the prisoners' dilemma.

Our example about sellers who are unable to combine effectively to raise prices should serve as a warning that prisoners' dilemmas, while frustrating to the acting parties, can produce desirable consequences for others. A prisoner's dilemma is not the same thing as a social problem.

Prisoners' dilemmas would not exist in the absence of transaction costs. The parties would make binding contracts with one another to assure that they ended up in the northwest square rather than the southeast one. One contract would specify that the bowling fan described above forfeits *three* hours in the lanes if he fails to put in a faithful two hours per week Doing His Duty. It thereby becomes in his interest to Do His Duty, and in everyone else's interest to Do Their Duty, because they are all constrained by similar contracts; and the society enjoys life in the northwest square. As you realize, however, it would be much too costly to devise, write, negotiate, record, monitor, and enforce such contracts. (Who can tell for sure whether the bowler is putting in a faithful two hours or just going through the motions?) Transaction costs thereby prevent us from doing what we all want to do.

We work at the problem, however, in an infinite variety of interesting ways. It would take another book to describe all the formal and informal institutions that evolve in a society as people try in their varied social exchanges to control the negative effects of prisoners' dilemmas. We use smiles, frowns, customs, conventions, formal and informal contracts, deposits, and even constitutions. You can very usefully think of the Constitution of the United States as an institution that functions to control prisoners' dilemmas, by constraining the private interests of people who claim to be serving the public interest.

THE LIMITS OF POLITICAL INSTITUTIONS

If all this is unsettling to those for whom it is an article of faith that the government takes care of the public interest, it may be time to question this article of faith. Perhaps it stems from the habit of equating "government" with "nation" and extending to the former the reverence felt for the latter. Or it may be a result of our belief that government is the last resort and therefore must be an effective resort, since we don't like to admit to any unsolvable problems. There's a popular bit of deductive reasoning that also leads toward this conclusion. It asserts that all social problems are the result of human behavior, that human behavior can be altered by law, and that government makes the laws, from which the argument concludes that government can solve all social problems.

Alexis de Tocqueville offered a more realistic view in *Democracy in America* (Volume I, Part I, Chapter VIII): "There is no country in which everything can be provided for by the laws, or in which political institutions can prove a substitute for common sense and public morality."

ONCE OVER LIGHTLY

Economic theory assumes that the actions of government follow from the decisions of citizens and government officials who are paying attention to the marginal costs and marginal benefits to themselves of alternative courses of action.

The distinguishing characteristic of government is its generally conceded and exclusive right to use coercion. To coerce means to induce cooperation by threatening to reduce people's options. Voluntary cooperation relies exclusively on persuasion, which secures desired behavior by promising additional options.

Coercion is useful to the members of a society, because it can sometimes secure the production of goods that everyone values at more than the cost of supplying them, but which would not be supplied through purely voluntary cooperation.

A supply failure of this sort is likely to occur when there is no low-cost way of confining supply of a good to those who pay for it, or of preventing demanders from becoming free riders.

Coercion may be able to secure the supply of such goods by lowering transaction costs.

The traditional activities of government turn out on examination to be largely actions aimed at reducing transaction costs and overcoming free-rider problems.

The coercive activities of government presuppose voluntary cooperation. Persuasion precedes coercion because, in the last analysis, citizens and government officials must be persuaded to employ coercion in particular ways. This implies that the limits on the effectiveness of voluntary cooperation that justify coercive action by government are limitations also on the effectiveness of the government's coercive action.

Positive externalities thoroughly permeate the political process in a democratic government. They make it unlikely that citizen voters will be adequately informed or that elected or appointed officials will consistently act in the way that the information available to them tells them they ought to act.

QUESTIONS FOR DISCUSSION

1. In what general, systematic way do the interests pursued by officials in government differ from the interests pursued by people in the private sector? Consider the following cases:

(a) The president of a state-owned university and the president of a privately owned university.

(b) A member of the U.S. House of Representatives who aspires to a seat in the Senate and a traveling sales representative for a large business corporation who wants a job as sales manager at one of the firm's plants.

(c) A prominent political figure who wants to become president of the United States and a prominent actor who wants to receive an Academy Award.

(d) An urban police officer and a uniformed guard employed by a private security firm.

(e) A grant-awarding official in the Small Business Administration and a loan officer in a bank.

2. In each of the following examples, what are the significant differences between government-owned and nongovernment-owned enterprises? Why do you think the government owns the enterprises mentioned? What different forms does competition take in the case of government-owned enterprises? In what different ways do they operate because of their government ownership?

(a) Investor-owned utilities and utilities owned by states or municipalities.

(b) State colleges and private colleges.

(c) City-owned intraurban bus companies and interurban bus companies like Greyhound and Trailways.

(d) Forest Service campgrounds and privately owned campgrounds.

(e) Public libraries and private bookstores.

3. A frequent argument in support of government-produced goods is that they are vital to social welfare and therefore their provision cannot safely be left to the "whims" of the marketplace. Does this explain why parks and libraries are usually municipal services, whereas food and medical care are usually secured through the market? Can you suggest a better explanation to account for these cases?

4. A feature story in *The Wall Street Journal* of May 23, 1979, carried this headline: "Washington PR Staffs Dream Up Ways to Get Agencies' Stories Out."

(a) How does a director of public affairs in a government agency differ from the director of advertising or public relations for a soap manufacturer?

(b) Why do the departments of Defense, Transportation, Agriculture, and others of the federal government spend millions of dollars trying to influence public opinion? Isn't it true, at least in a democracy, that public opinion is supposed to control the actions of government agencies?

5. Should the managers of business corporations, in their official capacities, accept social responsibilities beyond the responsibility to increase the net income of the corporations which they run?

   (a) Do they have a moral obligation to go beyond what the law requires in order to advance such causes as race and gender equality, a clean environment, better public transportation, good government, and so on? Why or why not?

   (b) Who will pay the costs if corporation managers shoulder such responsibilities? Who will review their decisions to be sure that the decisions they make really are in the public interest?

   (c) Why might the president of a large corporation want to contribute $1 million of corporate funds to a hospital-building program in the city where the corporation is headquartered? What personal benefits and personal costs accrue to the president from such a gift?

6. Advocates of government regulation often make their case by attacking "unrestrained" or "unbridled" competition. Is competition *ever* "unrestrained"? What were some of the important restraints on competition that operated in the U.S. economy in the nineteenth century when, according to some accounts, competition was "unrestrained"?

7. Critics of government regulation often try to make a case for the "free" market. Are markets ever completely free? Free from what? Is a market "unfree" if participants operate under laws that prohibit the use of dishonest weights and measures? Laws that prohibit misleading advertising? That prohibit price increases which have not been approved by a government agency? Where do you draw the line between free markets and unfree or regulated markets? Why do you draw it where you do?

8. The graph in Figure 14D pretends to show the net revenue (during some time period) that the proprietor of a grocery store expects from stocking four categories of merchandise: milk and dairy products (*M*), canned and bottled staples (*S*), fresh produce (*P*), and frozen foods (*F*).

   (a) How many units of each will he want to stock?

   (b) Now pretend that the four curves show the net satisfaction that the proprietor expects to receive from pursuing the four objectives of more money (*M*), enhanced status (*S*), greater personal power (*P*), and family well-being (*F*). How far will he pursue each goal?

   (c) What general differences would you be inclined to expect between the "satisfaction curves" of a person in business and a person in government service, or running for public office, or in the ranks of the clergy, or teaching school, or working as a medical researcher?

9. The text warns about the dangers in speaking of government as an "it" that can be manipulated, like a tool, to do whatever we want done. Isn't it also misleading to use the word "we" the way it's used in the preceding sentence? Who are the "we" who want government to do this or that? Ev-

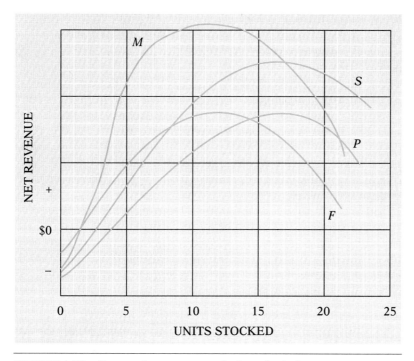

FIGURE 14D   Expected net revenue of a hypothetical grocery store

eryone? The majority? All informed and public-spirited citizens? Those who share my interests and my understanding of the situation? What do people mean when they say, "We must use government to control the effects of selfishness and greed"? Who is supposed to control whom in this vision of the way society works?

10. Guy Weyer is a former farmer turned suburban developer who built 50 houses on a 40-acre corner of his farm. He now rents these houses out.

   (a) If one of Guy's tenants calls a meeting at which 26 of the 50 tenants vote to reduce the monthly rents by $100, is Guy morally or legally obligated to abide by their decision?

   (b) If the 26 tenants simply withhold $100 of their monthly rent, does Guy have a moral and legal right to evict them?

   (c) If the evicted tenants refuse to move, what moral and legal means are open to Guy to get them out?

   (d) Suppose that the 26 tenants first form a local government, then reduce the rents by majority vote, and finally pass an ordinance prohibiting evictions. Would this make any difference in the answers you give to the questions above?

(e) What is the difference between a legitimate and an illegitimate government or government decision? Is a democratic government one in which the majority rules? Are there any limits to what a majority may do in a democracy?

(f) The principle of majority rule requires a prior determination: majority of *whom?* Who ought to be entitled to a vote in matters such as those discussed above? Property owners exclusively? All residents over 18? Tenants, with one vote per house rather than one per resident? All adults in the country, with Guy Weyer's tenants forming just a small part of a much larger set of voters? What different consequences would be likely to emerge from these different ways of distributing voting rights?

(g) If you are incapable of imagining a legitimate distribution of voting rights other than one-vote-per-adult, consider the distribution of voting rights in a condominium association or a country club. What about the distribution of voting rights among those who own the stock of a corporation? Why do we observe these different ways of assigning voting rights?

11. Use the definitions of coercion and persuasion offered in the text to evaluate the following actions. In order to decide whether an option was added or subtracted, we must know what options people possess initially, or what their property rights are to begin with.

(a) A prospective employee with strong religious objections to working on Sunday is told he must consent to Sunday work if he wants the job. If he consents because he very much wants the job, has he been persuaded or coerced?

(b) Your employer says you will be fired if you smoke anywhere at all during working hours and so you reluctantly give up smoking from 9 to 12 and 1 to 5 on weekdays. Were you persuaded or coerced?

(c) You very courteously ask the student who lives just below you to please play her stereo at a lower volume from 7 to 10 in the evening when you're trying to study. She refuses on the grounds that she isn't playing it loud enough to prevent you from studying. So you stomp on the floor in the middle of the night when she's trying to sleep. She agrees after two weeks of this to adjust the volume as you requested. Was she persuaded or coerced?

(d) Are electricity users persuaded to pay more or coerced into paying more when their local electric utility raises its rates?

(e) You consider parking your car illegally in a loading zone but finally decide against it because you fear you'll be ticketed. Were you persuaded or coerced into finding another parking space?

(f) A homeowner offers to let you park on the street in a way that blocks his driveway if you agree to pay him $1. You pay and park. Were you persuaded or coerced?

(g) Are you being persuaded or coerced in your decision about how much to contribute at the office to the United Way if you know that the amount of each pledge will be posted on the bulletin board?

(h) Does the umpire in a baseball game secure cooperation among the players by persuasion or by coercion?

12. Does either persuasion or coercion enjoy any inherent advantages over the other as a way of inducing cooperation?

(a) People who are cooperating because they have been persuaded usually want to maintain the relationship. Those who have been coerced will typically be looking for ways to sever the relationship. What does this imply about the level of transaction costs that will be associated with cooperative endeavors in each case?

(b) Coercion can be used to deny people the opportunity to engage in voluntary cooperation. Does this occur? Why should anyone want to use coercion to prevent others from cooperating on a voluntary basis?

13. Adam Smith assigned to the sovereign or commonwealth the duty of "erecting and maintaining those public institutions and those public works, which, though they may be in the highest degree advantageous to a great society, are, however, of such a nature, that the profit could never repay the expense to any individual or small number of individuals, and which it therefore cannot be expected that any individual or small number of individuals should erect or maintain" (*The Wealth of Nations*, Book V, Chapter I).

(a) How does this description of the goods that government should supply differ from the text's description of goods subject to the free-rider problem?

(b) Smith discusses four public institutions or works that at least partially satisfy his criterion: those "for the defence of the society . . . for the administration of justice . . . for facilitating the commerce of the society, and those for promoting the instruction of the people." How does Smith's assignment compare with the duties generally assigned to governments today? Is there any major duty of government that Smith overlooks?

14. The text discusses the problem of creating a police force for a community solely on the basis of voluntary cooperation. Isn't it the unwillingness of some people to cooperate on a strictly voluntary basis that makes a police force desirable in the first place? Aren't burglars and similar lawbreakers behaving as free riders?

15. Should the members of a volunteer fire department refuse to put out a fire in the home of someone who has refused to contribute to the firefighting service? (Assume that no property of subscribers is in danger.) What damage would they be doing by putting out the fire?

16. Is the free-rider problem a source exclusively of social *problems?* Doesn't the free-rider problem also prevent people from cooperating to take unfair advantage of others? Why do cartels generally break down unless they can enlist the support of government with its coercive powers?

17. "Of the 34,937 members in the cooperative eligible to vote, only 737 voted in the election of trustees, and 483 of these cast absentee ballots." Do these data indicate that the members don't support the cooperative? Do you think better trustees would be selected if more members voted?

18. Most automobile drivers probably exceed the legal speed limits somewhat when they think they can get away with it. Does this imply that they would vote for higher speed limits if given a chance?

19. Why do some people who drink alcoholic beverages vote in favor of legal prohibition?

20. Here is the opening sentence of a newspaper editorial lamenting the tiny turnout for a public hearing on improving the high schools in a large U.S. city: "Given the number of people who complain about public education, it's amazing how few attend meetings to tell the schools how to do better." Is it really surprising that many complain but few attend meetings?

    (a) What is the cost of complaining? What is the cost of attending a meeting?

    (b) What is the probability that a concerned citizen who spends an evening at a public hearing will actually be able to influence policies in a large urban school district?

    (c) The relative benefit-cost ratios of complaining and attending would seem to provide an adequate explanation for the facts lamented by the newspaper editorialist. But how can we explain the behavior of "activists," those few people who seem always willing to turn out for meetings on even the most inopportune occasions? Are there satisfactions other than that of actually affecting public policy that people can obtain through political participation?

21. Most parent–teacher associations have a hard time getting people to attend meetings and do other work for the associations.

    (a) Why does this not imply either that parents don't care about their children's education or that they don't think the PTA accomplishes anything?

    (b) Why is attendance usually better among teachers than among parents?

    (c) Why do a few parents choose to be very actively involved in the PTA?

22. Hospitals often find it not worth their while to hold down their costs, because reductions in costs produce lower reimbursement payments from government as well as a lower quality of patient care. A letter to *The Wall Street Journal* (February 24, 1982) complains about this attitude on the part of hospital administrators:

[E]very health care provider looks no further than his own checkbook. . . . If all providers would look to the size of the jar rather than the one jelly bean they have plucked from it, there would be bigger and better beans for everyone.

How does this illustrate both the free-rider problem and the "if each of us would only" fallacy?

23. Each of the ten families on a suburban block is likely to have its own power lawn mower. Why don't families more often share a single lawn mower? Try to enumerate the principal transaction costs that stand in the way of such a cooperative arrangement.

24. It's difficult for entertainers to supply their services exclusively to those television viewers who are willing to pay for the entertainment.

   (a) How do entertainers nonetheless manage to secure payment for providing their services to television viewers? Think through the way in which the free-rider problem is handled in network television. To whom do entertainers sell their services? Through what sequence of transactions do viewers receive the entertainment? How is the free-rider problem handled at each stage?

   (b) Some homeowners today try to get cable-television programs without subscribing by picking up the signal from satellites, using their own receiving dishes. How does the use of scramblers and decoders by pay-television companies illustrate the acceptance of transaction costs to eliminate free riders?

25. If running laps around the football field improves the conditioning of athletes and makes them more effective players, why do so many players try to get away with running fewer laps than the coach orders? Who receives the benefits and who bears the cost of such conditioning activities? Are coaches likely to order their players to run a more-than-optimal number of laps?

26. When a government agency requires households or businesses to submit detailed reports on their activities, the costs are borne by those who must prepare the reports and the benefits (in the form of additional information) are received entirely by the agency.

   (a) How does this explain the expansion of government-required paperwork despite a general consensus that such paperwork is already excessive?

   (b) Do you think the requirements would decline if agencies were required to use funds from their budget allocations to compensate those who must submit the forms?

   (c) Should teachers be required to read and comment on all papers that they require their students to write?

27. If positive externalities create free-rider problems to the extent suggested in this chapter in the analysis of charitable programs, why do United

Way campaigns work as well as they do in so many American cities? Are there elements of coercion in United Way fund drives, either in obtaining people to work on the campaign or in inducing people to contribute? What might be the advantages and disadvantages of having local government assume the welfare functions currently performed through the United Way?

28. Why do our courts require citizens who have been selected for jury duty to serve whether they want to or not? Couldn't courts obtain as many jurors as they require on a voluntary basis if they raised the fee for jury duty? Why don't we raise the fee, staff juries with volunteers, and stop imposing the heavy costs of jury duty on so many people who must abandon other valuable activities to do their "jury duty"? How do you suppose the composition of juries would be affected by such a move to a system of all-volunteer jurors? Is it legitimate to use coercion in this case because serving on a jury is every citizen's duty? If so, why don't we fine people who don't vote? Isn't voting a citizen's duty? Even better, why not fine people who fail a rigorous current affairs test *or* do not vote? That way we would coerce citizens into casting an informed vote. Or would we?

29. Should we have laws that require homeowners to insulate in order to save energy?

   (a) How will homeowners benefit from improved insulation? Should homeowners insulate if the cost to themselves of doing so exceeds the benefit to themselves?

   (b) How do others in a community benefit from the decision of some to insulate and thereby reduce their consumption of energy? Do these spillover benefits justify a subsidy to encourage homeowners to insulate? Who would lobby for such a subsidy?

30. Would you agree that the U.S. Constitution describes the property rights of the president, members of Congress, and Supreme Court justices?

   (a) Why does the Constitution prohibit Congress from lowering the salaries of the president or of federal judges during their terms of office?

   (b) Are we likely to be governed better or worse during a president's first term than during the second? (The Constitution prohibits a third term.)

   (c) Would you expect more statesmanlike decisions from members of the House of Representatives, who must stand for reelection every two years, or from justices of the Supreme Court, who are appointed for life?

   (d) Would you expect more statesmanlike decisions from the U.S. Congress if all members were selected by a lottery to serve six-year terms and then retire?

31. Do the decisions of people now living take any account of the demands of future generations for natural resources? Do these decisions take *ade-*

quate account of the demands of future generations? Is government likely to take *better* account of the demands of future generations? Evaluate the contention that government must serve as the steward of natural resources for future generations.

32. The Constitution of the United States gives Congress the power to establish post offices.

   (a) Can you think of any reasons why the government should assume responsibility for providing a system of postal service? Were there better reasons in 1789 than there are today?
   (b) Congress has passed "private-express statutes" that give the Postal Service a legal monopoly over letter carrying. Why should the government prevent firms from competing with the United States Postal Service in the delivery of letters?
   (c) Who would be likely to put pressure on Congress to defeat any bill that was introduced to repeal the private-express statutes?

33. Could the problem of producer dominance in the legislative process be solved by creating a government agency charged with the task of representing consumers in legislative hearings?

34. If everyone who uses public parks dislikes seeing litter on the ground, the parks won't necessarily be free of litter. The dilemma presented here assumes that each park user has the choice of either tossing litter on the ground or walking to a trash barrel to dispose of the litter. There are many park users, however, so that one less act of littering will make no discernible difference. *Everyone* (or *almost* everyone) must walk to the trash barrel if the park is to be unlittered and attractive. The matrix of Figure 14E shows the results for each park user of the possible choice combinations.

   (a) Each person who puts litter in the trash barrel is assured of bearing a cost, called effort; but whether this person will also receive the benefit of beauty depends on what all other users do. If each user aims at the maximum personal net advantage (benefit minus cost), the "society" may well end up in the southeast square. Why?
   (b) If each user definitely and strongly preferred the northwest square to the southeast square, would that be sufficient to move the "society" to the northwest square? What would each user want to do, under our narrow assumptions, upon finding that the "society" had achieved the situation described in the northwest square? Assume that a single act of littering will not make a noticeable difference. How would this reproduce the less desirable situation described in the southeast square?
   (c) How could "mutual coercion mutually agreed upon" produce the more desirable outcome of the northwest square?
   (d) In the real world, why do people not always behave as this question assumes they all behave? Why will people with no fear of prosecution

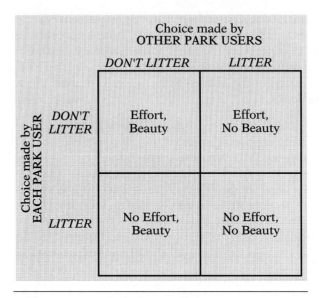

FIGURE 14E   The park users' dilemma

sometimes go to considerable "effort" to avoid littering even though they expect to obtain no "beauty" from it? An example might be a tourist leaving a national park campground.

(e) How many similar situations can you think of? Do they lead to the southeast square? If not, why don't they?

35. Nature Conservancy is the name of a national organization that tries to identify and then purchase endangered habitat in order to preserve it.

(a) Nature Conservancy makes its purchases with funds that have been donated by people who want endangered habitat preserved. How does the free-rider problem hinder Nature Conservancy's fund raising?

(b) Why is the free-rider problem less likely to hamper Nature Conservancy in obtaining gifts from corporations than from individuals?

(c) Nature Conservancy accepts gifts of land as well as money, including prime residential or business property. If you were running such an organization, how would you use commercially valuable urban property to promote the preservation of endangered rural areas?

36. By using the concepts of this chapter, can you explain the continuing use of violence (war) as a way of resolving disputes between nations?

37. If all Americans preferred living in racially integrated neighborhoods, would residential neighborhoods in the United States become integrated? They probably would if that were the only preference Americans held. But if the preference for racially integrated neighborhoods is only one part of their preferences, we may have a Prisoners' Dilemma.

(a) Visualize a city whose population is 50 percent black and 50 percent white. Suppose further that no one objects to living next door to someone of the opposite color, but that they all object to having neighbors of the opposite color on both sides and will move if they find themselves in that position. Will a segregated or integrated housing pattern emerge under a system of voluntary exchange? Why? If integrated housing is considered a good thing, how could it be achieved under these circumstances?

(b) It isn't as obvious but it's almost as inevitable that a severely segregated housing pattern will eventually evolve if the citizens of this city wait to move until their neighbors on *four* sides are of the opposite color. How could such a community give effect to the desire of each citizen to live in a racially integrated community?

(c) Do or should residents of an area have the right to encourage or discourage purchasers in order to achieve or maintain a racially integrated neighborhood? Do they thereby violate the rights of would-be sellers and purchasers who are prevented from arranging a mutually beneficial exchange because the purchaser is the wrong color?

(d) The private developer who built Starrett City in Brooklyn wanted it to be a racially integrated neighborhood. To achieve that goal, Starrett City adopted racial quotas, reflecting the percentages of different racial groups living in the area. In 1988 the Supreme Court declined to review an appellate court decision holding that the quotas violate the Fair Housing Act of 1968, which prohibits racial discrimination in housing. Should racial discrimination by private parties that aims at achieving residential integration be illegal?

38. Why do people sometimes provide valuable services without asking for or even being willing to accept payment, whereas at other times they will insist on being paid for a service that costs them nothing to provide?

(a) Why do managers of urban skyscrapers sometimes charge a fee just for letting people look out the windows on the top floor?

(b) Why do managers of department stores never charge a fee to let people who have no intention of buying anything walk through their stores before Christmas to enjoy the displays?

(c) Why don't people who landscape their premises in a beautiful way charge a fee to those who pass by and enjoy it? Are there ways of collecting benefits from passing spectators other than charging them a fee for looking?

(d) Why don't city residents ask for a contribution to defray expenses when they are stopped by tourists seeking directions? Are such tourists imposing costs on the people whom they stop?

(e) If you were flagged down on a highway by a motorist with a flat tire who said that his jack was broken and asked to borrow yours, would you cooperate? Would you ask to be paid for your services? Would you accept a payment of $5 afterwards if the motorist insisted strenuously? If you would absolutely refuse the money, might you nonetheless accept his offer to buy you dinner at a pleasant restaurant a few miles up the road? Assume that you've found him good company, that you do want to have dinner, and that the dinner will cost considerably more than $5.

(f) Suppose your elderly neighbor injures her back so that she cannot mow her lawn. You know this and so you quickly mow her lawn while doing your own. How would you react if your neighbor, grateful for your kindness, came over that evening and offered you a $10 bill? Would you be less surprised and affronted and more likely to accept if the gift she offered was a $15 bottle of wine? Why?

THE LIMITATIONS OF ECONOMICS

The possibility of civilization depends largely on how well societies work. What does the economic way of thinking reveal about the working of society? Is there anything of importance that it conceals?

If you can bring yourself to return to the first chapter of this book, you will find a brief discussion of the biases of economic theory. You might want to read that section again, now that you've completed the book. Are those really biases? Or are they something more like useful working hypotheses?

WHAT ECONOMISTS KNOW

The economic way of thinking employs such concepts as demand, opportunity cost, marginal effects, and comparative advantage to order familiar phenomena. The economist knows very little about the real world that is not better known by business executives, artisans, engineers, and others who make things happen. What economists do know is *how things fit together*. The concepts of economics enable us to make better sense out of what we observe, to think more consistently and coherently about a wide range of complex social interactions.

This turns out in practice to be a largely negative kind of knowledge about mostly impersonal transactions. The economic way of thinking, as you may have noticed, contributes relatively little to a better understanding of relationships within the family or other small groups where people can know one another well enough to cooperate on a personal basis. Economics mostly explains how cooperation occurs among people who don't know one another at all, but who nonetheless manage to work together with extraordinary effectiveness. Perhaps you also detected, as you read through the chapters of this book, a greater emphasis on what *should not* be done than on what *should* be done. But negative conclusions are important. The economist Frank Knight used to defend the heavily negative character of economic reasoning with a quotation: "It ain't ignorance that does the most damage; it's knowin' so derned much that ain't so."

Too many people "know" how to solve pressing social problems. Their mental picture of the economic universe is a simple one, in which intentions can easily be realized and the only obstacle to a better society is therefore a lack of good intentions. But social actions have consequences that run far beyond those that can be easily predicted or foreseen. Restricting textile imports into the United States, for example, does, for the present at least, protect the jobs and income of textile producers; that's clear enough. But it takes a tutored eye to notice that this will shift even more income away from other Americans, by raising textile prices, reducing American export opportunities, and in general inhibiting the exploitation of comparative advantage. Again, it is easy to see that rent controls hold down the money payments that tenants must make to landlords. But how many advocates of such controls are aware of the alternative payments that tenants will have to make, of the new forms of discrimination that will replace discrimination on the basis of money price, and of the short- and long-run effects on the supply of rental housing?

Nonetheless, people easily become impatient with those who warn against the inadvisability of actions that will make matters worse without proposing solutions of their own. And in a society such as ours, accustomed to the almost miraculous accomplishments of science and technology, the demand for "doing something" tends to exceed by a wide margin the supply of genuine solutions to social problems. We have probably erred in assuming that social problems can be handled in the same way that we manage technological problems. We admit that conflicting interests create hard problems for social policymakers. But we still underestimate the difficulties in the way of bringing about planned social change, largely because we underestimate the complexity of social systems, of the networks of interaction through which behavior is coordinated in a society and people are induced to cooperate in the achievement of their goals.

Perhaps that's why economic theory often treats proposals for reform of the economic system so unkindly. It's not that economists are themselves uninterested in reform, much less that they're the paid lackeys of the privileged classes. But economic theory, by revealing the interdependence of decisions, calls attention to the unexamined consequences of proposals for change. "It won't work out that way" is the economist's standard response to many well-intentioned policy proposals. Realism is not necessarily conservatism, but it often looks quite similar. And there is a sense in which knowledge does promote conservatism. Even physicists have been accused of hopeless conservatism by would-be inventors of perpetual-motion machines.

BEYOND MERE ECONOMICS

John Maynard Keynes once proposed a toast to economists, "the keepers of the possibility of civilization." The *possibility* of civilization—that is all. The efficient allocation of resources and effective social cooperation on complex tasks enlarge the realm of possibility, but they do not by themselves guarantee the progress of civilization. A well-coordinated and smoothly functioning society gives individuals more opportunity to choose; it does not guarantee that they will choose well. The economic way of thinking, especially in a democracy, is an important preliminary. But it is no more than that.

Economists are for the most part prepared to admit that the concepts they employ sometimes distort the reality they study. And they are willing to submit their analysis and conclusions to the test of rational criticism. But some point of view is indispensable to any inquiry, in the physical sciences as well as the social sciences. If the economic way of thinking sometimes leads to distortions, to misplaced emphasis, or even to outright error, the appropriate corrective is rational criticism. The application of that corrective has frequently altered the conclusions of economics in the past. It will probably continue to do so in the future.

Glossary

Definitions or explanations of the terms listed below may be found on the pages whose numbers are printed in the index immediately after these terms in **bold type.**

Adjudication
Capital
Cartels
Coercion
Commercial society
Comparative advantage
Competition
Deadweight costs
Demand, concept of
Demand, law of
Demand, price elasticity of
Economic way of
    thinking
Efficiency
Entrepreneur
Externalities (spillovers)
Free riders
Futures (contracts)
Government

Hedgers
Human capital
Income and wealth
Inflation
Interest
Investment
Legislation
Marginal analysis
Marginal cost
Marginal revenue
Markets
Monopoly
Negotiation
Net revenue
Nominal versus real interest
    rates
Oligopoly
Opportunity cost
Persuasion

Positive externalities
    (spillover benefits)
Predatory pricing
Price searchers
Price takers
Profit
Property rights
Public interest
Rationing
Residual claimant
Rules of the game
Scarcity
Shortage
Speculation
Sunk costs
Supply, price elasticity of
Supply and demand process
Surplus
Transaction costs

Index

455